Girls Make Media

Girls Make Media

Mary Celeste Kearney

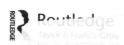

Routledge

Taylor & Francis Group
New York   London

Routledge is an imprint of the
Taylor & Francis Group, an informa business

Published in 2006 by
Routledge
Taylor & Francis Group
270 Madison Avenue
New York, NY 10016

Published in Great Britain by
Routledge
Taylor & Francis Group
2 Park Square
Milton Park, Abingdon
Oxon OX14 4RN

Printed in the United States of America on acid-free paper
10 9 8 7 6 5 4 3 2 1

International Standard Book Number-10: 0-415-97278-7 (Softcover)
International Standard Book Number-13: 978-0-415-97278-9 (Softcover)
Library of Congress Card Number 2005029586

Library of Congress Cataloging-in-Publication Data

Kearney, Mary Celeste, 1962-
  Girls make media / by Mary Celeste Kearney.-- 1st ed.
      p. cm.
  Includes bibliographical references and index.
    ISBN 0-415-97277-9 (hardback : alk. paper) -- ISBN 0-415-97278-7 (pbk. : alk. paper)
  1. Mass media and girls--United States. I. Title.

P94.5.G57K43 2006
302.230835'2--dc22   2005029586

informa

Taylor & Francis Group
is the Academic Division of Informa plc.

Visit the Taylor & Francis Web site at
http://www.taylorandfrancis.com

and the Routledge Web site at
http://www.routledge-ny.com

To my parents,

Celeste Tomczak Kearney and Terrence J. Kearney

Na zdrowie. Sláinte.

Contents

Preface

This project began in 1993 with my introduction to Riot Grrrl, a feminist youth culture that emerged somewhat simultaneously in Olympia, Washington, and Washington, D.C., in 1991 and spread quickly to other cities, including Los Angeles, where I was pursuing my Ph.D. in media, gender, and cultural studies. Shortly after becoming aware of Riot Grrrl, I read Angela McRobbie and Jenny Garber's essay, "Girls and Subcultures," the pioneering text of culture-oriented Girls' Studies.[1] It is no exaggeration to say that my exposure to these two things—one cultural and the other academic, but both radically political—transformed my life.

Through my engagement with Riot Grrrl zines and music, which privilege girlhood as a unique and powerful form of identity, I found a means for reengaging with my boisterous, girlish self. Moreover, I began to understand why I felt alienated from hegemonic feminism and many older feminists. Though I was in my early thirties at the time, I still felt very much the adolescent as a result of my postponement and, in some cases, rejection of many signifiers of middle-class adulthood: a career, marriage, children, and home ownership. Still battling pimples, impassioned about rock music, and saddled with debt that would keep me dependent on my parents and the federal government for the next several decades, I was inspired by riot grrrls' adamantly youthful perspective and was encouraged to think critically about the relationship of age and generation to other components of identity.

In McRobbie and Garber's article, I found an explanation for why girls don't appear in many studies of youth culture, and why female youth are typically excluded from the cultural practices to which their male counterparts are unquestioningly entitled. In addition, I found a theoretical means for merging analyses of gender and generation and exploring the unique cultural practices associated with female youth.

Yet, since McRobbie and Garber's study analyzed only British girls' involvement in youth culture, and their historic overview ended in the late

1970s, I was left curious about U.S. female youth culture, particularly its most recent incarnations. As a result, I decided to change my dissertation topic so that I could focus more specifically on Riot Grrrl as a feminist youth culture. My initial objective in studying this community was to understand its reclaiming of girlhood as a form of social, cultural, and political agency, as well as its reconfiguration of feminist ideologies and practices through attention to age and generation. Yet the more exposure I had to Riot Grrrl, the more intrigued I became with riot grrrls' production of media texts, which typically reconfigure and subvert the discursive practices used by the commercial media industries to represent girls.

After completing my dissertation, I became increasingly aware of girls' engagements with media production in other youth cultures as well as a variety of extracurricular programs across the United States. In fact, it was the dramatic rise in girl-made media, girls' media education programs, and girl-specific media technologies during the late 1990s that inspired me to look beyond Riot Grrrl to the larger sphere of contemporary U.S. girls' media production.

The ideas in this book were in gestation for over a decade before they materialized in the form they are now. As a result, they have transformed greatly in response to changes in girlhood, youth culture, technology, education, and my own life. In fact, it would not have been possible for me to research and write the book you hold in your hands when I first learned about Riot Grrrl and read McRobbie and Garber's essay. You'll have to keep reading to understand why.

Acknowledgments

Despite having my name on its cover, *Girls Make Media* is the result of a collaborative process involving many generous individuals who have contributed to its form, content, and spirit, often without their knowledge. First and foremost, it would have been impossible to imagine, much less research and write, this book if not for the many girls who are altering the landscape of contemporary U.S. popular culture through their involvement in media production. Their zines, music, films, and websites have encouraged me to believe more than ever in the power and potential of female youth, and have given me hope for the future during a time of disturbing social upheaval. In particular, I want to thank the girls I surveyed for my chapters on zines and web design, as well as the students of Girls Making Headlines 2001 who participated in my study of their workshop.

I'm also very grateful to the women who graciously answered my questions about their efforts to improve girls' media production, especially Andrea Richards, author of *Girl Director*; Deborah Fort from Girls Film School; Deborah Aubert from Girls Inc.; Amanda Lotz, Sharon Ross, and Diane Zander from Girls Making Headlines; k. bradford from It's a She Shoot; Laura Donnelly from Latinitas; Malory Graham from Reel Grrls; and Misty McElroy from the Rock'n'Roll Camp for Girls. In addition, my thanks to the staffs of Girls Inc. and the Girl Scouts of the U.S.A., who shared their organizations' materials for improving girls' media literacy, and of the Experience Music Project, for providing information from their Riot Grrrl Retrospective.

For his guidance and patience during the book's revision, Matthew Byrnie at Routledge has my sincere thanks. I'm grateful also to the anonymous readers who carefully reviewed my first manuscript and provided me with helpful suggestions for shaping it into a book. In addition, thanks to Mark Rogers and Michael Kackman, who prepared the book's images, as well as to Shannon Baley, who created the index, and Carolyn Cunningham, who helped with proofreading.

Special thanks go to Caren Kaplan, who first exposed me to critical theory and gender studies at Georgetown University and remains an inspiring role model to this day. In turn, I am extremely grateful to the Critical Studies faculty at the University of Southern California's School of Cinema-Television, especially David James and Lynn Spigel, who were instrumental in helping me hone my approach to media and cultural studies, and Marsha Kinder, whose support of my work has continued long since I departed from USC. I'm honored not only to have worked with USC's fine faculty, but also to have studied alongside some of its best students, especially Eric Freedman, Janice Gore, Vicky Johnson, Christie Milliken, Jim Moran, Bhaskar Sarkar, Alison Trope and Karen Orr Vered, all of whom kept my critical abilities sharp and my glass full during the dog days of doctoral studies.

I'm blessed to have landed a job at the University of Texas at Austin, where my approach to the study of media, culture, and gender has been expanded considerably through interactions with my stellar colleagues in the Department of Radio-Television-Film, as well as the Center for Women's and Gender Studies. I've also been very fortunate to work with super smart and passionately political students who have challenged me to think outside my own box by sharing their knowledge and experiences. Though the administrative members of universities are rarely acknowledged in texts such as this, I'm very grateful to the overworked and underpaid RTF staff for all their labors on my behalf, particularly Susan Dirks, whose efforts to support me and my work have been Herculean.

During my many years of working on this project, friends have bolstered my spirits with supportive chats, nourishing meals, and stress-relieving cocktails. My thanks and love to each of you, in particular, Pamela Chandran, Eva Eilenberg, Nancy Jones, and Cindy Sarver, who witnessed the start of this book in Los Angeles, as well as Jill Dolan, Stacy Wolf, and my neighbors in the "2-3" hood, who helped me celebrate its completion in Austin.

My family, which has alternately shrunk and expanded during my writing of this book, has been enormously supportive of my journey in academe, despite the fact that it has left me too busy and too poor to be able to visit with them often. To Christy, Terry, Mauri, Tom, and Samantha: Thank you so much for your sisterly and brotherly love and encouragement, and for making your homes mine as well so many times over the years. To Elise, Eric, Patrick, and Jack: Thank you for letting me play auntie and not reminding me that I'm a grownup. And to Michael, whose belief in and care of me during the completion of this book were extraordinarily loving and selfless: I have struggled to string together words that can express how grateful, honored, and happy I am to have you by my side, but nothing sounds as right as "Hello, you're my very special one," unless it's "bom, bom, bom."

And, finally, to my parents, Celeste and Terry, who nurtured my expressive and reflective abilities as a child by giving me my first diary, camera, typewriter, and musical instrument, and never hesitated exposing me to new things simply because I was a girl: As I grew up, you encouraged my pursuit of an education and a career that would enrich my life and expand my horizons, and lightened the load of my development as an intellectual through your continual love and support, the kind of which I can never possibly repay. This book is dedicated to both of you with much love, gratitude, and admiration.

My work on this book was supported by the University of Texas at Austin through a Research Assistantship from the Department of Radio-Television-Film, a Dean's Fellowship from the College of Communication, and a Summer Research Assignment from the Office of Graduate Studies.

Introduction
Producing Girls

In 1998, a series of commercials titled "Break the Rules" was released to promote the Independent Film Channel (IFC), a new U.S. cable television enterprise devoted to broadcasting non-Hollywood fare. At the center of this series is a director named Christie, a figure meant to symbolize the cutting-edge, rebellious spirit of IFC and the films it airs. In the first commercial, for example, actor Matt Damon asserts that Christie has "amazing, raw, real talent," while studio executive Bingham Ray refers to the new director as "a phenomenon."[2] Despite the conventional use of "Christie" as a name for females, in the absence of the filmmaker's visual representation when this dialogue is spoken, viewers are encouraged to recall the stereotypical image of a film director: a man. When Christie finally appears in the form of child actor Hallie Eisenberg, humor is created through the dissonance caused by the convergence of the adult male director stereotype in the viewer's mind with an image onscreen of a young girl actively involved in film production (Figure 1). More specifically, laughter is elicited from viewers through the commercial's excessively stereotypical construction of Christie as a female child in the mature

Figure 1 Christie, the fictional director of *Horses are Pretty*.
"Break the Rules" campaign, Independent Film Channel, 1998.

and sophisticated realm of filmmaking. For instance, Christie appears in close–up discussing her new, girlishly titled film, *Horses Are Pretty*, while in a subsequent scene adult actors rehearse the young director's puerile dialogue: "You shut up," "No, *you* shut up," "I said it first," "No you didn't. *I* said it first."

My reason for focusing here on IFC's "Break the Rules" campaign is its reliance on and reproduction of stereotypes about both girls and media production, in particular the common belief that female youth are culturally unproductive. Indeed, these commercials are most amusing if viewers believe that girls do not or cannot make films, even within the "rule-breaking" realm of independent cinema the spots promote. Christie and the commercials in which she appears are funny, in other words, because she is so out of place in the boys' club of filmmaking.

And yet, outside the fictional world created for the IFC series, female youth are actively defying stereotypes of girls' puerile interests and lack of cultural productivity on a daily basis. In fact, over the past decade, the number of young female filmmakers has risen exponentially. And they are not alone. Alongside the growing number of girl directors has been a dramatic increase in girl zinesters,[3] girl musicians, and girl web designers.[4] Although American girls have always been culturally productive, using various media to express themselves creatively and communicate with others, more girls are engaged in cultural production today than at any other point in U.S. history, largely as a result of the development of entrepreneurial youth cultures, a renewed focus on young people's media education, and, perhaps most significantly, the increased availability of inexpensive, user-friendly media technologies for amateurs.[5] As Gladys Ganley notes:

Until a few decades ago, the media were basically the mass media—
the newspaper, magazine and book publishers, radio broadcasters,
movie and record producers, and that post–World War II newcomer,
television. Even in the most liberal democracies, because of the lack
of technical means and/or prohibitive costs, individuals and small
groups had few and quite laborious methods of expression, and the
scope of these was sorely limited. … The possibilities for individuals
to play a more active role began to change significantly when … the
parade of personal electronic media started.[6]

In contrast to previous generations of female youth, whose forms of communication and creativity were largely restricted to writing and the domestic
arts, girls today are using virtually every medium currently available, including
film, music, periodicals, and the Internet, to express themselves, explore their
identities, and connect with others. In turn, contemporary girl-made cultural
texts circulate well beyond their producers' bedrooms, long understood as the
primary location for girls' creative endeavors. In fact, during the early 1990s,
numerous records, zines, and films created by female youth were introduced
to the larger pool of American popular culture. By the end of that decade, several of those recordings had received second releases, many of those zines were
being mass-produced and archived at libraries, and a considerable number of
those films were appearing on television and in international film festivals.
Meanwhile, female youth became active participants in the digital revolution
of the late 1990s, not just through emailing, chat rooms, and instant messaging, but also by engaging in web design, producing their own websites. As a
result of the increased presence of girl-made media, American popular culture is becoming further diversified and democratized.

The rise of girls' media production over the course of the past decade
should not go ignored. Indeed, it demands further attention, particularly by
those individuals interested in challenging the conventional gender and generational dynamics of media culture. Though several scholars have recently
done research in this area,[7] *Girls Make Media* is the first book-length study
of contemporary U.S. girls' media production. With the intent of broadening
scholarship on girls' culture in a variety of ways, this book connects contemporary girl media producers and girl-made media to the lengthy history of
girls' cultural production; relates the rise of girls' media production in the
late twentieth century to transformations in technology, education, and youth
cultures; explores multiple forms of girls' media texts and analyzes their relationship to commercial cultural products targeted to female youth; and examines how multiple ideologies of identity, not just sex and gender, impact girls'
access to media technologies, their involvement in media education, and their
creation of media texts.

Girls Make Media builds upon work begun by Angela McRobbie and Jenny Garber, who in the late 1970s launched the field of Girls' Studies by insisting on attention to sex and gender in analyses of adolescence and youth cultures.[8] I want to contribute to this project by providing an in-depth examination of girls' media production, a considerably understudied component of contemporary female youth culture. My approach, therefore, is somewhat unique, as the majority of scholars within the burgeoning field of culture-oriented Girls' Studies unconsciously reproduce stereotypes of girlhood and girls' culture as consumer oriented by focusing primarily on texts created for female youth by the commercial media industries and ignoring girls' productive cultural practices. As I have argued elsewhere, a continued focus on girls' consumerist practices by Girls' Studies scholars risks reproducing conservative ideologies of sex and gender that link females and femininity to the practices of consumerism and males and masculinity to the practices of production.[9] Moreover, by not addressing girl media–makers and the cultural artifacts they create, Girls' Studies scholars risk reinforcing the popular notion that adults are the only producers of culture.

In arguing for more attention to girls' media production, I am not claiming that girls' consumerist behaviors are insignificant or of lesser importance than the productive cultural practices in which they engage. At a time when consumerism has achieved a privileged position in the everyday lives of most individuals, and female youth are understood as one of the most lucrative consumer niches, it is of utmost importance that research on girls' consumption practices be conducted. In addition, I am not suggesting that consumerism is an inherently negative activity that reinforces passivity and false consciousness. Like production, consumption has no intrinsically positive or negative value. In fact, several studies have demonstrated that girls' consumption of commercial media products can be beneficial, particularly in assisting girls' with the development of their identity and social relations.[10] In turn, research shows that girls' collective participation in public activities centered on commercial media texts, such as going to the movies or attending musical concerts, has an important social function, helping female youth to express themselves assertively and to form relationships with other girls.[11]

My point here, therefore, is not to privilege girls' productive cultural practices over their consumer behaviors. Indeed, more thought needs to be given to how these activities are highly interdependent. Since girl media producers often appropriate and reconfigure commercial media texts when making their own films, music, websites, and publications, studies of the cultural artifacts girls create allow us to examine the ways in which they negotiate the various products of the culture industries. Moreover, by examining the ways in which girls' acts of cultural production are related to their acts of media consumption, we can better understand how traditional conceptions of cultural practice are being troubled by those who resist the strict oppositions of production/consumption, labor/leisure, and work/play in their everyday practices.

Today, girls as young as five years old make media. Most of the girl media producers discussed in this book, however, are between the ages of twelve and twenty-one.[12] I use the terms "girls" and "female youth" to describe these individuals, since most, even those in their early twenties, are still in what Joseph Kett refers to as a "semidependent" status, living with or financially dependent on their parents.[13] Moreover, many contemporary female youth tend to identify with such monikers rather than "young women," a term applied to this group by many older feminists who repudiate "girls" because of its association with men's infantilization and subjugation of adult females. As I discuss in Chapter 2, many contemporary female youth have reclaimed girlhood as their primary identity, often using it as a site for initiating cultural and political action. To use labels for this group to which its members do not ascribe would therefore run counter to my own political values.

My reasons for focusing on female youth between the ages of twelve and twenty-one are not related only to this group's current dominance of girls' media production. Considerable feminist research has shown that around the age of twelve, and often earlier, girls are encouraged by a variety of individuals and social institutions to privilege the traditional practices of femininity over all other activities available to them. Moreover, studies show that female youth of this age are encouraged to identify as heterosexual beings and to position procreation and the attraction of male attention as the primary goals of their adult lives. In fact, adolescence is the life stage when most girls' experiences are increasingly narrowed and oriented toward such practices. Contemporary girls who make media are therefore evidence of a notable transformation in gender and generational politics. Indeed, their investment in the role of media producer is deemed legitimate despite their engagement with tools historically naturalized as masculine and involvement in practices long dominated by adult men. Yet, in order to understand fully the radical nature of girl media producers, it is necessary to consider the larger systems of power their identities and practices subvert.

In 1984, Barbara Hudson wrote the first academic essay to explore at length the traditional ideological dynamics of "growing up girl" in a patriarchal society. In her essay, Hudson analyzes the gender and generational discourses that have shaped the lives of teenage girls for the past one hundred years, arguing that the convergence of such discourses has resulted in "feminine adolescence" being a virtually impossible identity to achieve and maintain.[14] On the one hand, she theorizes, this difficulty arises from the naturalization of adolescence as masculine since its emergence as a new life stage at the turn of the twentieth century.[15] As she notes, "All of our images of the adolescent—... the restless, searching youth ... ; the sower of wild oats, the tester of growing powers—these are *masculine* images."[16] Furthermore, adolescence has been constructed as masculine through an opposition of the characteristics with which it is associated—independence, rebellious-ness, adventurousness, and increasing investments in power—to those that are understood as feminine—dependence, passivity, timidity, and an acqui-escence to power.[17] In other words, the connection between adolescence and masculinity has been cemented through the repeated discursive displacement and abjection of femininity. This phenomenon is perhaps most obvious in the rituals associated with male adolescence, particularly sports, fraternity hazing, and military training, which commonly involve the use of feminine or emasculating terms, such as "pussy" and "sissy," in order to reorient boys who exhibit unconvincing performances of masculinity. Interestingly, this socialization process has a pedagogic function for female youth also, who, through the logic of binary oppositions, learn that girls are both not boys and not masculine.

On the other hand, Hudson argues that it has been difficult for female adolescents to privilege their generational identity because gender, specifi-cally femininity, has historically been positioned as the "master discourse" governing their lives, a phenomenon first studied in depth by Simone de Beauvoir in *The Second Sex.*[18] Given the resiliency of the heterosexual patri-archal sex/gender system that conflates males with masculinity and females with femininity,[19] teenage girls' investments in their generational identity are typically subversive of their achievements of femininity. As Hudson puts it, "[I]f adolescence is characterised by masculine constructs, then any attempts by girls to satisfy demands of them *qua* adolescence, are bound to involve them in displaying [a] lack of femininity."[20]

Historically, girls have relied on two primary methods for achieving femininity. The first strategy involves avoiding all behaviors and activities conventionally associated with masculinity, an approach that helps girls to construct themselves as the "second sex" (i.e., not male) within a patriarchal society. This process of feminine socialization through emasculation intensi-fies as female youth enter puberty, a process during which physical traits bio-logically coded as "male" and "female" become more pronounced. Recalling her parents' attempts to emasculate her body, activities, and desires when she was a teen, Judith Halberstam helps us to understand how girls are socially positioned as feminine subjects:

> I was told that boxing was not appropriate for a girl my age and that
> I should pick out something more feminine. This was the first time
> that I remember being told that I could not do something because
> I was a girl. Unfortunately, many more prohibitions were to follow

with precisely this rationale. Soon it was soccer that was no longer appropriate for a girl "my age" ... Next came gender-appropriate clothes and all manner of social prohibitions.[21]

Concluding her history of emasculation, Halberstam poignantly recalls: "I personally experienced adolescence as the shrinking of my world."

It is important to note that Halberstam calls out adolescence as the culprit here. Indeed, though masculinity in younger girls is excused as an innocuous display of "tomboyism," historically teenage girls' masculine traits have been disparaged and punished. Halberstam explains this phenomenon by noting "[t]here is always the dread possibility ... that the tomboy will not grow out of her butch stage and will never become a member of the wedding."[22] As this reference to weddings suggests, the construction of teenage girls' masculinity as socially problematic begins to make sense when we consider that sexuality has traditionally been linked to gender. Historically, sexual relations have been deemed legitimate in heterocentric societies only when they occur between members of the opposite sex and lead to reproduction.[23] In order to ensure that the courtship rituals associated with such mating are less confusing for those involved, males are encouraged to display masculine traits, while females are encouraged to display the opposite, or feminine, traits. As a result of the homophobia inherent to this system, which commonly leads to erroneous conflations of gender deviancy with sexual deviancy, masculine teenage girls are assumed to be young lesbians and thus incapable of taking on the adult roles of wife and mother. Within heterocentric societies, therefore, teenage tomboys are understood as deviant with regard to not only gender and sexuality, but also generation. Thus, just as the bullying taunts of "sissy" and "fag" have been used to discourage boys' effeminate traits and reorient them toward heterosexual masculinity, "butch" and "dyke" are meant to discourage girls' masculine displays and reorient them toward heterosexual femininity.

In an effort to groom them into becoming proper ladies, girls of the middle and upper classes have long been told by their parents and other authority figures to avoid participating in activities that require strenuous labor and may result in sweating, getting dirty, and developing muscles—in other words, activities that result in girls appearing "unfeminine" (as well as poor). Offering an example of how these gender norms have structured, and limited, girls' cultural practices, Mavis Bayton notes:

Playing the flute, violin and piano is traditionally "feminine," playing electric guitar is "masculine." ... The very first steps in learning the electric guitar force a young woman to break with one of the norms of traditional "femininity"; long, manicured, polished fingernails must be cut down.[24]

Moreover, since one of the attributes stereotypically associated with males and masculinity is technical knowledge and skills, wealthy girls have been discouraged from taking an interest in cultural activities that rely on mechanical or electronic tools not affiliated with domestic activities. Sue Curry Jansen explains the roots of such socialization practices by drawing attention to the gendered division of labor in patriarchal societies:

> [The] constitution of the terms "woman" and "technology" are not separate practices; they are related terms in a vocabulary of power relations that defines the objects men make and manipulate and the work they do as "technical"; conversely, this vocabulary treats the objects women make and manipulate and the work they do as "nontechnical." ... This practice is also, of course, congruent with theoretical conventions in economics, sociology, and history, which consider men's paid labor as productive and part of a nation's economy, and women's unpaid labor as reproductive and outside calculations of gross national products. As a result of these constitutive practices, histories of Western technology have been histories of male activities.[25]

Cynthia Cockburn notes another result of this practice that is of far greater impact on the everyday experiences of human beings: "Technology enters into our sexual identity: femininity is incompatible with technological competence; to feel technically competent is to feel manly."[26]

Teen magazines, the primary media texts targeted to female youth, encourage nonengagement in certain forms of cultural practice by avoiding discourse that might connect girls with physical action or the use of masculinized technologies, a phenomenon particularly noticeable in such periodicals' discussions of popular culture. For example, Angela McRobbie notes that in spite of the overwhelming emphasis on pop stars in teen magazines, such texts do not provide girls with "information about how to set up a band, nor are they encouraged to learn to play an instrument. Genius of the type represented by the pin-ups, is, it seems, something that one is born with and something that girls seem to be born without."[27] In turn, she argues that "[c]ritical attention is shown neither to the music itself nor to its techniques and production. The girls, by implication, are merely listeners."[28]

The other primary strategy girls have traditionally used to display their investment in traditional gender norms is adhering to behaviors and practices commonly associated with women, particularly those of the upper class. As feminist scholars like Iris Young and Lyn Mikel Brown have demonstrated, girls' traditional feminine socialization has included learning how not to be men, that is, to take up less space, to be "seen and not heard."[29] From a young age, female youth are encouraged to manifest their diminution physically—by being thin, restricting their movement, and keeping their limbs close to their body—as well as sonically—by being silent and not asserting themselves. Arguing that such feminine traits are not inherent in females but rather socially produced—"One is not born, but rather becomes, a woman"[30]— Beauvoir brought public attention to this process over half a century ago, noting, among other things, the various messages young girls receive about controlling their behavior and interests:

> [T]he passivity that is the essential characteristic of the "feminine" woman is a trait that develops in [the young girl] from the earliest years. ... [S]he is dressed in inconvenient and frilly clothes of which she has to be careful, her hair is done up in fancy style, she is given the rules of deportment: "Stand up straight, don't walk like a duck"; to develop grace she must repress her spontaneous movements . ... In brief, she is pressed to become ... a servant and an idol. ... [T]he delights of passivity are made to seem desirable to the young girl by parents and educators, books and myths, women and men; she is taught to enjoy them from earliest childhood.[31]

Since the early twentieth century, cultural texts directed toward female youth have encouraged them to achieve femininity through the beautification of their bodies. As Beauvoir notes, "most often no quality is asked of them other than their beauty."[32] Yet this goal is difficult to untangle from the consumerist activities that support it. For example, in her study of the development of a commercialized girls' culture in the United States, Kelly Schrum notes that "[b]y the 1920s, advice literature emphasized beauty routines for high school girls. In the 1930s, some manufacturers and retailers began to recognized age-specific concerns, and with help from girls themselves, tried to match products with teenage uses."[33] With the ever-increasing number of films, magazines, billboards, and advice books drawing attention to the female body over the course of the early twentieth century, girls became both more concerned about their appearance and more interested in improving it through the purchase of cosmetics and fashions. As Joan Jacobs Brumberg puts it, girls are now encouraged to see their bodies as their primary "projects" and to expend considerable time, energy, and money on making themselves as attractive as possible.[34]

Introduced in the early 1940s and supported primarily by the beauty and fashion industries, teen magazines have become the chief medium through which girls' are taught that femininity is achieved through physical attractiveness and that girls' culture is primarily beauty culture. Such periodicals are not digested uncritically by their readers—indeed, they often serve as a discursive space for girls' fantasies. Nevertheless, the commercial discourse within these texts plays upon girls' insecurities of not looking good enough, while promising that if they wear the correct makeup, have the right hair-style, dress in the latest fashions, and, of course, have a thin but full-breasted figure, they will be considered attractive and therefore popular. Thus, teen magazines also function as disciplinary manuals, encouraging their young readers to adopt an ideology of self-improvement and to practice self-surveillance. Interestingly, a 1999 study of 500 girls reveals the possible effects of such discourse, reporting that girls who regularly read commercial magazines were far more likely to have their ideas about body image, as well as diet and exercise regimes, affected by such texts than girls who did not.[35]

The discourse in teen magazines that encourages girls to improve their appearance is typically extended far beyond their physical bodies. As Ellen McCracken notes, such periodicals' "preoccupation with physical appearance pervades many of the editorial pages—not only the beauty and fashion features, but fiction, articles, features, and even the food section."[36] Magazine advice columns, comprised of letters written to the editorial staff by female youth in pursuit of help with their appearance, personality, and relationships, function according to this logic of self-improvement also. Connecting such discourse to Michel Foucault's theories of social control,[37] McRobbie notes its broader effects, arguing that the advice columnist "could also be seen as part of a regulative system. The encouragement to write in, the compulsion to 'tell all' reveals a powerfully normative system at work."[38]

Research demonstrates that the commercial messages that encourage consumers to surveil, find imperfections, and make improvements in their bodies, personalities, relationships, and living spaces result in a greater tendency for negative self-appraisal among girls than among boys.[39] Moreover, it seems these continual messages of self-improvement contribute to girls' pursuits of perfection in many other activities besides beauty. Indeed, a considerable number of female youth, feeling perfection is required of them at all times, are consistently disappointed in their performance. As one of the fifteen-year-olds in Hudson's study noted, "Whatever we do, it's always wrong."[40] As a result, many girls do not risk involving themselves in practices in which they fear they will not perform well or cannot achieve quick and noticeable results. Such anxieties seem particularly heightened around activities that exist outside the conventional realm of females and femininity, including sports and media production. Indeed, Mary Ann Clawson found that female rock musicians typically lose interest in playing instruments during adolescence, avoiding commitment to such practices until their early twenties, the period when young women's self-confidence begins to increase after years of adolescent decline.[41]

Clearly, many contemporary female youth continue to privilege the roles and practices of traditional femininity while avoiding those associated with males, particularly girls who are invested in heterosexual patriarchy. As Lyn Mikel Brown argues:

> Certainly the costs of refusing conventional femininity (the hostility, ostracism, and even violence) as well as the rewards of at least performing such femininity (acceptance, pleasure, a seamless move into the dominant culture, good grades, and promises of security and safety) entice girls ... to embrace such notions of the ideal.[42]

And yet most girls today are also required to incorporate some aspects of masculinity in their gender display, a phenomenon that has been given little attention by Girls' Studies scholars. Yet, as McRobbie argued in 1993,

> there has been a dramatic "unfixing" of young women ... over the last fifteen years which has been effected in the social institutions and can be seen in the field of commercial mass culture and in the various youth subcultures. ... There is ... a greater degree of uncertainty in society as a whole about what it is to be a woman. This filters down to how young women exist within this new *habitus* of gender relations. ... It might even be suggested that ... girls ... have been "unhinged" from their traditional gender position.[43]

A considerable number of contemporary female youth are demonstrating their resistance to, if not refusal of, the traditional ideologies of gender and generation that have historically limited teenage girls' options for identity and experience to the feminine realm. Interestingly, Brown argues that younger girls typically do not display this form of resistance, because their investments in masculinity are tolerated as tomboyism, and their cognitive abilities preclude them from thinking abstractly about the contradictions of gender and generational norms.[44] I would argue that such resistance is also less noticeable among poor girls, since, as Beverley Skeggs notes, female masculinity has long been associated with and somewhat tolerated for working-class women:

> For working class women femininity was never a given (as was sexuality); they were not automatically positioned by it in the same way as middle and upper class white women. Working class women—both black and white—were coded as the sexual and deviant other against which femininity was defined.[45]

Since the late 1960s, when the concept of "women's liberation" helped to involve more women into the paid workforce of Western nations that were staggering economically, most middle-class parents have supported their daughters' college education and pursuit of careers, activities traditionally restricted to adult male elites because of their relationship to the patriarchal public sphere.[46] Moreover, in order to compete successfully with males in school (and later work), girls are actively encouraged by parents, teachers, and other adult mentors to develop qualities traditionally associated with masculinity, such as independence, confidence, assertiveness, and competitiveness.

One interesting result of the growing tolerance for girls' display of such masculine traits is that the range of cultural experiences legitimated today for female youth is no longer limited to the domestic and consumerist activities associated with mid-twentieth-century girls' culture.[47] Indeed, girls' involvement in historically boy-dominated activities, such as sports, subcultures, and media production, has increased substantially since the 1970s. Yet, only by acknowledging the new gender *habitus* that allows girls access to masculinity (and thus adolescence) can we fully understand how contemporary female youth make investments in such practices and participate in them without being discouraged or ridiculed by others. In other words, femininity can no longer be understood as the "master discourse" governing these girls' cultural experiences, as Hudson theorized in the mid-1980s.

Through their involvement in a cultural activity that subverts the restrictive roles and practices associated with traditional femininity, today's girl media producers are evidence of the new gender *habitus* McRobbie describes. Such girls are helping to expand the experiences of contemporary girlhood and thus the spectrum of identities and activities in which all females can invest, for by engaging with the technologies and practices of media production, they are actively subverting the traditional sex/gender system that has kept female cultural practices confined to consumerism, beauty, and the domestic sphere for decades.

When girls invest in the role of media producer, stereotypical notions of girlhood and girls' culture are altered radically, and so is the popular understanding of media production, an activity historically constructed as adult- and male-dominated. Indeed, the development of a highly culturally productive generation of female youth suggests that something very profound has changed in the structures of media culture. In her exploration of the political viability of female resistance in patriarchal culture, Kathleen Kent Rowe argues that a woman's "insistence on her 'authority' to create and control the meaning of [her representation] is an unruly act *par excellence.*"[48] I want to take Rowe's argument one step further, noting that in a patriarchal *and adultist* society where each young girl is at least doubly deprivileged as a result of her age and sex, those female youth who insist on their authority to create and control their own representations, particularly representations that do not adhere to traditional notions of girlhood, exponentially multiply the subversive potential of female unruliness to which Rowe points. For as Clemencia Rodriguez argues when mapping the stakes of media production for society's most deprivileged members, this activity implies having the opportunity to create one's own images of self and environment; it implies being able to recodify one's own identity with signs and codes that one chooses, thereby disrupting the traditional acceptance of those imposed by outside sources; it implies becoming one's own storyteller, regaining one's own voice; it implies reconstructing the self-portrait of one's own community and one's own culture; ... it implies taking one's own languages out of their usual hiding places and throwing them out there, into the public sphere, and seeing how they do.[49]

Invading domains of adult male power and privilege using not just pens and paper, but computers, video cameras, and musical instruments, young female media producers are the newest generation of cyborgs, the interfaced human/machine organisms whom Donna Haraway boldly predicted would lead the feminist movement into the twenty-first century.[50]

This is not to say that girls who make media are not besieged by the social and psychological problems associated with female adolescence, nor that they are unaffected by the various oppressions that result from a deprivileged status associated with race, class, ethnicity, sexuality, or ability. Indeed, as revealed in many of the media texts discussed in this book, girls often use the creative and communicative practices of media production to give voice to and work through such difficulties. Recognizing that what is represented in commercial popular culture has little to do with their identities and experiences, many girl media producers rely on the practices of appropriation and *détournement*[51] to reconfigure commercial cultural artifacts into personalized creations that speak more directly to their concerns, needs, fantasies, and pleasures, a practice bell hooks refers to as "talking back" and relates to the politics of liberation. As she argues, for disenfranchised individuals,

true speaking is not solely an expression of creative power, it is an act of resistance, a political gesture that challenges the politics of domination that would render us nameless and voiceless. ... Moving from silence to speech is for the oppressed, the colonized, the exploited, and those who stand and struggle side by side, a gesture of defiance that heals, that makes new life, and new growth possible. It is that act of speech, of "talking back" that is ... the expression of moving from object to subject, that is the liberated voice.[52]

Through their insistence to be both seen and heard, girl media producers are a disruptive force, and we do well to consider the changes to popular culture and dominant society their presence is provoking.

Before becoming overly celebratory, it is crucial to point out that the contemporary world of U.S. girl-made media is not as diverse as it could and should be. In fact, the ratio of middle-class to working-class girl media producers today is strikingly similar to that of adults during the foundational periods of all forms of media production. This phenomenon is not surprising when we consider that making media typically requires access to expensive forms of technology and training in complex technical and aesthetic practices. Today, most girl media producers are from upper-middle-class families, and therefore have direct access to personal computers, video camcorders, and musical instruments within both their homes and schools. In addition, such girls have a considerable amount of disposable leisure time that allows them to develop and perfect the various skills required for media production.

In contrast, poor girls have little access to media technology, particularly at home. Although some public schools, libraries, and recreational centers in working-class neighborhoods make computers, filmmaking equipment, and musical instruments available to youth, girls in such communities often have difficulty finding transportation to these facilities. More significantly, poor girls have little leisure time for mastering the practices and skills of media production, since they are often called upon to help out with household chores after school and while their parents work. Indeed, older working-class girls are typically encouraged to hold down paying jobs when not in school to help support their families.[53]

Historically, the class imbalance that structured the larger pool of media producers was related directly to race. Yet, the number of middle-class people of color has increased substantially in the United States since the 1950s, thus challenging the common conflation of wealth and whiteness, and, with specific regard to the realm of culture, subverting media production's domination by white writers, filmmakers, and musicians. Nevertheless, the racial, classed, and gendered imbalances that have historically characterized adult media production continue to manifest themselves today in U.S. youth cultures, a phenomenon that severely limits the number of poor girls of color who produce media within these realms. For example, punk scenes continue to be dominated by hegemonic ideologies of race and gender despite criticisms of such dynamics by some of their participants, a situation that results in most punk media producers being white and male.[54] And while a considerable number of Asian, Latino, and African American youth involved in contemporary hip-hop culture participate in the creation of media, cultural production within this community has been increasingly dominated by males since the 1980s, leaving its female media-makers marginalized and confined to traditional, unthreatening forms of female cultural practice, such as singing and dancing.[55]

And yet, despite the conventional class, race, and gender dynamics that structure media production within youth cultures, rich white girls are not the only female youth making media today. Although youth cultures continue to be a primary training ground for young media producers, increased governmental and foundational support of school- and community-based media programs designed to strengthen job skills and bridge the "media divide" has resulted in a considerable number of working-class girls receiving training in media production. Unfortunately, however, because girls in poor communities, most of whom are not white, have less access to the various channels of media exhibition and distribution than their wealthy peers, far fewer of their media texts are in circulation, a situation that has resulted in the common misperception that most girl media producers are white and economically privileged.

In an effort to map and critically assess as much of the landscape of contemporary American girls' media production as possible, this book includes studies of media texts produced by a wide variety of female youth. Using an intersectional approach to identity,[56] I demonstrate how *all* girl-made media texts reveal negotiations of ideologies of race, class, and sexuality, not just those created by female youth who are disenfranchised by hegemonic ideologies of identity and thus are encouraged to bear the burden of that difference in public discourse. In other words, in addition to exploring how race, class, and sexuality are negotiated in media texts made by girls of color, poor female youth, and young lesbians, this book also investigates privileged girls' investments in whiteness, middle-classness, and heterosexuality, despite the fact that female youth with such identities rarely foreground them.

I am aware that my published analyses of girl media producers and their texts are acts that risk reproducing the historical imbalance of power between adults and youth, particularly with regard to issues of representation. For many of the girls discussed here, my privileged status as an upper-middle-class, heterosexual, white adult compounds that risk. My objective, however, is not to speak *for* such girls, but rather, as Trinh T. Minh-ha suggests, to "speak near by."[57] As this book repeatedly demonstrates, many girls now have access to the public sphere via the exhibition and distribution of their media texts. Nevertheless, some discursive locations continue to be out of reach for female youth. Academia, the site of this book's production, is one such place. Not yet formally trained in the theories and methodologies that help intellectuals make sense of human beings and the world, and lacking access to the structures of academic publication, it is difficult for girls to produce the type of study I present here.

This is not to say, however, that female youth do not possess critical skills, nor that they have nothing intelligent to say about their identities, their experiences, or the worlds in which they live. In fact, this book is a testament to the contrary. By involving girl media producers in my research through the practices of ethnography, I hope to help broaden critical analysis and discourse beyond the adults who have historically dominated this arena. Moreover, by drawing attention to the many female youth engaged in media production and the zines, films, and websites they create, I hope to motivate readers to seek out such texts themselves so as to experience first-hand the power of girls' critical ability as well as creative expression.

In order to facilitate readers' productive engagements with this book, I have divided its contents into chapters that are meant to build upon and speak to each other. The first chapter revives the marginalized history of American girls' cultural production prior to the mid-twentieth century, exploring transformations in girls' forms of creative expression in relation to larger changes in culture, education, and recreation over the past two centuries. Chapter 2 focuses on the emergence of the Riot Grrrl movement in the 1990s, and this punk feminist community's development on an infrastructure that motivates and supports girls' media production and distribution. Chapter 3 analyzes the recent introduction of girls-only media education curricula, exploring in particular its relation to the resurgence of both media literacy initiatives and the girls' advocacy movement in the 1990s. In light of the extreme importance that writing has played in the lives of many girls, the fourth chapter examines one of the newest forms of written text produced by female youth—the zine—and the relationship of such texts to both commercial teen magazines and girls' explorations of nonconformist identities. Chapter 5 analyzes the common themes and narrative strategies in contemporary girl-made movies, while also discussing the barriers that have discouraged previous generations of female youth from using film as a means for cultural expression. The final chapter examines girls' training and skills in digital media production through an ethnographic study of young female web designers and close analyses of the websites they create. In the Conclusion I discuss the differing levels of girls' activity in various forms of media production today, drawing attention to the relative dearth of girls' recorded music in contemporary U.S. society. In turn, I look to the future, theorizing the possible effects girl media producers and girl-made media will have not only on girlhood and female youth culture, but also on women's relationships to media industries and American popular culture at large.

I
Contexts

1
Delightful Employment
Girls' Cultural Production Prior to the Late Twentieth Century

With the old handicrafts coming back into favor and
new ones constantly being brought forward,
a girl's life may be full of delightful employment.

—Lina and Adelia Beard, 1904[1]

I wonder about all those secret superstars sitting alone in their
bedrooms writing in their diaries, playing the guitar, and feeling half
human because they're represented that way. Hoping a revolution will
come along and change things. Not realizing that they are the
revolution, and that their creations are the most powerful
weapon in the fight because they represent themselves.

—Sadie Benning, 1992[2]

At the turn of the twentieth century, Lina and Adelia Beard published several books about girls' handicrafts and recreation, including *The American Girls Handy Book: How to Amuse Yourself and Others, New Ideas for Work and Play: What a Girl Can Make and Do,* and *Indoor and Outdoor Handicraft and*

Recreation for Girls (Figure 2).[3] Sisters of Daniel Carter Beard, author of the popular *American Boys Handy Book*,[4] Lina and Adelia were key figures in broadening girls' leisure time and cultural experiences beyond the domestic handicrafts traditionally associated with the women's sphere, a significant development given the retrenchment of conservative gender ideologies during the Victorian age.[5] Indeed, although girls' productive recreational activities were in keeping

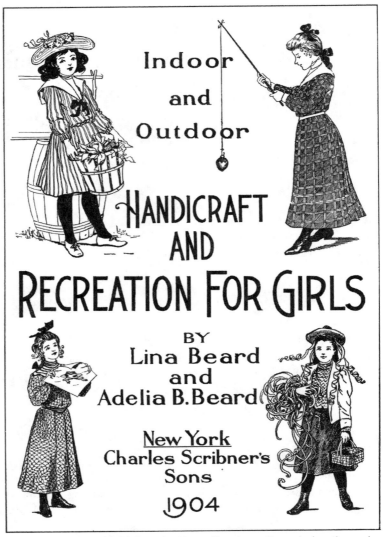

Figure 2 Promoting girls' productive cultural practices during the early twentieth century.

with the Puritanism commonly associated with Americans, the "delightful employment" recommended by the Beards nevertheless complicated the gendered and generationalized structures associated with cultural producers and production up to that point.

In the early 1990s, young video artist Sadie Benning similarly advocated productive recreation for female youth, linking it this time to the leisure spaces and activities of contemporary teens. Foregrounding girls' loneliness and isolation yet arguing that their bedrooms are potential sites of not only cultural production but political action, Benning's optimistic vision for late-twentieth-century female youth significantly challenged both popular representations and academic theories that suggest that girls' culture primarily involves the consumption of commercial media texts. Imbued with the "do it yourself" (DIY) spirit that has inspired a considerable number of amateur media producers, she encouraged girls' various forms of creative expression, clearly articulating the stakes of such cultural practice: the subversion of media stereotypes about their demographic through self-representation, their increased involvement in the public sphere and thus political discourse, and the further democratization of power in U.S. society.

Why a young women writing a hundred years after the first calls for girls' productive recreation would need to advocate so forcefully for contemporary girls' engagement in this form of cultural practice is a primary question grounding this chapter. To begin answering that question, greater attention must be paid to the connections between girls' earlier forms of cultural production and those in which they engage today, for as British cultural theorist Raymond Williams notes, "a new practice is not, of course, an isolated process."[6] In other words, if we hope to comprehend fully how the contemporary field of girls' media production has developed, we cannot study it apart from the larger history of girls' cultural practices and the various social factors that have both influenced its formation as well as complicated its development. Yet, in order to draw such connections we must first rethink the theories that have shaped the study of female youth culture to date.

IN THE BEDROOM: THEORIZING GIRLS' CULTURE

In the mid-1970s, Angela McRobbie and Jenny Garber broke new ground in both feminist scholarship and youth culture research with their study, "Girls and Subcultures."[7] Frustrated with the male bias of youth culture scholars, particularly their colleagues at the Birmingham Centre for Contemporary Cultural Studies, who tended to ignore girls and their unique cultural activities, McRobbie and Garber linked the subordination of female youth in male-dominated subcultures to girls' "structured secondariness" in patriarchal society.[8] In addition to exploring the marginal involvement and "alternative strategies" of girls in various male-dominated postwar British subcultures, they argued that "[t]he important question may not be the absence or presence of girls in the male sub-cultures, but the complementary ways in which girls interact among themselves and with each other to form a distinctive culture of their own."[9] Therefore, they asked, "If subcultural options are not readily available to girls, what are the different but complementary ways in which girls organise their cultural life?"[10]

In their attempt to answer this question, McRobbie and Garber looked back to the years following World War II, noting that girls "remained more focussed on home, Mum, and marriage than her brother or his male peers."[11] As they argued, female youth of this period were motivated by the commercial market to use their disposable income on products that could improve their appearance and provide them with entertainment within the home, thus developing a "culture of the bedroom" that included "experimenting with make-up, listening to records, reading the mags, sizing up the boyfriends, chatting, jiving."[12] Though Kelly Schrum has demonstrated recently that this form of female youth culture was active in the United States as early as the 1930s,[13] McRobbie and Garber's theory of girls' "culture of the bedroom" was nonetheless formative in drawing more attention to the structural differences in the cultural experiences of mid-twentieth-century female youth.[14]

Noting the continuation of girls' bedroom culture in later decades and focusing on 1970s' "teenyboppers," McRobbie and Garber argued that this culture offers female youth different possibilities for exploring identities, developing homosocial relationships, and interacting with cultural commodities than youth cultures dominated by boys. In particular, they argued that girls' bedroom culture has both individual and collective dimensions, is flexible in terms of membership, and operates primarily through girls' use of commercial media texts for the development of heterosexual fantasies and, in some cases, defensive strategies against authoritarian adults, especially teachers. Though their original study found some aspects of bedroom culture to be troubling, particularly girls' encouragement by the culture industries to privilege male popular musicians ("the subordinate, adoring female in awe of the male on the pedestal"),[15] in a revised version of their article, McRobbie and Garber backed away from such negative assessments of this culture in order to recuperate it for feminism and youth cultures. Reconfiguring girls' domestic cultural practices as "resistant," they argued:

> Girls who define themselves actively within these teenybopper subcultures are indeed being *active*, even though the familiar iconography seems to reproduce traditional gender stereotypes with the girl as the passive fan, and the star as the active male. These girls are making statements about themselves as consumers of music, for example.

If the next record is boring or simply bad, the future of the star is in jeopardy. If the stars are seen to disregard the fans, they are likely to lose their place in both the charts and the popularity stakes. Finally and most importantly, teenybopper culture offers girls a chance to define themselves as different and apart from both their younger and older counterparts.[16]

McRobbie and Garber's revised essay attempted to initiate an exploration of female youth as active cultural participants, and thus is indicative of British cultural studies scholars' privileging of resistance during this period. Yet, by continuing to focus primarily on the immaterial leisure activities of girls' bedroom culture, such as listening to records and daydreaming about stars, they ignored its material and productive components, such as letter-writing, scrapbook making, and newsletter production. Thus, McRobbie and Garber unwittingly reproduced an adultist and patriarchal construction of cultural activity wherein adult men are media producers and young females are media consumers.

Although McRobbie and Garber's theory of girls' bedroom culture as consumer oriented was formulated thirty years ago within a unique socio-historical context, this view remains dominant in contemporary U.S. society. Indeed, the connection between consumerism and female youth culture has been reproduced for many decades by the commercial culture industries, which encourage and profit from girls' frequent and carefree forms of consumption. More specific to my project here, most Girls' Studies scholars have reproduced the notion of girls' cultures as primarily domestic and consumerist also. In "Alice in the Consumer Wonderland," Erica Carter points to the problems associated with this approach, noting that feminist scholars who want to analyze the specific nature of female youth culture have "plunge[d], head-on at times, into the seething morass of capital flows, emerging with a proliferation of critiques of the commodities which pattern the fabric of girls' lives: advertising images, fashionable clothes, mass magazines, popular fiction."[17] Thus, in contrast to the many male youth researchers who have focused on the entrepreneurial subcultures dominated by teenage boys, most Girls' Studies scholars have ignored girls' productive cultural practices.

Contemporary American female youth are more involved in media production than any previous generation, a phenomenon that calls for a rethinking of theories of girls' culture as consumer oriented. Yet, these girls are not the first young females to be culturally productive. Indeed, there is a much longer history of girls' creative cultural practices that has been excluded from most analyses of American youth culture. Attention to this history not only provides a foundation for analyzing the rise of girl-made media in the late twentieth century, but encourages further theorizing of girls' cultural practices and relationships to the field of production according to specific socio-historical contexts.

ART/WORK: PREINDUSTRIAL FORMS OF GIRLS' CULTURAL PRODUCTION

American girls have long been involved in creative activities that, though often invisible to others, link them directly to the realm of cultural production. From preindustrial times until well into the early twentieth century, most girls' forms of cultural production, like those of the majority of women, were domestic in nature, largely as a result of the hegemony of patriarchal ideologies and social structures that relied on females' exclusion from the public sphere. As feminist cultural historian Kathy Peiss explains:

> Shaped by the sexual divisions that structured work, access to resources, and participation in public life, women's time differed from men's. Their leisure … tended to be segregated from the public realm and was not sharply differentiated from work, but was sinuously intertwined with the rhythms of household labor and the relationships of kinship. … Women had to fit their entertainment into their work, rather than around it.[18]

Connecting women's experiences to those of female youth, Joseph Hawes argues that "[g]irls in the pre-industrial world had few options. … [Their] vocation was to be domestic."[19] As a result, "[t]he roles of daughter and mother shaded imperceptibly and inevitably into each other," as girls developed into women who were confined to the domestic sphere and excluded from most forms of public life.[20] Female youth were prepared for their future roles through what Carroll Smith-Rosenberg describes as an "apprenticeship system," where older female relatives trained girls in domestic chores.[21] Thus, girls of this period had few opportunities to extend their experiences outside the family home and domestic tasks, a situation that was further reinforced by the construction of the agrarian family as an autonomous, self-sustaining economic unit. Poor girls options were especially limited, as they were expected to labor on behalf of their family or other families, and thus had few experiences that allowed them to transcend the roles and practices traditionally associated with the domestic sphere.

Though girls' place in the domestic "women's sphere" of preindustrial times has been analyzed by several historians, few scholars have taken into account the role socioeconomic status played in the cultural activities of female youth during this period. Wealthy adults typically hired servants to perform the labor-intensive and time-consuming tasks associated with the family home, and as a result their daughters had considerable time to engage, both as consumers and producers, in the various fine arts associated with the upper class. In contrast, girls from poorer families were responsible for sharing housekeeping and childcare duties with their sisters, mothers, aunts, and grandmothers, or were paid to be substitute homemakers via positions as domestic servants for rich families. As a result, such girls had little time to spend on leisure activities, not to mention little schooling in the fine arts and little capital to purchase the materials necessary for such forms of creative expression. Thus, poor girls' cultural productivity was confined largely to the domestic arts they learned from older female relatives: cooking, sewing, weaving, quilting, knitting, pottery, and candle making.[22]

Largely utilitarian in nature, the domestic arts of girls and women have long been disparaged as "handicrafts," products of manual household chores that allegedly do not require much intellect, reflection, or creativity to produce, and thus do not hold the same cultural status as the nonutilitarian artistic objects created by wealthy individuals. Indeed, given academia's historical privileging of the fine arts, the cultural practices associated with the working class have been ignored by most scholars. Fortunately, several contemporary feminist scholars have attempted to legitimize the cultural art/work of domestic females, noting the ways in which engagement in these practices facilitated girls' and women's creativity and self-expression, as well as provided them with opportunities to socialize with other females in activities not strictly linked to labor. For example, in Patricia Cooper and Norma Bradley Allen's collection of oral histories of female quilters raised in the nineteenth century, one interviewee recalls:

> In the summers we'd put up the frame on the screened porch, and when the work was done, Mama would say, "O.K., girls, let's go to it." That was the signal for good times and laughin'. We'd pull up our chairs around the frame and anyone that dropped in would do the same. ... Had to have a screened porch 'cause sometimes you'd quilt and visit till midnight by lamplight with the bugs battin' against the screen.[23]

One of the more fascinating aspects of domestic arts is their blurring of the traditional boundaries of labor and leisure, alienated work and creative expression. Carla Bittel notes, for example, that "[s]urviving rugs and coverlets show that clothwork was ... a medium for [girls'] creativity."[24] Other scholars suggest that the domestic arts also served a pedagogical function for female youth. As Cooper and Bradley Allen argue, for example, "The best elements of teaching were often combined over the construction of a quilt: early and often loving instruction, tradition, discipline, planning, and completing a task, moral reinforcement."[25] Jacqueline Tobin and Raymond Dobard have demonstrated that quilts made by slave girls and women had a far more radical purpose than assumed, their stitches, symbols, and patterns clandestinely signaling to slaves various methods for escape and routes to freedom.²⁶ Such quilts thus served social and communicative functions that went far beyond the objectives of personal creativity and autonomous expression privileged by upper-class artists and their critics.

KILLING TIME: WEALTHY GIRLS' RECREATION DURING THE EIGHTEENTH AND NINETEENTH CENTURIES

In preindustrial times, the education of girls, even those from wealthy families, was typically considered a waste of time, as female youth were expected to marry, have children, and be engaged in domestic responsibilities when they grew up. As a result of the Industrial Revolution, however, the everyday lives of most Americans changed dramatically. Advancements in technology, economics, science, and labor radically altered girls' experiences, expanding their opportunities for education, broadening their cultural practices beyond the domestic arts, and, by extension, allowing for their greater involvement in the public sphere.

The increased industrialization and modernization of the United States during the eighteenth century resulted in the decline in domestic and rural forms of production and a shift from handcrafted to mass-produced goods. In turn, industrialization lead to the substantial growth of the middle class, a social group comprised largely of artisans, shopkeepers, and various professionals. Unlike rural, agrarian families, the urban middle class of this period increasingly relied on manufacturers for household goods and furnishings, which in turn freed their time for other practices. One consequence of this phenomenon was an increase in the number of female youth with considerable time for engagement in nonlabor activities, which in turn resulted in many middle-class parents hiring private tutors for their daughters or sending them to school. The Revolutionary War transformed the lives of American girls even further. As Anita Reznicek notes, "a more liberal spirit toward the education of girls" emerged after the war, as it was believed that "the American mother needed to be educated to at least the standard that would prepare her male children for their duties as citizens, and her female children for marriage and motherhood."²⁷ Thus, in contrast to female youth from poorer families, who were educated only during those times when their families did not require their labor, wealthy girls were attending school on a regular basis by the mid-eighteenth century.

Yet, the schoolgirls of this period were no less trained in household tasks than the female youth who were too poor to attend classes, for girls' education was largely domestic. Mary Jaene Edmonds notes, for example, that "[t]he history of sampler making in this country is inextricably tied to the history of women's education, for samplers were made in classrooms and were often the first—and sometimes the only—step in a young ... woman's education."[28] As Edmonds demonstrates, samplers were meant as training tools through which girls could practice their alphabet and compositional skills, as well as perfect their needlework. At the same time, most girls infused their samplers with considerable creativity and used them as a medium for personal expression. Not surprisingly, then, such samplers were displayed prominently in their creators' homes.

As literacy among schoolteachers increased over the course of the eighteenth century, girls' education eventually expanded beyond the domestic arts to include other subjects, such as mathematics. By the mid-nineteenth century a formal education outside the family home was seen as essential for middle- and upper-class girls as a result of the common understanding that women were not only the primary teachers of children, but also morally superior to men, a view championed most strongly during this period by Catherine Beecher in such books as *A Treatise on Domestic Economy.*[29]

With the further development and proliferation of labor- and time-saving domestic technologies as well as household goods produced outside the family home, the lives of middle- and upper-class Americans changed dramatically during the Victorian era.[30] For example, the mass production of the sewing machine in the 1850s led to a considerable decline in domestic needlework.[31] Such forms of modernization offered girls of all classes more opportunities for nondomestic activities than ever before, thus challenging traditional ideas about the gendered roles and practices associated with the domestic sphere. In particular, girls of wealthy parents, who had few domestic responsibilities, had significant amounts of time to spend in various leisure activities, as Dinah Mulock commented in 1857:

> [They are] papa's nosegay of beauty to adorn his drawing-room. He delights to give them all they can desire—clothes, amusements, society; he and mamma together take every domestic care off their hands; they have abundance of time and nothing to occupy it.[32]

Only two years later, advice writer William Thayer argued, "Many [girls] who continue to reside with their parents, have several hours at their command each day. Some spend these hours in fancy work, music, and idleness. With not a few it may be almost a study in *how to kill time.*"[33]

As Foster Rhea Dulles notes, as a result of wealthy girls' (and women's) increased idleness during the Victorian period, "[d]elicacy became the hallmark of gentility, the sign and symbol ... of freedom from manual labor."[34] Yet, such forms of femininity were not available to all girls of this period. As Sally Mitchell notes, "[T]he mid-Victorian 'ideal' of womanhood ... excluded three-quarters of the unmarried female population, who labored in factories, on farms, in workshops and private houses."[35]

In an effort to fill wealthy girls' time and garner some of their fathers' income, several authors published guidebooks with suggestions for how wealthy female youth could occupy themselves, many of which were modeled on the Beard sisters' *American Girls Handy Book*.[36] Interestingly, these guidebooks contain instructions in traditional domestic arts, such as spinning, weaving, and pottery, as well as in nonutilitarian activities associated with the upper class and meant to beautify girls' surroundings, such as floral arranging and china painting. By broadening girls' cultural activity beyond feminine handicrafts and encouraging their productive recreational practices, such guidebooks helped to facilitate the gradual subversion of the gendered and generationalized structures conventionally associated with recreation and cultural production.

As a result of the rapid urbanization of the United States during the turn of the twentieth century, many members of the middle class felt increasingly alienated from nature and thus drawn to forms of recreation that took place away from their city dwellings and workplaces. A considerable number of camps and summer resorts in remote yet scenic locations were built during this period so that these Americans could rejuvenate themselves through walking, hiking, fishing, hunting, and canoeing.[37] Advocating outdoor recreation as a means to character building, several national scouting organizations for youth were introduced at this time, including the Camp Fire Girls, founded in 1910 by Charlotte and Luther Gulick, and the Girl Scouts, founded in 1912 by Juliette "Daisy" Gordon Low.

Interestingly, amateur photography became a common pastime among scouts and other youth during the turn of the twentieth century, particularly after Kodak's introduction of the small, portable $1 Brownie camera in 1900. With Kodak's encouragement, scouting organizations urged many young people to integrate photography with their other outdoor recreational practices.[38] Again, female youth were not excluded from this appeal, as a Brownie advertisement from 1902 makes clear: "Any schoolboy or girl can make good pictures with a Brownie Camera" (Figure 3).

Because Kodak's amateur cameras were relatively cheap and did not require much skill or literacy to operate, photography became one of the primary means by which girls of this period documented their lives and expressed themselves creatively. As an art form and means of communication that encourages interaction with the world outdoors, photography offered many female youth a mechanism by which they could participate more actively in nondomestic, public life, thus complicating the strictly gendered spaces, roles, and practices of the Victorian era.

Figure 3 Encouraging girls' engagement with photography and the world outdoors. Kodak advertisement, 1902.

A PEN OF HER OWN: THE PRIVILEGED PLACE
OF WRITING IN AMERICAN GIRLS' CULTURE

In 1929, Virginia Woolf published *A Room of One's Own*, a book that broke new ground by exploring the reasons that female genius, particularly in the form of literary talent, is not valued in patriarchal society.[39] Chief among Woolf's theories was that women were not afforded time and space to write, as their roles as unpaid domestic laborers left most with too many other tasks to accomplish, and little money of their own that could buy time away from household chores. Even without such encumbrances, a woman eager to write had few experiences to draw on that were not domestic, and even fewer women authors who could serve as her role models. Nevertheless, *A Room of One's Own* was meant to be optimistic. Indeed, in a letter to her friend G. Lowes Dickinson, Woolf explained that her reason for writing it was "to encourage the young women—they seem to get fearfully depressed."[40]

Although *A Room of One's Own* struck a chord with many women at the time (as well as since), Woolf was accused by some of perpetuating a type of elitism associated with male artists. As Mary Gordon argues, "The thesis of *A Room of One's Own*—women must have money and privacy in order to write—is inevitably connected to questions of class."[41] Nevertheless, Woolf's class-based definition of the female writer was historically correct: prior to the mid-twentieth century, women who expressed themselves via the written word were primarily of the middle and upper classes. Only these women had a substantial education in reading and writing, as well as the time, space, and capital to write unencumbered by the domestic labor poor women were required to perform (often in the homes of these writers).

Woolf focused primarily on women's writing in her book; yet, these class tendencies have existed for younger females also. Letter writing has long been understood as an essential skill for "ladies," and since the late 1800s schools and etiquette manuals have stressed good penmanship and well-crafted letters as the sign of a girl's proper upbringing. In turn, diaries have been a part of upper-class girls' culture since the eighteenth century, as religious leaders stressed their role in spiritual reflection and teachers advocated their usefulness in improving girls' handwriting and compositional skills.

As recreational activities that require little physical exertion or use of heavy equipment, and are primarily performed at home, letter and diary writing do not compromise girls' attempts at achieving the gentile form of femininity traditionally privileged for females in our society. Thus, despite furthering girls' education and broadening their experiences of the world, writing has not been seen as threatening to traditional gender (and generational) roles. Nevertheless, because it allows female youth to transcend, at least temporarily, their familial roles, spaces, and responsibilities, writing has a liberating effect on many girls. It is no surprise, therefore, that by the late eighteenth century, both letter writing and diary writing had become privileged activities in American girls' culture, a status they retain to this day. In order to understand this phenomenon, it is necessary to consider the various functions these particular means of communication have had in girls' lives over the past two centuries.

Writing has long been understood as a means for documentation, expression, and communication. Nevertheless, since written communication has been conceived differently according to historically specific conceptions of identity, girls have not always undertaken this practice in order to fulfill all three of these objectives simultaneously. For instance, prior to the twentieth century, female youth were encouraged to use writing as a form of social, rather than personal, documentation. Thus, wealthy girls of the eighteenth and nineteenth centuries used their letters primarily to record significant events rather than as a means of creative expression. As Kristine McCusker notes, teachers, parents, and etiquette advisors encouraged female youth "to write letters that were neither informal nor intimate. To [these adults], letter writing provided an opportunity to instruct girls in the importance of self-control, not self-expression."[42] Furthermore, since writing about oneself was seen as particularly inappropriate for girls and women, who were encouraged to put aside their own feelings in order to serve and care for others, guidebooks from this period, like Mrs. Farrar's *The Youth's Letter-Writer*, instructed wealthy girls to write letters with topics that would be of interest to readers.[43] Interestingly, letter writing was not constructed as a private form of communication during this period, as it is today. In fact, in the process of helping their daughters become better ladies, upper-class mothers often read and corrected their daughters' writing. In turn, girls' letters were sometimes read aloud to the family as a form of entertainment.[44]

Prior to the nineteenth century, girls' diaries, like their letters, emphasized formality and a reporting of events over personal expression. Diaries were of considerable significance among religious groups that valued personal belief and spiritual self-examination over external authority, such as the Puritans and Quakers, and religious leaders often presented diary writing as a way to build character. Thus, the diaries of many eighteenth-century girls functioned as documents of their writers' various struggles with piety and religious conversion, often containing lists of resolutions that revealed efforts to perfect themselves in the eyes of their parents, communities, and God. As Jane Hunter argues, "In the efforts of girls to be good and repress self, diaries seem to have had a moderating effect. Certainly keeping a diary which recorded successes and failures on the road to virtue was an additional incentive to be good."[45]

By the early nineteenth century, the disciplinary function of girls' diaries extended well beyond the spiritual realm, as advice experts encouraged wealthy parents to understand diary writing as a primary means for not only filling their daughters' time, but also teaching them the habits of organization and regularity. Therefore, girls were instructed to use their diaries to document, in correct chronological order, the events of their day, such as the weather, school activities, and social visits. Since girls' diaries were understood as documents of character building, they, too, were subject to parental inspection. As Hunter notes, "Clearly the journals [such advice experts] had in mind were semi-public family records rather than personal confessions. They were designed for self-grooming along prescribed lines rather than experimentation."[46] Thus, advice writers pointedly discouraged girls from using diaries to indulge their fantasies or entertain inappropriate ambitions. Containing their authors' expressivity via highly regulated, and adult-supervised, norms of behavior that would not disrupt the conventions of traditional femininity and upper-class propriety, "diaries offered [Victorian girls] a compromise—a way to release and contain rebellious impulses, however circumscribed, without breaking with families."[47] In other words, the media that fostered young females' communication also served as muzzles, keeping their voices safely out of the public realm, and ensuring that female youth would be seen and not heard.

Despite repeated encouragement to adhere strictly to social conventions governing feminine and upper-class behavior, girls of the late nineteenth century increasingly used their diaries and letters to express personal thoughts and emotions rather than to document their social and religious lives. For example, when describing the letters Victorian girls wrote to family members while they were away at boarding school, McCusker notes that "some girls … used letters to express their emotional anguish, anxiety, and affection. In fact, adolescent girls routinely used letters to convey their deepest feelings and thoughts about each other."[48] This shift in the function of girls' letter writing was due in part to various scientific discoveries, technological advancements, and social transformations that motivated a move away from religious dogma and toward secular philosophies of the human subject as rationale, inquisitive, and reflexive.

Hunter notes that although parents of the Victorian period often read their daughters' diaries, some girls had private journals that they used as a means of relaying events and describing feelings that were difficult or inappropriate to express verbally or in other, more public forms of writing, such as letters. Conceptualized as a form of private expression and means for self-discovery, diary writing was safer than speech, as the writer's thoughts and feelings, like her penmanship and grammar, did not need to be edited or censored for an audience:

In a Victorian world which celebrated civility, the diary could function as a conduit around awkwardness. ... For the same reasons that parents might encourage their daughters to write to them—as a way of communicating without the embarrassment of face-to-face expression—girls might use their diaries [as a means for] the keeping up of appearances.[49]

With the increased modernization of life at the turn of the twentieth century, girls' writing became more reflective, expressive, and intimate. Several social transformations contributed to this phenomenon, particularly the transition from a religious to a secular lifestyle for many Americans. In addition, both the popularization of feminist sentiment and the increased interaction between members of the opposite sex during this period contributed to a loosening of sexual mores, which, in turn, led to more girls expressing their sexual feelings through writing. As Jane Greer and Miriam Forman-Brunell note:

As peers and consumer culture became far more important and influential in the lives of American youth by the 1920s than before, high school–age girls ... included more intimate entries in their diaries. They included such topics as boys and sex along with franker entries on their bodies and how (through the use of hairstyles, clothing, and cosmetics) they could make themselves more sexually alluring.[50]

Interestingly, Greer and Forman-Brunell note that such early-twentieth-century diary writers often "drew upon the melodramatic language of movie and magazine romances" when describing their romantic fantasies about, or encounters with, boys.[51] This point is substantiated by Schrum, whose archival research found that "[s]choolwork and family appeared in [girls' diaries of this period], but movies shared a privileged space with dances, stimulating the most frequent, descriptive, and enthusiastic entries."[52] One possible reason for such melodramatic and enthusiastic rhetorical styles may have been diary writers' awareness of a potential audience. For example, Schrum notes that "[s]ome teenage girls shared diaries with real-life friends. ... Girls compared their entries and sometimes evaluated each other's reflections."[53]

Although wealthy girls attending boarding school during the nineteenth century improved their compositional skills by writing letters to their families, female youth of the early twentieth century increasingly used such skills to write letters to individuals not related to them and those who lived outside their local communities. For example, as a result of the introduction of scouting organizations, many middle-class female youth formed friendships with other girls who lived in different communities and wrote letters in order to maintain such long-distance friendships after camp. In turn, during World War I female youth were encouraged to write to soldiers overseas in order to lift their spirits and communicate news from back home. Similarly, the Student Letter Exchange, founded in 1936, encouraged thousands of American girls to write to "pen pals" in foreign countries so as to improve their compositional skills and stimulate their interest in other cultures. As a result of the popularity of these nonfamilial and increasingly heterosocial letter-writing experiences, many girls' social circles and worldviews were expanded well beyond their immediate circle of friends, schoolmates, and family members. Yet it was girls' increased interaction with the mass media during the early twentieth century that altered their cultural practices most profoundly.

WORKING GIRLS: NEW EXPERIENCES WITH LABOR AND POPULAR CULTURE

While middle- and upper-class girls gained more access to education and outdoor recreational activities in the United States during the turn of the twentieth century, the lives of poor girls changed more dramatically as a result of increased urbanization and the rise of mediated popular culture. Targeted as inexpensive laborers who could help build a modern nation, many young people uprooted themselves from rural, agrarian environments to take advantage of new commercial opportunities and lucrative, year-round employment in cities. As a result, poor families became fragmented, and young people became increasingly independent of parents. Thus, historian Joseph Kett relates the emergence of the concept of adolescence specifically to industrialization, noting that it was "roughly the period from 1820 to 1920, when the development first of commercial and later of industrial opportunities made it possible for young people to achieve adult economic status at relatively early ages."[54]

Interestingly, girls from poor families were just as likely as their brothers to leave home for more lucrative employment in metropolitan centers during this period. Indeed, Kett theorizes that "girls probably left agricultural communities at earlier ages than boys, for girls were less valuable on farms."[55] Once in the city, American working-class girls commingled with daughters of immigrant families who had moved to the United States to seek better jobs. Traditional employment for these "working girls" was as domestic servants; however, as a result of increased industrialization, bureaucratization, and consumerism during this period, factory, secretarial, and retail sales jobs became increasingly popular among female youth who preferred the higher wages, shorter workdays, greater freedom, and increased opportunity to meet new people (especially young men) afforded by these forms of work.[56]

Just as education gave wealthy girls of this period a chance to see beyond the roles of the women's sphere (even if many of them did not pursue a career alternate to it), labor outside the domestic sphere offered poor girls the opportunity to experiment with new forms of identity and social relations not associated with older women and traditional femininity. Middle-class girls eventually experienced such transformations in girlhood also as female-oriented white-collar fields, such as nursing, retailing, and teaching, expanded and the number of part-time, after-school jobs available for adolescents rose substantially. Moving less quickly from the role of daughter to those of wife and mother as a result of their engagements in the workforce, these working girls of the early twentieth century were the first to experience adolescence as a distinct phase between childhood and adulthood, a life stage Kett refers to as "semidependence."[57]

Because many working girls of this period had disposable income to spend as they wished, Kathy Peiss argues that they collectively "marked out a cultural terrain distinct from familial traditions and the customary practices of their ethnic groups, signifying a new identity as wage-earners through language, clothing, and social rituals."[58] Rather than participating in the recreational spaces traditionally associated with working men, such as bars and sports fields, these female youth became active participants in the public spaces that housed the "cheap amusements" of the early 1900s, particularly movie theaters, dance halls, and amusement parks. Peiss's attention to the commercial nature of working girls' entertainment during this period is key, for she draws attention to how the cultural practices of American female youth shifted from the production of domestic arts associated with the "women's sphere" to the consumption of entertainment made available by the culture industries. This phenomenon had a profound effect on American girls' culture throughout most of the twentieth century, as I discuss in more detail below.

As motion pictures began to receive more attention during the turn of the century, film-going became a primary activity for many urban, working-class residents, including female youth. For less money than a vaudeville show, movies provided girls with the opportunity to engage in cultural experiences outside their family homes and traditional gender roles. Moreover, parents were willing to let their daughters attend films because "[t]here was a widespread perception that the movies were a safe environment for daughters, in part because entire families attended in a neighborhood setting."[59]

The rise of American movie fan culture can be traced to this particular period, and this particular audience. As several cultural historians have demonstrated, it took Hollywood only a short amount of time to realize the popularity of film-going among female youth, soon capitalizing on such fans' enchantment with glamorous movie stars through commercial magazines directed to this particular demographic.[60] Indeed, as Schrum demonstrates, "[m]ovie fan magazines increasingly marginalized male fans between 1915 and 1920 as they replaced technical information on movie production with advice columns and recipes."[61] As a result, "fans and adolescent girls were thought to be synonymous" by the 1920s, and a decade later "the subscriber to the fan magazines was more than likely to be an adolescent girl."[62] In order to expand this market, marketers often took their promotional campaigns directly to female youth, passing out photographs of popular actors in schools and hosting publicity tours with young stars in movie theaters frequented by youth.

As film fandom grew over the course of the 1920s and 1930s, many girls collectively supported their favorite stars through the organization of fan clubs, most of which were highly productive. As Schrum notes, "Girls constructed their own fan culture through scrapbooks, letters, diary entries, decorations, and stories. They shared the accoutrements of movie fan culture with their friends—from photographs to magazines, gossip to fantasy—and formed strong bonds around them."[63] These girls' fan clubs came to function as an alternative "women's sphere" for many female youth, an interesting social development given the increased heterosociality among adolescents during this period as a result of the growth of both after-school jobs and public education.

With the mass production of radios, records, phonographs, and jukeboxes in the 1930s, recorded music became far more accessible to Americans than it had been previously. Many female youth became devoted fans of popular musicians during this period, often expanding their music-related practices well beyond those suggested by the recording industry. For example, girl music fans wrote poetry and essays that focused on their favorite performers, pasted photographs of them into lockets and school lockers, and dressed in ways that mimicked their style.[64] In addition, many girl music fans reworked favorite musical texts in ways that expanded their meaning for such consumers. Schrum notes, for example, that "teenage girls in Walla Walla, Washington, transformed 'out of date' records into fashion accessories, [while] girls in Omaha, Nebraska, embroidered the notes of their favorite songs on their skirts."[65] While many African American female youth of this period participated in jazz culture, white girls were drawn primarily to swing musicians, especially Frank Sinatra, who inspired a particular type of music-based fandom that would significantly shape the fan practices of female youth, and the media's representation of them, for several generations to come.[66]

FROM DEVOTEES TO TEENYBOPPERS: GIRLS' FAN CULTURES OF THE EARLY AND MID-TWENTIETH CENTURY

One of the most fascinating aspects of early twentieth-century girls' fandom is its high level of cultural productivity. As Georganne Scheiner notes, these "[f]ans not only wanted information about their favorite stars, they created it as well," openly challenging the stereotype of female youth as passive consumers of culture.[67] Many adolescent girls expressed their passion for cinema by writing letters to film studios and movie stars. Indeed, Leo Rosten's study of the 1940s' Hollywood film industry reported that "[a]bout 90 percent of all fan letters come from persons under 21; between 85 and 90 percent come from girls."[68] Yet, young female fans of this period expanded girls' expressive practices well beyond letter writing, creating scrapbooks, collages, and even film scripts in celebration of their favorite performers. Commercial movie magazines encouraged girls to send in such work for publication, thus providing some female youth with a public forum for expressing their devotion to particular stars.[69]

Yet girl fans of this period did not restrict their productive practices to the commercial sector. Through their organization of and involvement in fan clubs, many young females responded to the stars and films they so loved by creating their own periodicals, a significant development in the history of girls' written culture. For example, the Deanna Durbin fan club, founded in 1937 by four teenage girls, self-published a newsletter titled *Deanna's Journal*, which included biographical information on the young star, profiles of her family members, and editorial comments by the club's founders.[70] Such self-published newsletters are evidence of the proliferation of typewriters and mimeograph machines into middle-class American homes and schools during this period, not to mention the expansion of girls' education via the growth of the public school system. As a mechanism for collectively asserting their love of particular media texts and celebrities, as well as for displaying their creative talents in writing, drawing, and photography, girl-fan newsletters complicated their producers' relationships with the commercial culture industries and the public sphere, both of which had traditionally excluded members of this particular demographic.

Contemporary theories of fandom have heightened our awareness of the various ways in which media fandom troubles the distinction between consumers and producers, while also blurring the boundaries conventionally maintained between spectators and participants, and commercial and home-crafted.[71] For example, Henry Jenkins, expanding upon Michel de Certeau's theory of readers as "poachers,"[72] argues that fans broaden the spectrum of consumerist practices by creating a "participatory culture" through their various interactions with and appropriations from media texts. As he notes, "Fans possess not simply borrowed remnants snatched from mass culture, but their own culture built from the semiotic raw materials the media provides."[73] Similarly, John Fiske has used Pierre Bourdieu's theories of culture to analyze what he calls the "shadow cultural economy" of fans, an economy that is developed through fans' appropriation of commercially produced texts in the creation of their own cultural artifacts.[74] As Fiske notes:

> All popular audiences engage in varying degrees of semiotic productivity, producing meanings and pleasures that pertain to their social

situation out of the products of the culture industries. But fans often turn this semiotic productivity into some form of textual production that can circulate among—and thus help to define—the fan community. Fans create a fan culture with its own systems of production and distribution.[75]

Many of the cultural artifacts girl fans created during the first half of the twentieth century were produced in small quantities or, more typically, only once, and thus received little attention beyond their fan cultures and the publicity offices of film and recording studios. Nevertheless, by poaching from commercial texts and producing their own forms of media, these female youth challenged the gendered and generational dynamics that traditionally structured the entertainment industries. As Scheiner argues, being fans "allowed girls a specific form of cultural expression that offered them a public forum for what normally has been private discourse. It also enabled them not only to attain a form of cultural authority but to acquire and construct knowledge in their own way."[76] Perhaps most significantly, however, the young female film and music fans of the early twentieth century expanded the range of girls' cultural practices well beyond the realm of consumption, thus setting the stage for later generations' more direct engagements with media technologies.

Following World War II, girls' fan cultures transformed considerably largely as a result of various changes in U.S. society. For instance, as commercial teen culture increasingly privileged male celebrities and male-centered entertainment texts over their female counterparts, girls' fandom became constructed as a heterosexual enterprise. As a result, the stereotype of the romantically obsessed "teenybopper" emerged, and adults who did not understand their function in the lives of young females disparaged girls' fan activities. Several feminist scholars, including McRobbie and Garber, have attempted to recuperate girls' postwar fan practices, arguing that while they provided female youth with a means for expressing their burgeoning heterosexual desires, they also facilitated their bonding with other girls and resistance of traditional gender and generational norms.[77] At the same time, however, it is important to note that fan cultures of this period became far more consumerist and domestic in nature as retailers and marketers encouraged citizens to reinvigorate themselves and the economy through the practices of consumption.[78] Indeed, as manufactured products were increasingly positioned as superior to handcrafted goods, girls' fan cultures began to privilege engagement with mass-produced commodities, such as posters and magazines, over girls' own cultural artifacts, like scrapbooks and newsletters, thus resulting in a decline in girls' media productivity and the rise of a highly consumerist form of bedroom culture.

The ideologies associated with the postwar containment culture contributed to these transformations in girls' fandom also. With the retrenchment of traditional gender norms, female youth were encouraged not only to idolize young male celebrities, like Elvis Presley and the Beatles, but to identify with the housewife as the ideal form of feminine subjectivity and to understand the domestic sphere as the space in which their presence was most valued.[79] As a result, older girls, especially those of the middle class, began to focus less on hobbies that could be developed into professions, such as writing and photography, and more on those that would attract a male partner and produce a good homemaker, such as dieting and shopping. The rise of suburbia during this period also altered girls' fan cultures, as many young people became isolated from their classmates and friendship networks through both distance and a lack of transportation, a phenomenon that helped to produce the lonely, bedroom-bound teenagers Benning describes at the start of this chapter. Indeed, other significant social transformations had to happen before young female media producers emerged in numbers that rivaled those who developed fan clubs during the early twentieth century.

CHERRY BOMBS: GIRLS IN EARLY PUNK CULTURE

In a provocative article published in 1981, Lori Twersky punched holes in the heterocentric and androcentric stereotypes of girls' fandom that had become popular by that time. Arguing that girl fans are attracted to performers' assertive, confident subjectivity and that such power is not always, or even primarily, configured in (hetero)sexual terms, she asserted, "There are undoubtedly more female teenagers daydreaming of being Ann or Nancy Wilson [of Heart] than having daydreams of being [rock star girlfriends like] Bebe Buell, Britt Ekland, and Anita Pallenberg."[80] Cheryl Cline echoed this point a few years later noting that "[i]n the classic female sex rock fantasy, the heroine is a musician, a journalist, a photographer—not a groupie."[81]

Twersky's and Cline's assessments of girl fans' investments in cultural productivity point to a different sociohistorical context than that which led to McRobbie and Garber's theory of girls' bedroom culture. In particular, the development of several entrepreneurial youth cultures during the late 1970s, especially punk and hip-hop, motivated a considerable number of female youth to resist the heterocentric and consumerist dynamics of patriarchal femininity that limited girls' cultural practices and confined them to the domestic sphere. Indeed, while numerous young women of this era, especially lesbians, found women's culture a supportive site in which to express themselves creatively, many nonconformist female youth felt excluded from feminist agendas and discussions because of their age, race, class, and sexuality. Seeking out alternate arenas for their resistance to traditional gender roles and dominant society, many of these girls turned to punk and hip-hop because these youth cultures provided the heterosocial interaction that they found lacking in the separatist culture privileged by feminists. In turn, many teenage girls found punk and hip-hop to be useful arenas for experimenting with forms of identity, behavior, and cultural practice that differed from not only those privileged in mainstream society, but also those associated with feminism. Lucy O'Brien articulates this doubled resistance to patriarchy and feminism in "The Woman Punk Made Me":

> To find fresh meanings as a woman [in the 1970s] it was necessary to overturn the pastel shades of post-60s femininity and make an overt statement on a newly emerging, more aggressive understanding of female sexuality. Punk provided the perfect opportunity. ... It reacted against, yet at the same time re-defined 60s feminism.[82]

As O'Brien's and other feminist cultural historians' work suggests, girls were of central importance to the punk and hip-hop cultures of the late 1970s, and many were active media producers within these realms. Thus, it is important to look beyond the commercial bedroom culture associated with teenyboppers if we are to understand the complexity of and transformations in American girls' cultural experiences during this period.

Most histories and analyses of punk tend to privilege the various males involved in the development of this culture; however, several feminist scholars who were active in punk during the 1970s have helped to shed light on the productive roles female youth occupied in this community. For instance, Angela McRobbie has analyzed girls' roles in second-hand commodity exchange and how they intersect with the counterhegemonic ideologies and entrepreneurial cultural practices of punk. Foregrounding the gender politics involved in punk fashion and style, she argues that "girls played a central role, not just in looking for the right clothes but also in providing their peers with a cheap and easily available supply of second-hand clothes."[83]

The female entrepreneurs of early punk who received the most attention both within and outside this culture were musicians, largely because music was punk's most commodifiable art form and thus was quickly exploited by the commercial entertainment industries. Patti Smith of the Patti Smith Group, Debbie Harry of Blondie, and Tina Weymouth of the Talking Heads were some of the more popular performers to emerge out of New York's early punk scene during the mid-1970s. Though each of these musicians and the bands with which they are affiliated sought out contracts from corporate-owned recording labels, their personas, fashion choices, and performance styles challenged the gender roles and behaviors associated with 1970s' women's culture and commercial popular culture. As Vermilion Sands of the all-female band Mary Monday argued at the time, "We barf on old models of female behavior and interaction. We're women with some fucking guts, not fashion magazine poseurs."[84] The gender deviance suggested by female punk musicians' fashion and performance styles reflected their confidence within, while also likely mediating their frustrations with, a rebellious cultural milieu dominated by males.

During punk's peak in Britain during the late 1970s, a considerable number of young female musicians—including Poly Styrene and Lora Logic of X-Ray Spex, Siouxie Sioux of the Banshees, Pauline Murray of Penetration, Fay Fife of the Rezillos, Gaye Advert of the Adverts, and Jordan of Adam and the Ants—as well as all-female groups—including Snatch, the Slits, the Castrators, the Bloods, PMT, and the Bodysnatchers—gained public recognition not only by projecting images of powerful musicians, but also by foregrounding female, and often feminist, perspectives in their music making (as well as in their band names). Far more politically active than their American counterparts, these British performers often combined their art with political activism through their affiliation with groups like Rock Against Racism and Rock Against Sexism.

Meanwhile, female performers involved in the American "no wave" movement of the late 1970s, such as Ikue Ile Mori of DNA, Pat Place and Adele Bertei of the Contortions, Conny Burke and Nancy Arlen of Mars, and Lydia Lunch of Teenage Jesus and the Jerks, played a mix of avant-garde and punk music in sex-integrated bands. Adopting the more aggressive stance associated with working-class British punks, these female "no wavers" helped to further legitimate performances of female masculinity within this community. As Bertei notes:

> No Wave was when women started playing instruments in bands. It was liberating: we were just like the boys, finally, we could do what the fuck we wanted to do, without any sexist bullshit. ... We'd wear tight black jeans, Doc Martens, T-shirts and leather jackets, and very short hair. ... It was a very defiant look.[85]

As older American punk bands, like Blondie and the Talking Heads, continued to perform and record throughout the late 1970s and early 1980s, punk culture expanded across the country, especially on the West Coast. In contrast to British punk culture, all-female groups were rare in American punk scenes of this period. More typically, female musicians performed in coed bands, as was the case for Exene Cervenka of X, Phranc of Nervous Gender and Catholic Discipline, Jennifer Miro of the Nuns, Penelope of the Avengers, Dee Dee Semrau of UXA, Poison Ivy Rorschach and Miriam Linna of the Cramps, and Laura Kennedy and Cynthia Sley of the Bush Tetras.[86]

Punk was clearly a male- and music-dominated culture in the 1970s. As Helen Reddington recalls, "The scene was as volatile as it was encouraging; ... [h]owever, it was the quantity of productive activity and the breadth of its spread that made the environment so encouraging for female musicians."[87]

But musicians were not the only girls inspired. Many female youth turned their identification with punk culture into other forms of media productivity that helped to build and sustain this community's counter hegemonic infrastructure. Although some young women, like Caroline Coon, Nicole Panter, Sophie Richmond, Christine Robertson, and Barbara Harwood, became active behind the scenes by managing punk bands, others joined bands or started their own. Dave Laing explains girls' feelings of confidence in playing music by drawing attention to the culture's repudiation of romance and love, themes long dominant in popular music, as well as its privileging of an amateurist aesthetic:

> Punk's deliberate refusal of romance as a theme for songs meant that it could avoid one of the most potent sites of gender stereotyping. ... Similarly, punk's stance against the cult of instrumental virtuosity had the side-effect of undermining one of the main sources of male dominance in musical performance: the general rock assumption that women were not capable or competent to play "properly." ... It wasn't, then, punk rock itself which was positively anti-sexist, ... but its negative operations opened up greater possibilities for [women's radical] work within popular music.[88]

As Sharon Cheslow, a member of Washington, D.C.'s early punk community, recalls, "the whole attitude of punk at that time was, anyone can do it! You didn't need to know how to play, all you had to do was pick up an instrument. ... You know, our guy friends are doing it, why can't we?"[89] Reddington argues that a "chain of enablement" based on friends sharing equipment help to spread this DIY spirit, as young people did not have to make much investment in performing, either literally in instruments or figuratively when trying on their new identity as a musician.[90]

Jon Savage notes how the principle of amateurism also governed the making of punk fanzines, thus offering female youth, even those with minimal literacy, a means for expressing themselves and reconfiguring girls' written culture:

> The point was *access*: anybody with a certain command of English ... could make their statement. The economics were simple: the cost of photocopying ... would just be met by the cover price. ... The fanzine was the living exemplar of this access aesthetic.[91]

Many female punks of the 1970s asserted their "do it yourself" spirit and identification with punk performers through self-published fanzines, like *Let It Rock*, created by Wendy Blume, and *More-On*, created by Crystal Clear, Vinyl Virgin, and Sarah Shoshubi, thus continuing the tradition of girls' fan writing in a new context.[92]

Despite the popularization of the DIY ethos among early punks, not all female punks had the time, capital, education, or interest to engage in the various forms of cultural production modeled by their community's most popular entrepreneurs (many of whom had college and art school backgrounds). Thus, young female musicians and zinesters should not be seen as representative of all girls involved in this community. Indeed, as a result of the gender dynamics of this period, most girls were limited to their role as music and fanzine consumers and to their personal development of spectacular fashion and makeup styles.

B-GIRLS: FEMALE YOUTH IN EARLY HIP-HOP CULTURE

The gender dynamics that structured and limited the experiences of young female punks also shaped the roles and practices of girls in 1970s' hip-hop culture, with most female members of the community participating only as consumers. Yet, as several feminist historians have demonstrated, a considerable number of girls, particularly African American girls, were actively involved in the development of hip-hop's countercultural economy.

Nancy Guevara's essay, "Women Writin' Rappin' Breakin'," is pioneering in this regard, uncovering the gendered history of early hip-hop, while also pointing to the various forms of delegitimization negotiated by girls and women associated with this community:

> Black and Latina daughters of immigrant working-class parents belong integrally to the social landscape in which hip-hop first developed. ... The political significance of hip-hop is extended and deepened by the presence and active participation of the women of the hip-hop subculture, who must fight not only the prevailing prejudice against racially oppressed groups and working-class art, but the critical double standards applied throughout Western culture to women artists. ... In addition, women's struggle for recognition in hip-hop is sabotaged by the tendency of the media to ignore, negate or stereotype their participation.[93]

Through oral histories Guevara restores numerous female artists to hip-hop, and women's history, including graffiti writers like Lady Pink (Sandra Fabara) and Lady Heart (Gloria Williams), rappers like Lisa Lee (Lisa Counts) and Roxanne Shanté (Lolita Shanté Gooden), and breakdancers like Baby Love (Daisy Castro). Though Guevara respectfully refers to such artists as "women" and many refer to themselves as "lady," it is important to recognize that many early hip-hop entrepreneurs were teenagers. Baby Love, for example, was only thirteen when she joined the Rock Steady Crew of breakdancers, while Shanté was fourteen when she recorded "Roxanne's Revenge," her famous response to UTFO's "Roxanne, Roxanne."[94] According to Guevara, Lady Pink "was a consummate graffiti writer by the ... age of fifteen," and Lady Heart spent long hours practicing her writing skills during her high school years.[95] Robin D. G. Kelley explains such girls' involvement in hip-hop by noting that "music and the arts offered women more opportunities for entry than the highly masculinized and sex-segregated world of sports," the other primary arena for poor young people's play-work.[96] Moreover, hip-hop provided working-class girls with a means of safe and respectful self-commodification that differed radically from prostitution, the most accessible and lucrative, yet also most disrespected, form of labor for poor females.[97]

Following Guevara's lead, many contemporary historians of hip-hop have made a special effort to reclaim other teenage girls and young women who helped to build this culture. For example, Tricia Rose notes that early hip-hop history includes such female DJs and producers as Jazzy Joyce, Gail "Sky" King, and Spinderella.[98] Other scholars demonstrate how female youth involved in hip-hop have used this community as a primary forum for creatively expressing their experiences as African American girls. For instance, Murray Forman argues:

> Rap's popular profile and its increasing appeal among teenage girls (as listeners and performers) makes it well suited as a cultural form of expressivity which focuses attention on black women's experiences and issues of concern to women generally. ... [T]he music also provides an important medium through which women's sexual desires and fantasies can be defined and shared, disrupting the often recurring scenario whereby women are cast as passive objects of an active masculine libidinal drive.[99]

Similarly, Rose notes that "black women rappers are carving out a female-dominated space in which black women's sexuality is openly expressed. ... They affirm black female working-class cultural signs and experiences that are rarely depicted in American popular culture."[100]

Despite such resistant reconfigurations of black female identity, Rose notes that hip-hop girls "are uncomfortable with being labeled feminist" because they "perceiv[e] feminism as a signifier for a movement that related specifically to white women ... [and] an antimale position."[101] Yet, Forman argues for a way of rethinking hip-hop females' reconfigurations of feminism:

> [B]lack women in Rap have begun to generate their own discourse of empowerment, which achieves two important aspects of the black feminist agenda. First, they have continued to carry the experience of being black and female from the private to the public domain, giving a new form to black women's testimony and amplifying the domi-

nant issues in their lives. Secondly, through their public presence and articulation, they have provided influential role models for an entire generation of female fans, creating a binding force in an increasingly cohesive network of sisterhood, if not feminism.[102]

Imani Perry adds to this view, arguing:

> [C]laiming of the body and its desires is one of various ways in which women are carving an empowered space in hip-hop. Included in this movement are the appropriation of male spaces, the discussion of traditionally feminist issues against male domination and the personification of folk heroes to characterize themselves. ... [M]any seem to at once reclaim private sexuality from males and to construct a culture of female grooming and dress that is separate from popular notions of femininity that frequently have White women's looks or attributes as their template.[103]

Thus, much like punk, hip-hop provided an alternate place for girls' resistance to both patriarchal and feminist constructions of femininity during the 1970s, as well as a space for their more active engagement in cultural production.

PART OF THE BOYS' CLUB: PATRIARCHY AND SEXISM IN EARLY PUNK AND HIP-HOP

Given the gendered structures that have traditionally discouraged girls from investing in male-dominated youth cultures, it is important to explore how girls who participated in early punk and hip-hop were forced to negotiate the patriarchy, sexism, and misogyny dominant within those cultures. As Michael Brake argues, such regressive gender politics have much to do with male adolescents "subscrib[ing] to the cult of masculinity" through their involvement in youth cultures.[104] Indeed, teenage boys often reproduce patriarchy through their conscious and unconscious marginalization and exclusion of girls from the spaces, practices, roles, and institutions associated with such cultures. For example, Kelley states:

> Participants in and advocates for ... Hip Hop ... erect gender boundaries to maintain male hegemony in the areas of production, promotion, and performance. ... [G]ender boundaries within Hip-Hop were vigilantly policed at all levels of production. Young men often discouraged or ridiculed women emcees; such women were often denied access to technology, ignored, or pressured by gender conventions to stay out of a cultural form identified as rough, profane, and male. Indeed, one might argue that rap music's misogyny is partly a function of efforts of male Hip Hop artists to keep it a masculine space.[105]

Rose similarly notes the patriarchal gender dynamics that structured early hip-hop cultural production while also connecting them to larger society. For example, in arguing that few female DJs have become "major players" in the hip-hop community, she points to girls' socialized technophobia, the gender-segregated vocational tracking in public schools, and the exclusionary enclaves males develop around technology.[106]

Patriarchy, sexism, and misogyny were evident in early punk culture also. O'Brien argues, for example, that "women suffered the same discrimination they had always done. ... While there were men wrestling with questions of masculinity and feminism, there were just as many content to leave it unreconstructed."[107] Although punk's patriarchy was demonstrated in the male domination of virtually all its forms of cultural production, sexism and misogyny were perhaps most evident in male musicians' song lyrics and delegitimization of female performers. As O'Brien remembers from her experience in the band Catholic Girls:

> During gigs there were regular cries of: "fuckin cows, who do you think you are?", while at one pub gig we barely got through the first number when a brick was thrown through the front window, tables were overturned, and Wild West bar-room mayhem ensued. ... Contrary to myth, punk was not necessarily woman-friendly, and it was hard to make an impact as a female musician.[108]

Interestingly, O'Brien also points to the discrimination and oppression punk females faced outside their culture as a result of their resistance to patriarchal gender codes and privileging of bondage gear: "For many punk women the streets became a battleground, as if by dressing in a certain way you gave up your 'rights' as a woman to be respected and protected."[109] Such mistreatment likely led many female punks to further valorize the aggressive, masculine attire, language, and behavior stereotypically associated with working-class male punks: "[W]omen often relied on a fierce sense of individuality to buttress themselves. ... Carving a definitive style separate from male expectation ... meant embracing 'ugliness.'"[110]

Though they demonstrated an independent attitude, assertive sexuality, and level of cultural engagement rarely associated with members of the "fairer sex," punk and hip-hop girls of the 1970s were largely ineffectual in subverting the patriarchal values traditionally associated with male-dominated youth cultures. Thus, we should be wary of romanticizing girls' experiences in these cultures during this period. Nonetheless, female punk and hip-hop participants clearly developed new forms of identity, body politics, and cultural practice that differed radically from most feminists and mainstream girls of that period, while also directly challenging the feminine subjectivity privileged by the commercial culture industries. Indeed, as McRobbie suggests, there were political benefits for the girls involved in these communities:

> I'm not arguing that if girls were doing the same as some boys [in youth cultures] ... all would be well. ... Yet the classic subculture does provide its members with a sense of oppositional sociality, an unambiguous pleasure in style, a disruptive public identity, and a set of collective fantasies. As a prefigurative form and set of social relations, I can't help but think it could have a positive meaning for girls who are pushed from early adolescence into achieving their feminine status through acquiring a "steady." ... For many of us ... , escaping from the family and its pressures to act like a real girl remains the first political experience.[111]

Those girls who "escaped" from home through their involvement in the early punk and hip-hop cultures helped to unlock doors that disaffected female youth would push wide open two decades later.

CONCLUSION

As demonstrated in this book's Introduction, the barriers to girls' engagement in cultural production are numerous and complex, and they have successfully discouraged many generations of young females from being involved in such activities. Yet a considerable number of female youth from previous eras were culturally productive, helping to pave the way for contemporary girls' active engagement in media production. The domestic arts, for example, offered even illiterate female youth a means to express themselves creatively during preindustrial times; letter and diary writing expanded girls' expressive practices during the eighteenth century and beyond; and entrepreneurial fan and youth cultures of the twentieth century provided girls with an opportunity to produce their own media texts, as well as to consume others made by their peers.

And yet, as significant as these forms of "delightful employment" are to the larger history of American girls' cultural productivity, few of them provided earlier generations of female youth with enough access to the male- and adult-dominated public sphere so as to transform traditional gender and generational norms that continued to discourage other girls from investing fully in such activities. Indeed, as a result of their disenfranchised status, girls' creative expression via such practices was consistently disparaged, marginalized, and ignored, leading to the silencing of this history until quite recently. Girls' preindustrial handicrafts, for example, were largely confined to the domestic sphere, understood as utilitarian, and subordinated to the fine arts. In turn, girls' diary writing became increasingly privatized by the early twentieth century, to the point that young female scribes were encouraged to use their journals to keep their thoughts and emotions tucked out of sight. Though largely homosocial and often highly productive, girls' fan activities were made unthreatening to dominant society during the postwar era through the consistent framing of such fans as young females pining for male celebrities.

During the late 1970s, however, a new *habitus* of gender relations began to emerge in Western societies,[112] altering girls' relationships to masculinity and male-dominated forms of cultural practice in ways unprecedented for any previous generation. In turn, the broad diffusion of inexpensive media technologies and entrepreneurial youth cultures during this period allowed more girls to gain access to the tools and infrastructures of cultural production than ever before. As a result, a considerable number of female youth became actively engaged in media production, demanding their right to be both seen and heard and gradually transforming both girlhood and girls' culture in the process. When punk girls of the late 1980s eventually became frustrated with the patriarchy and sexism that dominated their community, they combined the ideologies and practices of their culture with those of feminism, thus laying the groundwork for the emergence of Riot Grrrl—the first feminist youth culture.

II
Sites

2

Brought to You by Girl Power
Riot Grrrl's Networked Media Economy

BECAUSE we girls want to create mediums that
speak to US. ... BECAUSE every time we pick up a
pen, or an instrument, or get anything done,
we are creating the revolution. We are the revolution.

—Erika Reinstein[1]

We use [media] as a way of denying history, of ignoring messages in
our upbringing telling us that [girls] can't do certain stuff. WE CAN
DO ANY STUFF. ... DO STUFF. DO IT. DO–IT–YOURSELF.

—*RIGHT NOW. RIOT GRRRL*[2]

Coming to critical consciousness about their doubly subordinated position as
female youth in the early 1990s, some teenage girls and young women involved
in the U.S. punk scene began to speak out about their complicated relationship
to the patriarchy, adultism, and heterocentrism perpetuated by commercial culture as well as the countercultural community with which they were
affiliated.[3] Enraged by various imbalances of power that often result in young

51

females being victims of child abuse, sexual abuse, and self-abuse, not to mention classism, racism, and homophobia, these girls decided to unite with other female youth who had similar experiences and concerns. They began to communicate, they began to organize, and within a year they created a movement that spread internationally via their self-produced media texts, particularly music and zines. The name eventually attached to this movement was Riot Grrrl, and its members' call to action was "Revolution Girl Style Now!"

In my first study of Riot Grrrl, I analyzed representations of this movement in the commercial press, focusing on the strategies by which its ruptural sociopolitical force was discursively contained, dismissed, and ignored in an effort to downplay and eliminate its various threats to dominant ideologies and social relations.[4] In particular, I drew attention to mainstream journalists' reliance on the now conventional and explicitly commercial framework for representing punk, foregrounding this culture's music and style over its other practices, particularly political activism. Noting that Riot Grrrl's connections to punk music had been privileged in academic analyses also, my second study of this community focused on its relationship to earlier sociopolitical movements, especially feminism, whose impact on Riot Grrrl had to that point been subordinated or ignored by other scholars.[5] In this second analysis, I examined connections between riot grrrls' political ideologies and cultural practices and those of 1970s' feminists, demonstrating that the "do-it-yourself" (DIY) ethos motivating riot grrrls' political and cultural activism is not affiliated only with punk culture.

One of the chief catalysts for the dramatic rise of girl media producers in the United States during early 1990s, Riot Grrrl remains a primary site for contemporary girls' media production a decade and a half after this community's emergence. In order to explore Riot Grrrl's impact on the development of girls' culture and girls' media in the United States, I return here to a more conventional framework for its analysis—youth culture studies. In particular, I am interested in Riot Grrrl's construction of the first economy for girls' media production, as well as its reliance on and reconfiguration of the countercultural ideologies, practices, and infrastructures formed previously by punks and feminists.

TOWARD THICK DESCRIPTIONS OF YOUTH CULTURE PRODUCTION

In the late 1970s, two texts published by British cultural studies scholars transformed the manner in which youth cultures are analyzed: Dick Hebdige's *Subculture: The Meaning of Style*, and *Resistance through Rituals: Youth Subcultures in Post-War Britain*, a collection edited by Stuart Hall and Tony Jefferson.[6] The significance of these books to youth studies cannot be exaggerated, for they offered new approaches to analyzing youth culture formations, particularly in relation to style and class, which broadened scholars' interpretations of such communities beyond conventional frameworks, such as delinquency.

Nevertheless, the theories of postwar subcultures elaborated in these texts present numerous difficulties for the study of contemporary youth cultures. Scholars who studied these earlier youth cultures, for example, could not predict the broad geographical diffusion and thus class blurring of youth culture memberships that were made possible in the 1980s and 1990s via the introduction of global media enterprises, such as MTV, and new communications technologies, such as the Internet. More specific to my project here, such scholars were unable to foresee the dramatic rise of cultural productivity in youth cultures during the late twentieth century, typically presenting such entrepreneurship as specific to the middle-class counterculture of the late 1960s and early 1970s, and less significant to, or possible within, the working-class spectacular subcultures in which many of them were personally invested.[7] Indeed, most theories of subcultures developed in the late 1970s do not give much attention to young people's cultural productivity, outside of the creative reconfigurations subculture members make of commercial commodities. Indeed, though Hebdige notes that "[t]he existence of an alternative punk press demonstrated that it was not only clothes or music that could be immediately and cheaply produced from the limited resources at hand," he does not engage in an analysis of the various productive processes that were integral to 1970s' punk culture.[8] Commenting on this oversight by subcultural theorists, Angela McRobbie notes that "so much attention was put on the final signifying products of the subculture and the permutations of meaning produced by these images, that the cultural work involved in their making did not figure into the analysis."[9] Unfortunately, this tendency has continued more recently in much of the research associated with "post-subcultural studies."[10]

Few individuals would disagree with the fact that the documentation and study of youth cultures often necessitate certain exclusions as attempts are made to define and understand disparate and sometimes contradictory agents, practices, events, ideologies, and institutions associated with such communities. Nonetheless, as Gilbert Ryle and Clifford Geertz have argued, cultural analyses must involve more than "thin descriptions" that interpret only surface details of social phenomena.[11] If scholars are to appreciate fully the various influences on and components of any one cultural phenomenon, if we are to produce "thick descriptions," then we must be willing to see past the most obvious cultural signifiers.

Given that studies of youth cultures continue to privilege such communities' most visible and audible components, we must think beyond the dominant frameworks on which we have come to depend for making sense of such cultures in order to understand young people's active engagements with the tools and practices of media production. As McRobbie argues:

> To ignore the intense activity of cultural production ... is to miss what is a key part of subcultural life, that is the creation of a whole way of life, an alternative to higher education, (though often a "foundation" for art school), a hedonistic job creation scheme for the culture industries. ... Subcultures are often ways of creating job opportunities as undocumented, unrecorded and largely "hidden economy" sector subcultures stand at one end of the spectrum of the culture industries, and the glamorous world of the star system and entertainment business at the other.[12]

As McRobbie suggests, the various spaces established in youth cultures for the creation, reproduction, exhibition, promotion, and distribution of media texts operate as important training grounds for young people, and thus deserve greater attention from scholars studying such cultures. Indeed, the critical shift from text to economy, and from consumption to production, that McRobbie advocates can help to facilitate a deeper understanding of the cultures young people create for themselves. The remainder of this chapter, therefore, is an exploration of the countercultural infrastructure developed by Riot Grrrls in order to inspire and sustain young females' involvement in media production. In order to understand the larger cultural transformations that led to the development of this infrastructure, however, it is necessary to consider the longer history of counter hegemonic media economies in the United States, for here we find the ideologies, practices, and structures riot grrrls have used to build their own.

DOING IT THEMSELVES: THE DEVELOPMENT OF ENTREPRENEURIAL YOUTH CULTURES

The mid-twentieth century was a period characterized by considerable social unrest that called into question traditional systems and structures of economic and political power in the United States. Numerous young people were radicalized by the social movements that emerged during this era, as African Americans spoke out about racism and fought for their civil rights, and middle-class white youth, particularly those involved in Students for a Democratic Society, transformed the class-based politics of the Old Left into the New Left. In turn, political unrest in Korea, Vietnam, and Cuba, as well as many colonized, "third world" countries, ignited in many young Americans an oppositional perspective on U.S. society and foreign relations that could not be contained by either the market or the government. From the gradual expansion and fragmentation of the New Left, civil rights movement, and antiwar movement during the late 1960s and early 1970s, other politicized groups emerged, including the women's liberation movement, whose members repudiated sexism, misogyny, and patriarchy while advocating women's rights, as well as the gay liberation movement, whose members fought for social recognition and the decriminalization of their sexual practices.

With a belief that their groups' viewpoints were either ignored or misrepresented by the media industries, members of these sociopolitical movements attempted to establish some control over popular culture and representational politics by independently producing their own forms of media. This phenomenon was greatly facilitated by the introduction of more amateur media technologies during this period, as well as the diffusion of the DIY principle of counterhegemonic cultural production developed in France in the 1950s by the Situationists International.[13] Such practices of self-representation significantly heightened the visibility of disenfranchised groups to those outside their community, and thus altered the terrain of not only American politics, but also popular culture.

More specific to my project here, the social movements of the mid-twentieth century developed new practices for the creation, promotion, and distribution of media that opposed those traditionally privileged by the commercial culture industries and significantly shaped the entrepreneurial youth cultures that would develop out of such counterhegemonic communities. For example, activist media producers from this period privileged authentic expression over professional aesthetics and encouraged their audiences' active participation in media culture, thus setting in motion the ongoing, integrated circuit of production-consumption-production that Walter Benjamin saw as necessary for the development of radical media.[14] In turn, the organizations that sustained such producers were typically antihierarchical and anticorporate, relying on collaborative work and consensus decision making. Because their objectives were not profit motivated, these organizations were also noncompetitive and networked with other activist media producers, thus facilitating the broad diffusion of counterhegemonic ideas during this period.

The entrepreneurial youth cultures that developed in the wake of these social movements were not as explicitly politicized as the activists of the mid-twentieth century. Indeed, though the members of such youth-based communities similarly desired social change, the primary realm for their practices was culture, not politics. Helping to explain the development of this trend since the postwar period, Paul Willis notes:

> Young people are in the vanguard of seeking pleasure, fun, autonomy and self-direction—and this quest is increasingly focused in and on leisure, in and on the hidden continent of the informal. They seek possibilities there, in their own way, which have formerly been open

only in the more glamorous public worlds of artists, writers and the truly "leisured" classes.[15]

Moreover, as young people grew increasingly disenchanted with politics during the 1970s, many activist organizations began to privilege personal liberation through counterhegemonic lifestyles over direct political action, thus facilitating the development of youth-based countercultures in the late twentieth century. With the increased proliferation of inexpensive, user-friendly amateur media technologies during this period, young people were increasingly able to create their own media texts, and as a result considerably expanded young people's options for both leisure and labor.

In "Shut Up and Dance: Youth Culture and Changing Modes of Femininity," McRobbie asserts that "things were never the same after punk." She explains:

> The turning point it marked was one where youth subcultures, in whatever guise they had taken, no longer could be seen as occupy-ing only a "folk devil" position in society. There were too many of them, they were increasingly able to counter whatever charges were made against them by the mass media since they had at their dis-posal, partly as a result of the availability of cheaper technology, the means to defend themselves and to discuss the issue with at least a wider audience than themselves.[16]

Clearly, punk has provided an opportunity for many youth to respond to the commercial culture industries through their own production of media texts. But the "turning point" to which McRobbie refers should not be associated with punk. This honor belongs to the hippie counterculture that developed a decade earlier. Emerging out of the milieu of social unrest during the mid-twentieth century, hippies adopted and reconfigured many of the ideolo-gies, activities, and structures developed earlier by activist media producers, including the DIY ethos, the practice of self-representation, and the formation of an alternative media economy. In doing so, the hippie counterculture was the first community to afford a large number of American young people the opportunity to commodify their leisure practices outside the commercial cul-ture industries. Yet, it was not the last.

STRUCTURALLY DIFFERENT: GIRLS' PRACTICES IN 1980S' PUNK AND HIP-HOP CULTURES

As discussed in the previous chapter, the punk and hip-hop cultures that emerged in the late 1970s similarly advocated counter hegemonic forms of cultural practice and served as primary places for young people's training and involvement in various forms of media production. Yet, unlike the hippie counterculture, which reaffirmed patriarchal ideologies of sex and gender and thus marginalized females within its various sites of media production, the early punk and hip-hop communities attracted many girls interested in cultural production, especially nonconformist female youth who felt excluded from not only mainstream culture, but also the "women's culture" developed by feminists during this period. As the revisionist historical work of such feminist scholars as Lucy O'Brien, Helen Reddington, Angela McRobbie, Nancy Guevara, and Tricia Rose makes clear, girls were of central importance to the new media economies built by punks and members of the hip-hop community during the late 1970s.[17]

Yet the gender dynamics of punk and hip-hop manifested themselves quite differently in the subsequent decade, resulting in different opportunities for media production for the female youth involved in these two cultures. As hip-hop became further commodified in the 1980s, and rap became its most privileged cultural form, many girl DJs, graffiti writers, and breakdancers went underground, becoming less visible than they had been during hip-hop's formative years when roles, practices, and identities were less formalized, professionalized, and structured by traditional gender politics. As a result, girls' interests in spinning, writing, and breaking—the most male-dominated and masculinized forms of hip-hop culture—declined considerably during this period.

By the mid-1980s, therefore, the two hip-hop artistic roles most legitimated for and inhabited by girls were rapper and background dancer, both of which encourage the females who embody them to privilege heterosexual patriarchal performances of femininity, especially sexual attractiveness, over cultural innovation and technological expertise. This situation was further exacerbated by the recording industry's growing reliance on music videos as promotional texts during the 1980s. In this image-oriented performance context, female rappers and background dancers were pressured into adhering to the gendered and racialized representational politics that have historically constructed women of color as hypersexualized.[18] Thus, as the infrastructure supporting rap music became further dominated by the corporate-run recording industry, fewer female artists were allowed to deviate from traditional gender norms, and even fewer had control over their representation, much less their careers.

As Gayle Wald suggests when arguing that with whiteness comes "a social entitlement to experiment with identity," the white female punks of the 1980s had far more privilege in rebelling against gender norms since their femininity was already affirmed as a result of their dominant racial identity and its associated privileged class status.[19] In contrast, girls of color who participated in the hip-hop community did not have such license for "gender bending" since their deprivileged racial, and often class, status encouraged conformity to traditional ideologies of gender. This phenomenon had a direct effect on not only the degree to which girls in punk and hip-hop deviated from traditional forms of femininity, but also their modes and level of cultural productivity within those scenes.

For example, because displays of female masculinity were more legitimated in punk than hip hop, punk girls had greater access to forms of cultural expression long dominated by males and gendered masculine, such as playing electronic musical instruments. In turn, because punks had built a strong, geographically dispersed infrastructure for the production, promotion, and distribution of media by the early 1980s, girls within punk scenes were somewhat insulated from the patriarchal values of the commercial market that tend to position females as "women" first and thus require their privileging of traditional modes of feminine subjectivity and cultural practice. As Donna Gaines argues, "Punk/hardcore was uglier [than previous youth cultures], less conducive to marketing, and so gave the alternative industry time to develop its economic base and sphere of influence (radio, warehouses for bands, and performances, fanzines, squats, etc.)."[20] But perhaps most significantly, punk culture privileged amateurist aesthetics and the DIY ethos over the professional standards required by the commercial market, and thus opened doors for girls that had long been closed to them.

As a result of the convergence of these various ideologies within punk culture, female punks of this period had not only more access to the broad spectrum of cultural practice than hip-hop girls, but also more opportunities for counterhegemonic gender performances that further eased their legitimization as media producers within male-dominated scenes. This phenomenon helps to explain why the first national entrepreneurial female youth culture, Riot Grrrl, emerged out of 1980s' punk culture. But this is only half of the story.

In drawing attention to the significant opportunities for cultural production girls had within punk in the 1980s, I do not mean to suggest that this community was not marked by patriarchy and sexism during this period, nor that girls within its various scenes felt safe, respected, and supported. In fact, punk culture became more male-dominated and at times virulently misogynist over the course of the 1980s as it moved underground and developed into "hardcore." As a result, many female youth were discouraged from participating in this community. As Cynthia Connolly recalls:

> I had a really great time, at least for a while. But when moshing became violent and extremely masculine, there was nothing funny about it. I hated going to shows when it became so violent and insane. As it got more and more Hardcore I got more and more disinterested. By '83, I was 100% disinterested. Most women I knew bailed.[21]

Many of the girls who stayed, however, became radicalized via the disturbing gender politics of the youth culture they were helping to build. In turn, as Women's Studies curricula and gender studies proliferated in the U.S. academy over the course of the 1980s, many of the young women who were part of the punk community became formally educated in feminist theory and brought that knowledge to bear on their critique of youth cultures and dominant society.

Nevertheless, most of the female youth associated with punk during the 1980s found it difficult to connect the ideologies, practices, and aesthetics privileged by feminists during that period with those of their subcultural scenes. For example, Lois Maffeo recalls:

> When I was at Evergreen [State College], there was a core group of about six or seven strong girls that were my age, almost like a gang; they were highly intellectual, very feisty and really tough. They were having reading groups … like a feminist consciousness-raising group, … [but] I think they were rejecting traditional feminism of the time. … There was a local radio show which played womyn's music like Holly Near, and these girls' response was against that kind of formalized feminism which they regarded as awful and boring— I felt the same way.[22]

As Maffeo's recollections of her feisty "girl gang" suggests, female youth of the late 1980s reconfigured feminist ideologies and practices in relation to punk (and vice versa), and in doing so helped to ignite a countercultural movement whose explosive power further fractured the sexism of male-dominated punk while also deconstructing the adultism of feminism. Indeed, it was their potent combination of feminist critique and punk practice that helped give rise to the first entrepreneurial female youth culture—Riot Grrrl.

"REVOLUTION GIRL STYLE NOW!": RIOT GRRRL'S COUNTERCULTURE EMERGES

Riot Grrrl unofficially formed during the summer of 1991 in Washington, D.C., where members of Bikini Kill (Kathleen Hanna, Billy Karren, Tobi Vail, and Kathi Wilcox) and Bratmobile (Molly Neuman, Erin Smith, and Allison Wolfe) were temporarily living while on break from college in the Northwest.[23] There they met several influential and active media producers in the D.C. punk community, including Ian MacKaye of the band Fugazi and Dischord label, as well as Sharon Cheslow, Jenny Toomey, and Jen Smith. Following a race riot that erupted in the neighborhood where they were staying, Smith suggested that the male-dominated punk scene could use a "girl riot." In an attempt to form a community with other female youth whose lives included playing or consuming punk music, Wolfe and Neuman of Bratmobile started a new zine called *Riot Grrrl*. As Neuman recalls: "We had thought about *Girl Riot* and then we changed it to *Riot Grrrl* with the three 'r's' as in growling. It was a cool play on words, and also kind of an expression about how there should be some kind of vehicle where your anger is validated."[24] According to Hanna, the commercial press used the zine's title as the moniker for this new punk feminist movement, and eventually the female youth who were part of this community adopted the name as their own.[25]

In addition to using their music and zines to spread the message of "Revolution Girl Style Now,"[26] Hanna and some of the other members of Bikini Kill and Bratmobile began to solicit female youth active in the D.C. punk scene for weekly get-togethers. As Hanna recalls:

> I wanted to meet these other women and figure out how we could network with each other—you know, people who are not only feminist, but are also resisting capitalism through creating their own mediums like fanzines and music that's [distributed] through small labels.[27]

Much like the consciousness-raising groups initiated by feminists in the late 1960s, these Riot Grrrl meetings allowed female youth to explore their experiences of sexism, misogyny, and homosexuality, often considered taboo discussion material in mixed company, much less the various clubs they frequented that were dominated by straight male punks. Indeed, for many of the girls involved, these meetings presented the first opportunity to connect personal experience to larger systemic problems, such as patriarchy and heterocentrism. By helping to construct a community built on female solidarity, Riot Grrrl meetings were a powerful rejection of dominant society's encouragement for girls to compete with one another.

Another significant event in early Riot Grrrl history occurred when the female members of Bikini Kill, Bratmobile, Heavens to Betsy, Kreviss, Tiger Trap, 7 Year Bitch, Mecca Normal, and the Spinanes united during the "Love Rock Revolution Girl Style Now" event, or what has come to be known as "Grrrl Night," at the 1991 International Pop Underground convention in Olympia. These bands' collective, all-female performance, as well as their strong affiliations with punk and feminism, motivated them to understand their music as a political medium that would help them to critique sexism within the punk community and society at large, while also encouraging girls to relinquish their ties to patriarchal forms of femininity. From Heavens to Betsy's "Terrorist," which addresses the imbalance of power between the sexes that often leads to sexualized violence,[28] to Bratmobile's "and i live in a town where the boys amputate their hearts," which focuses on the domestic containment of female youth,[29] to Bikini Kill's "Double Dare Ya" call for girls to "stand up for your rights,"[30] the songs of early Riot Grrrl musicians repudiated stereotypical constructions of girlhood by constructing a bold and unruly form of subjectivity historically discouraged in female adolescents. As Hanna sings in Bikini Kill's "New Radio": "I'm the little girl at the picnic / Who won't stop pulling her dress up / It doesn't matter who's in control now / It doesn't matter cuz this is new radio."[31]

As Hanna argued early on, "Revolution Girl-Style [means] taking control and participating in the music scene [and] trying to inspire participation from other girls in the community."[32] Thus, in the face of a commercial culture that reinforces female complacency and consumption over assertiveness and production, many of the young women involved in the formation of Riot Grrrl directly and forcefully challenged girls to be culturally and politically active. As Jean Smith of Mecca Normal recalls, "I talked a lot during those years. I almost talked more than I performed, in between songs, and just said to women, 'Get a guitar, get your friends together, and do this!'"[33] Similarly, Neuman remembers how this DIY spirit impacted her life and those of other female youth around her: "It was as simple as someone going, 'You should do a fanzine' or 'You should start a band.' At that point it was like, 'Okay, that's what we should do.'"[34]

The zines produced during the early years of this movement carried the message of girls' cultural productivity far beyond their creators' communities. *Bikini Kill: A Color and Activity Book* (referred hereafter to as *Bikini Kill #1*), one of the first zines associated with the Riot Grrrl movement, encouraged female youth to see joining a band as a viable option for using their time and enacting social change (Figure 4):

1. Cuz its fun
2. Its a good way to act out ... behaviors that are wrongly deemed "inappropriate" ...
3. To serve as a role model for other girls
4. To show boys other ways of doing things and that we have stuff to say
5. To discuss in both literal and artistic ways those issues that're really important to girls.
   — naming these issues, specifically, validates their importance and other girls' interest in them
   — Reminds other girls that they aren't alone
6. To make fun of and thus disrupt the powers that be.[35]

Similarly, *Riot Grrrl #8* declares,

> You don't have to take shit from anyone. Be who you want, do what you want. Don't be pushed to the back at shows if you want to be in the front. Don't stop doing something just because someone says you

Figure 4 Challenging girls to be culturally and politically active.
Bikini Kill's first zine, 1991.

can't do it, or doesn't encourage you. Go skateboard, write a zine,
form a band. Make yourself heard![36]

As zines and music disseminated the Riot Grrrl message throughout the
punk community in the early 1990s, the commercial press became aware of
this movement and began documenting it for those outside. Although wary of
this attention by dominant culture, riot grrrls demonstrated their media savvy
by purposefully exploiting reporters in order to disseminate their "girl power"
message. For example, during an early interview for the *LA Weekly*, Hanna

lied to journalist Emily White, stating that riot grrrls existed nationwide and naming several cities that already had Riot Grrrl "chapters."[37] By manipulating the information communicated by the press about this movement, Hanna hoped to challenge girls to form their own Riot Grrrl groups if there was none in their town. Her plan worked. As White's article was reprinted in other periodicals, groups of riot grrrls emerged in cities across the United States. Meanwhile, some riot grrrls collaborated with the staff at *Sassy* magazine to distribute information about this movement and its cultural products, especially music and zines.[38] As Joanne Gottlieb and Gayle Wald have argued, "Possibly, the riot grrrl movement would have been significantly diminished had it not been for its careful coverage in [*Sassy*], which gave a mass audience of teenage girls access to a largely inaccessible phenomenon in the rock underground."[39]

Though riot grrrls eventually imposed a commercial media blackout in 1992 to prevent the further misrepresentation of their movement, Jessica Rosenberg and Gitana Garofalo support the view that their community's exposure through the mass media was useful, noting, "Many girls became acquainted with the [Riot Grrrl] movement through the mainstream media rather than the punk rock underground."[40] Lea Thompson confirms this point, recalling that "the first time I heard about riot grrrl in *Newsweek* I was really excited and wanted to get involved. I then wrote to some grrrls in the Chicago area that I discovered in the *Chicago Tribune*."[41] Thus, while many riot grrrls have objected to the commercial media's exploitation of their community, others have noted that without such attention, Riot Grrrl would have defused early on. Vail argues, for instance, "Riot grrrl still exists all over the world, [w]hich I think probably wouldn't have happened without the media coverage. And that's pretty exciting."[42]

It is important to note that Riot Grrrl received some of the media attention it did not only because of its original members' spectacular style and confrontational music, but also because this movement emerged at the same time that Seattle "grunge" bands, like Nirvana, and "women in rock," like Courtney Love, were being touted in the music press as rock's newest saviors and its most lucrative commodities. Because Riot Grrrl's emergence and scenes were not independent of these phenomena (which, in turn, are not mutually exclusive; many popular female rock musicians of the 1990s had roots in the Northwest), this radical girl movement was easily understood, and thus publicized, as a chapter in both of these larger musical narratives.

As Riot Grrrl's "Revolution Grrrl Style Now!" battle cry was further diffused by the zines and music associated with this movement, as well as by the commercial press, riot grrrls began organizing annual conventions so that girls could meet each other, discuss issues of concern to feminist youth, and experience a counterculture created by other teenage girls and young women.

Thus, another significant event in this community's early history is the first Riot Grrrl convention, which was held in 1992 in Washington, D.C. Modeled on the women's music festivals introduced by feminists in the 1970s, the convention provided a public forum for riot grrrls' performance and consumption of music, as well as their discussion of such issues as rape, racism, domestic violence, self-defense, and fat oppression.[43] As the movement's "girl power" spirit diffused across the United States, Riot Grrrl conventions were held in subsequent years in such cities as Omaha, Boston, Los Angeles, and New York City. Meanwhile, as a result of Riot Grrrl music and zines being distributed more broadly and the commercial press documenting this community more frequently, smaller gatherings of riot grrrls began to emerge in suburban and rural areas, as well as overseas. With the increased penetration of personal computers and modems into most schools and many middle-class homes during the 1990s, riot grrrls eventually turned to the Internet and World Wide Web to meet, converse, and organize.

Now transgressing local, regional, and national boundaries and moving between schools, clubs, political rallies, and the Web, Riot Grrrl can be likened to what Benedict Anderson calls an "imagined community."[44] Such reliance on a virtual, imagined identification with other like-minded girls not living in close proximity exists primarily because of the common view today that it is impossible for many female youth to have a "room of one's own" where they can physically meet and bond with other nonconformist girls.[45] The imaginary community of Riot Grrrl thus provides female youth with both a network of supportive friends and a forum for discussing their personal problems, larger social issues, and visions for a better future without fear of censorship, silencing, or retaliation.

FROM GIRL TO GRRRL: RIOT GRRRL'S RECONFIGURATION OF GIRLHOOD AND FEMALE YOUTH CULTURE

Despite the significance of bands like Bikini Kill and Bratmobile to the formation of Riot Grrrl, this movement has never been confined only to the "rock underground," as Gottlieb and Wald suggest in the first academic analysis of this movement and many other scholars and journalists have repeated.[46] While music has been an important expressive and networking tool within this community, other cultural artifacts, like zines and films, have been produced by riot grrrls also. Yet, to see Riot Grrrl as only a cultural community precludes understanding it as a political movement. As Corrine Tucker of Heavens to Betsy argues, "The whole point of riot grrrl is that we were able to rewrite feminism for the 21st century. We took those ideas and rewrote them in our own vernacular."[47]

With the knowledge that "growing up" and "becoming a woman" often means leaving the self-confidence and homosocial bonds of girlhood behind, Riot Grrrl dares female youth to stand up for themselves, for their rights, and for each other. As Misty, creator of the zines *Just Like a Girl* and *I Can't Get Far Enough Away*, writes:

> Wimmin need to learn that power is not given, we have to take it. We need to realize that we don't have to stand around and be treated like this. Don't let anyone control you or dictate your life to you. ... No one can save you from your oppression except yourself. GIRLS UNITE![48]

Similarly, Lailah Hanit Bragin argues that Riot Grrrl is about "getting girls to do it for ourselves, changing the stuff going on in our lives, change it ourselves because we can't wait for someone else to do it."[49] Yet, at the same time that Riot Grrrl champions the individual empowerment of female youth, it recognizes the need to maintain a supportive community where girls can safely learn assertiveness and self-confidence in the company of like-minded female youth. As Rosenberg argues:

> For many, Riot Grrrl is a community in which girls can transgress and challenge something they don't believe in and still feel comfortable; when girls feel alone because they disagree with the cultural majority, they have a network of people they can turn to and rely on.[50]

Thus, in addition to rewriting feminism, as Tucker suggests, riot grrrls are reinventing girlhood and girls' culture for a new millennium.

As discussed in the Introduction, Barbara Hudson made a convincing argument in the mid-1980s that feminine adolescence exists as a paradox for teenage girls, since adolescence has been gendered masculine and the performance of traits associated with that life stage thereby undermine girls' attempts to achieve femininity.[51] Yet, by recuperating the traits of independence, rebelliousness, and assertiveness normally associated with adolescence (and masculinity), while at the same time celebrating the innocence, playfulness, and homosociality typically associated with girlhood—in other words, by putting the "grrr" into "girl"—riot grrrls refuse the double bind that traditional ideologies of gender and generation have historically created for female youth.

As Wald's work on whiteness in rock culture suggests, however, we must be mindful of how the gender deviance displayed by riot grrrls is a privilege to which only middle-class white girls have access.[52] Indeed, the gender (and generational) trouble celebrated within Riot Grrrl may be the primary reason for its lack of appeal to poor female youth and girls of color, whose performances of gender and generation are structured quite differently as a result of their disenfranchised status and encouragement to achieve legitimacy within middle-class white society. Nevertheless, as McRobbie suggests, riot grrrls are evidence that contemporary girlhood has become "unhinged" from traditional femininity, a phenomenon that has afforded a considerable number of female youth more access to the broad spectrum of gender identities and behaviors than girls of earlier generations had.[53]

In addition to reconfiguring girlhood, Riot Grrrl has also revolutionized girls' culture. Indeed, though Riot Grrrl can be linked to previous female youth cultures in several ways, particularly in its function as a primary site for girls' homosocial recreation, communication, and support, in contrast with earlier girls' cultures, riot grrrls have developed a somewhat virtual global community with considerable distance from the domestic sphere and the privatized realm of girls' bedroom culture. Furthermore, riot grrrls typically have an oppositional relationship to the commercial media industries that shaped the cultural practices of most twentieth-century female youth cultures. Although, riot grrrls value the centrality of homosocial bonds, they often move far afield from the heterosexual fantasies of romance commodified by the commercial media industries for female youth. In Riot Grrrl, boys are not on the side; they are often subordinate to girls and, sometimes, removed from the equation altogether. Thus, in many ways, Riot Grrrl has emerged as the feminist youth culture that, in 1980, McRobbie could only dream about:

> To the extent that all-girl subcultures, where the commitment to the gang comes first, might forestall [the search for boyfriends] and provide their members with a collective confidence which could transcend the need for "boys," they could well signal an important progression in the politics of youth culture.[54]

Since "girl love" is advocated continuously in Riot Grrrl music, zines, and visual art, it is important to consider how its more obvious meaning—lesbianism—further signifies Riot Grrrl's radical transformation of both girls' culture and girlhood.

We should be mindful, however, of the class privilege that allows riot grrrls to develop a nonheterocentric, noncommercial, and nondomestic female youth culture. As McRobbie and Jenny Garber argue:

> The middle-class girl student has more time, a more flexible timetable, three or four years in which marriage is positively discouraged, and finally, a softer environment, a more total experience not so strictly demarcated into work and leisure, which allows for the development of *personal* style.[55]

Moreover, in comparison to poor girls, middle-class female youth are typically privileged with not only more education, but also greater access to the tools of media production, which in turn contributes to their confidence when using such technologies and involvement in entrepreneurial youth cultures. Indeed, by the mid-1990s, most middle-class adults were encouraged to believe that personal computers and video cameras were essential household appliances, which means that most female youth involved in Riot Grrrl have access to such media equipment well before they come in contact with it at school or in local community organizations.

With little time and disposable income to invest in such youth cultures, working-class girls more often involve themselves in recreational activities within their homes. The culture of the bedroom works for such girls because, as McRobbie and Garber argue, it "does [not] rely on a lot of money. Its uniforms are cheap, its magazines are well within the pocket-money weekly budget, its records are affordable and its concerts are sufficiently rare to be regarded as treats."[56] Though this construction of the commercial products used by girls to form bedroom culture as "cheap" is disputable today, poor girls have ready access to a broad range of cultural commodities purchased and shared by friends and family members. Unfortunately, working-class girls' continued investments in bedroom culture reveal the hegemony of heterocentric, patriarchal ideologies in their lives, a phenomenon less true for contemporary middle-class female youth who have other options for cultural practice. Indeed, despite the broad proliferation of feminist ideologies over the past three decades, the cultural experiences of most poor girls today are virtually the same as those studied by McRobbie and Garber in the 1970s.

Given the structural differences of middle-class and working-class girls' lives, Riot Grrrl's ability to fully transform girlhood and female youth culture seems unlikely. Indeed, class has long marked the cultural experiences of the female youth who participate in this community, as riot grrrl Erin McCarley notes:

> As a middle-class girl, I have access to canvas and paint. I can use my dad's camera. If you're working class, you [may not] have access. There are many talented people who don't have access. It's a privilege to be in a band because of the equipment.... You need money to press the vinyl; tapes are not acceptable to some people. I really wanted to make a zine with my photography, but photos look like shit when they're photocopied. I have access to a scanner, but not directly, so it's a hassle. I don't have the resources.[57]

At the same time, however, it is important to note that most riot grrrls champion punk's working-class ethos and practice the voluntary poverty historically associated with disaffected middle-class youth. As a result, most of the musicians, zinesters, and filmmakers within this community practice a "bare bones" approach to cultural production that contrasts dramatically with that of the commercial media industries. By privileging amateurism in both their equipment and aesthetics, Riot Grrrl media producers send a message to other girls that the independent production of culture is possible, even for those female youth with minimal capital, education, or access to technology. Therefore, as cultural theorist Walter Benjamin would argue, riot grrrls have put an "improved apparatus" for media production at the disposal of female youth.[58] It is no surprise then that Riot Grrrl has become one of the primary sites of contemporary American girls' cultural productivity.

AN IMPROVED APPARATUS: RIOT GRRRL'S NETWORKED MEDIA ECONOMY

The creation and maintenance of Riot Grrrl's community is due in large part to the circulation of girls' self-produced media products, which disseminate the "Revolution Girl Style Now!" message and signal a rebellion against not only girls' subordinated social position, but also their complicated economic position as one of the primary target groups for the fashion, beauty, and culture industries. Unlike most American youth, whose cultural identities and experiences are connected primarily to the consumption of commodities mass-produced by capitalist industries, riot grrrls attempt to oppose and exist outside the institutions that support commercial youth culture by creating the music, magazines, and other creative products they consume.

Championing the DIY ethos of punk culture and living the "females-can-do-anything" attitude of feminists, Riot Grrrl media producers have boldly seized control of the tools and practices related to the creation, reproduction, exhibition, promotion, and distribution of media texts in order to offer representations of girlhood alternate to those mass-produced by the commercial culture industries. In the process, they have motivated thousands of other female youth to do the same. The first issue of Bikini Kill's self-titled zine, significantly subtitled "An Activity and Coloring Book," seems to have set the stage for such cultural productivity: "We are not special, anyone can do it. encouragement in the face of insecurity is a slogan of the revolution."[59] The second issue of *Bikini Kill* was more explicit: "[Girls] must take over the means of production in order to create our own meanings."[60] In its now-famous manifesto, *Bikini Kill #2* addressed the various reasons why female youth should get involved in media production:

> riot grrrl is ... because us girls crave records and books and fanzines that speak to us, that we feel included in and can understand our own ways. ...

> because we must take over the means of production in order to create our own meanings. ...

because doing/reading/seeing/hearing cool things that validate and challenge us can help us gain strength and sense of community that we need in order to figure out how bullshit like racism, able-body-ism, age-ism, species-ism, classism, thinism, sexism, anti-semitism and heterosexism figures in our own lives.

because we see fostering and supporting girl scenes and girl artists as integral to this process.[61]

Noting the broad effect of Riot Grrrl's DIY/girl power ethos, one riot grrrl, Spirit, argues:

Riot grrrl—the idea, the movement, the non localized group, whatever—inspired literally hundreds of girls to do zines, start bands, collectives, distributions, have meetings etc. ... Our networking through mail, the internet, through music, through zines and through the punk scene keeps us closely knit and strong.[62]

Though Spirit describes the collective power Riot Grrrl ignited, other riot grrrls have commented on the sense of individual agency this movement has inspired in them, encouraging them to produce their own media. Indeed, riot grrrls' explorations of assertiveness, confidence, and agency, traits rarely afforded female youth in the public sphere, are evident in much of the writing and imagery associated with this community. For example, Ciara Xyerra notes in her zine, *A Renegade's Handbook to Love & Sabotage*, "riot grrrl ... shook me out of my fear that i was too young, too inexperienced, too female, too stupid for people to want to hear my voice."[63] Similarly, Witknee writes in her zine, *Alien*:

since i've been doing zines, my self-esteem has improved rapidly. before and in the beginning (of my 'zine years') i was very insecure and unconfident with my opinions, i felt i was worthless and nothing i thought had any importance. by publishing my work and making it public i began to extinguish the latter and relearn the importance of speaking out and expressing myself. *alien* has been my tool to confidence and self-assurance.[64]

The revolutionary aspect of girls' cultural production, as commented on by Witknee, is noted also by Renee, who politicizes this practice in her zine, *Stumble*: "Just by going out and doing a zine says something—it means that this thing called 'empowerment' is in effect. Time to make a statement. And it ain't no feeble attempt. These zines scream 'i am making a difference.'"[65] Hanna first articulated this sense of individual girls enacting social change in *Bikini Kill #1*:

I was like, okay I can sit here in my apartment and be really pissed off and beat the shit out of my pillow or something or I can get my anger out by making this little xerox thing about what I was thinking [a flyer about sexual harassment], so I did. It made me feel a lot better, I mean if just one woman reads it and feels like she knows what I'm talking about, then it's totally worth it. I think the idea that one person can do stuff is really important.[66]

In order to fully comprehend and appreciate the revolutionary nature of Riot Grrrl's various media texts and counterculture, it is necessary to first comprehend the larger infrastructure in which such texts are created, reproduced, exhibited, promoted, and distributed. When riot grrrls like Spirit discuss their movement's "networking" practices, therefore, we need to consider the various meanings of this term. Indeed, I would argue that in order to comprehend Riot Grrrl's sociopolitical significance more fully, we need to understand networking not only in the traditional sense—as a social and communicative practice that brings human beings together (the privileged meaning for this term in other studies of Riot Grrrl)[67]—but also in the sense the broadcasting industry use—as an infrastructural system and set of practices that use communications technology to connect consumers with a variety of media producers and their texts.[68] When viewed through these two perspectives, Riot Grrrl's networked media economy reveals its coterminous objectives to bring girls together and to broadcast the movement's "Revolution Girl Style Now" message through a variety of technology-based channels.

Though most researchers studying the production of culture focus on the commercial culture industries,[69] three sectors constitute the larger field of cultural production, even for youth cultures: the *micro* sector, often referred to in popular discourse as "alternative," "independent," or "underground";[70] the *commercial* sector, typically described as "mainstream," "mass," or "corporate"; and the *governmental* sector.[71] Individuals can potentially engage in six primary activities of cultural production within each of these sectors: *production, reproduction, exhibition, promotion, distribution*, and *consumption*.[72] Although not all of these activities and sectors come into play in the production and diffusion of every artifact produced within a youth culture, a study of Riot Grrrl's networked media economy demonstrates that considerably more interaction and interdependency exists between these various activities and sectors than most analyses of youth cultures suggest.

Zines

Part of a long tradition of counterhegemonic print media, zines are the Riot Grrrl artifacts most closely affiliated with the micro sector of cultural production. As discussed in more detail in Chapter 4, because zines are typically created by a single individual or a small group often within a home, zine production is commonly represented as a "cottage industry" and zine editors (or "zinesters," as they are popularly known) as autonomous producers. Nevertheless, because zinemakers typically rely on the technologies of amateur print production (typewriters, word processors, personal computers, desktop printers), their use of tools originally developed for the commercial sector suggests that their engagement in media production is never fully independent from dominant society. Zinemaking moves beyond the domestic sphere and micro sector of cultural production when the activities of reproduction, promotion, and distribution come into play. For instance, many zinesters rely on the technologies of print production and reproduction accessible to them at work to create their zines, and many others use commercial photocopying businesses to reproduce their texts (even if such businesses are not remunerated). Many zines are sold or traded via direct means so as to keep the boundaries of this economy secure. Yet, the distribution of zines often necessitates interacting with the governmental sector. Indeed, most committed zinesters have subscriptions lists and thus must rely on the state-controlled postal service to distribute their work via the mail. By the late 1990s, many zines were being sold via independent, online distribution services (commonly referred to as "distros"), another practice that connects zinesters to both the governmental and commercial sectors of cultural production.

In an effort to keep the production and reproduction of their zines as independent of commerce and the government as possible, riot grrrl zinesters typically create their zines at home either individually or with a small group of friends. Moreover, in keeping with the counterhegemonic ethos of punk and other leftist cultures, riot grrrls interested in producing (and reproducing) zines often "scam" the use of print and reproductive technologies from their work establishments (an anti-industrialist practice of cultural bricolage the French refer to as *la perruque*),[73] or from commercial photocopying establishments. According to Hanna, several of the earliest Riot Grrrl zines were produced through such practices: "Molly [Neuman] worked as a secretary for a Senator or something, and a group of us girls would go to her office late and stay all night, xeroxing *Riot Grrrl* on his copier!"[74] In turn, Vail writes in *Jigsaw #5*:

> it's not because I'm dumb that I don't own a xerox machine ... this fanzine reflects certain things which are true to my relationship to the means of production, mainly it's not in my hands ... and I don't have a computer either, but mostly because they're ugly, but also because of no job and I still don't understand how I can possibly pay for the cost of printing this, I need a scam, maybe someone can help me, yeah, so keep it in mind.[75]

Like zines produced in other communities, Riot Grrrl zines are typically distributed via the mail (either through requests or subscriptions), though they are also traded by their creators at musical events and conventions, and sold through consignment at independent music stores, bookstores, and countercultural boutiques. Interestingly, shortly after the emergence of Riot Grrrl as a tangible movement, Hanna and Vail had the idea to start a press that would reproduce and distribute zines made by members of this community. Perhaps because of their commitments to touring and recording at the time, a different group of girls in the Washington, D.C. area founded Riot Grrrl Press in the early 1990s (Figure 5). GERLL (Girls Empowered Resisting Labels and Limitations) is another girl-run zine distribution service associated with the Riot Grrrl movement. Though now defunct, both of these presses were extremely significant in disseminating this community's early print media to interested readers, especially those who did not have access to meetings, conventions, and online groups. Today, many Riot Grrrl zines are sold via mail-order distribution services, many of which now exist on the Web.

As mentioned above, *Sassy* magazine was quite influential in bringing Riot Grrrl zines to the attention of female youth who were not part of this community by publishing reviews of these texts in its "Zine of the Month" column during the early to mid-1990s. Yet, most Riot Grrrl zinesters advertise their zines in other girl-made zines, thus further solidifying and expanding the personal and infrastructural communication network of this movement. In an effort to motivate more female youth to produce their own zines, several women affiliated with the Riot Grrrl community, and influenced by the concept of feminist mentoring, have created workshops on zinemaking, such as those taught at various Girlday and Ladyfest conventions. Other young

Figure 5 A crucial link in Riot Grrrl's early networked media economy. Riot Grrrl Press's mail order catalog, 1993.

women wanting to encourage more girls to get involved in zinemaking have published zines, articles, and books that outline the basic techniques involved in paper and digital zine production, and direct readers to the many girl-made zines associated with this community.[76] In order to motivate further communication and support among girl zinesters, many of the female-run zine distros, including Grrrl Style! and Pander Zine Distro, have created "member boards," where girl zinesters gather to discuss various issues related to zines and zinemaking.

Music

In contrast to zinemaking, the creation, reproduction, exhibition, and distribution of musical recordings requires the use of far more sophisticated and expensive forms of media technology, and thus far more interaction with the commercial sector of cultural production. This reality calls into question the use of the term "independent" to describe music created in the micro sector of cultural production. For instance, musical performance necessitates, at minimum, the use of musical instruments produced within the commercial sector. When music is performed for a large group, musicians must also rely on amplification equipment manufactured for use within commercial venues, such as bars and clubs. Though many amateur musicians rely on inexpensive, used (as well as borrowed and stolen) equipment, because many performers affiliated with the independent music scene prefer older and less sophisticated instruments and amplification equipment (which produce a "low-tech" sound homologous with their culture's values), such equipment has become somewhat fetishized and is often quite expensive to acquire.[77]

The recording of music similarly necessitates the use of technology originally manufactured for the commercial recording industry, such as tape decks and mixers, as well as the assistance of individuals trained in the use of such equipment. Although the DIY, amateur aesthetic privileged in punk performance typically applies to the recording and mixing processes as well, with musicians independently recording and mixing their own work via inexpensive technology produced for nonprofessionals, many punk musicians rely on the recording, distribution, and promotion services provided by record labels associated with the independent music scene. The reproduction of independently recorded music connects these musicians most closely to the commercial sector since it requires their (or their label's) reliance on commercial businesses that mass-produce and package vinyl records, cassette tapes, and compact discs.

Perhaps as a result of the naturalized masculinity of electronic musical equipment and thus girls' and women's discouragement from engaging with such technology and the discourse associated with it,[78] few references to riot grrrls' instruments and amplification equipment appear in either commercial or alternative accounts of this community. Indeed, Andrea Juno's collection, *Angry Women in Rock*, is one of the few texts that identifies women rock musicians' equipment. For example, Juno cites Hanna as using a Sure Vocal Master P.A. circa 1960, a SM 57 microphone, and a green Hagstrom bass with two pickups.[79] Some riot grrrls have attempted to involve female youth in musical production even if they had little access to equipment, reminding girls that sounds are not just created through commercially produced instruments. For example, a writer for the zine *RIGHT NOW. RIOT GRRRL* argues:

> Getting guitars; some girls have bits of equipment, and some of us have money, and some of us can get things cheap—we'll figure out ways. And if all that fails, we got loud voices and we can always find things to hit, things that make good sounds ... blocking out boring boyrock, getting more and more ways of saying our thing that's been ignored for centuries.[80]

The promotion of music requires public performances, either live, via shows, or mediated, via radio or television. Many musicians associated with Riot Grrrl effectively model their movement's DIY, "girl power" spirit by booking their own performances and crewing their own equipment. In an effort to further democratize the independent music scene, especially for young girls, Riot Grrrl bands typically privilege the pro-amateur and anti-adultist ethos of punk culture by having an all-ages policy for their performances, or by performing in venues that normally allow for a general audience. Maffeo connects this strategy to the independent music scene developed in such places as Olympia, Washington, and Washington, D.C., while also attesting to the close relationships between many clubs, independent producers, and small record labels:

> Young people [in Olympia during the 1980s] were starting to feel incredibly empowered because there were places to put on shows; in a lot of towns there's no place for kids to play music or gather or do anything. Here there was this setup that all these people had worked hard to achieve: there was a club, a place you could record, a place you could dub off all your cassettes (K [Records] was trying to be as open as possible about letting people use their equipment).[81]

More significantly, perhaps, musicians associated with Riot Grrrl reconfigure the traditionally masculinized spatial and behavior dynamics of punk gigs by encouraging girls to come to the area in front of the stage and prohibiting mosh pits from forming. In doing so, such musicians demonstrate their adherence to the traditions of feminist musical practice, which emerged as part of 1970s' women's culture.[82]

As is the case with many young musicians, numerous performers and bands affiliated with Riot Grrrl only play live, never recording their music. Since the digital recording of music and mass-production of CDs were expensive practices in the early 1990s when this community first developed, Riot Grrrl bands that did record their music (like many other independent musicians of that period) tended to produce their work on cassette tapes and vinyl discs, releasing their work in CD format only if money and consumer demand permitted. These practices are still adhered to by a considerable number of musicians who self-identify as riot grrrls. Most Riot Grrrl performers who record their own music distribute it themselves at live music events, though some sell their music via mail order or small, independent record stores also.

Several Riot Grrrl–affiliated musicians have worked with independent labels owned and run by punk females, such as Echo, Candy-Ass, Chainsaw, Horse Kitty, Simple Machines, and Villa Villakula. In an effort to promote female-run independent labels among riot grrrls and other interested female musicians in the mid-1990s, Tinuviel from Villa Villakula distributed a "Grrrl Record Label Directory" via email that contained over thirty U.S. companies owned or run partly by women. Nevertheless, the earliest-formed and most popular bands associated with Riot Grrrl—Bikini Kill, Bratmobile, Heavens to Betsy, and Tiger Trap—relied on established labels that had grown out of the 1980s' punk scene, particularly K Records, Dischord, and Kill Rock Stars, to record, promote, and distribute their work. Indeed, it is likely that due to their participation in the Olympia and Washington, D.C. punk scenes since their teenage years the members of early Riot Grrrl bands had connections to the older countercultural entrepreneurs who owned the clubs and bars and ran the record production and distribution companies affiliated with those cities' independent music scenes. This phenomenon likely contributed to these bands' higher level of exposure than other Riot Grrrl musicians in both the independent and commercial press.

At the same time, however, it is important to note that the distributors of Riot Grrrl music typically demonstrate the same values as the performers they support, thus allowing for the fluid continuance of amateur aesthetics and counterhegemonic practices throughout the practices of reproduction, promotion, and distribution. For example, Tinuviel has described her first office as "a portable typewriter in a field of blueberries."[83] Though Villa Villakula became successful in a relatively short time ("my office was now my bedroom closet"), Tinuviel kept to the "low-tech" strategies championed by those working in the independent music community and larger micro sector of cultural production:

> I had a bunch of records. Now i was trying to figure out how to sell them, where to advertise, get the mail order into the mail basically all by myself. Occasionally a friend would come over for a few hours

> and help with mail order or promotional mailings. A couple of times
> i hooked up with other small Boston labels to send out promo pack-
> ages to radio & press. I really liked working with others who had
> similar DIY visions and aesthetics.[84]

Indeed, Tinuviel, who is also an artist, took her adherence to the DIY ethos as far as creating the covers for her label's various recordings. For instance, for the *Move into the Villa Villakula* album, she drew the cover illustration, silk-screened all 1,000 copies in her apartment, sent them to various distributors, and set up a mail-order system for those without access to the records in local music stores.[85]

During the early 1990s, Riot Grrrl music was independently distributed via mail-order catalogs, as well as noncorporate music stores. However, as these musicians became more popular, their record labels turned to other commercial enterprises to promote such musicians. For example, Kill Rock Stars agreed to collaborate with *Sassy* to market one of the label's compila-tion discs after the magazine's staff noted that "[t]he majority of our readers still have no access to Bikini Kill or ... Bratmobile unless they live in D.C., Olympia, or New York City."[86] As digital technologies became more afford-able in the late 1990s, online distros provided yet another commercial source for the promotion, selling, and buying of Riot Grrrl music. Operating outside commercial systems of reproduction and distribution, many riot grrrls make compilation tapes of their favorite bands' music that they share with friends. Such tapes function much like chainletters, connecting female youth and spreading the "Revolution Girl Style Now" message.

In the spirit of feminist mentoring, several women associated with the independent music scene have held workshops on performing music, while others have published guidebooks specifically related to buying musical instruments and producing records. For example, Jenny Toomey and Kristin Thompson of Simple Machines created the twenty-four-page "Introductory Mechanics Guide to Putting Out Records," which was published in 1991 as part of Dischord's larger guide to independent music production, *You Can Do It*. Although not read only by girls affiliated with Riot Grrrl, Thompson and Toomey's document received such interest that over the course of eight years, the authors printed over 10,000 copies. Due to its overwhelming popularity, the "Mechanics Guide" was digitized in 1996 and placed on the Web, where it now appears in its sixth edition.[87] Other women have attempted to offer cheap, accessible guidance in musical production for girls also. For example, in the mid-1990s, several riot grrrls collaboratively published a zine titled *Girls Guide to Making a Band and a Record*. More recently, Erin McCarley has produced a zine titled *Girls Guide to Touring* as a resource for female musi-cians interested in booking their own tours and promoting their music.

Film and Video

The national (and international) distribution of Riot Grrrl music and zines has been quite influential in encouraging female youth to create other forms of cultural expression, including film and video projects. Indeed, Sadie Benning, a young filmmaker much celebrated in the early 1990s for her pixelated Fisher-Price visions of adolescent lesbianism, has indicated that the inspiration for her video, *Girl Power*, came from her contact with Riot Grrrl music and zines:

> [W]hen I heard Bikini Kill and when I read these zines, it was so much what I had wanted when I was in high school. It really creates a break in the chain, you know, being able to have words to put upon things that are happening to you and knowing that we all exist and finding one another.[88]

As she reported in a 1992 interview, "[R]ight now my heroes seem to be girl bands—Fifth Column, Tribe 8, Bikini Kill, L7, Bratmobile. I worship girls who make girl power, creatin sexy girl sweat, and pumpin girly sounds."[89] Riot Grrrl's messages of empowerment and self-sufficiency have also led to Benning's creation of her own zines, including *Teenage Worship*, as well as her participation in such bands as All Girl Action and Le Tigre.[90] In turn, many of the female youth associated with Riot Grrrl have found Benning to be an inspiring role model. For instance, articles about and interviews with the young video-maker appear in *Jigsaw* and *Girl Germs*, two zines that were crucial to the development of the Riot Grrrl movement.

In addition to Benning, several other young female filmmakers have been affiliated with and inspired by the Riot Grrrl movement, including Tammy Rae Carland, Sarah Jacobson, Miranda July, Maria Maggenti, Lucy Thane, and Alex and Sylvia Sichel. Like Benning, these filmmakers have relied on the music of Riot Grrrl–associated bands to sonically represent their films' messages of girl power and girl love. For instance, Thane's documentaries of contemporary punk feminism, *She's Real Worse than Queer* and *In March 1993, Bikini Kill Toured the UK. It Changed My Life*, include a considerable amount of footage of Riot Grrrl bands performing, as well as female youth being energized and inspired by such music. Narrative and experimental films inspired by Riot Grrrl include punk feminist music and performers also. For example, Maggenti's *The Incredibly True Story of Two Girls in Love* foregrounds one of its protagonist's admiration for such riot grrrl bands as Bikini Kill, while *All Over Me*, by the Sichel sisters, features a real-life female rocker, Leisha Hailey of The Murmurs, as well as a fictional all-girl punk group, The Coochie Band. The use of such music and performers in independent films focusing on teenage girls is a notable attempt to move beyond the formula of studio-produced female-centered teenpics, which continue to rely on the music of male performers to construct their soundscapes, while also positioning boys as girls' main role models and objects of desire.

Despite the presence of these young female filmmakers, it is important to note that, unlike zinemaking or musical performance, the production of audiovisual texts requires not only considerable expense, due to the cost of renting or buying camera and editing equipment, but also considerable interaction with the capitalist sector of cultural production. Indeed, virtually all of the practices involved in film and video shooting, postproduction, and exhibition require sophisticated technology originally produced for commercial purposes. Although the introduction of camcorders in the 1980s and digital video cameras in the late 1990s have considerably reduced the high level of capital, skill, and equipment needed for amateur movie production, the technology involved in video production and editing remains quite expensive for most youth, and thus prevents many girls from actively engaging in this form of media production. (In addition, as I discuss in more detail in Chapter 5, the tools and practices of film production have been naturalized as masculine for so long that many female youth do not consider film or video to be forms of media with which they can engage.)

Nevertheless, the young women filmmakers associated with Riot Grrrl have attempted to keep the costs of producing their audiovisual projects to a minimum, working with technology that is inexpensive and contributes to the amateur aesthetic privileged by punks. For example, when asked to describe her equipment and editing style during an interview for *Jigsaw*, Benning noted:

> I have a 8mm video camera, and an 8mm small little deck that cost like 400 dollars, and an editor controller that cost a hundred dollars, and I edit between the deck and the camera. I plug the fisher price [camera] right into the deck, and record onto 8mm, and then edit between the two. It's so bare bones. I have one channel of sound, and if I want to have music and voice over, I have to have my boom box and be turning it up, and saying the lines, and then be turning it down.[91]

Foregrounding her "bare bones" approach to sound and image editing, Benning specifically distances herself from commercial filmmaking, while also noting the professional standards that often constrain directors:

> I also appreciate the limit of it because I respect what I do have. And that's the thing about people in film and video who care so much about technical things and all the things you can do with money, who concentrate so much on the medium, and not on exactly what they want to get across, or what they really care about, or themselves.[92]

Unfortunately, by having her videos screened primarily in places associated with elite culture, like college campuses and the Museum of Modern Art, and distributed through companies that charge extremely high rental and purchase fees, like Video Data Bank and Women Make Movies, Benning has prevented many girls from seeing her work.

In order to bring attention to female filmmakers and their work, as well as provide resource information for those interested in making movies, Tina Spangler introduced her zine, *femme flicke*, in the early 1990s. Though not directly affiliated with Riot Grrrl, Spangler has been instrumental in promoting the work of filmmakers associated with this community. Indeed, *femme flicke #5* has a special section called "Grrrls on Film" about movies related to the Riot Grrrl movement, including Thane's documentary about Bikini Kill's tour of the United Kingdom.[93] In turn, the zine has proven to be an important source of information, informing aspirational filmmakers about guidebooks on film production and histories of female filmmakers, as well as directing readers toward movies created by women. The impact of Spangler's zine on girls' feelings of confidence and legitimization as filmmakers has been significant. For example, a letter published in *femme flicke #7* reads:

> I am an 18-year-old girl spending the summer in Chicago taking a film course at Columbia College. And I brought my only issue of *Femme Flicke* with me to keep as a reminder that I actually might be able to do this (and give me good references on films to look for).[94]

Spangler and other female zinesters have played an active role in promoting the film and video work of riot grrrls and other young independent female directors; however, the distribution of movies beyond members of this community has usually been quite difficult. For example, though Jacobson's film, *Mary Jane's Not a Virgin Anymore*, was screened at the Sundance Film Festival, she was unable to secure a distribution contract. As she put it, "Distributors didn't believe in an audience made up of young straight girls and the boys who love them."[95] Nonetheless, because her films were popular on the festival circuit, she decided to self-distribute, selling them "mail order like a record, sending out copies for review to different magazines," as well as putting up flyers in urban areas.

In turn, the DIY and pro-girl spirit of Riot Grrrl motivated performance artist Miranda July to create an independent company in 1995 called Big Miss Moviola, which distributes female-produced films on video compilations (Figure 6). As July notes, she was inspired "when I realized there must be thousands of worthwhile girl-made movies out there that you just can't run down to Blockbuster to rent."[96] July refers to these compilations as "chainletters," because they work in a similar way: Filmmakers send a copy of their film or video to her, and she reproduces it on a video cassette with nine other mov-

Figure 6 An alternative distribution system for female filmmakers. Big Miss Moviola promotional flyer, 1995. Courtesy of Miranda July.

ies. July then distributes the compilation to all contributors, as well as those non-contributors interested in purchasing it. Noting that Big Miss Moviola is a "non-selective institution working with, not against, the more commercial opportunities that are available to women moviemakers,"[97] July programs the chainletters to include films and videos from both amateur and professionally trained female filmmakers, thus leveling the playing field of female filmmaking while helping to democratize the medium. Whereas other independent film distributors typically marginalize young and less experienced filmmakers, July ensures that girl-made movies do not remain within the closed community of their creators' friends, schoolmates, and family members. Indeed, in the spirit of democratic communication that fuels countercultural practice, July encourages her consumers to "[m]ake bootleg copies of this tape!"[98]

In an effort to motivate networking among female filmmakers, each Big Miss Moviola chain letter is accompanied by a directory (also referred to as a "viewer's digest"), which includes information contributed by the filmmakers about their work and interests, as well as information about July's related media projects. Through the inclusion of the artists' addresses, the directories help female filmmakers who may feel isolated to communicate and bond with others. As July writes in the directory for the first compilation, *Velvet Chainletter,* "The Directory is important. It's the reason why Big Miss Moviola is more about communication than presentation. The participants can give each other feedback if they want and they will also get letters from non-participants who bought the tape."[99] In the late 1990s, July changed the name of this project to Joanie 4 Jackie and created a website through which visitors can read about the films, watch clips, purchase the chain letters, and communicate with the filmmakers.[100] Aligning her project within the countercultural scene of Olympia, July now distributes the Joanie 4 Jackie tapes through K Records.

Although Joanie 4 Jackie emerged from July's experiences in the independent and Riot Grrrl communities of the Pacific Northwest, it is important to note that her development of this distribution service would not have been possible without July's engagement with the commercial sector of cultural production. For example, she has actively worked to open her project to individuals outside those scenes, perhaps most significantly by agreeing to appear as *Sassy* magazine's first "Sassiest Girl of the Month" in 1996. As she writes in the first chain letter's directory:

> [T]his project is going to be defined by it's media coverage. It's about media: who get's to be seen, who represents who, what do you watch on your TV. ... [Y]ou too can be a Big Miss Moviola Publicist. Call your local newspaper and ask them to interview you today. Really.[101]

Though July originally reproduced the chain letters herself on used video cassettes purchased at second-hand stores, she now relies on commercial video duplication services to mass-produce copies of the tapes, which has sometimes resulted in attempted censorship of the films she distributes. Relating one such incident in the directory for the *Underwater Chainletter*, July demonstrates that she is one of the few participants in the punk feminist media community who has drawn attention to her connections to the capitalist sector of cultural production:

> While Big Miss Moviola is underground, girl-powered and everlasting: ... I am always making pacts with and kissing the straight worlds ass; I am often making decisions that both help me/you and also fuck us over. The things that are difficult for me with Big Miss Moviola are probably the same kinds of things that are frustrating for you as a moviemaker or as an active, smart woman. So then you know what I mean when I say that it is all worth it and it will never be enough.[102]

In addition to exhibiting the Big Miss Moviola films at various arts and educational institutions, July has other cinematic projects, including Joanie 4 Jackie 4 President, a program to teach film and video production techniques to girls and women. July describes the Portland, Oregon, version of the program as "specifically for teenage girls, since dismissing teenagers is part of the conspiracy that wants to keep women silent."[103] (As discussed in more detail in Chapter 3, several other young women interested in feminist mentoring and supportive of the Riot Grrrl community have introduced workshops in filmmaking for girls in recent years.)

In order to involve non–filmmakers in her cinematic vision of cultural transformation, July has also created "The Missing Movie Report." For this project, she asked girls and women to describe spontaneously the film they would most like to make. (As she argues, "Some of the most incredible movies ... will never be made, but that's not a reason to forget about them.")[104] July recorded such cinematic fantasies on audiotape, and then compiled them into a poster that includes the respondents' pictures and brief descriptions of their unmade films. Fully embracing and further disseminating the leftist DIY message, July encourages Big Miss Moviola consumers to start their own Missing Movie Report and get involved in filmmaking. As she states in all of her projects, "This is a challenge and a promise."

RIOT GRRRL'S EFFECTS: THE PROLIFERATION OF GRRRL POWER CONSCIOUSNESS

In May 1993, Nina Malkin reported in *Seventeen* about the "rumblings of an internal rift between Riot Grrrl's vehemently militant faction and the less hard-core groups."[105] Focusing her article on one Riot Grrrl "drop-out," Malkin used this girl to highlight the failings of this movement's ideologies and practices. That same fall, journalist Ann Japenga authoritatively asserted (in the past tense, no less) that "[Riot Grrrl's] credo—that young women should support each other rather than competing as society urges them to do—was lost in the transition, and the movement was reduced to a kicky little clique defined almost exclusively by fashion."[106] Similarly, Lorraine Ali reported in 1995 that the Riot Grrrl "scene never erupted" and "the only traces of riot grrl-dom outside its insular core are cutesy mutations of its once ironic fashions in perky teen magazines."[107]

Over a decade has passed since Malkin's, Japenga's, and Ali's pronouncements of Riot Grrrl's demise. Yet, this community is still active and productive, though little indication of that appears in dominant society or commercial popular culture, largely due to riot grrrls' media blackout in 1992. In fact, much Riot Grrrl activity remains underground and thus imperceptible to mainstream journalists and commercial trendsetters in search of the "next best thing." As Tamra Spivey asserted in an interview in 1996, "I get so much pleasure when the media types go, 'Oh, Riot Grrrl, that's passé.' There were nine conventions last year. Did you hear about that, Mr. Media?"[108]

Perhaps more significant than its continual presence in the U.S. for over a decade has been Riot Grrrl's diffusion across the globe. Although a Riot Grrrl posting circulated in 1995 on the Internet listed twenty-six U.S. Riot Grrrl groups and one Canadian group, a web-based directory last updated in 2004 listed twenty-nine U.S. groups, four Canadian groups, six UK groups, two European groups, and one Brazilian group.[109] Thus, in spite of mainstream journalists' misrepresentations of Riot Grrrl as a thing of the past, this movement continues to grow in numbers and become more geographically diffuse as female youth around the world are coming together to support one another, organize political events, and form their own countercultural scenes.

Although few of the original founders self-identify as riot grrrls today, many young women involved in this movement have noted its particular significance for younger girls, who benefit greatly from bonding with other girls and educating themselves about misogyny, homophobia, sexual abuse, and commercial beauty culture, as well as media technology and practices. As Bragin argues:

> Riot Grrrl's crucial. It's saving girls' minds. There are so many different ent situations that girls face. ... Riot Grrrl needs to be there for girls who are young, because they need help now, because you can't wait until you're old and abuse has already happened.... Riot Grrrl has been successful in making girls have revolutions in their lives. It carries out to people they know. As long as they continue spreading their ideas, Riot Grrrl will continue to be effective.[110]

As Bragin suggests, often involvement in Riot Grrrl is a preliminary step for female adolescents attempting to regain the confidence, assertiveness, and self-respect they lost due to abuse or the onset of puberty. Yet, unlike members of the contemporary girls' advocacy movement who use middle-class standards to help female youth besieged by the traumas of growing up female,[111] riot grrrls motivate other girls to find their own voice in a safe and supportive community of similarly disaffected young females emboldened through feminist and punk ideologies.

Because of its affiliations with and historical legacies in other counter hegemonic communities, Riot Grrrl helps to facilitate girls' critical awareness of identity, power, oppression, and social relations. Like feminist consciousness-raising groups, Riot Grrrl's meetings, workshops, concerts, and conventions allow female youth to share their personal experiences with others, thus helping girls to produce an assertive and expressive identity, while also creating a common knowledge of the larger systemic problems associated with being young and female in a predominantly adultist, patriarchal, capitalist, and heterocentric society. For adolescent lesbians and bisexual girls especially, Riot Grrrl's nonjudgmental, queer positive community is a safe haven from the homophobia they experience in everyday life, as well as the ageism they experience in the larger lesbian and gay community.

As several women formerly associated with Riot Grrrl have reported, the initial potency girls feel upon becoming involved with Riot Grrrl often loses its effect as they grow, learn, and change. Indeed, many older riot grrrls feel as if this group no longer addresses their needs and concerns, and suggest that they will soon move on to different communities. For example, at eighteen, McCarley stated:

> Even now I don't feel like I'll feel as committed to Riot Grrrl in a year as I do now. I don't want to feel committed to Riot Grrrl. I mean, it has

done a lot for me personally, but as a movement, I'm starting to feel it's almost a moot point.[112]

Recalling early Riot Grrrl meetings, Toomey notes that she often felt distanced from younger girls in this community because of her age:

> The level of discussion was not really what I was interested in. I could see how important it might be for the younger girls, but I had a college degree in women's studies and just wasn't that interested in talking about boyfriends, slamdancing, or stuff like that.[113]

Other young women once associated with Riot Grrrl have distanced themselves from the movement also, yet often for reasons other than age differences. For example, Mimi Nguyen indicates that as much as Riot Grrrl was a positive force in her life at one point, this community never worked for her as an Asian American woman. Although she argues that "Riot Grrrl is amazing in so many ways: as confrontation, as education, as performance, as aesthetic, as support, as theory, as practice, etc.,"[114] she also notes some riot grrrls' uncritical racial and class biases:

> [I]t's important for me as a feminist of color to critique Riot Grrrl for the ways in which it has (or hasn't) dealt with differences of race and class. In that aspect rather than presenting an *alternative*, Riot Grrrl totally parallels "mainstream" Euro-American feminism. Gender is presumed to be a social category that can be separated from race, class, or even nation. ... A lot of the subjects white girls talk about in their zines I just don't relate to. Basically I grew up *counter-appropriating* what I could.[115]

Ultimately, Nguyen decided to leave Riot Grrrl for new areas of cultural and political activism, and she notes that she is not alone in making this transition: "I've ... met a lot of women who were once involved in Riot Grrrl and punk and have since moved on to other subcultural spaces (or created their own), and that's been amazing."[116]

Similarly, Jen Smith, who helped launch Riot Grrrl by advocating a "girl riot," has discussed her alienation from this community. Recalling the first convention and the movement that grew out of it, she notes:

> It was fun, and, if only for a moment, it felt like liberation. ... Yet, despite my compassion and enthusiasm, I still felt weary. The urgency of some of the women was alienating to me. There seemed to be an overwhelming specter of patriarchy. Implicit to the sense of power we were cultivating was a constant rejection of white male authority. Though I would concur that a vigorous examination of these issues

will always be necessary to subvert old definitions of power, it seemed to me that a lot of energy was spent in anger and rejection.[117]

Falsely suggesting that Riot Grrrl is a movement of the past, Smith privileges what she believes to be a more "positive" culture developed by older punk feminists since the mid-1990s. In particular, she focuses on the SPRGRL Conspiracy Convention held in Portland, Oregon, in June 1996. Noting the organizers' emphasis on inclusivity and accessibility, as well as the convention's many workshops related to teaching young women productive skills, Smith argues:

> From my perspective, the SPRGRL Conspiracy is concrete evidence of the "image past" Riot Grrrl, and marks a transition in youth feminist culture. It is a turn toward an attitude of independence rather than simple repudiation, and is firmly entrenched in the power and inspiration of a feminist community.[118]

Though hesitant to celebrate Riot Grrrl, consider it a viable community in the present, or credit the many productive female youth associated with it, Smith does acknowledge that it is "[p]robably due to the anger and reactionary struggle of these earlier incarnations of Riot Grrrl ... [that] women are currently more free to explore not only the terrors and frustrations but also the possibilities of their lives."[119]

In an effort to spread the girl power message and motivate female youth to participate in the public sphere, other young women supportive of Riot Grrrl have developed workshops and other events for female youth. One of the more significant one-time events was Free to Fight!, organized in 1995 by Jody Blyele (of the band Team Dresch and Candy-Ass Records), Staci Cotler, and Anna Lo Bianco, self-defense teachers who are also active in Portland's independent music scene. In an effort to help girls and women empower themselves in the face of abuse, the organizers of Free to Fight! ("an interactive self defense project") produced an album that includes the music of diverse female performers, women's memories of abuse, women's stories of thwarting sexual harassment, and helpful tips on how to act assertively and defensively. Produced by Candy-Ass and distributed by Revolver in early 1995, the *Free to Fight!* album (modeled after the popular 1970s' children's album, *Free to Be You and Me*) is accompanied by a seventy-five-page zine that includes more stories of women's abuse, tips on defensive behavior, and information about the performers, as well as illustrations and cartoons that further the Free to Fight! message.

In order to make the project as interactive as it was inclusive, the zine, whose text and images were created by thirty women, also includes a page with only the words, "My Story ... ," thus encouraging readers, at the minimum, to connect with the various stories of abuse or self-defense and write their own. More important, the zine serves as a guidebook to help women learn assertive behav-

ior and self-defense techniques in order to protect themselves. As the introduction to the zine states, "[D]on't forget to practice your moves during the musical
numbers on the record (or meditate on your inner strength). Don't be shy."

With a goal of spreading their message to as wide an audience as possible,
the organizers distributed the album and zine through both independent record
stores and feminist bookstores, and profits from album/zine sales were used to
fund free self-defense classes for girls and women. In addition, the organizers
decided to take their project on the road as the Free to Fight! Tour in the summer of 1995 after having a successful release show in Portland earlier that year.
The organizers' intent was to reach as many girls and women as they could,
even if that required their cooperation with the commercial sector. As Blyele
stated, "We want 'Free to Fight' to get to as many people as possible. We want to
get on 'Oprah.' We want as many women to come to our shows and to have the
album. That's the goal, period."[120] In addition to promoting musicians, the tour,
funded in part by sales from the album/zine, included self-defense workshops
led by Alice Stagg, a martial artist and self-defense instructor who toured with
the bands.

In order to continue to educate, motivate, and form networks with other
young feminists, several young women supportive of or formerly affiliated
with Riot Grrrl have organized conventions for young feminists, including the
Southern Girls Convention, first held in 1999 in Memphis, Tennessee. Ladyfest,
introduced in 2000 in Olympia, was produced in twenty-five different cities
over the next four years.[121] These conventions, typically held in the summer and
including a weekend's worth of musical performances, film screenings, poetry
readings, activist meetings, educational workshops, and support groups, are
often organized by women affiliated with local punk scenes, and take as their
model earlier Riot Grrrl conventions, which were modeled on feminist conventions of the 1970s. For instance, Lili Kotlyarov-Montoya, one of the organizers
of the first Riot Grrrl convention, decided to organize Ladyfest D.C. in 2002,
since she "thought it would be cool to have a 'Ten Years Later' event."[122]

In addition to organizing conventions, workshops, and tours, former (and
older) riot grrrls have also participated in the further expansion of a punk feminist infrastructure. For instance, musicians formerly associated with Riot Grrrl
have formed new bands, such as Le Tigre and Sleater-Kinney.[123] In turn, new
record labels and distribution companies have been founded. For example,
Tammy Rae Carland and Kaia Wilson introduced their independent label, Mr.
Lady, in the mid-1990s, selling women-made films, music, and magazines. In
addition to developing the means for marketing and distributing their own
work, Carland and Wilson's reasons for starting Mr. Lady included wanting to
bring greater exposure to women musicians and filmmakers, noting that "to
purchase and view work by ... peers ... is not easy to do unless you maybe live
in a big city or go to college."[124] In turn, because most independent film distri-

bution companies, such a Women Make Movies, charge expensive rental and purchase fees, Carland and Wilson wanted "to make buying videos more like buying a couple of cds or a nice book."[125] Moreover, they see their service as providing an opportunity "to cross the audience borders between music and visual work in an attempt to break down notions that one media is more accessible and the other more elitist."[126]

Like many other independent record distributors, Mr. Lady expanded from a mail-order business to a web-based distro by the late 1990s. Although Carland and Wilson's website is devoted to the sale of Mr. Lady merchandise, many other online distros managed by punk feminists have emerged in the past five years that sell products independently created by many different individuals. (Given the vast numbers of zines produced by female youth in recent years, it is not surprising that zines are primary items on most of these websites.) The introduction and maintenance of such online distros as Grrrl Style Distro, (her) riot distro, and Screamqueen Distro are evidence of the increased presence of personal computers and modems in middle-class girls' lives, as well as the further engagement of digital media technologies by members of punk scenes, especially young women. As Doreen Piano argues, the punk feminist managers of these distros

> facilitat[e] an alternative Net-economy by galvanizing the subculture in ways that traditional distribution methods could not, and also by making the distribution and consumption of feminist goods accessible to a broader market, thus helping to create feminist pockets or zones in cyberspace.[127]

In addition, she notes that "by choosing to buy individually produced products made by their peers," the visitors of punk feminist distros link shopping to activism, thus challenging common assumptions about women's passive complicity in consumer capitalism. In turn, by requesting feedback and programming hyperlinks to bulletin boards and chat rooms, these distros challenge skepticism about the Web as a mechanism for radical communication, organizing, and culture.

Though few of the former riot grrrls who have organized these various businesses and events discuss it, their age, education, experience, and cultural capital has allowed them to interact with sectors of society normally inaccessible to the female youth who continue to drive the Riot Grrrl community. Most notably, their use of digital technologies to communicate, organize, and manage business and cultural events indicates a level of access to computers and other digital equipment not afforded to most girls. Moreover, by having access to other countercultural organizations and activist groups, these young women have been able not only to garner a larger audience for their texts, events, and businesses, but to build a stronger infrastructure for the punk feminist community.

In turn, though few acknowledge it openly, several of the women artists, performers, and cultural entrepreneurs who were once affiliated with Riot Grrrl have received grants from private foundations, such as the Rockefeller Foundation, and government organizations, such as the National Endowment for the Arts, to support their work, thus connecting them, in sometimes awkward ways, to the very structures of power and privilege that many riot grrrls and members of the larger micro media community oppose. Nevertheless, these convergences between independent producers and the more conservative sectors of commerce and government point to the complex interactions and interdependencies operating within contemporary media cultures. More scholarly attention to this phenomenon would help to challenge the conventional construction of youth cultures as autonomous spheres untainted by capitalism and the state.

CONCLUSION

Significant transformations over the past decade have broadened the concept of female youth culture beyond its traditional understanding as a bedroom culture where girls consume commodities mass-produced for them by the capitalist culture industries and fantasize about future heterosexual relationships. Although many American girls, particularly those of the working class, undoubtedly continue to construct their cultural experiences according to this particular paradigm, the Riot Grrrl community is powerful evidence that a considerable number of female youth today, especially disaffected middle-class white girls, are rejecting the naturalized story of girlhood by actively seizing control of the means of media production and creating new forms that more directly express their specific concerns, desires, and pleasures.

The importance of Riot Grrrl's independently produced media texts cannot be overstated, particularly in their reformulation of girlhood, feminism, and youth culture, their connection of disaffected girls across the world, their proud declaration and broad dissemination of the DIY ethos and girl power message, and their encouragement of female youth to understand themselves as active cultural agents and to seize the tools of media production. Indeed, it is because of these various aspects that Riot Grrrl's cultural artifacts exemplify Walter Benjamin's point that a text is most progressive when it "is able, first, to induce other producers to produce, and, second, to put an improved apparatus at their disposal."[128]

Some older punk feminists have distanced themselves from Riot Grrrl; yet, it is clear that this movement has a profound effect on the various female youth and young women who participate in it. Regardless of how long they affiliate themselves with Riot Grrrl, or see it as politically and culturally viable, many girls have experienced this community as a social, cultural, and political space, a subaltern counterpublic free from the patriarchy, sexism, and homophobia of most youth cultures, as well as from the adultism associated with the hegemonic feminist movement. As Nguyen wrote in 2000, several years after moving beyond Riot Grrrl:

> I was asked to give a guest lecture about riot grrrl for a class on "Feminism and Popular Culture" at [the University of California,] Santa Cruz. My eight pages of notes arrayed before me and mostly ignored for the duration of the class, and I was inspired by riot grrrl all over again, reading out loud from *Bikini Kill* (both the band and the fanzine). I mean, what else could I possibly feel when uttering [excerpts] from the *Riot Grrrl Manifesto*[?] ... It's still worth fighting for, I think.[129]

As a feminist youth culture where girls learn to see themselves and other female youth as intelligent, powerful, creative, and self-sufficient, Riot Grrrl serves a critical function in the lives of many girls alienated from commercial culture, feminist culture, and punk culture, and thus marks a ruptural moment in the histories of each of these larger social formations. Moreover, the fact that most of the earliest riot grrrls are still active in their local punk scenes and the larger micro media community attests to Riot Grrrl's ability to collectively energize and sustain female youth as media producers. Nevertheless, other sites have emerged in the past decade that allow girls to gain training in cultural production and thus legitimacy as creative agents. The next chapter, therefore, explores the rise of girls' media education programs at the turn of the twenty-first century.

3

Girls' Media Education

Critical Viewing or Control of the Image?

While we can't control every media image in our environment, we all can and should do more thinking about what we're looking at and listening to. ... This is especially true when those images and messages are displayed ... where captive audiences have no choice and young, easily influenced minds (read: kids) are watching.

—Girls, Women + Media Project[1]

We need to train our girls to think differently about media, to think about becoming the director, the person who controls the image.

—Margaret Caples[2]

Entrepreneurial fan and youth cultures, particularly those organized around film and music, have proven to be nourishing training grounds for U.S. girls interested in media production. Another, and more recently formed, site for the development of young females' cultural productivity is the pool of extracurricular girls-only media education programs that have been introduced since the early 1990s. Unlike youth subcultures, which usually attract older adolescents and young adults interested in counterhegemonic values, identities, practices, and communities, girls' media education programs do not have such a narrow contingency. Designed to improve all girls' interest in, access to, and involvement in media production, such programs appeal to a broad range of female youth and thus typically have diverse student populations. Nevertheless, preteen girls are especially attracted to such programs because of their limited ability to participate in the spaces and activities associated with most youth subcultures.

This chapter is devoted to an analysis of the rise in girls' media education programs in the United States during the 1990s. Though the various individuals and organizations that have developed these programs have the similar objective of improving girls' relationships to the media, their methods for achieving this goal reveal an ideological affiliation with one of two broader social formations: the *girls' advocacy movement*, whose history is over one hundred years old but has been reenergized recently by reports of adolescent girls' self-esteem problems; and the *grrrl power movement*, which has emerged from the broad diffusion of "do-it-yourself" (DIY) values and practices associated with activist media organizations and, more specifically, Riot Grrrl. These two perspectives, respectively expressed in the epigraphs to this chapter from the Girls, Women + Media Project and Margaret Caples, executive director of Chicago's Community Film Workshop, are the primary objects of analysis in this chapter, and I trace their influence through case studies of several girls-only media education programs introduced in the 1990s.

GIRLS' MEDIA LITERACY: TEACHING FEMALE YOUTH ANALYTICAL SKILLS

Over the past decade, several organizations associated with the girls' advocacy movement have introduced after-school media literacy programs to facilitate girls' critical media analysis. Girls Inc., an organization almost a century and a half old, has developed two different curricula for girls' media literacy: Girls Re-Cast TV, introduced in 1995, and Girls Get the Message, introduced in 2002. Girls Re-Cast TV was developed specifically in response to reports about the negative effects of television on girls' self-esteem, and it guides female youth through a series of viewing and listening exercises, as well as questions designed to increase their awareness of television representation. The objectives for the Girls Get the Message curriculum is a bit more expansive:

> [A] national program that encourages girls and other media consumers to evaluate the messages in media such as television shows, films, CDs, newspapers, websites, music videos, magazines and video

games. ... Girls learn to "read" media messages with a critical eye as they consider issues of ownership, media business and the roles of women and minorities "behind the scenes" in media careers.[3]

Girls Inc.'s two media literacy programs are based on two assumptions: first, commercial media primarily represent females in stereotypical, unrealistic ways that endanger girls' self-esteem; and second, few progressive depictions of female youth and adult women can be found in commercial media texts. For instance, in its "Facts: Girls and Media" brochure, the organization states in bold letters: "TV consistently portrays stereotyped images of women and men."[4] Moreover, Girls Inc.'s programs reproduce the problematic notion that realism is the most progressive aesthetic strategy. For example, in the "Action Kit" used in the Girls Re-Cast TV program, girls are asked to "watch TV, look closely at people's eyes, hair, clothes and skin. Listen to their tone of voice and how they respond to each other. Notice what they do, where they live and where they go to school. Does it look like your life?"[5] Reproducing a perspective on media culture that has historically been linked to leftist social movements and is commonly held by disenfranchised individuals seeking positive representation, the Girls Get the Message curriculum states that "[t]he program helps girls recognize stereotypes in media and differentiate between those stereotypes and their own lives."[6]

Girls Inc.'s attempts to facilitate girls' critical understanding of the relationship of gender and media are to be commended. As David Buckingham notes when describing the benefits of such programs:

> By confirming or questioning the accuracy of television representations, explaining and supplementing what is shown, and offering advice about whether television should be taken as a model of real-life behavior, they are helping children to develop a more complex and nuanced understanding of the relationships between the medium and the real world.[7]

Nevertheless, the questions and comments posed by Girls Inc. to female youth via its media literacy curricula suggest the teaching of an outdated and reductive understanding of media representations as direct reflections of, and thus direct influences on, reality. Indeed, the objectives of its media literacy curricula echo much of the discourse circulated by feminists in the early 1970s about the need for more "positive" and "realistic" representations of women, ideals which were largely shaped by white, middle-class, heterosexual women.[8] By constructing their programs' objectives in this way, the developers of Girls Inc. media literacy curricula demonstrate their lack of exposure to or training in contemporary theories of the relationship of gender to media representation and consumption. As a result, the female youth who participate in Girls Inc.'s programs are not motivated to problematize realist aesthetics or to understand fantasy as a primary component of media production and reception. Moreover, since Girls Inc.'s curriculum developers assume that each media text has only one meaning that is solely produced by its creator, the girls addressed by such curricula are not encouraged to understand media texts as inherently polysemous, or to consider consumers as actively participating in the meaning-making process.

More disturbingly, however, despite its rhetoric of girl empowerment, the media literacy curricula developed by Girls Inc. does not encourage female youth to produce their own media texts, an activity that would allow them to directly challenge media representations they find problematic.[9] Despite calling their Girls ReCast TV curriculum an "Action Kit," the only active practice advocated by this program is girls writing to media industry professionals about their concerns with particular texts. This sort of dialogue is important for increasing girls' participation in popular culture; however, it does not motivate them to see that culture as larger than the commercial media industries. More recently, the Girls Inc. website has added an activity where female youth can produce a treatment for a new television show.[10] Though helping to facilitate girls' creativity, this activity limits their involvement in media production to its most traditional form: writing. No attempts are made to motivate girls' engagement with cameras or other technologies that create televisual texts.

The media literacy initiatives developed by the Girl Scouts of the United States of America similarly focus on developing girls' critical abilities at the expense of providing information on media technology and hands-on media experience, especially for younger girls. For example, after the Girl Scouts' national office introduced the Media Savvy Interest Patch in 1999, a California chapter of the Girl Scouts formed an alliance with the Museum of Television and Radio in Los Angeles to produce a workshop for scouts on television genres and girls' representation within this medium. Similarly, a Texas chapter of the Girl Scouts collaborated with the Austin Children's Museum in 2001 to produce a workshop on video for young scouts.[11] Although both of these workshops included components that facilitated the development of girls' critical viewing skills and knowledge of media technology, neither entailed practical experience in the creation of audiovisual texts. Indeed, by organizing the workshops around adult practitioners who discussed media analysis and technology but did not facilitate the scouts' engagement in such activities, these two workshops reproduced the conventional understanding that media criticism and production are practices in which only adults engage.

To my knowledge, the only nationwide effort on the part of the Girl Scouts to encourage female youth to produce their own media texts appears in a guidebook called *Media Know-How*, which was published in 1999 and is specifically directed to older Cadette and Senior Girl Scouts.[12] Unfortunately, the book's suggestions on how to make a magazine, website, or television program do not provide female youth with enough information to effectively start, much less complete, exhibit, and distribute such media projects. For example, while the guide for producing a television show includes directions on preparing the basic elements of a script, its directions on videotaping the program are minimal, and the only instruction on editing suggests "quick cuts" to make the show "more dramatic and exciting."[13] Although the limited amount of instruction offered by this guidebook is concerning, it is important to note that the Girl Scouts operates almost entirely via volunteer assistance and, therefore, would have a difficult time instituting a nationwide curriculum in media production for all its troops.

The Girl Scouts' and Girls Inc.'s narrow focus on developing girls' critical viewing skills has been replicated recently by several other girls' advocacy organizations. For example, according to informational discourse for Girls, Women + Media Project's "What Can I Do?" program, the only ways in which girls can participate in today's media culture are establishing a media literacy group, going on a "media diet," making intelligent decisions about media consumption, and giving feedback to media industry professions via letters.[14] Interestingly, other girls' advocacy organizations encourage female youth to confine their media critiques to diary or journal writing, one of the most traditional, and conventional, forms of girls' media production. For example, the Girl Power! program kit, produced by the U.S. Department of Health and Human Services, includes a diary for girls to use, and the "Girl Power! How to Get It" and "Girl Power! Keep It Going" activity guides suggest that girls use writing for purposes of self-reflection. In other words, girls are encouraged to see writing as a means to "dump" their emotions privately rather than as a form of public expression.

By critically analyzing and assessing these various girl-centered media literacy curricula, it is not my intention to suggest that they are not useful for female youth. Indeed, they have helped to develop many girls' analytical skills and awareness of media representation, and thus broadened their literacy beyond printed texts. Such skills are necessary for participating in a society where media are ubiquitous. Nevertheless, most girl-centered media literacy programs are not committed to facilitating girls' involvement in forms of creative expression and communication that might increase their audience and expand their cultural experiences beyond stereotypical female activities that result in them being seen and not heard. Indeed, while the girls who participate in such programs develop skills and knowledge that help them critique media texts, they also gain a skewed perspective of media culture that may actually limit their understanding of the opportunities for resistance, opposition, and subversion afforded by self-representation. In order to understand why these programs have been structured in this way, it is necessary to consider their roots in the larger fields of media pedagogy and girls' advocacy.

TEACHING CRITICAL VIEWING SKILLS: MEDIA LITERACY INITIATIVES IN THE UNITED STATES

Media pedagogy is now many decades old, having emerged alongside various advancements in media technology and developments in educational philosophy and instructional practices.[15] This field can be divided roughly into three different approaches to media used by instructors: *integration*, *production*, and *analysis*.[16] The *integration* of media into schools includes two different strategies: first, incorporating media texts, such as newspapers and films, as supplemental learning materials, and second, incorporating media technologies, such as television and the Internet, as alternative channels for delivering information to students. *Production*-oriented media education curricula involve facilitating students' knowledge and skilled use of various media technologies for purposes of documentation, communication, and creative expression. The *analytical* approach to media pedagogy, commonly referred to as "media literacy," entails teaching students' critical skills for analyzing and evaluating media texts. Comprehending the differences between these approaches is essential for understanding contemporary girl-centered media education programs in the United States.

Many scholars trace the history of media literacy initiatives in the United States to the late 1920s and early 1930s and connect it contextually to the rise of mediated popular culture. It was during this period that research on children's cinema attendance and the effects of film on youth was first conducted,[17] leading to adult concerns over the amount of young people's film consumption, and eventually the development of educational guides to accompany school screenings of particular films. Adult fears about young people's media consumption were reignited in the 1950s with the publication of Fredric Wertham's *Seduction of the Innocent*, which linked children's comic book reading to juvenile delinquency.[18]

The first formal media literacy program was introduced in 1959, when Marshall McLuhan, strongly influenced by F. R. Leavis and similarly conservative and pessimistic about the media's effects, proposed such a curriculum for eleventh graders to the Canadian National Association of Educational Broadcasters.[19] Concerns over children's television viewing reinvigorated media literacy initiatives in the United States in the early 1970s, particularly after the Surgeon General's Scientific Advisory Committee on Television and Social Behavior published a report in 1972 that connected young people's antisocial behavior with their viewing of violence on television.[20] Followed the next year by a Ford Foundation report calling for more attention to mass media in public classrooms,[21] the Committee's report inspired the development of several media literacy initiatives over the course of the 1970s, including four "critical viewing skills" programs for elementary and secondary students funded by the then U.S. Department of Health, Education, and Welfare.[22]

While media education efforts in Canada, Australia, and Great Britain received increasing support from teachers, parents, and government officials in the 1980s, media literacy initiatives in the United States deteriorated during this period, largely as a result of decreasing federal funding, as well as repeated calls by conservatives for a return to "basics" in elementary and secondary education. Since the early 1990s, however, media literacy classes for youth have experienced phenomenal growth in the United States. In fact, while only twelve states had such curricula in 1999, that number expanded to forty-nine within only two years.[23] This development is due in part to increased support from governmental and private agencies, as well as from new grassroots organizations composed of teachers and media activists, such as the Center for Media Literacy and Alliance for a Media Literate America. In addition, the virtual ubiquity of media in contemporary popular culture, as well as parents' heightened concerns about the potentially negative effects of their children's consumption of commercial media have contributed significantly to the recent resurgence of media literacy initiatives. It is somewhat ironic, therefore, that commercial interests have impacted the proliferation of media literacy curricula also. For instance, CNN, Channel One, and Cablevision each have a media literacy curriculum that, not surprisingly, appeals to young people as consumers of these various media enterprises.

Until quite recently, media literacy programs in the United States have vastly outnumbered production-oriented media education curricula. The lack of practical, hands-on production components in such programs has been rationalized as a result of teachers' minimal training in media technology and production practices, teachers' unwillingness or inability to integrate media into their current lesson plans, schools' limited access to or funds for equipment, the minimal amount of time allotted for individual subjects in the average school day, and a belief that students, particularly younger children, will merely replicate what they see in commercial popular culture.[24] Middle-class adults' concerns about teachers privileging the development of young people's technical/vocational skills over analytical/professional skills, as well as the potential valuing of popular culture over the fine arts and humanities, have also contributed to students' lack of training in media production in most schools.

The dominance of media literacy curricula in the United States can also be connected to the reemergence of conservative social agendas during the late twentieth century, particularly "family values" and "back to basics" curricula that focus on reading, writing, and arithmetic.[25] Wendy Ewald and Alexandra

Lightfoot suggest a connection between contemporary teachers' avoidance of training in visual arts and their privileging of other forms of literacy:

> Nearly every day we're warned about the bad effects on children of what they see. Little or no thought, though, is directed to the benefits of positive visual stimulation. ... [O]nce their nursery school days are over, we stop engaging them in visual play ..., very little attention is paid to their visual skills.[26]

In response to this pedagogical conservatism, many contemporary media educators have argued against the analysis-only approach that structures media literacy programs. For example, Kathleen Tyner labels media literacy as a "protectionist" form of media pedagogy that is both apolitical and theoretically antiquated.[27] As she and other media education scholars note, this approach has roots in the anti-popular culture sentiments of elite cultural critics and social reformers from past decades. Critiques of popular culture as formulaic entertainment meant to stultify the masses and keep them subjugated for their role as laborers within a capitalist economy can be traced back to the 1930s and critical theorists such as Max Horkheimer and Theodor Adorno.[28] Film and radio were the first forms of mass media to receive such criticisms; yet with the introduction of television in the 1950s, it, too, came under attack by cultural conservatives. Anti-television rhetoric as articulated by such scholars as Neil Postman continued in the decades that followed with the global transformation of popular culture via the proliferation of American commercial television.[29] As Tyner notes, "The need to protect children from television, as though it represented an electronic form of toxic waste, was the clear impetus behind the critical viewing skills programs in the 1970s."[30]

As a result of their particular perspective on commercial media culture, media literacy advocates have developed what Roger Desmond refers to as a "deficit" model of media pedagogy, "promoting their programs as prophylactics for a host of diseases that have not been supported by existing media research."[31] Tyner explains:

> The rationale for ... media literacy goes something like this: If only children could be given the skills and awareness to uncover the manipulative strategies of media, they would be able to discern the good media from the bad media and recognize the bad media for the unmitigated trash that it really is and summarily reject it.[32]

The protectionist approach to media literacy thus borrows the rhetorical strategies of conservative social movements of the past, positioning media culture as a cesspool and media literacy as an inoculation against such pollutive forces.

The rhetoric of media literacy advocates also reductively reproduces now debunked theories about media consumers' passive acceptance of what they see and hear. As David Sholle and Stan Denski note, "[media literacy] approaches are limited by their reliance on a theory of the media-audience link as one of activity-passivity."[33] In constructing young people without critical viewing skills as passive victims of the commercial culture industries, media literacy advocates seem unaware of the work of cultural studies scholars, such as Henry Jenkins, who have demonstrated that consumers play an active role in making meaning of media texts.[34]

Though few scholars of media education explicitly address it, the protectionist approach in media literacy initiatives demonstrates the strong influence of middle-class tastes and values. In fact, the most vocal advocates for children's media literacy are conservative, middle-class parents, teachers, and government officials whose construction of commercial media culture as churning out violent and sexually explicit drivel for the masses has been shaped by their place in what John and Barbara Ehrenreich refer to as the "Professional Managerial Class" (PMC).[35] Emerging as a result of shifts in the U.S. economy during the late nineteenth century, the PMC developed as a means for managing and controlling the everyday practices of the working class. As a result of the PMC's "expropriation of the skills and culture once indigenous to the working class," considerable antagonism exists between its members and those of the working class. Such antagonism is expressed in the "[r]eal-life contacts between the two classes ... [and] the relation of control which is at the heart of the PMC-working class relation: teacher and student, ... manager and workers, social worker and client, etc." Indeed, as the Ehrenreichs argue, the paternalist ideals relied upon by members of the PMC in shaping working-class labor and leisure ultimately reproduce the imbalances of power and privilege that contribute to the proper functioning of capitalism.

As Laurie Ouellette argues, members of the PMC have regularly called for media reform in the United States by advocating "public service alternatives ... that could transform the masses into better, more discriminating citizens."[36] Dismissing the entertainment function of popular culture while championing the mass media's role as educators, members of the PMC have played a major role in the development of not only government-controlled broadcasting enterprises, such as the Corporation for Public Broadcasting, but also media-based school initiatives, like media literacy. As a form of analytical training, media literacy is intended to give students mastery over commercial media culture by providing them with the tools necessary for finding the harmful messages in such texts. Once young people see the manipulative and formulaic nature of mass media, it is believed, such texts will be demystified, and youth will turn toward more legitimate forms of culture, such as literature, thus reproducing the taste culture Pierre Bourdieu associates with the middle class.[37]

Despite their relationship to the history of cultural reform, as David Buckingham argues, media literacy curricula typically reproduce an especially patronizing and missionary approach to pedagogy that further disempowers youth:

> By and large, students are seen to be particularly at risk from the negative influence of the media, and as seemingly unable to resist their power; while teachers are somehow assumed to be able to stand outside this process, providing students with the tools of critical analysis which will "liberate" them. In each case, media [literacy] is regarded as a means of counteracting children's apparent fascination and pleasure in the media. ... Media [literacy] will, it is assumed, automatically lead children on to an appreciation of high culture, to more morally healthy forms of behavior, or to more rational, politically correct beliefs. It is seen to offer nothing less than a means of salvation.[38]

Moreover, as Sholle and Denski suggest, by constructing hierarchies that privilege the fine arts over commercial popular culture, media literacy programs do little to encourage students "to draw upon their experience and knowledge, and to connect their education with political practice, or to be critical and active citizens in a democracy."[39]

In spite of such criticisms, the protectionist approach adopted by media literacy advocates continues to dominate the majority of contemporary media education programs in the United States, and most educators place little or no emphasis on improving young people's knowledge about and engagement with the technical tools and creative practices that produce media. The foregrounding of critical ability over technical and creative abilities can be seen in virtually all forms of media literacy discourse, from guidebooks directed to parents concerned about their toddlers' overexposure to media to the world's most prestigious departments of critical media studies. For example, in *Screen Smarts: A Family Guide to Media Literacy*, Gloria DeGaetano and Kathleen Bander describe twenty-three different activities for improving children's media literacy; yet only one of these activities involves learning about and using film technology.[40] At the other end of the spectrum, graduate programs in critical film and television studies have traditionally avoided incorporating production courses into their curricula despite increasing the number of theory and criticism courses required of students majoring in media production.

The privileging of the mental processes of critical analysis over the manual practices of creative production in media literacy curricula not only results in students being only partially informed about media culture, but also continues to reinforce the often impenetrable wall that separates media analysis from media production and, more generally, theory from practice. Moreover, the valuing of intellectual over practical ability echoes, and thus reproduces, the dominant class dynamics that structure the larger realms of education, labor, and leisure.

There is little doubt that the dramatic increase in media literacy curricula in the United States since the early 1990s has contributed considerably to the recent rise in girls' media education. Yet the introduction of girls-only media literacy programs also reveals the influence of feminist research that shows that female youth, especially adolescents, are uniquely disadvantaged in patriarchal societies and thus need special assistance in order to be socially and psychologically healthy individuals. Thus, in order to fully appreciate the introduction of girls' media literacy curricula in the 1990s, it is necessary to understand its relationship to the much longer history of female-centered social reform initiatives in the United States.

MAKING LADIES: WOMEN'S SOCIAL REFORM AND THE RISE OF GIRLS' ADVOCACY

In *The Grounding of Modern Feminism*, feminist historian Nancy Cott expands the popular understanding of the origin of feminism by arguing that the movement was composed of not one but three different areas of activity, each of which had ties to different ideologies that in turn gave rise to different and often contradictory approaches to feminist politics and theory. The first area of feminist activity, initiated in the early nineteenth century, was comprised of women's volunteer service, which included benevolent, charitable efforts in welfare and social reform.[41] This work greatly influenced the emergence of what came to be known as the *woman movement* of the mid- to late nineteenth century, and has distinct ties to the PMC analyzed by the Ehrenreichs. The second area of feminist activity emerged during the late nineteenth century and entailed more explicit efforts to gain women's equal rights with men in legal, political, economic, and civil matters, a form of activism that later became known as *suffragism*. The third and most recent area of feminist activity comprised less distinct and more broad-ranging practices surrounding the emancipation of women from customs and laws that kept them subordinate to men in society and culture. This last area emerged in the early part of the twentieth century and was identified as *feminism* (borrowed from the French *feminisme*) to distinguish it as not only a political movement, but also an ideology for social change.

Like Cott, Barbara Ryan traces the roots of the woman movement to the social reform movements of the early 1800s that emerged in response to the dramatic social transformations resulting from the Industrial Revolution.[42] As she demonstrates, it was through their involvement with widows, prostitutes, unmarried mothers, and working-class girls that middle-class women reform-ers of this period began to understand gender oppression as a systemic social problem: "In a remarkable turn of events, philanthropist women identified with 'deviant' women, emphasizing the similarities with women rather than the dif-ferences."[43] Indeed, women involved in social reform during this period began to understand themselves and other females as part of a "sex category."[44]

Although activists of the early woman movement addressed female youth, girls were typically excluded from later feminist initiatives, particularly suffra-gism, which focused on women achieving equality with adult white males in the public sphere. Nevertheless, women reformers' interest in female youth was reignited in the late nineteenth century as a result of the further industrializa-tion and modernization of the United States. As discussed in Chapter 1, ideolo-gies of gender and generation changed dramatically during this period as more female youth left home for work and education, activities that brought them further independence from parents and greater interaction with males and the public sphere. Such transformations in the behavior of female youth led to con-siderable public concern, as can be seen in periodical articles from this era that focused on the threat the "modern girl" posed to the traditional American way of life.[45] Indeed, many conservatives believed that with an increasing num-ber of female youth attending high school and college, postponing or refusing marriage and motherhood, and taking an increasingly active role in the paid labor force, the traditional structure of the family, and perhaps American soci-ety as a whole, was in severe danger. As Joseph Hawes notes:

> Reformers, whether feminist or not, worried about "the new girl" and proposed new courses for high school and college girls to promote traditional ends ... champion[ing] classes in "domestic science" to teach girls how to be effective wives and mothers.[46]

In light of the "cult of true womanhood" ideology that was prevalent at this time,[47] Hawes argues that "[t]he professionalization of motherhood was essen-tially a defensive reaction to the emergence of young women in the late nine-teenth century."[48]

Public concern with female youth did not end with the turn of the twen-tieth century, however, for adolescent girls garnered just as much, if not more, attention in the early 1900s by reformers and, increasingly, intellectuals, who deemed to know what was best for them. For example, in his ground-breaking text, *Adolescence*, published in 1904, G. Stanley Hall argued adamantly for girls' education in and adherence to the "natural" roles of wife and mother.[49] As Kathy Peiss suggests in her study of early twentieth-century working girls' culture in New York, such traditional views on adolescent femininity were related to prevailing middle-class values during this period, especially those of the woman movement, which, despite advocating women's emancipation, also privileged motherhood and domestic life. As Peiss notes, "By the 1880's, women had pushed a gender-based ideology of domesticity, moral guardian-ship, and sisterhood from the realm of home and family into the public arena. Protecting womanhood and the home became public and political issues."[50]

The sex-based homogeneity privileged in the nineteenth-century wom-en's sphere strongly influenced the ideology of "sisterhood" that developed among middle-class women reformers of the early twentieth century, who believed that working girls "needed places to find womanly support, mutual aid, and practical advice."[51] Feminists and other reformers of this period saw working girls' forms of recreation and entertainment—especially their partic-ipation in the heterosocial spaces of dance halls, amusement parks, and movie theaters—as unique social problems. In response, organizations like the Girls' Friendly Society, the Young Women's Christian Association (YWCA), and what eventually became known as the Girls Clubs of America (and later Girls Inc.) created alternative recreational spaces for such female youth. Based on middle-class women's clubs, the social centers created for working girls dur-ing this period stressed service and self-improvement, while also focusing on domesticity, purity, and female solidarity.

Despite some clubs' accommodations of working girls' cultural prefer-ences, the poor and often immigrant female youth who were their supposed beneficiaries often felt patronized by the bourgeois Anglo women who brought to these clubs their class, ethnic, and racial biases. Indeed, as a result of the growing awareness of the economic oppression of the lower classes, working girls increasingly abandoned these clubs and became members of labor orga-nizations and trade unions.[52] Through their work experiences, many female youth were able to form relationships with men outside the supervision and conservative moral codes of their families and social reformers. Thus, many working-class girls of this period retreated from the female-only, improve-ment-oriented spaces of girls' clubs to the heterosocial spheres of working-class leisure and entertainment, such as dance halls and movie theaters. As a result, "[t]hese young women pioneered new forms of public female behavior, which the dominant culture ultimately incorporated and popularized."[53]

Though women reformers constructed urban working girls as a social prob-lem, for many women involved in the burgeoning feminist movement of the early twentieth century, these girls became modern heroines. As Peiss notes:

> What had been seen as rowdy girls' deviant behavior in the mid-nine-teenth century was evaluated more ambiguously by the early 1900's. Flamboyant fashion, assertive sexuality, and close social interaction between the sexes held their appeal by being not quite respectable.[54]

By the 1920s, the young, independent females who went to college, worked outside the home, drank, smoke, and publicly displayed their sexuality had become models for a new type of female subjectivity that directly challenged traditional modes of domestic femininity. Yet, as was the case with turn-of-the-century working girls, this new form of youthful female subjectivity was seen by many individuals, including some older feminists, as the antithesis of the type of femininity advocated by the cult of true womanhood, and thus a harbinger of the decline of civilized femininity. As Paula Fass notes in *The Damned and the Beautiful*:

> Gazing at the young women of the period, the traditionalist saw the end of American civilization. ... Its firm and robust outlines, best symbolized by the stable mother secure in her morality and content in her home, were pushed aside and replaced by the giddy flapper, rouged and clipped, careening in a drunken stupor to the lewd strains of a jazz quartet.[55]

Although some feminists recognized the positive effects of liberation upon female youth, other women involved in the women's movement were vehemently opposed to the shallow self-indulgence they saw among female youth during this period. For example, Charlotte Perkins Gilman argued that rather than "mastering birth control and acquiring 'experience,'" modern young women should devote themselves to their roles as wives and mothers.[56] As Fass notes, "It was the new definition of equality that was most troubling, for it was apparently not the same thing that the old feminists had in mind."[57]

As the lifestage of adolescence drew more public attention in the first decades of the twentieth century, the concept of youth became increasingly dissociated from college-aged individuals and centered on those attending high school. As a result, social reformers of this period expanded their initiatives to address the social needs of younger girls. Significant to this development was the introduction of several scouting organizations for female youth, including the Camp Fire Girls in 1910 and the Girl Scouts in 1912. Interestingly, though the founders of both of these organizations demonstrated considerable influence by the women's reform movement of the nineteenth century, encouraging girls' training in domesticity and community service as a way of preventing the erosion of "true womanhood" and thus the decline of American society, they also demonstrated the increasing proliferation of feminist sensibilities during the early twentieth century, encouraging female youth to reach their full potential through involvement in outdoor recreation, civic activities, and career development.

In their early years, both the Camp Fire Girls and the Girl Scouts were designed primarily for middle-class female youth who had the disposable time and income to spend participating in such organizations. Yet both organizations altered their objectives in later decades so as to assist poor girls also. For example, "[d]uring the Depression, the Girl Scouts joined with other women's and youth organizations to respond to the needs of girls and the 'hard times' of the country, including a project to work with Dust Bowl migrant girls."[58] In turn, the Camp Fire Girls made a special effort in the 1960s to assist disenfranchised girls. After receiving a substantial grant from the Department of Health, Education, and Welfare, the organization was able to establish groups in poor urban communities, rural areas, migrant worker camps, and Native American reservations.[59]

GIRLS' SELF-ESTEEM CRISIS: RESEARCH ON FEMALE ADOLESCENCE AND THE RESURGENCE OF GIRLS' ADVOCACY

Despite the strength of the social reform movements of the late nineteenth and early twentieth centuries, it was not until the 1990s that popular discourse constructing female youth as "troubled" reached another crescendo. This resurgence of girls' advocacy is intrinsically related to a concurrent increase in research on girls' loss of self-esteem during adolescence. Though other feminist scholars had worked in this area previously,[60] it is Carol Gilligan's book, *In a Different Voice*, which is most often cited as the spark that ignited feminist research into adolescent girls' psychological development.[61] Gilligan's book, published in 1982, countered traditional patriarchal theories of developmental psychology by inserting sex and gender into psychological research on identity and morality and by paying specific attention to the "different voice" of females. In agreement with the cultural feminist perspectives that dominated feminist scholarship during this period, *In a Different Voice* furthered an understanding of social and psychological development based on sexual difference by advocating for the legitimization of women's unique voices and perspectives. More significant to the construction of contemporary girlhood, Gilligan argued that adolescence is especially difficult for girls who, unlike most boys, struggle between contradictory social messages that encourage them to simultaneously attach to and separate from other individuals.

Following the publication of *In a Different Voice*, Gilligan continued her research in adolescent girls' psychology, coauthoring and coediting several books on this subject in the early 1990s.[62] In the wake of this work, several other publications emerged that continued, and often reconfigured, Gilligan's theme of adolescent girls' uneasy psychological development, including the American Association of University Women's report, *Shortchanging Girls, Shortchanging America*, Myra and David Sadker's *Failing at Fairness: How Our Schools Cheat Girls*, Peggy Orenstein's *SchoolGirls: Young Women, Self-Esteem and the Confidence Gap*, and Mary Pipher's *Reviving Ophelia: Saving the Selves of Adolescent Girls*.[63] Unlike Gilligan's and other feminist researchers' previous work in this area, many of these later books were published by trade presses, such as Penguin, Scribner's, and Doubleday, and thus received enough national promotion, as well as critical attention, to make them bestsellers. It is these later books that are largely responsible for rekindling the girls' advocacy movement during the 1990s.

Studies of adolescent girls' unique and often disturbing developmental experiences have been important and necessary, especially in bringing to public awareness issues long unaddressed by educators, psychologists, social workers, and public policy makers. Indeed, since few girls have access to the channels of communication that would get their stories heard by a large number of people, this research has helped shed considerable light on the social and psychological difficulties associated with adolescent girlhood. In turn, it has led to a recognition that female youth are disadvantaged in activities that have been traditionally dominated by males or that privilege masculine behaviors.[64]

At the same time, however, the narrow focus on adolescent girls' troubled psyches during the 1990s contributed significantly to the popular construction of female youth as victims of the developmental process, not to mention traditional gender ideologies. Indeed, as Lyn Mikel Brown argues, many of the studies conducted during that period focused overwhelmingly on adolescent girls' loss of self-esteem during adolescence, and "passed over the clarity and strength of girls' voices" in Gilligan's and Brown's earlier studies, thus ignoring one of their primary findings: "that girls actively *resist* dominant cultural notions of femininity, particularly at the edge of adolescence."[65] Michelle Fine and Pat Macpherson echo Brown when arguing that such studies

> have been persistently committed to public representations of women's victimization and structural assaults and have consequently ignored, indeed misrepresented, *how well young women talk as subjects*, passionate about and relishing their capacities to move between nexus of power and powerlessness. That is to say, feminist scholars have forgotten to take notice of how firmly young women resist— alone and sometimes together.[66]

Indeed, the message in a considerable number of these studies is reminiscent of nineteenth-century women reformers: girls are not able to overcome their troubles without adult help.

One example of such discourse appears in Joan Jacobs Brumberg's *The Body Project*, which argues, "Adolescent girls simply are not mature enough, or sufficiently in control of their lives, to resist all the social and commercial pressures they face in our hypersexual, televisual environment."[67] Interestingly, she connects "the current vulnerability of American girls" to "the decline of the Victorian 'protective umbrella' that sheltered and nurtured them well into the twentieth century."[68] Ending her book with a chapter titled, "Girl Advocacy Again," Brumberg's solution to this problem is "to fashion a new strategy of girl advocacy that acknowledges the convergence of earlier sexual maturation with current cultural imperatives."[69] Her view on who should be in control of such a movement is clear: "[F]emale professionals—particularly social workers, psychologists, nurses, doctors, and teachers like myself—need to create a national forum for developing a code of sexual ethics for adolescent girls in a postvirginal age."[70]

The construction of girls as passive, silent victims who need to be saved by older feminists is perhaps most evident, however, in Pipher's bestseller, *Reviving Ophelia*, which is significantly subtitled *Saving the Selves of Adolescent Girls*. As Pipher notes in the preface:

> One dilemma came up again and again [for parents of female youth]: How could we encourage our daughters to be independent and autonomous and still keep them safe? How could we inspire them to take on the world when it was a world that included kidnappers and date rapists? Even in our small city with its mostly middle-class population, girls often experienced trauma. How could we help girls heal from that trauma? And what could we do to prevent it? … What can we do to help them? We can strengthen girls so that they will be ready.[71]

In ways quite similar to the conservative discourse about the problems of the "modern girl" in the early 1900s, many of the analyses on girls' self-esteem crisis at the end of that century were class as well as race biased. In fact, the "problem girls" of most popular books on the self-esteem crisis are overwhelmingly white and middle-class, though rarely do the authors of such studies explicitly address race and class as variables in this psychological phenomenon.[72] As Julie Bettie argues about studies like Pipher's, "gender appears here as the most significant dimension of girls' selves, and race/ethnicity and class as dimensions of subjectivity are analytically subordinate to gender."[73] Moreover, much of this research relies on reductive notions of subjectivity that privilege the modern ideal of a centered, rational, self-determining, adult subject. Indeed, by championing ways for girls to become well-adjusted women or, better yet, good feminists, some scholars researching female psychological development demonstrate a tendency similar to that of women reformers of the early twentieth century who prescribed an "appropriate" (i.e., middle-class) lifestyle for female youth in order to make them socially acceptable young ladies. Yet, as Rachel Orviro asks rhetorically: "How can we be Superwoman without having been Supergirl?"[74]

CONTEMPORARY GIRLS' ADVOCACY: RECONFIGURING FEMINIST AGENDAS, SAVING FEMALE YOUTH

The dramatic increase in academic interest in girls' psychological and social development in the 1990s contributed to a moral panic about female adolescence at the turn of the twenty-first century, the degree of which matched public concern about young female sexuality in the 1920s.[75] In particular, this research led to a resurgence of the girls' advocacy movement, reinvigorating organizations developed over a century earlier to assist female youth. The current promotional discourse for Girls Inc., for example, reveals that the organization's earlier concerns about girls' etiquette and social welfare have been substituted recently by those about the social and psychological difficulties of contemporary girlhood:

> Growing up in a male-dominated culture, many girls face enormous pressure to judge their self-worth based on narrow standards of physical attractiveness; to put others ahead of themselves; and to conform to damaging notions of femininity that promote passivity and self-sacrifice while discouraging autonomy and pursuit of their dreams. By contrast, Girls Inc. welcomes girls into our centers to expand their minds, strengthen their bodies, and fortify their spirits.[76]

Similarly, promotional discourse for the Girl Scouts of the U.S.A. has been retooled in light of the popularization of girls' self-esteem crisis:

> Girl Scouts of the USA is the world's pre-eminent organization dedicated solely to girls—all girls—where, in an accepting and nurturing environment, girls build character and skills for success in the real world. In partnership with committed adult volunteers, Girl Scouts cultivate their full individual potential. The qualities they develop in Girl Scouting—leadership, values, social conscience, and conviction about their own self-worth—serve them all their lives.[77]

The increase in research and public discourse about adolescent girls' self-esteem problems during the 1990s also inspired the launching of several new girls' advocacy initiatives, all of which have similar goals of assisting the social and psychological development of female youth. For instance, Nell Merlino helped to reinvigorate the Ms. Foundation's National Girls Initiative (founded in 1989) by developing Take Our Daughters to Work Day in 1992 in an effort to inspire girls' career pursuits. The Ms. Foundation has also sponsored Girls Speak Out, a workshop series begun in 1994 by Andrea Johnston to improve girls' self-esteem and assertiveness.[78] Other girls' advocacy initiatives that have sprung up in the past decade include the Empower Program of Washington, D.C., which was founded in 1994; the Hawai'i Girls Project in Honolulu, founded in 1996; and GENaustin (Girls Empowerment Network, Austin) in Texas, also founded in 1996.[79] The Ophelia Project, launched in 1997 in Erie, Pennsylvania, has now spread to several other U.S. cities.

Also influenced by studies of adolescent girls' loss of self-esteem, the U.S. Department of Health and Human Services, under the leadership of Donna E. Shalala, initiated its Girl Power! campaign in 1996 in an effort "to galvanize parents, schools, communities, religious organizations, health providers, and other caring adults to make regular, sustained efforts to reinforce girls' self confidence, by providing girls with positive messages, meaningful opportunities, and accurate information about key health issues."[80] In 1997, Girl Power! joined with the American Association of University Women, Big Brothers Big Sisters of America, the YWCA of the U.S.A., Girls Inc., the Girls Scouts, and GirlZone (a web magazine for female youth) to host a series of empowerment conferences for female youth called Sister-to-Sister Summits.

As the title of the Girl Power! program suggests, the formation of contemporary girls' advocacy organizations and programs have not developed in a cultural void. The motto of "girl power" originated within the Riot Grrrl community during the early 1990s, and Shalala's adoption of that term reveals the wide-spread and long-term effect of that community's ideologies and practices. Indeed, as I suggested in the previous chapter, there now exists an international grrrl power movement. Yet, rather than focusing on the power female youth already possess but may have difficulty accessing, as riot grrrls do, girl advocacy initiatives, like Girl Power!, stress the future empowerment of female youth through adult intervention, and thus unwittingly construct girls as disempowered in the present. As demonstrated in my analyses of Girls Inc.'s and the Girl Scouts' media literacy curricula, this discursive framing of girlhood has had a significant impact on girls' advocacy organizations' perspectives on media pedagogy. Yet it is important to note that this is not the only approach used today in girls' media education, as an analysis of other girls-only media programs reveals.

GIRLS' MEDIA EDUCATION: TEACHING FEMALE YOUTH TECHNICAL AND CREATIVE SKILLS

Motivated by their own difficult educational experiences, several women educators have recently introduced extracurricular programs in order to facilitate girls' direct engagement with the tools and practices of media production. These after-school programs move beyond the protectionist approach of the media literacy movement, and instead promote girls' active involvement in popular culture and public discourse through training in both media analysis and production. Though numerous programs with this objective have been introduced over the past decade, I am primarily interested in analyzing those that facilitate girls' training in forms of media production that have historically marginalized female involvement, particularly filmmaking.

k. bradford, a poet, filmmaker, and performance artist, started It's a She Shoot in Austin, Texas, in 1994.[81] A promotional announcement describes the program as "a feminist film and video class that covers cinematic concepts, narrative strategies, video production techniques, hands-on camera work and basic A to Z instruction for making your own video."[82] Though bradford, who has an M.F.A. in creative writing from the University of Texas, developed this filmmaking class for adult women, she expanded the program in 1996 so as to include female youth. Her interests in helping girls and women gain knowledge in the practices of film and video originally stemmed from her involvement in Austin's feminist community, particularly Women's Access to Electronic Resources (WATER), a grassroots, cultural feminist project that facilitated women's training in radio, video, and computers. bradford's first girls-only It's a She Shoot class took place in 2000, following her involvement in Grrrl Action, a summer-long writing and performance workshop for adolescent girls developed by graduate students from the University of Texas and sponsored by the Rude Mechanicals, an Austin-based theatre collective. bradford felt a film production class for the Grrrl Action participants was a natural extension of the creative context in which these female youth learned to "come to voice" by embracing their own "girl power."

According to bradford, her reasons for developing a girls-only workshop also stemmed from her "inherent interest in girls." Although she feels unable to separate female youth and adult women in her feminism, bradford is aware that girls have unique needs as a result of their age and generational status, though her perspectives on this phenomenon seem more in line with Riot Grrrl than the girls' advocacy movement. bradford is not opposed to coed workshops; however, she developed a girls-only program in video production because she feels teenage girls (and boys) should have alternatives to mixed-sex educational environments where they have a tendency to perform for members of the opposite sex. Moreover, as a self-identified feminist and part-time "drag king," bradford reports that the creation of female-only spaces, where patriarchally defined gender behaviors can be actively and safely subverted, feels "instinctive" to her.

It's a She Shoot's six-week program is not as formally structured for students as most other after-school media education workshops, as bradford wants girls to "arrive at their own voice" and therefore does not "like to steer them too much." bradford stresses her role as a facilitator, not expert, and in turn has provided an opportunity for her students' further female mentoring via the volunteer help of several other young women. In the program, girls work both individually and collaboratively on various elements involved in film production, including storyboarding, scriptwriting, cinematography, directing, and editing. Since the program privileges filmmaking practices and aesthetics, It's a She Shoot focuses less on media analysis than other media education programs developed for girls. Nevertheless, bradford indicates that gender issues are regularly integrated at different points in the curriculum, particularly during girls' brainstorming for and writing of film projects.

It's a She Shoot was originally created to assist women in the low-income and primarily Latino and African American neighborhoods of East Austin. Although bradford attracts economically disadvantaged students through her program's sliding tuition scale, she notes that mostly white, middle-class female youth between the ages of thirteen and seventeen have enrolled in the program. It's a She Shoot is currently funded by the Austin Film Commission, yet Bradford has plans for expansion through financial support from governmental agencies and other private foundations. Nevertheless, she is fearful that her original vision for racial and economic diversity in the program may be adversely affected by the stipulations that often accompany such funding.

Reel Grrls, a media education program for teenage girls in Seattle, Washington, was founded by Malory Graham in January 2001 (Figure 7).[83] A program director for the larger 911 Media Arts Center's Young Producers Program, Graham, who has a B.A. in video production/media arts from Hampshire College, realized the need for a girl-centered media education curriculum after several of the female youth enrolled in one of the Center's other projects expressed interest in having more time to focus on female-specific issues. As Reel Grrls' website indicates, the program's curriculum and promotional discourse show the impact of the media literacy and girls' advo-

Figure 7 Combining girls' critical media analysis and production. Reel Grrls class, 2005. Courtesy of Malory Graham.

cacy movements, yet are also influenced strongly by the production-oriented model of media pedagogy discussed later in this chapter:

> By teaching teenage girls how to be critical television watchers and then producers of their own media, we are giving them a voice in an arena where they are heavily targeted as consumers but where their artistic expression is seldom heard or seen. ... Because of the influential role of media in girls' lives, we believe that it is critical to give young women the skills to critically evaluate the media they are exposed to and then to empower them to produce their own media.[84]

Though some girls have told Graham that the title of the program is "dated" as a result of the broad diffusion of the terms "grrl" and "grrrl" during the mid-1990s, she chose the name "Reel Grrls" specifically because of its connotation of grrrl power initiatives, such as Riot Grrrl, as well as radical feminist art initiatives, like the Guerilla Girls.[85] As she argues, "I don't want this to be just about the cliché of 'Let's give the girls a video workshop so they can talk about body image and feel good about themselves.' I want them to get angry and push things further."[86]

Graham's decision to develop a girls-only media education program was based on her experience with the skewed gender dynamics she noted in coed youth filmmaking workshops: "Boys seem to be more comfortable with technology and in a mixed-gender setting 'take over' operating equipment," whereas girls have a tendency to "take a backseat," feeling more comfortable being looked at than getting behind the camera and looking for themselves. A strong supporter of single-sex education, Graham nevertheless understands the differences in boys' and girls' learning styles as a result of socialization, with female youth encouraged to a greater degree than their male peers to "work collaboratively, use lateral hierarchy, and empathize with their subject matter."

With students typically between the ages of fourteen and eighteen, Reel Grrls attracts a slightly older group than It's a She Shoot. Graham's reasons for focusing on this age group are related to her perception of generational differences in girls' abilities and interests. For example, she feels that female youth between the ages of nine to twelve have a greater need for discussing body image issues, while older girls aged fourteen to eighteen are more media savvy, more comfortable with technology, and thus more willing to engage actively with the practices of media production. Nevertheless, Graham has noticed that the younger girls in the program tend to learn about filmmaking more quickly, and that students of all ages seem more comfortable handling technology if they have experience using computers.

With 70 percent of the students in the program being nonwhite, and several poor girls attending on scholarship, Reel Grrls has a more diverse mix of female youth than most girls-only media education programs, no doubt the result of recruitment efforts by the staff, as well as stipulations from funding agencies. Unfortunately, with this diversity come problems, which Graham attributes to both ethnic and cultural differences. For example, although white, middle-class students in Reel Grrls have had little problem engaging in dramatic exercises meant to elicit personal reflection and expression, Native American girls have ridiculed such games as a "white girl thing." In turn, Graham has noticed conflicts developing between "mainstream" girls and those who identify as "alternative" and are more apt to be critical of commercial media and traditional gender norms.

Like bradford, who describes her approach to girls' media education as "low-tech" and "guerilla," Graham says that Reel Grrls has a "down and dirty" approach to training girls in the tools and practices of film production. In an effort to create an intergenerational but all-female learning environment, Reel Grrls relies on the help of several twenty- to twenty-five-year-old women volunteers, some of whom are former students of the program and are now interested in mentoring younger girls. In addition, Reel Grrls invites independent female artists to talk about their work and to collaborate with students on projects. Graham describes herself and the various women who function as Reel Grrls' volunteers as "co-creators" with the students.

To date, the most ambitious media education program for female youth is Girls Film School, which began as a one-day workshop in 1999 and is now a two-week residential course (Figure 8).[87] Girls Film School was founded by Deborah Fort, a professor in film production at the College of Santa Fe in New Mexico who has an M.F.A. in filmmaking from the San Francisco Art Institute. According to the school's website:

> The objective of this program is to extend the knowledge and skill base of high school girls. The introduction to moving image arts provided by this program affords participants the opportunity to expand their vision and encourage them to consider this field as a viable future. … It is our hope that, through public screenings of professional films by women filmmakers as well as the exhibition of the participants' final projects, the absence of women in technology and media will be brought to the foreground, and women of all ages will be assisted and encouraged to contribute their voices and exert their personal influence in the media industries.[88]

In focusing the school's objectives on drawing attention to the subordination of women in the media industries, as well as increasing the number of females choosing filmmaking as a career, Fort demonstrates the influence of liberal feminism on her values and goals. The rhetoric of girls' advocacy also permeates the promotional discourse for Girls Film School. For example, its website contains references to Pipher's *Reviving Ophelia* and the American

Figure 8 Preparing girls for careers in media production.
Girls Film School class, 2005. Courtesy of Girls Film School™.

Association of University Women's report on how schools "shortchange" female youth.

Like many founders of media education workshops for female youth, Fort was inspired by other single-sex schools, particularly a girls-only science camp that her niece attended at Smith College. In turn, she has long been disturbed by the gender dynamics of the college-level film production courses she teaches, where she sees men "take over" and unconsciously limit women's access to equipment and the more prestigious roles associated with filmmaking, such as director and cinematographer. Moreover, Fort has been frustrated by the minimal number of young women interested in film production degrees: "I've often had classes with only one or two women; sometimes none at all."[89] As a result, she has developed concerns that girls are ignoring film as a viable medium for their creativity and communication:

It's a wonderful mode of expression that incorporates every single aspect of youth, of the world. There's sound, there's images. You can work in an abstract way, you can work in a very literal, realist way. You can do documentary, you can do fiction. ... It has endless possibilities for creative expression.[90]

Elsewhere Fort has stated, "This program is really about finding one's personal creative voice and mode of expression, and each girl exploring her own unique way of perceiving the world."[91]

Housed on the campus of the College of Santa Fe and using the facilities of the Moving Image Arts Department, Girls Film School has enormous advantages over workshops for female youth located within community media arts centers, such as Reel Grrls, or those organized in the homes of their instructors, as is the case for It's a She Shoot. Moreover, the school's advisory board includes well-known film professionals, such as producer Gale Anne Hurd, screenwriter Danny Rubin, and actor Ali McGraw, whose status in the Hollywood film industry has helped the school attract funding and equipment from Eastman Kodak, Apple Computers, the National Endowment for the Arts, and the Academy of Motion Picture Arts and Sciences. With such support, Girls Film School has been able to garner more funding, resources, and guest artists than the vast majority of other media education programs for girls.

Girls Film School currently attracts female youth between the ages of fifteen and eighteen, whom Fort finds are somewhat more confident than junior high students and "at a level of maturity where they can engage with media in an intense way." Like Reel Grrls and It's a She Shoot, the school is female centered and nonhierarchically structured and focuses on intergenerational collaboration between adult instructors, college-aged mentors, and teenage students, which Fort believes accounts for the quick shift in girls' self-confidence in using media technology. In turn, like Graham, Fort sees a connection between girls' experience in using computers and their comfort in engaging with film equipment. Nevertheless, she states that girls who do not have much access to technology "jumped all over it" at Girls Film School.

Attesting to the school's effort to educate more girls who do not normally have access to film technology at home, over 50 percent of the students are nonwhite, and Fort has cultivated a relationship with the Institute of American Indian Arts in Santa Fe in order to provide Native girls with mentors like themselves. As with Reel Grrls, the racial composition of Girls Film School is likely due to grant stipulations also. Yet despite Fort's commitment to diversity and the school's sliding tuition scale, the ratio of wealthy to poor girls in the school has increased dramatically over the past three years. Not surprisingly, therefore, Fort indicates that most conflicts develop from girls' class and cultural differences, especially the "mainstream"/"alternative" opposition Graham has noticed between some of Reel Grrls' participants.

Interestingly, although support from members of the Hollywood film industry might suggest that Girls Film School is producing students with conventional filmmaking interests, Fort has concerns that the single-sex program is helping to shape filmmakers who may not only be unwilling but unable to participate in the male-dominated commercial film industry. Nevertheless, Fort states that she "now knows that this [experience] is different and can work," thus suggesting that an alternative film culture composed largely of women—what Claire Johnston calls "women's counter-cinema"[92]—may blossom further with the rise of graduates from girls-only media education workshops. Regardless of where the students situate themselves culturally, as one of the school's mentors argues:

> This school and this camp are really going to open the doors for a lot of young women coming out of high school. They learn to work with each other, from different backgrounds, prejudices and even generations. At the center of our program is the artist aspiring to find her voice.[93]

Though not specifically devoted to facilitating *girls'* media education, Street-Level Youth Media in Chicago has offered several programs exclusively for female youth. For instance, the organization developed a ten-week-long Girls Only program in 1997 that was funded by the Girl's Best Friend Foundation.[94] More recently, Street-Level has introduced several programs for young females, including Real Extraordinary Females, for girls ages eight to thirteen, Female Action Voicing Change, for female youth ages fourteen to twenty-two, and The Mothership, for teenage mothers. Another girls-only program offered by Street-Level is Female Link, which brings together girls from different communities and organizations for collaborative media-making projects. Each of these programs integrates training in media analysis and production. Attesting to Street-Level's influence by the girls' advocacy movement and production-oriented media education initiatives, its girls-only curricula focus on facilitating girls' confidence and competence in expressing their own voices and opinions through media production, as well as discussions of issues of interest to female youth, such as women in hip-hop. As the organization's promotional discourse states, "by addressing and creating work about particular issues relevant to young women, [Female Action Voicing Change] participants develop the confidence to be their own advocates who are able to articulate their needs and concerns in a constructive manner."[95]

Another recent girl-centered film production workshop to emerge is Divas Direct, a ten-week program that teaches high school girls how to storyboard, film, edit, and produce a movie. Organized by the San Diego Women Film Foundation, the objectives of this workshop are quite similar to the other girls-only programs discussed previously, reflecting the combined perspectives of the girls' advocacy and grrrl power movements. In addition to reporting statistics on the low percentage of women in the Director's Guild of America (12.2 percent), recent promotional materials for the program state:

Through the mentorship of women filmmakers in San Diego, the young women will create, produce, film and edit multiple P.S.A.'s [public service announcements] that will address teen concerns and issues prevalent to today's young women. Through this program, we hope to break female stereotypes and create social change by promoting women into positions of leadership and give them experience in jobs that are male-prevalent.[96]

Several other production-oriented media education workshops for female youth were introduced during the 1990s but are no longer in operation. For example, Girls Making Headlines was a workshop conducted in Austin, Texas, during the summers of 2000 and 2001.[97] Part of a larger joint venture in youth media education organized by the Austin Museum of Art and the University of Texas's Department of Radio-Television-Film, Girls Making Headlines had objectives quite similar to those of Girls Only, Reel Grrls, It's a She Shoot, and the Girls Film School. As described by Sharon Ross, one of the three graduate students who designed the workshop:

[T]he goal of the class was to teach [female youth] to analyze how girls are represented in the mainstream media. ... As a corollary to this, the production skills we were teaching them were geared to providing them with the tools to counter those representations they didn't like with work of their own.[98]

Thus, in addition to facilitating girls' critical analyses of the media, the instructors developed a component of the workshop that entailed the students' production of a television news magazine devoted to issues of importance to girls.

Though the majority of girls' media education workshops focus on film and video production, several programs have emerged in recent years to help motivate girls' involvement in other forms of media production. Latinitas, for example, was founded in the early 2000s to encourage Hispanic girls to see journalism as a current vocation and possible career.[99] Initially developed as a concept for Latina girls' magazine for a course on Latinos and media at the University of Texas, Latinitas was eventually brought to life as a webzine in January 2003 by two of the project's creators, Laura Donnelly and Alicia Rascon. As Latinas, Donnelly and Rascon were frustrated with the negative representation of Hispanic girls and women in the commercial mass media, and recognized the need to provide young Latinas with a webzine that both affirmed their identity and inspired them to be creative and expressive. Later that year, Donnelly and Rascon expanded their mission, creating Haciendo an Ezine, free community workshops in web design, and Club Latinitas, an after-school program designed to inspire young Latinas' interest in journalism. In

2004, Latinitas launched the Teen Reporter Intern program to ensure that the webzine's content would be meaningful to and useful for adolescent Latinas.

Donnelly and Rascon's active efforts to facilitate Latina girls' interest in media, journalism, and web design are related to their awareness that Latinos make up less than two percent of the newsroom staff nationwide, despite their dominance as the largest racial minority group in the United States. Moreover, as a promotional flyer for the program argues, girls from traditional Hispanic families

> are not encouraged to set goals to be independent and ambitious in their careers. They are encouraged to seek a partner with those qualities. … They see the heroic, creative, and interesting crafts, like music, hip hop performance, breakdancing, technology, studio art, etc. as boys' things. Few … see a future for themselves in creating.[100]

As a result of this dynamic, Donnelly and Rascon

> felt it necessary … to equip the girls with tools of their own, therefore generating an "army" of sorts of future journalists. Teaching them to use the digital technology to do so also diminishes that digital divide chasm a bit for each girl we work with.

Cosponsored by various community organizations, such as the Hispanic Mother-Daughter Junior League and the Lone Star Girl Scout Council, the Latinitas web design workshops draw students from all class backgrounds. Nevertheless, since a considerable number of these students come from poor families that do not own computers or have high-speed Internet access, Donnelly and Rascon make a special point to hold the workshops in community recreational centers in working-class Latino neighborhoods. Most of the students are familiar with surfing the Web, but very few have experience in creating websites. The workshops typically last three hours, during which time students learn how to create their own e-zine via free online authoring software. Recognizing the potential vulnerability of young girls in cyberspace, instructors also facilitate students' knowledge about web safety. Like Reel Grrls and Girls Film School, the Latinitas workshops operate through the support of women volunteers interested in mentoring Hispanic girls. As Donnelly notes, "We are a young group and mostly Latina, which I think instills a confidence in the girls that they can do it, too."[101] A relatively young organization in comparison to the other girls' media education initiatives discussed here, Latinitas hopes to expand its outreach programs in the near future by securing funding from private foundations.

As the statements above reveal, the organizers and instructors of girls' media education workshops are primarily women who want to use their power and privilege as adults to help facilitate girls' increased critical and creative abilities. The majority of these women are under the age of thirty-five, unmarried (many are feminists and some are lesbians), childless, and have formal training in the visual arts or media studies. Their identity seems to have had a strong effect on their approach to both girls and media culture. For example, unlike many girls' advocates, the instructors and organizers of production-oriented girls' media education programs do not have an oppositional relationship to mediated forms of popular culture (though they express a similar concern about its increasing commercialization). Instead, they see media technologies as powerful tools for girls' communication, self-representation, and identity exploration. Nevertheless, as a result of having little to no formal training in media production and analysis prior to college or graduate school, the organizers of these girls' media education programs understand the need to train female youth in such practices at a young age so as to broaden the options for their future choices in both labor and leisure. Moreover, since few of these women educators had much support for their media interests at a young age, they see themselves as important role models and mentors for female youth interested in participating more actively in media culture.

Many of these educators have been radicalized to issues of age and generation via their exposure to or association with Riot Grrrl or the broader grrrl power movement. Thus, unlike girls' advocates, who tend to construct female youth as media and gender victims who are waiting to be empowered by adults, these young feminist media educators understand girls to be powerful cultural agents with unique ideas and perspectives that deserve expression via various forms of media. Rather than simply arming female youth with critical viewing skills, therefore, these instructors take girls' empowerment one step further by facilitating their sustained access to, training in, and engagement with media technologies. With girl-centered curricula facilitated by girl-positive instructors, the programs these women educators have created provide their young female students with spaces where they can create work that allows them to be heard and not just seen.

MEDIA EDUCATION AS CRITICAL DEMOCRATIC PEDAGOGY: YOUTH PRODUCERS IN AND OUTSIDE THE CLASSROOM

Girl-centered media education programs that include production training have clearly been influenced by the grrrl power movement; yet, they are also continuing the legacy of practice-oriented media pedagogy. Indeed, a considerable number of contemporary media educators and scholars, particularly in Canada, Australia, and Great Britain, have been advocating students' simultaneous education in media analysis and media production since the late 1980s. In contrast to the protectionist perspective of most media literacy advocates, media educators have what might be called a "promotionist" approach, which is grounded not only in different perspectives on education and the media, but also on a different understanding of young people and their abilities. Desmond calls this an "acquisition" model since educators focus on students' increased opportunities to acquire knowledge through media education.[102]

The promotionist/acquisition model of media pedagogy owes its development to the influence of critical democratic pedagogy,[103] an approach introduced by Paolo Freire in the 1970s that constructs education as a student-centered political practice leading to young people's increased critical consciousness and thus their more engaged participation in education and society.[104] In turn, teachers have gained greater exposure to critical theory over the past three decades, which has provided them with the means for analyzing the structures, relations, and functions of power in society and culture. Thus, rather than understanding the media as directly reflective of society and influential on consumers, as most media literacy advocates do, media educators approach media texts as social constructs that contain multiple and often contradictory messages, and thus elicit multiple and often contradictory responses. Indeed, in dramatic contrast to media literacy advocates, media educators do not have an oppositional stance to commercial media culture, but rather understand it as intrinsic to contemporary young people's pleasure and identity formation and thus as a useful site for developing critical consciousness. Stanley Aronowitz, echoing the rhetoric of the British cultural studies movement, points to the radical dimension of integrating popular culture into schools by noting its relationship to the deprivileged social status of youth:

> Clearly, for those who want to generate an emancipatory pedagogy the task has changed since the days when judgments of the Frankfurt School dominated their thinking about mass culture. It is not a question of unmasking television or rock music as forms of domination that reproduce the prevailing set-up. Instead, we are engaged in a program of reclamation, to rescue these forms as the authentic expressions of generations for whom traditional culture is not available.[105]

In keeping with the principles of critical democratic pedagogy, media educators acknowledge and respect young people as intelligent, engaged members of society who are far more media savvy than previous generations of youth, as well as most teachers. Thus, media educators refuse to position themselves as more enlightened than youth, and instead see their role as mentors, facilitating, supporting, and promoting the students in their classrooms. Moreover, media educators are sensitive to the multiple and often contradictory forms of subjectivity and experience that shape young people's identities and values, and thus are wary of encouraging a unilateral perspective when facilitating their development of critical analysis and creative expression.

For media educators, training in the tools and practices of media production is intrinsic to developing media-literate and critically conscious students whose participation in democratic communication can help to transform media culture. For example, Peter Greenaway argues that learning about media is

> best supported within an ... environment where the pedagogy is more conducive to the encouragement of an active "hands on" learning approach, [which] allows students creative expression and links the understanding of how a visual text conveys meaning with experiential learning in making their own visual messages. ... [T]o teach the analysis of text without any experience in the making of text is similar to teaching reading but not writing.[106]

Thus, much as English/language arts educators help to further students' competency in both reading and writing, while understanding that the two practices are not inseparable, media educators facilitate young people's competency in media by immersing them in both media analysis and production. Many scholars of media pedagogy advocate this approach also. For example, Tyner argues that curricula that include a media production component offer

> an opportunity for experiential, collaborative problem-solving that enhances media analysis skills. Media-making also takes a refreshing approach to media representation as an entry point for the discussion of a range of aspects inherent to the construction of the media. ... [Media production] offers a space for students to define and redefine their own "problems" with the media and to explore their own relationship with the media.[107]

Similarly debunking arguments against practical education made by conservative media literacy advocates, Buckingham and Julian Sefton-Green note that

> [i]n terms of teaching about popular culture, ... the production of texts may in fact have much greater potential than is often assumed. Far from serving merely as a form of training in technical skills, or as a means of illustrating predetermined theoretical insights, practical production may offer students the potential for a much more genuinely active and playful relationship with popular culture than can be achieved through analytical critique.[108]

In turn, media educators argue that hands-on experience in media production offers opportunities for young people's development of media literacy beyond critical viewing, thus problematizing the perception that such programs are an "educational dumping ground" for low-ability students.[109] In addition to developing students' technical skills that might expand their job

opportunities, as traditional vocational-technical ("vo-tech") classes do, production-oriented media education programs offer the possibility for students
to further develop their communication skills and creative abilities, to learn to
work collaboratively with others toward a shared goal, and to think critically
about their own lives and the world in which they live. Indeed, despite the
fact that minors are not afforded the rights adults are, engagement in media
production facilitates young people's active participation in public dialogue
about important social issues, including the manner in which members of
their communities are represented in popular culture.

This perspective on media education is grounded in an awareness of
media culture as a dominant socializing force in contemporary U.S. society,
and thus how crucial it is for all citizens, including young people, to participate fully within this realm. Indeed, much like the activist media producers
discussed in Chapter 2, advocates of production-oriented media education
curricula argue that facilitating young people's skills in self-representation is
a necessary requirement for the full development of democratic communication and participatory democracy. As Tyner argues:

> [A] sophisticated and powerful vision of literacy shows potential to
> enable each person to at least join the debate by skillfully negotiating
> within the existing power structure, as well as outside it. And this is
> why it is urgent that everyone has access to literacy in its most power-
> ful forms.[110]

Many educators working within media arts programs in Canada,
Australia, and Great Britain have called for a greater integration of critical
analysis and creative practice in media education curricula since the 1980s.
Unfortunately, the United States has lagged far behind these other countries
in this regard. Yet the tide seems to be gradually turning, largely as a result of
increased communication between media educators and scholars from different countries via international publications, conferences, and professional
organizations devoted to media pedagogy. For instance, in a 1992 meeting
organized by the Aspen Institute and jointly attended by media educators
from the United States and Canada, the National Leadership Conference on
Media Literacy collectively defined media education as "the ability of a citizen
to access, analyze, and *produce* information for specific outcomes," a definition influenced considerably by one adopted earlier by the Ontario Ministry
of Education.[111]

As a result of various grassroots organizations advocating the integration of media analysis and production, the media education curricula recently
introduced by several states' departments of education now require training
in media production. For example, in addition to privileging critical viewing
skills, the contemporary Texas Essential Knowledge and Skills (TEKS) media

education standards include a component for grades four through twelve (ages nine to eighteen) that in part requires students to "produce visual images, messages, and meanings that communicate with others."[112] Such curricula expand public education in media production beyond the informal training grounds of student publications and broadcast initiatives, as well as beyond the vo-tech programs found in many working-class schools, thus providing a much broader spectrum of students with such knowledge and skills.

In addition to the recent rise in media production classes in secondary schools, a number of community-based workshops and programs in youth media education have been introduced over the past decade, as the various girls-only programs analyzed above suggest.[113] Modeled on older community-based media initiatives, such as Appalshop's Appalachia Media Institute (founded in 1969) and Educational Video Center (founded in 1984), these new programs have been developed to facilitate young people's training in the tools and practices of media production, while also promoting their critical skills, stimulating their creativity, and encouraging the expression of their unique identities and experiences. Though often located within urban communities and primarily serving disadvantaged youth, these workshops have more than just vocational training in mind. As Brian Goldfarb notes:

> The objective is to use video production to provide a means for working through the social and psychological issues that play a role in these students' ability to make it through the school system and life, and to help students make meaningful connections to their communities through the production process. ... The projects tend to be exercises in political consciousness-raising, addressing less overtly the agendas of workforce preparation and academic learning that are nonetheless intended outcomes of the curriculum.[114]

Oddly, despite their progressive beliefs about pedagogy, communication, and power, virtually none of the theorists of media education mentioned above have discussed how gender relates to training in media production.[115] Yet, an extremely significant component of the contemporary production-oriented media education movement is the rise of girls-only initiatives, like Reel Grrls and Latinitas. These programs have been introduced primarily because girls' difficulties in learning the tools and practices of media production have not been addressed in most coed classrooms and community-based workshops. How single-sex media education programs provide girls with unique opportunities for not just career but also social, psychological, and political development thus deserves greater attention.

GIRL POWER?: PROBLEMATIZING EMPOWERMENT
DISCOURSE IN MEDIA PEDAGOGY

Reflecting on the various outcomes of the media production workshops offered by the Educational Video Center (EVC), founding director Steve Goodman writes:

> In contrast to their teacher-centered classes, students [at EVC] consistently report that they feel more positive about themselves, their work, and their community. A powerful sense of engagement and excitement surrounds them when they are out on the streets talking with their peers, and talking about subjects of immediate importance to them. They have a sense of ownership over their work when they get to decide the subject of study. And they feel tremendous pride when they present their projects and answer questions at public screenings attended by their friends, family, and teachers.[116]

Like Goodman, educators facilitating girls' training in media production often demonstrate the success of their programs by pointing to the further enhancement of their students' assertiveness, self-esteem, and social engagement. Indeed, the term "empower" appears in the promotional discourse for many of these programs. Reel Grrls' slogan, for example, is "empowering young women through media," while the stated goal of Divas Direct is "to empower San Diego's young women to become leaders by inspiring them through film."

Recently, several scholars have begun critiquing media educators' use of such "empowerment" discourse. For example, Tyner questions the resiliency of power that students gain in production-oriented programs that do not include a component on developing critical consciousness:

> At best, the esteem accrued through media production is a result of completing a project from beginning to end with adults who care. At its worst, the good feeling produced by working in an endeavor that approximates broadcast media simply is a borrowed esteem that defers true empowerment in order to keep students busy in activities that are self-absorbing and that keep them out of trouble in class. True self-esteem that enables students to give back to their communities grows out of a mastery of skills, but also out of identifying, analyzing and overcoming the daily erosion of human dignity in an unjust society.[117]

Buckingham reiterates this point, noting that "production must be accompanied by systematic reflection and self-evaluation. ... Media education aims to produce *critical* participation in media, not participation for its own sake."[118]

Scholars like Tyner and Buckingham are wise to question the ability of training in media production alone to empower youth, particularly since few educators agree on what this term means, how it is manifested, and how it can be measured. Indeed, there has been much dialogue among media educators and scholars over the past decade on the difficulties of evaluating such programs in general. As Jenny Grahame notes:

> Among the many conventional wisdoms underpinning the practice of media education, the claims which are most fiercely defended are often the hardest to evaluate. ... [E]vidence of the value of hands-on experience of media production is notoriously difficult to assess.[119]

Despite such concerns, particularly those relating to the degree of students' increased self-esteem, I would argue that when we consider young people's individual relationships to power, a different perspective on the potential for growth through training in media production emerges. In particular, we must take into consideration students' status in the social hierarchy as determined by their age, sex, race, class, ethnicity, and sexuality.

For instance, because media technologies have been developed and dominated by men for decades and thus are typically gendered masculine, boys do not question their entitlement to participate in media production and recognize this as one of many forms of vocation and labor in which they can eventually engage. The same is not true for girls and women who therefore tend to find media production a liberatory practice since it allows them to transgress the gender roles and practices associated with their sex. At the same time, adults dominate the media industries, and, except in the cases of extreme talent, youth are typically excluded from this sphere. As a result of this dynamic, participation in media production is typically far more emancipatory for young people than it is for older individuals. Since girls are both young and female, and therefore have at least a doubly deprivileged status in the world of media production, their education in and use of media technologies, regardless of an accompanying education in media analysis, are potentially more liberating than they are for either boys or women. Yet the self-esteem boost that can be gained from engaging in media production is perhaps most substantial for female youth who are marginalized as a result of their racial, ethnic, class, or sexual identity. As Goodman notes:

> [A]verage citizens, and especially youth of color, are not expected to use professional-quality equipment and to be engaged in the more serious business of gathering news and producing documentaries. This is still considered to be the sole province of mainstream media institutions. ... It is a shift in power relations for traditionally marginalized teenagers to also do so.[120]

Unfortunately, the skewed gendering and generationalizing of media technologies and practices that give boys and men a sense of entitlement to the role of cultural producer have contributed significantly to most girls' minimal interest in media production, particularly those forms that require engagement with sophisticated and often heavy electronic equipment, such as that used in filmmaking. As Tanya Doriss, assistant director of Girls Film School, notes: "Most of the students come into the program with the idea of being an actress. They come in thinking that that's what women do in film. They don't realize the myriad jobs they can do in the film industry."[121]

As explored in the Introduction to this book, girls' constant encouragement to achieve femininity through appearance improvement and heterosexual activities also contributes to their disinterest in engaging in media production, as well as their lack of confidence and, in some cases, competence when using media technologies. As the work of Gilligan and other feminist developmental psychologists suggests, these problems are usually magnified for teenage girls, whose self-assurance becomes increasingly difficult to maintain once they enter adolescence. While I want to avoid labeling such female youth "victims," particularly since many girls successfully negotiate and overcome such problems, I do think it is necessary to acknowledge that, as Barbara Hudson argues, girls often have a difficult time negotiating the contradictory demands of normative gender and generational identities, and thus have special needs when learning how to participate in male- and adult-dominated activities, such as media production.[122]

In interviews I conducted with educators who teach girls media production, several noted that many of their students have no problem approaching and using media technology, particularly those who already possess skills necessary for multiple forms of media production, such as writing, photography, and acting. In turn, as noted above, some instructors indicated that girls with computer experience are more comfortable using other forms of electronic media technology, such as video cameras. Nevertheless, several educators reported that some girls' problems with self-confidence could negatively affect their self-perception as technically competent. For example, Diane Zander, one of the founders of Girls Making Headlines and an instructor who has worked with both female and male youth in media education programs, reports:

> Dealing with … self-esteem issues is something I find mostly in girls, rather than boys: boys just do it without considering that they can't, but girls sometimes lack the confidence to think they're capable. I don't want to generalize, because there are plenty of girls who go at it fearlessly, but the ones who have fear [about using media technology] have always been girls. … Fighting the prejudices they already hold about women and technology is always a challenge.[123]

Donnelly of Latinitas similarly notes the gender imbalance in technical confidence: "[B]oys are less shy about getting online and creating their own project. Some, not all, of the girls need a little prodding. Also, the boys never express doubt that they could create a website. Some of the girls do."[124]

Many instructors commented on how the gender dynamics of coed workshops can affect girls' confidence with media technology also. As both Graham and Fort suggest above, struggling with boys for access is one of the biggest problems female youth face in such classes. Similarly, Zander discusses the skewed gender dynamics in youth filmmaking workshops: "[M]ore boys jump in immediately, as if in competition for the limited equipment. They want to touch it, play with it, press all the buttons. Some girls hang back, because they are blocked from participating since the boys have grabbed everything."[125] Such observations echo those of Danish media educator Kirsten Drotner, who in 1989 found that "[b]oth boys and girls initially saw video as a technical and hence a male medium. Not unexpectedly, I found that without adult direction the boys would take charge of the lighting, the props, and the camerawork."[126]

In addition to girls' acquiescence to boys during the production process, both Zander and the other cofounders of Girls Making Headlines found their students' attempts to achieve normative femininity posed difficulties for their engagement in the program. For example, Ross notes that "some girls worry about how they 'appear' to boys in that age group [and] so will 'act accordingly'—flirting, deferring power, etc."[127] As Fort discusses, this dynamic often continues well into young adulthood and college-level film production classes: "I'd see women who were very competent kind of defer to men, neither of them being conscious of it."[128] Again, these observations support those of Drotner who found that, while boys and girls are equally imaginative in planning media production projects, "the girls restrained themselves from putting their ideas into action. Unlike the boys, they wanted to rehearse what to say, when to move, and how to leave the scenes. ... The boys were generally more playful ... and less afraid of making a fool of themselves in front of their friends."[129]

In light of many girls' hesitancy and lack of confidence in using technology, particularly when boys are present, most media educators working with female youth understand the need to take extra measures to provide such students with a supportive environment that facilitates their assertiveness, their creativity, and what Tyner calls their "mastery of skills." Film professors Anne Orwin and Adrianne Carageorge note, for example, that showing films made by women and inviting female role models to speak about their work gives female students "encouragement ... through seeing what other women have accomplished."[130] This strategy is used in most girls' media education programs to considerable effect, broadening girls' knowledge of women's culture as well as their pool of potential mentors and role models. Yet the primary strategy used by educators to create a nurturing, noncompetitive environment for female youth learning about media is to exclude males from such work-shops. Providing a girls-only class was extremely important to the founders of Girls Making Headlines, as Zander notes:

> Simply offering an all-girl class makes the class possibly more attrac-tive to girls, as something special for them. ... Once you get them there, ... there's also the possibility of talking to young girls about media and the absences they see in it. We talked a lot about what kinds of images of girls were out there, and what kind of images were not. ... I doubt these kinds of conversations would be possible with boys, especially at the ages of 9–13. ... [H]aving an option of same-sex learning where kids can grapple with the gendered part of their existence is important.[131]

Similarly, Donnelly of Latinitas asserts, "We prefer to work with girls since we feel they are the least encouraged to explore technology."[132]

The creation of girls-only after-school programs in media education is understandable within the longer history of sex discrimination in conven-tional school environments and feminist educators' responses to this problem. Though Title IX has helped to increase American girls' access to sports and some academic subjects historically dominated by males, most contemporary media education classes in the U.S. are coed and continue to be dominated by male teachers and students. Furthermore, because this law prohibits sex-based discrimination in educational institutions receiving federal funding, attention to girls' special needs via single-sex programs is not possible in pub-lic schools. Thus, extracurricular girls-only media education workshops are understood as a necessary intervention to increase girls' interest in, access to, and engagement with media technologies.

The formation of girls-only media education programs must also be con-textualized in relation to the larger history of marginalized groups' various tactics for empowerment and control, specifically separatism. For example, many feminists have argued that females in patriarchal societies need to sepa-rate, at least temporarily, from males in order to gain control of their bodies, ideas, and practices. Marilyn Frye notes the radical dimension of this tactic when used by women, yet we can understand its power for any disenfran-chised group:

> When women separate (withdraw, break out, regroup, transcend, shove aside, step outside, migrate, say *no*), we are simultaneously controlling access and definition. We are doubly insubordinate, since neither of these is permitted. And access and definition are funda-mental ingredients in the alchemy of power, so we are doubly, and radically, insubordinate.[133]

Yet, as Orwin and Carageorge argue, girls-only media education classes are not designed only to compensate for the present gender-imbalanced conditions of girls' lives; single-sex learning environments also allow development of a different type of media producer:

> In educating women to work in [the male-dominated industries of media production], we must decide whether to prepare them to accept the world on its terms and help them to be accepted within that world, or to give them tools to be their own creative mentors and perhaps alter the dynamics and values of that world.[134]

The separatist philosophy grounds the vast majority of girls' media education workshops and demonstrates the residual effects and thus potency of cultural feminist ideologies on many women media educators.

As Zander suggests, another strategy for creating a supportive environment for girls' media education, as well as more critically aware female media producers, is to privilege female-oriented issues in such workshops. Amanda Lotz, another cofounder of Girls Making Headlines, reiterates this point: "[C]reating a girls-only space seemed critical to making [a] space that was open to thinking about being a girl and expressing it."[135] As substantiated by their students, raising critical consciousness about gender is a noticeable result of girls-only media education workshops. When I asked the Girls Making Headlines' participants if the workshop would have been different had boys been included, all students who responded to this question answered in the affirmative, and the majority noted that it would have been more difficult to include female-centered subjects because male youth are not interested in or care about such topics. When asked if they would prefer a girls-only or coed media workshop, one ten-year-old stated, "I would probably take a girls' class because I'm more comfortable working with girls, but I might take a co-ed class for the variety."[136] Another participant responded that her favorite part of the workshop was that no boys were involved. Girls who have enrolled in other girls-only media workshops concur. For example, one of the participants in Girls Film School notes: "I think if boys were here, boys would tend to show off more and jump in front of the camera. [We girls] don't have to hold back at all. [We're] not hiding behind them."[137] Another Girls Film School student argues that the absence of boys in the program "makes it much easier to concentrate."[138] As these girls confirm, Tyner's criterion that media education workshops should help students "identify, analyze, and overcome the daily erosion of human dignity in an unjust society" in order for them to gain "true self-esteem" is achieved in girls-only programs through a particular focus on gender.

Attesting to the increased sense of power media education can provide for female youth, virtually all of the media educators whom I interviewed for this project reported that girls' training in media production strengthens their self-confidence, particularly in relation to seeing themselves as cultural agents. As Clarissa Moore, the teaching assistant for Girls Making Headlines, states, "It was rewarding for them to know that THEY made this cool video, practically by themselves."[139] In turn, Ross notes: "[T]hey learned how to DO things. The finished product was something you could tell they were proud of!"[140] A graduate of Reel Grrls reveals this feeling of accomplishment also: "It's an amazing feeling, to look at a video and say, 'I did that.'"[141] Similarly, students at Girls Film School demonstrate that such feelings of accomplishment are not the dead-end forms of empowerment critiqued by Tyner. As Fort notes:

> At the end of the session, they'll often say they have different ideas about what they imagine themselves doing in the future. ... It's really exciting to see how their thinking changes, especially as they start working with technology. ... We've had a number of girls tell us they'd never considered college as a possibility for themselves ... then after the program, they really started thinking about it.[142]

Other instructors have noted a general increase in girls' assertiveness that is not specifically related to media production. Reel Grrls instructor Lucia Ramirez states, for example: "These girls are incredibly articulate now. When we first started, these girls were very quiet. They were shy."[143] Many of the female youth who enroll in such workshops are similarly aware of an increase in their assertiveness and confidence. As one seventeen-year-old Girls Film School student reported, "[The camp] really helped me to open up to people and tell them stuff that I had never told anybody before."[144] Another girl enrolled in the school noted, "It helped build my self-confidence a lot, just talking and interacting with people. I actually took my skills and made a film of my own ... , which I'd never considered doing before."[145] In turn, students enrolled in the Reel Grrls program have been quoted as saying, "I'm more self-confident," "I got rid of stage fright," and "I'm coming to grips with my strengths."[146] Students in Latinitas workshops express similar feelings, noting, "This workshop really helped me see my future a little better" and "Because of the club, I want to make my own magazine someday."[147] Even girls who are not yet negotiating the difficulties of adolescence report experiencing a boost in their self-esteem from engaging in media production workshops. For example, an eleven-year-old participant in Girls Making Headlines noticed an increase in her confidence simply through her contact with media technology, stating that, for her, the best part of the class was simply "[w]alking around campus with a tripod on my shoulder. It made me feel important."[148] As Graham explains, "Technology is the great equalizer."[149]

It is extremely difficult to discern the origins or duration of the self-esteem boost girls gain through media production without doing a lengthy study of numerous programs. Nevertheless, reports from instructors and participants of girls' media education workshops demonstrate that girls' active engagement with tools and practices traditionally dominated by adult males is, at the very least, one of the small steps they can take in becoming comfortable with technology, engaging actively with culture, expressing themselves in a new way, and feeling confident and proud of their accomplishments. Moreover, as many of the projects made by these girls have gained attention outside their local communities via their presence in film festivals, cable television shows, and the Web, their producers are indeed "giving back to their communities" and engaging in the processes of public dialogue that Tyner and other media education scholars see as necessary for participatory democracy.

Although most media education workshops for girls are relatively new and thus have not yet trained many students, several graduates of Reel Grrls and Girls Film School not only have returned to those programs to mentor younger students, but have enrolled in college or other programs where they can continue their education in media production. The Reel Grrls website includes a page devoted to its graduates' current pursuits, which include writing original screenplays, directing films and videos, apprenticing at a television station, and attending media production programs at the college and university levels. With their hearts firmly set on participating in the media industries as adults, or their feet firmly planted on that ground already, many graduates of these programs demonstrate that the self-confidence, critical consciousness, and comfort with technology that they developed in girls-only media education workshops have contributed to an increased sense of themselves as powerful cultural agents. As Jamie Wheeler, a graduate of Reel Grrls, argues: "I want to change the world, and media is the best way to do it because media controls society. If I'm behind the camera, I can control it."[150]

CONCLUSION

The increase in media education initiatives as well as the resurgence of the girls' advocacy movement contributed significantly to the introduction of media literacy and media education programs for American girls in the late 1990s. Nevertheless, because the girls' advocacy movement continued its conservative legacy, the media literacy curricula first developed by such organizations rarely moved beyond teaching girls to protect themselves from media representations that will negatively affect their self-esteem. Though there is little doubt that training in such programs contributes significantly to girls' intellectual growth, such an approach ultimately limits girls' development as engaged citizens and cultural agents. Indeed, by not facilitating girls' involvement in media production, such curricula tend to reproduce the gender and generational ideologies that keep female youth limited to the feminized position of consumer.

Fortunately, over the past few years, some girls' advocacy organizations have recognized these problems and begun to implement programs that expand girls' engagements with media beyond critical viewing. For example, in 2003, Girls Inc. received a $600,000 grant from the Time Warner Foundation to expand its media education initiatives through the creation of a high-school-level program that includes instruction in the tools and practices of media production.[151] To develop this new curriculum, Girls Inc.'s Associate Director of National Programs, Deborah Aubert, who has a M.A. in media ecology, consulted with Graham of Reel Grrls. The twelve-lesson Girls Make the Message curriculum was tested in several pilot sites during 2004, and will be distributed, along with light kits, digital video cameras, and computers with editing software, to all eighty of the organization's U.S. locations by 2006.[152] Once students at those sites begin learning the new curriculum, Girls Inc. will have put into action the largest production-oriented media education initiative for female youth in the history of the world. Girls Make the Message is sure to have a profound effect on American girls' culture, which has privileged writing above all other forms of media production for over a century.

III

Texts

4
Grrrl Zines
Exploring Identity, Transforming Girls' Written Culture

The world did not say to her as it did to them,
Write if you choose; it makes no difference to me.
The world said with a guffaw, Write? What's the good of your writing?

—Virginia Woolf[1]

When I started *Ben Is Dead* in 1988, I hadn't a clue what a "zine"
was—there weren't many. I was just looking for a forum and escape,
and without any background in writing or editing—or reading
other "zines"—I found myself creating a magazine of my own.
No one said I couldn't.

—Darby Romeo[2]

Exploring the various forms self-representation might take for female youth,
Lyn Mikel Brown ponders the following questions:

What would it mean for a girl—against the stories read, chanted,
or murmured to her—to choose to tell the truth of her life aloud to

another person at the very point when she is invited into the larger cultural story of womanhood—that is, at early adolescence? To whom would a girl speak and in what context? Who would listen to the story she dares to author? What does she risk in the telling?[3]

As Brown notes, for girls to speak about their experiences as girls would mean their refusal to comply with "the established story of a woman's life."[4] In light of the many contemporary media texts created by girls that critique the dominant myths of girlhood mass-produced by the commercial culture industries, I would argue that a considerable number of female youth are refusing the established story of a *girl's* life also. Indeed, when telling their own stories, many girl media producers reveal not only their resistance to dominant constructions of girlhood but also their interests in exploring nontraditional forms of young female identity.

As discussed in Chapter 1, writing has long served a primary role in American girls' culture, providing female youth with a means for documentation and self-expression, as well as communication with others. Although this written culture was originally associated with upper-class white girls, the democratization of education in the United States after World War II has resulted in an increase in the number and diversity of young female writers, as well as an expansion of the formats in which their writing appears. No longer confined to diaries and letters, girls today produce a variety of written texts, including not just short forms, like poetry and song lyrics, but also long forms, like novels and memoirs.

In order to limit the scope of my analysis of contemporary girls' written culture, this chapter focuses specifically on zines, handmade publications that are produced and distributed by individuals or small groups independent of the commercial publishing industry.[5] My interest in studying zines stems from the fact that they are the primary type of media created by contemporary American girls. Moreover, zinemaking is the form of media production most accessible to the largest number of girls. Unlike electronically mediated forms of cultural expression, such as films and websites, which can be difficult and expensive for youth to create, zines, in their most basic form, require only paper, writing implements, and elementary composition skills. In turn, zine reproduction via mimeograph or photocopying requires minimal skill and expense, and such texts can be easily and cheaply distributed by hand or the postal system.

I am also interested in analyzing girls' zines because the level of production of such texts has risen exponentially over the past decade. This phenomenon is due to several factors. Perhaps most significantly, Riot Grrrl's continuous encouragement for female youth to produce their own media has inspired a considerable number of girls to become actively involved in making zines.

In addition, zines have received considerable attention from the commercial media since the early 1990s, thus motivating many girls who are not affiliated with youth cultures to see zinemaking as a viable means for networking and creative expression. Furthermore, feminist critiques of and girls' resistance to teen magazines—the primary commercial media texts directed to this specific demographic—has inspired many female youth to self-publish print media that better address their interests, needs, concerns, and desires.

A TIME FOR SASSY VOICES: CONTEMPORARY TEEN MAGAZINE CULTURE

As female youth physically mature, become critically conscious, and enter the economic market as consumers, they are encouraged to seek out cultural texts that can help them negotiate the liminal and often troubling experiences of adolescence and, more importantly, their entrance into womanhood. As Kate Peirce argues:

> [I]t can be argued that teenage girls are dependent on teen maga-
> zines for information about their lives. These magazines are the only
> medium targeted specifically to them and their popularity suggests
> that the magazines meet one or more needs, which increases depen-
> dency. ... There is not an overabundance of magazines targeted to
> that age group so the magazines that do exist are read by hundreds of
> thousands of teenage girls.[6]

Although commercial teen magazines have been the primary form of mass media produced specifically for girls for over sixty years, a consider-able number of contemporary female youth feel alienated from such texts. Some girls' opposition to teen magazines is likely the result of their exposure to feminist ideologies, as well as the by-now popular critique of commercial media texts as reproductive of patriarchal ideologies. In turn, since the 1980s, teen magazines have considerably decreased the amount of participation their readers can have in the creation of such texts, having curtailed the publication of girls' fiction, poetry, and essays, a long-standing practice since the 1940s. As a result, contemporary teen magazines have eliminated one of the primary realms in which previous generations of female youth positioned themselves publicly as media producers.

In March 1988, a new periodical for girls called *Sassy* was introduced in the United States. Through its employment of young feminist editors and writers, *Sassy* privileged nonconformist constructions of girlhood and female youth culture over the traditional discourses of heterocentrism, self-surveil-lance, appearance improvement, and narcissistic consumerism relied on by other commercial teen magazines, such as *YM*, *Teen*, and *Seventeen*. Indeed, the original publisher and editors of *Sassy* were determined to create a periodical for intelligent, discerning young readers that broke free of the boy-crazy, shopaholic, beauty-obsessed clichés of American teenage girlhood. Although fashion and beauty, the mainstays of female-oriented periodicals, were not disregarded in *Sassy*'s original format, such content was considerably subordinated by the original editorial staff, who concentrated on the unique problems of contemporary female youth, such as sexual abuse, depression, eating disorders, and AIDS. Controversial topics considered taboo by most teen magazine publishers, like rape and feminism, were also featured regularly. Indeed, it was *Sassy* editors' insistence on providing information to teenage girls about the harsh realities of young female life in contemporary society that made this magazine stand apart from other teen periodicals.

In addition to providing content typically ignored by other commercial teen magazines, the original *Sassy* staff embraced Riot Grrrl's notion of "girl power," boldly highlighting girls' acts of cultural engagement through such reader-produced columns as "It Happened to Me" and "Stuff You Wrote," as well as by foregrounding girls' various forms of media production.[7] For example, the monthly column, "What Now," featured reviews of zines and drew attention to female youth who were actively producing their own media. Perhaps *Sassy*'s largest step toward recognizing and encouraging girls as active producers of culture was its annual "Reader Produced Issue" (introduced in 1990), which allowed female youth to take over creative control from editors and participate in different aspects of magazine production, including writing, layout, and photography. By encouraging its readers' participation, *Sassy* resurrected practices that, though introduced in teen magazines as early as the 1940s, had long since been abandoned by most commercial periodicals targeting the young female demographic.

In light of the girl power spirit that informed their practices, *Sassy*'s original staff confirmed Angela McRobbie's theory that editors and journalists working for contemporary teen magazines "have asserted their commitment to gender-equality and to creating a more confident femininity," and "attempt to integrate at least aspects of ... political or feminist discourses into their work."[8] *Sassy*'s staff mirrored many of the progressive values Janice Winship noted in British girls' magazines of the 1980s, where feminist topics, such as self-defense, eating disorders, sexist language, and alternatives to marriage, were "taken up pragmatically, translated into the practical and individual skills of the street-wise."[9] Although she discourages a conclusion that contemporary teen magazines are promoting only feminist ideologies, Winship nevertheless argues that "there is still a cultural level at which feminism *is* taken for granted. The magazines don't so much assume that the feminist case has been won as that it goes without saying that there is a case."[10]

The transformations that occurred within *Sassy's* pages and editorial board during its last two years of publication (1994–1996) attest to the commercial publishing industry's continued uneasiness with troubling traditional gender roles and modes of representation. After firing *Sassy's* original editorial staff in 1994, Petersen Publishing Company abruptly stopped publication of the magazine in 1996, despite readers' protests. Appropriating *Sassy* from the hands of feminists (both editors' and readers'), Petersen's plan to be "forward in fashion, beauty and entertainment" led many girls to look elsewhere for periodicals that more directly engaged their specific concerns, needs, and pleasures.[11]

As a result of *Sassy's* initial success in appealing to a more diverse demographic of girl readers, several other feminist-oriented teen magazines were introduced in the mid-1990s, including *Teen Voices, Empowered,* and *blue jean magazine,* all of which were dedicated to valuing girls and their experiences through means other than commodity consumption, heterosexual romance, and beauty enhancement. As Kim Whiting, the publisher of *Empowered,* argued in her welcome message to readers:

> You deserve a magazine that talks about more than catching a guy and keeping him happy, diets and looking good because you are so much more than these things. This magazine is about your dreams, about the wonderful things that you are, just the way you are, and the amazing things you can achieve. It is a place for you to unite, hear about the lives and ideas of others, ask questions, share, support, learn, empower, laugh and create.[12]

In turn, *blue jean magazine* described itself as "an alternative to the fashion and beauty magazines targeting young women. *blue jean magazine* is advertising-free, and you will find no beauty tips, fashion spreads, or supermodels on our pages."[13] Similar in both form and content to *Empowered* and *blue jean magazine, Teen Voices* has been described by one of its editors as "an interactive, educational forum [that] serves as a vehicle of change, improving young women's social and economic status. *Teen Voices* provides an intelligent alternative to glitzy, gossipy fashion-oriented publications that too often exploit the insecurities of their young audience."[14]

Unlike commercial teen magazines, which are produced by adults with little input from girls, *Empowered, Teen Voices,* and *blue jean magazine* were created with the help of teen editors and journalists, and thus signified a unique development in contemporary periodicals for female youth. Encouraging their readers to create alternative forms of media and communication networks,[15] these magazines provided girls with opportunities for participating actively in culture and society without relying on the traditional ideologies of heterosexuality, consumerism, and self-improvement repeatedly reinforced by commercial teen magazines.

NEW MEDIA FOR NEW GIRLS: THE RISE OF GIRLS' ZINES

Unfortunately, most of the feminist teen magazines introduced in the mid-1990s were defunct by the end of that decade. Indeed, as of this date, only *Teen Voices* is still in circulation.[16] It is in this context of change within the publishing industry, particularly the minimal attention given to nonconformist female youth and their interests, that the phenomenal rise in girl zinemaking must be located. Indeed, it seems no coincidence that since the majority of these feminist-oriented magazines became unavailable, a considerable number of girls have been motivated to publish their own zines, many of which spend considerable space skewering commercial teen magazines. For example, in the second issue of her zine, *Nolite te Bastardes Carborundorum*,[17] Nikki analyzes the promotional discourse written by *YM*'s editors:

> I think I'm going to puke every time I hear *YM* mentioned. They just WANT girls to be so STUPID. Or maybe they just *expect* it. "beauty, new fashions, and (of course) guys." Like *they* know anything about beauty. Their idea of beauty is an anorexic person from Somalia covered with pounds of make-up. Their "new fashions" are just whoever paid them the most money to show their clothes off to hundreds and thousands of teenage girls who get sucked in because magazines like *YM*, and the society around, tell girls that they won't be accepted if they DON'T buy the newest thing. ... And this is the part I really hate, "and (of course) guys!" Of course! That makes me so sick. They tell girls that guys are the *only* really important thing. Like thats the only reason girls are here, to be objects and property for men. ... O yes, we must put on our make-up and smile at everyone or no one will like us. Come on! There's so much more to LIFE![18]

Even *Sassy*, understood by many girls and women to be the first feminist teen magazine in the United States, has not been spared critique by female zinesters, particularly after the magazine's editorial staff was replaced by a new publisher in the mid-1990s. For example, the premiere issue of Lisa Jervis's *Bitch* contains a special section titled "*Sassy* Sucks," which criticizes the revised magazine for its narrow representation of girls and reproduction of patriarchal standards of female beauty.[19] Similarly, a writer for *Little Big Sister Zine #2* asserts:

> I'm sure most of you have heard of that trendy teen magazine called *Sassy* in which the newest fashions are displayed and the latest social and health issues are dealt with in an oh-so-sassy way. Well, I'm hear to say it's all just bullshit. ... [I]f you think *Sassy* is such an enlightened magazine then think again.[20]

Other female zinesters have responded to girls' commercial magazine culture by devoting part or all of their zines to parodies of such periodicals, often employing the irreverent discourse and confrontational aesthetic strategies associated with punk in order to critique teen magazines' conservative ideologies and moral discourse. For example, after losing *Sassy*'s "Reader Produced Issue" contest, Darby Romeo and her collaborators on *Ben Is Dead* decided to put out their own "Very Essential Super Extra-Special *Sassy* Issue" in 1994.[21] Using *Sassy*'s conventional layout and rhetorical style, *Ben Is Dead #23* reveals its creators' general distaste for commercial teen magazines, as well as their conflicted pleasures in reading *Sassy*. The zine also provides readers with more distance (as well as more ammunition) to critically assess the dominant discourses and representational strategies of commercial teen magazines, a point that is hammered home in Amanda Burr's contribution, "Competition? What Competition?":

> After *Sassy* was launched with the mission of ignoring the traditional formula for women's magazines, the other magazines looked so outdated that they had to make some superficial changes. Like, they tried to be more on top of entertainment and loosen up their tone. But they read like cheap knock-offs and have no souls. *Sassy*'s purpose really is to inspire girls to be opinionated and informed and rebellious and funny, while other magazines don't have a clue. They just want to sell sell sell.[22]

Inspired by both *Sassy*'s rebellious spirit and the "do-it-yourself" (DIY) ethos of the zine community, the creators of *Ben Is Dead #23* encouraged their readers to move beyond commercial teen magazines by including both an extensive list of zines made by female youth,[23] as well as an article on how to create electronic zines ("e-zines").[24] By promoting girls' self-publication—that is, by motivating their readers to move from readers to writers—Romeo and her staff attempted to expand not only girls' written culture, but popular culture at large. Given the thousands of girl-made zines that have been introduced since *Ben Is Dead #23* left bookstore shelves, it seems their dream has come true.

Since the early 1990s, the number of zines created by female youth has increased exponentially. Although contemporary girls' zines are often associated with riot grrrls,[25] many of these texts are produced by female youth affiliated with other counterhegemonic cultural and political scenes, such as anarchism and skateboarding.[26] Riot grrrls helped to inspire this growth in girl-made zines during the early 1990s by creating girl-run mail-order businesses, like Riot Grrrl Press, and by holding zinemaking workshops at annual conferences. *Sassy* helped to ease girls' access to zines (as well as inspire their own zinemaking) in the 1990s by regularly publishing reviews of zines, as well as their creators' addresses. Since the mid-1990s, zine production, distribution, and workshops have been expanded beyond the Riot Grrrl community by women zinesters who want to strengthen the infrastructure that motivates and sustains female zinemaking practices. For example, several women-run online zine distribution companies ("distros"), like Pander and Grrrl Style!, have been introduced during the past decade,[27] and some older female zinesters, such as those involved in Grrrl Zines a Go-Go, hold workshops in zine production for teenage girls and young women.[28]

Although there is little doubt that Riot Grrrl's DIY/girl power spirit and networked media economy are of primary significance to the rise of girl-made zines over the past two decades, several other factors have been influential also. For instance, because magazines are the primary media texts directed toward female youth by the commercial culture industries, and girls have self-published fan newsletters since the 1930s, zines are a natural extension of traditional forms of girls' culture. Thus, zinemaking is not a male-dominated cultural practice in which female youth have recently become involved, as many believe. Moreover, since zines do not require the use of sophisticated and heavy equipment that has traditionally limited girls' involvement as media producers, such texts have proven to be an inviting and inexpensive format for female youth who want to participate in the broader sphere of cultural production. These two factors—zines' historical connection to girl's culture, and the easy accessibility of zines as a medium—have contributed greatly to the dominance of zines in contemporary girls' media production.

The various political ideologies engaged and nonconformist identities performed in girls' zines suggest that many of their producers are over sixteen years of age. Nevertheless, many younger girls are actively involved in zinemaking also. Indeed, although most of the early female punk fanzine editors were in their early twenties when they began producing these texts, many contemporary girls become involved in zinemaking much earlier in life, often while they are in junior high or middle school. For example, Robin Crane of *Sweetheart*, Serra Rose Sewitch of *Moon Fuzz*, Emilie Feingold-Tarrant of *Girl Infinity*, and Kristy Chan of *Wild Honey Pie* and *Riot Grrrl Review* started publishing zines when they were thirteen.[29] Responses to two surveys I conducted—one of female distro owners and the other of participants in distro message boards— indicate that most contemporary girls are between the ages of fourteen and twenty when they make their first zine.[30]

The young age of girl zinesters today should not come as a surprise if we remember that adolescents who live with their parents, particularly those of the middle class, have more disposable time and income to spend on creative cultural projects than adults. Moreover, young people who do not have access to transportation often find their cultural practices limited to what they can do within their homes. That a considerable number of teenage *girls* have become active participants in the zine community is not surprising if we consider the dearth of media texts that address female youth as intelligent, powerful, and creative individuals, as well as the privileged place writing has had in female youth culture for over two hundred years.

The history of zines is often traced back only as far as the punk fanzines of the late 1970s. Nevertheless, such self-publications have a longer and more complex history in a variety of marginal cultural groups, such as science fiction fans of the late 1930s, the Beat poets of the 1950s, and the underground press of the 1960s and 1970s.[31] Although the earliest zine producers were typically white males, and this group continues to dominate zine culture, an increasing number of females and people of color have become involved in zinemaking since the late 1980s. Most contemporary zinesters are teenagers and young adults who feel alienated from dominant society and commercial culture. Zines are an attractive medium for such youth, because they require minimal education and technical skill to produce, and their main ingredients (paper and writing implements) are inexpensive, as well as easily accessible, manipulable, and transportable.

Zines are primarily produced and consumed by members of the middle class, a social group that for generations has been encouraged to privilege written texts, such as novels, magazines, and newspapers, over the broad array of other cultural artifacts that circulate through their everyday lives. Indeed, despite the phenomenal rise of literacy among all classes of U.S. youth since World War II, contemporary middle-class teenagers and young adults continue to participate in written culture to a far greater extent than do poor youth, who, in continuing the legacy of working-class culture, tend to privilege nonliterary cultural practices, such as dance, sports, and popular music, that do not require traditional forms of literacy.

Despite the class dynamics of zine culture, in keeping with the anti-industrial, anti-commercial ethos of countercultural production, zines are typically created via relatively inexpensive and unsophisticated means: handwritten or typewritten text, hand-drawn illustrations, and text and images cut from commercial media texts. Unlike the "slick" (i.e., professional, technically enhanced, big budget) magazines that dominate the publishing industry, zines typically are created at home and reproduced via mimeographs or photocopiers. In this way, zinesters often remain independent from the practices and technologies associated with professional presses and commercial publishers. With the increased availability of personal computers, as well as word processing and desktop publishing software, an increasing number of zine producers are using digital technology to typeset and format their material. Nevertheless, these electronic, technologized practices are often frowned upon by zinesters interested in steering clear of the commercial, industrial sector of culture and expressing themselves as authentically as possible.

The independent, DIY ethos privileged by zinesters has important connections to the anti-industrial, anti-capitalist practice known in France as *la
perruque*.[32] Zine producers often rely on illicit means for creating, reproducing, and distributing their texts, appropriating office time, space, equipment,
and supplies, as well as postage and photocopying services from their places
of work. Other zinesters "scam" the means of zine production and reproduction from commercial photocopy businesses. In addition, zinesters freely use
text and images mass produced by the commercial media industries, refusing
to adhere to policies meant to protect intellectual and artistic property. Such
text and images are rarely reproduced in their original forms, however, as
zinemakers deconstruct and reassemble such materials to produce new meanings (a practice known as *détournement*, which is discussed in further detail
below). In order to avoid criminal prosecution and censorship for such practices, many individuals who make zines do not reveal their real identities and
use nicknames by which they are known in the zine community. In addition,
zinesters typically use post office boxes instead of home addresses, change the
titles of their zines, and accept only cash or stamps as payment.

As these various practices suggest, making zines affords young people an
opportunity to rebel against dominant social institutions and to explore alternative cultural economies and counterhegemonic identities even during what
are considered the mundane practices of reproduction and distribution. Since
historically female youth have not had much license to digress from dominant
culture and normative subjectivities, I am interested in examining how zinemaking, as a creative practice involving fantasy, facilitates girls' explorations
of different forms of identity, particularly those that subvert the established
stories of girlhood.

PAPER TRY OUTS: WRITING AS A PRACTICE
OF IDENTITY EXPLORATION

In addition to documentation, communication, and expression, the three
objectives of writing discussed in Chapter 1, a fourth and equally important
function of writing is the *exploration of identity*. Just as the development of
writing as a means for personal expression has been connected to the nineteenth century and new conceptions of the subject as rationale, inquisitive,
and reflexive, the notion that writing can be used as a means for identity
exploration can be connected to the reconceptualization of human subjectivity resulting from the conditions of postmodernism. As Fredric Jameson has
argued, postindustrialism, late consumer capitalism, and the rise of information technologies have destabilized the Cartesian notion of the unified and
coherent subject.[33] Understood as fragmented, multiple, and contradictory,
identity is now conceived not as something inherent or essential, but rather

as dynamically and pluralistically constituted via an individual's various rela-tionships with other people, as well as different ideologies, roles, practices, and institutions. In other words, as an individual's social, geographical, and historical contexts change, so does her or his identity.[34]

Poststructuralist theorists consider discourse—the effect of symbolic practices that construct meanings and organize human experiences—to be the primary mechanism for constituting identity. In describing this contem-porary conceptualization of identity, Stuart Hall argues:

> Perhaps, instead of thinking of an identity as an already accomplished historical fact, which ... discourses then represent, we should think, instead, of identity as a "production," which is never complete, always in process, and always constituted within, not outside, representation.[35]

At the same time, however, Hall is careful to qualify this notion of identity as an abstract, discursive construction, since it makes problematic such concepts as authority and agency, which have been considered vital for engaging in public debate and thus politics. Bringing social constructionism and discourse theory together with historical materialism, therefore, Hall reminds us:

> The practices of representation always implicate the positions from which we speak or write—the positions of *enunciation*. ... We all write and speak from a particular place and time, from a history and a culture which is specific. What we say is always "in context," *posi-tioned*. ... [I]dentities come from somewhere, have histories. But, like everything else which is historical, they undergo constant trans-for-mation. Far from being eternally fixed in some essentialist past, they are subject to the continuous "play" of history, culture, and power.[36]

Recent reconceptualizations of identity as discursive have radically trans-formed the study and practices of self-representation. Indeed, rather than approaching cultural production as a mechanism for the expression or docu-mentation of a "true" or "authentic" self, such practices are understood as par-ticipating in the process of identity construction. As Hall argues, by the late twentieth century a new phase of cultural practices had begun in which pro-ducers, understanding essentialized forms of identity as impossible and thus unrepresentable, explore the formative role the media play in (re)producing and questioning identities.[37] In other words, in the process of "representing" them-selves, cultural producers experiment with different identities.

Within this new realm of what Hall calls the "politics of representation," conceptions of writing have changed also. As Barbara Crowther argues in rela-tion to contemporary girls' diary writing, for example, "[S]ome of what is going on in diary discourse is a kind of performance in front of a mirror, seeing how things look, trying out poses and voices."[38] Similarly, in a survey I conducted with young female zinesters, virtually every one of the respondents indicated that exploring her identity was a primary reason for her zinemaking. In turn, several answered "identity" when asked which topics are discussed most often in girls' zines.[39] Indeed, it seems that one of girls' primary purposes for creating zines is personal exploration, and often this objective is given priority over others, such as networking and community building, particularly upon writers' initial entrance into the practices of media production. Darby Romeo notes, for example: "[My] zine became a tool for me to move around the world. A signpost marking time so I could see where I was at, and where I might want to go. … *Ben Is Dead* … has always been about discovery … and creating new worlds for oneself."[40] As the young females who create zines are often adolescents transitioning from girlhood to womanhood, such texts provide a space for their creators' initial exploration of nontraditional identities, especially those that may be deemed inappropriate for individuals of their sex and age and thus are rarely permitted public expression. As Stephen Duncombe notes, "Zines … allow people, if only for a short time, to escape the identity they are born into and circumscribed by and to become someone else. … Zines offer a space for people to try out new personalities, ideas, and politics."[41]

Interestingly, in his study of thousands of contemporary zines, Duncombe noticed that the zinesters most likely to use their texts for exploring identity were females and people of color, individuals "acutely aware of the constraints of identity as defined by others."[42] Duncombe's observation is supported by Teresa de Lauretis, who similarly argues that the "double vision" of marginalized individuals comes from their experience of knowing that their social group is not represented accurately in public discourse.[43] Using women as an example, she notes their awareness of "the discrepancy, the tension, and the constant slippage between Woman as representation, as the object and the very condition of representation, and, on the other hand, women as historical beings, subjects of 'real relations' …"[44] De Lauretis suggests that this form of perception increases the potential for a critical understanding of identity's social construction, and thus an appreciation for, if not enactment of, de- and reconstructed identities and their emancipatory potential. Though neither de Lauretis nor Duncombe explicitly do so, it is important to consider the phenomenon of "double vision" in relation to our media-saturated postmodern context, which has raised the stakes for individual involvement in representational practices. Indeed, I would argue that disenfranchised individuals have "triple vision" given that through their consumption of texts produced through the culture industries, they are made acutely aware of the norms of identity that they are encouraged to adopt as ideal but will never achieve.

Since most scholars studying girls' zines have focused on the interpersonal, communicative function of such texts, very few analyses draw attention to the many other functions zine production can serve in their creators' lives, such as identity exploration. For example, although Marion Leonard notes how zinemaking typically takes place in the "private space of the bedroom," which becomes a "site of activity ... integral rather than incidental to the text itself," her analysis of girls' zines is framed primarily by a discussion of how such texts function outside the domestic sphere, collectively forming what she refers to as "the riot grrrl network."[45] Similarly, Ednie Kaeh Garrison explores zines' function in the development of Riot Grrrl as a transnational community, while also positioning such texts in the larger context of what she calls "third wave feminist networking."[46] And while Michelle Comstock's analysis of girls' zines includes a discussion of girl zinesters as "postfeminist authors" who employ writing "as a tactic for critical or alternative subject formation," her discussion of this process focuses primarily on how such writers use their traumatized bodies as sites of collective gender performance.[47] Moreover, like Leonard and Garrison, Comstock privileges a conception of zinemaking as "a site of collective struggle and interactivity" that produces what she refers to as "the grrrl zine network."[48]

Leonard's, Garrison's, and Comstock's constructions of zines as primarily community media seem largely and, in some cases, unconsciously informed by the ubiquitous rhetoric of dialogue and collective action circulating within the zine and Riot Grrrl communities. As Leonard notes, "Publications produced by those involved in riot grrrl reveal a ... range of collective terms," including "support network," "a group of women (grrrls) who work together," and "a community of cooperative young women."[49] In addition, these scholars' framings of girls' zines as primarily social media are informed by dominant approaches for studying activist media and countercultures, the majority of which have been strongly influenced by Marxist theories of culture and power, and thus tend to be interested in the broader social, rather than personal, functions and effects of media production and consumption. In particular, studies of girls' zines as community media follow a path previously charted by Henry Jenkins in *Textual Poachers*, one of the first contemporary analyses of fan culture. Of enormous influence on other scholars' approaches to studying the productive practices of media consumers, Jenkins's text primarily concerns fan culture, and thus focuses more on the ability of fanzine writers "to speak from a position of collective identity, to forge an alliance with a community of others in defense of tastes which, as a result, cannot be read as totally aberrant or idiosyncratic" than how their zinemaking provides them with an opportunity for exploring their individual identity.[50] Thus, while he notes that "[t]he astounding array of different fan stories, the relatively low barriers of entry into fan publishing, and its status as a cottage industry encourage us to see fan writing in highly individualized terms," Jenkins's ultimate concern is with "how writing becomes a social activity for these fans" and how "[f]an writing builds upon the interpretive practices of the fan community."[51]

By foregrounding the dominant framing of zines as social media, I do not mean to dismiss or reject zines' significance in the formation and maintenance of communities and collective forms of identity. Indeed, as I discuss in Chapter 2, zines were essential to the emergence and solidification of the Riot Grrrl community, as well as its transnational development. Nevertheless, it is important not to downplay the nonsocial and noncollective functions of such texts, for while communication is a primary goal for most zinesters, it is not their only or most privileged objective. Therefore, more attention should be paid to how the production of such texts functions in the lives of their individual producers, for zinemaking typically begins as diary and letter writing do—with a singular writer.

In an effort to reconceptualize the practice of zinemaking from a psychoanalytic and thus personal perspective, Fred Wright argues that "zine publishers create their publications because of the psychological need to produce and consolidate a sense of identity for themselves, an impulse that operates simultaneously in the Lacanian registers of the Symbolic, Imaginary, and Real."[52] In light of poststructuralist theories of subjectivity and discourse, however, I would amend Wright's thesis to say that the practices of writing allow zine producers to explore and experiment with identities, not consolidate them. Thus, in my own analysis of girls' zines, I am less concerned with examining those forms of discourse that work to construct the girl zinester as an intelligible self than I am with discerning how female youth use zines to "try out" various forms of identity.

FANTASY ROLES: EXPLORING IDENTITY THROUGH MEDIA PRODUCTION

Within contemporary media and cultural studies, identity exploration has been analyzed primarily in relation to consumers and practices of consumption.[53] Yet several scholars have demonstrated that media producers also explore identity in the process of creating cultural texts. For example, Constance Penley has used theories of fantasy to examine female *Star Trek* fans' experimentation with identity in their artwork and writing. Such theories, she argues, allow scholars "to describe how the subject participates in and restages a scenario in which crucial questions about desire, knowledge, and identity can be posed, and in which the subject can hold a number of identificatory positions."[54] Influenced primarily by Jean Laplanche and Jean-Bertrand Pontalis's rereadings of Sigmund Freud's theories, Penley foregrounds fantasy as a broad range of interrelated psychical phenomena—from conscious daydreams to unconscious scenarios—that form a psychical reality not opposed to but rather structuring material reality.[55] In keeping with Laplanche and Pontalis's theory of fantasy as "the stage-setting of desire,"[56] Penley posits fantasy as a psychical performative space or site—what Elizabeth Cowie refers to as "a *mise en scène* of desire"[57]—in which individuals can try on several identities simultaneously, including those ostensibly at odds with their sex, race, sexuality, and age.[58]

As Penley argues, through their creation of fantastic scenarios that place the bodies of Kirk and Spock (the lead male characters in *Star Trek*) in sexually intimate encounters,[59] female *Star Trek* fans explore their desire for empowered identity and egalitarian heterosexual (and heterosocial) relations. In other words, the women's construction of such scenarios "allows for a much greater range of identification and desire for the women: in the fantasy one can *be* Kirk or Spock (a possible phallic identification) and also still *have* (as sexual objects) either or both of them since, as heterosexuals, they are not *un*available to them as women."[60]

By employing poststructuralist theories to analyze media producers' use of fantasy, Penley has helped to reinvigorate the study of media authorship, which traditionally, and problematically, has been grounded in conceptions of subjectivity as centered, stable, and authentically reflected in texts. Some scholars who are members of socially marginalized groups, such as women, homosexuals, and people of color, have resisted the use of such theories because they subvert the notion of essentialized identities upon which such groups' counterhegemonic politics were originally grounded. Yet other deprivileged scholars have embraced theories that posit identity (like truth and reality) as constructed and thus available for de- and reconstruction according to alternate values. For example, Richard Dyer argues that the poststructuralist position on identity has a "political edge over the apparently more inspiring universalist positions":

> While the latter seem to have more immediate political power to mobilize people round an identity apparently rooted in an essential human type, social constructionism returns control over [identity] to those who live it. It does this by identifying the fact that the latter are not those currently in control of it and indicating the cases and ways in which they are or can be. Those cases and ways include forms of *cultural production* …[61]

Pausing for emphasis, Dyer continues, arguing:

> —but one can have no concept of socially specific forms of cultural production without some notion of authorship, for what one is looking at are the circumstances in which counter-discourses are produced, in which those generally spoken of and for speak for themselves.[62]

Elaborating further on the relationship of marginalized identity and authorship, Dyer argues that studies of the relationship of an author's identity to the texts s/he produces are "haunted" by the dubious figures of both the author, whose status as the master meaning–maker has been thoroughly debunked by numerous reception studies scholars, and the marginalized subject, whose deprivileged and essentialized identity has been constructed by those with the privilege of individuality.[63] Refusing to let go of either of these problematic figures, Dyer attempts to resolve this haunting, arguing:

> [I]t still matters who specifically made a film, whose performance a film is, though this is neither all-determining nor having any assumable relationship to the person's life or consciousness. What is significant is the authors' material social position in relation to discourse, the access to discourses they have on account of who they are.[64]

In addition, Dyer notes that the concept of authority cannot be ignored when considering texts produced by disenfranchised individuals, because

> [t]he idea of authority implied in that of authorship, the feeling that it is a way of claiming legitimacy and power for a text's meanings and affects, is indeed what is at issue. They are about claiming the right to speak ... , claiming a special authority for their image.[65]

As a way of solving the conundrum caused by merging authorship studies with poststructuralist theory, Dyer suggests that "both authorship and [identity] become a kind of performance, something we all do but only with the terms, the discourses, available to us, and whose relationship to any imputed self doing the performing cannot be taken as read."[66] Dyer's theory of authorship as performance is useful for analyzing texts produced by deprivileged individuals since it posits authors' identities as implicated in their cultural productions, yet maintains that these identities are neither stable nor all-determining. Moreover, he does not let go of the material bodies involved in such performative practices, arguing that authors have access to particular discourses that are made available "on account of who they are."[67]

Wendy Hollway further clarifies the processes through which discourses are made available to individuals, and thus helps to round out Dyer's insights about media authorship as a performative practice involving the exploration of identity. Hollway begins by noting that "[d]iscourses make available positions for subjects to take up,"[68] yet qualifies this statement by arguing that all positions (identities) are not made equally available to all individuals. Rather, because discourses of identity are constructed through various mechanisms of social organization, individuals are encouraged to "invest" in particular discursive positions that relate to their bodies (Dyer's "who they are") and result in "some satisfaction or pay-off or reward ... for that person."[69] This concept is useful for thinking through the different levels of access individuals have to different discourses as a result of their position within social hierarchies as determined by such demographic characteristics as sex, race, class, ethnicity, sexuality, and age. For example, in his study of homosexual forms of cinematic authorship, Dyer focuses on such individuals' access to discourses associated with lesbian/gay subcultures.

In an effort to resist critiques of discursive determinism, and acknowledge psychoanalytic theories of desire, Hollway accounts for change in this system by arguing that "discourses coexist and have mutual effects and that meanings are multiple. This produces choice, though it may not be simple or conscious."[70] To push Hollway's theories a bit further, although our bodies transform somewhat minimally over the course of our lives, the material conditions of our lives (i.e., the spatial, temporal, and social contexts in which those bodies are located) change constantly and sometimes in dramatic ways. Where we are and when and with whom and under what specific circumstances all impinge upon the discursive positions/identities that are available for our investment and exploration at any given moment. Thus, I would add that discursive access is determined also by the relationship our bodies have to particular sociohistorical contexts. Moreover, the process of discursive investment is complicated by psychological and intellectual development, particularly the accumulation of education and experience that, as Pierre Bourdieu argues, provide each individual with a certain amount of cultural capital and thus a specific degree of access to the spectrum of discursive positions.[71]

According to Judith Butler, "discourses present themselves in the plural, coexisting within temporal frames, and instituting unpredictable and inadvertent convergences from which specific modalities of discursive possibilities are engendered."[72] In societies rich in signifying practices and sophisticated communications technologies, such as the United States, multiple discourses are in circulation at all times. Thus, Hall argues that "as the systems of meaning and cultural representation multiply, we are confronted by a bewildering, fleeting multiplicity of possible identities, any one of which we could identify with—at least temporarily."[73] An important question remains, therefore: How do individuals determine which identities or discursive positions are worth their investment? What mechanisms encourage our privileging this identity over that identity at any given time, and are such mechanisms purely discursive?

Although it is extremely difficult, if not impossible, to explore all the variables impinging upon any one person's identity investments, I would argue that we can limit our study of this phenomenon to a particular range of discourses and discursive practices. Many contemporary linguists have studied identity performance in the most mundane and routinized discursive acts, such as conversing with friends.[74] Yet the processes of identity exploration are often more explicit, and thus easier to discern, in those practices that privilege discursive experimentation, such as the production of media texts. As Cowie argues:

Fantasy has, of course, never been simply a private affair. The public circulation of fantasies has many forms, from the publishing of psychoanalytic case studies, to feminist articles such as those appearing in *Heresies*, or speaking-out in consciousness-raising groups; and anthologies such as *My Secret Garden* which, besides their pseudoscientific claims of extending human knowledge, are also offering forms of circulation of fantasy just as much as do the letters in … *Penthouse*, etc. But by far the most common form of public circulation of fantasy is what Freud described as "creative writing."[75]

As media texts that combine the confessional aspects of diary writing, letter writing, and "speaking-out in consciousness-raising groups" with the more conventionally fantastic characteristics of creative writing, girls' zines provide a rich resource for studying young females' various discursive explorations of identity. In particular, these texts demonstrate their creators' strong interest in sex and gender. Indeed, though girl zinesters have multiple identities that are available for their investment, many of these media producers use the discursive position of "girl" to express and represent themselves authoritatively. This phenomenon is not surprising if we consider Barbara Hudson's theory that female youth are socialized to privilege their sex and its associated gender identity above all else.[76] Nevertheless, girl zinesters typically do not reproduce conventional constructions of girlhood in their texts. Keeping in mind Butler's theory that hegemonic forms of identity can be subverted by varying the repetition of the discursive acts that make such identities intelligible, I am particularly interested in examining the strategies developed by girl zinesters to block the dominant discursive construction of female youth as appearance-oriented, boy-obsessed shopaholics.[77]

FROM GIRL TO GRRRL: EXPLORING FEMALE IDENTITY THROUGH ZINEMAKING

Though most male-written histories of punk ignore girls' involvement as cultural producers, several female punks were active in zinemaking during the late 1970s and early 1980s, including Wendy Blume of *Let It Rock*, and Crystal Clear, Vinyl Virgin, and Sarah Shoshubi who coedited *More-On*. Like other punk periodicals of that period, most zines produced by these female punks functioned as fanzines, and thus primarily included interviews with punk musicians and reviews of shows and recordings.[78]

During the mid- to late 1980s, a significant number of zines produced by teenage girls and young women, including Laura MacDougal's *Sister Nobody*, Donna Dresch's *Chainsaw*, and Tobi Vail's *Jigsaw*, began to privilege autobiographical writings alongside fan discourse, thus helping to develop the genre now widely known as "personal zines" or "perzines." Through the process of autobiography, many of these writers used their zines to explore the unique, and often uncomfortable, position of females within punk culture. As Mark Fenster argues, fanzines provided a space for female punks' "ongoing process of producing, within forms of representation, a range of possible identities."[79] The performative function of such zines was extremely significant to lesbians who participated in 1980s' hardcore culture, as the patriarchal and homophobic ideologies dominant within punk scenes at that time severely limited such girls' public displays of sexuality. This combination of music, autobiography, feminism, and queer politics continued into the early 1990s in zines associated with the Riot Grrrl movement, such as *Bikini Kill*, *Girl Germs*, and *Riot Grrrl*.

As a result of the diffusion of the girl power spirit beyond the Riot Grrrl community, not to mention the significant increase in zine production by individuals not affiliated with the punk community, many contemporary girl zinesters have limited the amount of fan-based musical discourse in their zines, injecting their texts with far more autobiographical writing than those created by previous generations of female zinesters. This personal aspect of contemporary girls' zines is significant to their function in their producers' lives. As alternatives to commercial teen magazines that present consumerism, appearance improvement, and heterosexual romance as the primary activities in which girls should be interested, zines allow young females to develop other interests through their creative abilities, while also providing a space to explore their identity.

Sarah Dyer, creator of the comic *Action Girl*, and one of the first people to produce a directory of girl-made zines,[80] has argued that while the exploration of female identity was present in many women-produced zines prior to the 1990s, this particular discourse became a primary focus for many girl zinesters by the mid-1990s:

> Riot Grrrls got so much press and hype that people thought that all girl zines were Riot Grrrl zines. I tried to let people know that Riot Grrrl zines are part of a larger movement of girl zines, which are zines by girls which are specifically about being a girl and the "female experience." I started *Action Girl* in 1992, and it wasn't until the next year that I really started seeing what you might call girl zines. Up until that, it was mainly zines about music, literature, art, etc. that happened to be by women.[81]

While I do not want to discount Dyer's important differentiation between Riot Grrrl zines and the broader category of what she calls "girl zines," for purposes of clarity, I use the term *grrrl zines* to identify those texts that foreground an exploration of female identity and experience, and *grrrl zinesters* when referring to the producers of such texts. Grrrl zinesters' emphasis on femaleness is evident in the multiple female-specific discourses that appear in the pages of their zines, including female history and role models, female pride/affirmation, female bodies and health, female beauty standards and body image, female sexuality, female reproductive issues, violence against females, girlfriends and female-centered communities, and female representation in commercial popular culture. Interestingly, grrrl zinesters' repeated engagement with these discourses suggests greater interest in their femaleness than their femininity (or masculinity), that is, their membership in a particular sex category as a result of their physical bodies rather than the gender performances enacted through those bodies.[82]

Recalling Hollway's and Dyer's theories of discursive investments, the fact that grrrl zines are dominated by sex-specific discourse is not surprising given that this is the discourse to which girls most have access on account of "who they are." Within patriarchal societies, all girls and women are aware of their subordinated and "Othered" social position as a result of their "not male" sex categorization. The appearance of a broad range of female-specific discourses in girls' zines indicates, therefore, that many grrrl zinesters use their texts as a means for exploring an identity that continues to be disparaged within both dominant society and the smaller, male-dominated groups to which such girls belong, including the zine community. At the same time, however, grrrl zinesters' focus on female identity is also the result of the racial and class politics of the zine community, which mimic those of dominant society and allow white, middle-class females to isolate their sex from other components of their identity. In the counterhegemonic world of zines, femaleness becomes the identity through which these otherwise privileged girls understand oppression, and thus the site from which many of them launch their critiques of dominant society. Not surprisingly, this uncritical isolation of sex from other modes of identity has been criticized by many girl zinesters who are not white and middle-class and who experience their deprivileged identities as inseparable. As Indian American Ani Mukherji writes in *Split Lip*, "I wish to make it clear that almost no part of my identity exists independent of my ethnicity. One of the key elements of privilege is the failure to recognize yourself as a group."[83]

Though female identity is a dominant discursive framework within grrrl zines, many female youth who produce these texts reveal their savvy about zinemaking as a mechanism for experimentations with, rather than simply reflections and thus reproductions of, identity. Indeed, some grrrl zinesters are quite explicit in their awareness of identities as socially constructed. For example, in *Bikini Kill #2*, Kathleen Hanna asks, "How much of my life comes from what i've been taught? Is there anything 'natural' about me? ... If there is nothing natural about me, i might as well be the best construct ever."[84] Thus, while grrrl zinesters valorize girls and women through female-specific discourses, they also broaden the meaning of femaleness by exploring various forms of unruly female identity in their texts.

Opportunities for exploring nonconformist identities differ greatly in relation to a person's position within dominant social hierarchies. Thus, as Gayle Wald argues, white girls have more opportunities for legitimate forms of gender bending than do girls of color.[85] Yet, because zines are a primarily textual medium and thus lack a direct, indexical relationship to the human bodies that create them, they can function as a discursive space for any girl's fantasizing about and exploration of nontraditional identities. Indeed, although white girls tend to dominate grrrl zine culture and its experiments with oppositional identities, the number of African, Asian, and Latin American female zinemakers has been growing since the 1990s. Perhaps the best evidence of this are the two zine collections edited by Mimi Nguyen, *Evolution of a Race Riot* and *Race Riot #2*,[86] which contain numerous selections from nonwhite girl zinesters, as well as the various zine distros that are run by and for teenage girls and young women of color, such as C/S Distro and Mamas Unidas Distro.[87] These female youth also demonstrate an interest in exploring nonconformist identities, even though they are aware that it may come with a price as a result of cultural differences. As Sisi from *Housewife Turned Assassin* notes, "[A]s a 22 year old Chicana womyn, I know I have felt ostracized through my youth by my peers because I listened to 'alternative'/'punk' music, and vocalized the unpopular ideas behind it."[88] Why such girls would become active within the zine community and what opportunities it provides them through identity exploration is an important question to consider.

EMBRACING UNRULINESS: EXPLORING NONCONFORMIST FEMALE IDENTITIES THROUGH PUNK AND FEMINISM

Grrrl zines reveal contemporary American girls' access to a much broader range of feminist ideologies than that available to previous generations of female youth. For instance, liberal feminism shapes grrrl zinesters views on sex and gender equality, particularly the right of females to have access to the same roles, spaces, and practices as males, including zinemaking and other forms of public expression. Grrrl zinesters also engage with cultural feminism by privileging female-specific discourses in their texts and creating a girl-dominated space within the larger zine community. In turn, grrrl zinesters demonstrate the influence of poststructuralist feminism through their recognition of the social construction of sex and gender and rehearsals of nontraditional identities in the pages of their texts. Unfortunately, too few grrrl zinesters demonstrate an awareness of identity as multiply constructed and experienced, which suggests both their privileged social status as well as their lack of exposure to or unwillingness to embrace U.S. third world feminism.[89] Though many female youth involved in zine culture are bisexual or lesbian and therefore explore their sexuality alongside their sex and gender, by comparison very few nonwhite and poor girls of color make zines; as a result, race and class are only rarely considered as significant, inseparable components of identity.

Each of the feminist ideologies addressed above importantly shapes the content of grrrls' zines; yet, when one considers the aesthetic practices that are used to express and frame such content, these texts suggest that punk operates as a strong influence also. Rarely acknowledged by theorists of feminist politics and culture, punk has had a considerable impact on contemporary feminist ideologies, especially for teenage girls and young women raised during the 1980s and 1990s when this youth culture was broadly diffused beyond its original urban locales. Indeed, while many female youth involved in early punk resisted being identified as feminists (despite their pro-female and anti-patriarchal attitudes), many contemporary girls who participate in this culture attempt to merge their punk perspectives with feminism, thus producing what many call "punk feminism." As a culture known for its anarchic, unruly, offensive tendencies as well as its youthful perspective, punk provides female youth with a different form of rebellion than that associated with older feminists.

Knowledge of the various ideologies and aesthetic practices associated with punk culture helps in discerning how punk converges with feminism in the form and content of grrrl zines. The countercultural political perspectives and aesthetic practices associated with punk have roots in various avant-garde artists and radical political movements of the early twentieth century, particularly Dada and the Situationist International.[90] Through their unconventional forms of art and activism, the participants of these movements critiqued industrial capitalism and attempted to ignite new forms of revolution.

The Dada movement emerged in Europe during the late 1910s largely in response to the effects of World War I. As John Walker notes, "The spectacle of supposedly civilized nations butchering one another in the trenches prompted a violent critical reaction: Dadaists sought to shock and provoke the public, to undermine and satirise the regimes they detested."[91] Commenting on the Dadaists' deliberate rejection of the traditional aesthetics used to motivate contemplation, Walter Benjamin theorized:

> Their poems are "word salad" containing obscenities and every imaginable waste product of language. The same is true of their paintings, on which they mounted buttons and tickets. What they intended and achieved was a relentless destruction of the aura of their creations ... dadaistic activities actually assured a rather vehement distraction by making works of art the center of scandal. One requirement was foremost: to outrage the public. ... [T]he work of art

of the dadaists became an instrument of ballistics. It hit the spectator like a bullet.[92]

In an attempt to spark social critique through new forms of art and media, the Dadaists developed insurgent, confrontational aesthetic practices through a focus on taboo topics and social outcasts, as well as the use of nonsensical, sensationalist, and offensive discourse. In turn, Dadaists privileged a practice known in French as *détournement* (literally, the diversion of footsteps), which involves appropriating objects, text, and images from their original contexts and placing them in different contexts, often by juxtaposing them with other material that seems unrelated.[93] Such strategies of decontextualization, juxtaposition, and reconfiguration resulted in what Max Ernst called an "explosive junction," a profound disruption and thus subversion of normative meanings through the creation of unintended affiliations and meanings. Connecting the aesthetic practices of the Dadaists to the sociohistorical context of early industrial environments, where sudden jolts and explosions were common occurrences, Benjamin similarly noted that these artists intentionally used jarring, confrontational aesthetics in order to prevent audiences from making traditional meanings and to force them into seeing new connections between disparate objects, ideas, and experiences, a process he referred to as a "shock effect."[94]

Another countercultural movement that had considerable impact on punk ideologies and aesthetics was the Situationist International, a group of radical European artists and writers which was active from the late 1950s to the early 1970s.[95] Growing out of the *Internationnale lettriste* and borrowing from Dadaist and Surrealist aesthetic strategies, the Situationists developed unique methods for critiquing everyday life in capitalist, industrialized society through the use of inexpensive reproductive media technologies. Creating mimeographed flyers and periodicals filled with agit-prop slogans meant to inspire social critique and revolution, the Situationists were perhaps the first truly media-savvy counterculture. Yet, rather than present themselves as leaders of a new revolution, the Situationists developed a political philosophy based on participatory action that encouraged each citizen to launch her or his own critique of dominant political and economic regimes and the material reality of everyday life, an ethos that later became known as "do it yourself."

In an effort to communicate their rejection of commercial culture and dominant society, punks have drawn on these earlier unorthodox ideologies and aesthetic strategies in their development of what Dick Hebdige labels a "style in revolt" or "revolting style."[96] Borrowing from Dadaists and Situationists, punks express their social alienation and outrage by rejecting the traditional aesthetic practices, by embracing abject social figures and taboo practices, and by creating new meanings for conventional objects and symbols via *détournement*. Through these insurgent, confrontational aesthetic practices, punks have produced their own shock effects in contemporary society. Perhaps most evident in fashion, punk's revolting style can be seen in its other cultural artifacts also. For example, commenting on late 1970s' British punk art, Hebdige notes:

> Even the graphics and typography used on record covers and fanzines were homologous with punk's subterranean and anarchic style. The two typographical models were graffiti which was translated into a flowing "spray can" script, and the ransom note in which individual letters cut up from a variety of sources (newspapers, etc.) in different type faces were pasted together to form an anonymous message.[97]

Although the aesthetics of Dada and Situationism are obviously residual within punk culture, it is necessary to connect the development of punk style to its specific sociohistorical moment. As Hebdige argues, the punk music, fashions, and publications that emerged in Britain during the late 1970s drew on the "rhetoric of crisis" that permeated British society as a result of rising conservatism, racism, unemployment, and poverty:

> [T]he punks were not only directly *responding* to increasing joblessness, changing moral standards, the rediscovery of poverty, the Depression, etc., they were *dramatizing* what had come to be called "Britain's decline" ... . In the gloomy, apocalyptic ambience of the late 1970s ... it was fitting that the punks should present themselves as "degenerates"; as signs of the highly publicized decay which perfectly represented the atrophied condition of Great Britain. The various stylistic ensembles adopted by the punks were undoubtedly expressive of genuine aggression, frustration and anxiety.[98]

Although the punk scenes that developed in the United States during and after the 1970s have been less political than cultural, American punks have demonstrated a similar desire to revolutionize society through the reconfiguration of popular cultural forms that were already important components of youth culture, particularly music, fashion, and magazines. For Hebdige, this strategy, which differs greatly from those employed by Dadaists and Situationists, allows punks to communicate with a larger group of individuals: "[Punk] statements, no matter how strangely constructed, were cast in a language which was generally available—a language which was current."[99] At the same time, however, punks reject the bourgeois values of commercial popular culture that they feel stifle creativity and authentic expression. Instead, punks favor anarchic expressions of alienation from and disgust with dominant society.

In light of the considerable influence of Dada and Situationism on punk aesthetic strategies, it is important to note that a significant aspect of punk culture is its further development of these earlier groups' valorizations of amateurism and the DIY ethos. Regularly disparaged by the cultural elite because of its traditional association with those who have little experience or education and thus little cultural capital and social status (i.e., youth and the poor), amateurism has been privileged over professionalism by punks in an effort to further democratize aesthetic practices. For example, in describing punk zines from the 1970s, Hebdige notes:

> The language ... was determinedly "working class" (i.e. it was liber-ally peppered with swear words) and typing errors and grammatical mistakes, misspellings and jumbled pagination were left uncorrected in the final proof. Those corrections and crossings out that were made before publication were left to be deciphered by the reader. The overwhelming impression was one of urgency and immediacy, of a paper produced in indecent haste, of memos from the front line.[100]

Though the Dadaists and Situationists celebrated amateurism, punks alone seem to have connected this aesthetic specifically to *youth*, as the label they use to identify themselves suggests.[101] In doing so, they call attention to, while also rejecting, the adultism inherent in the standards of professionalism that structure dominant society and commercial culture. By dismissing the con-ventional standards for artistic expression and success, and repeatedly invok-ing the DIY mantra, punk culture has motivated many young people without formal training or talent to become actively involved in media production.

Though many scholars who study punk do not focus on its connections to preindustrial cultural aesthetics and practices, I would argue that punk clearly has links to the carnival culture developed in early modern Europe.[102] Indeed, it is through attention to carnival culture's social critiques that we can understand young people's investments in punk as a viable counterculture. In particular, punk exhibits signs of carnivalesque hybridization through its practices of juxtaposition and *détournement*, as well as its inversion of "low" (i.e., taboo, debased, and abject) culture over elite, "high" culture.[103] As Mary Russo argues, carnivalesque aesthetics have an explosive effect similar to that associated with Dada:

> The categories of carnivalesque speech and spectacle are heteroge-neous, in that they contain the protocols and styles of high culture in and from a position of debasement. ... It is as if the carnivalesque body politic had ingested the entire corpus of high culture and, in its bloated and irrepressible state, released it in fits and starts in all man-ner of recombination, inversion, mockery, and degradation.[104]

Although the practices of carnival culture were typically contained through a reaffirmation of social order and hierarchy, as Russo argues, "[t]he extreme difficulty of producing lasting social change does not diminish the usefulness of these symbolic models of transgression."[105] In turn, though Peter Stallybrass and Allon White are hesitant to attribute long-term political efficacy to inversive aesthetics, they see considerable potential in the carnivalesque practice of recombination: "Hybridization ... produces new combinations and strange instabilities in a given semiotic system. It therefore generates the possibility of shifting *the very terms of the system itself*, by erasing and interrogating the relationships which constitute it."[106]

Until recently, male theorists interested in counterhegemonic cultural practices like carnival rarely drew attention to the gender dynamics involved in such activities. Nevertheless, several feminist scholars have reconfigured theories of carnival culture in order to explore the political efficacy of women's various transgressive and unruly acts within a patriarchal context. For example, in arguing that the topsy-turvy world of carnival culture was instrumental in preindustrial social critique, Natalie Zemon Davis asserts:

> [T]he image of the disorderly woman did not always function to keep women in their place. On the contrary, it was a multivalent image that could operate, first, to widen behavioral options for women within and even outside marriage, and, second, to sanction riot and political disobedience for both men and women in a society that allowed the lower orders few formal means of protest. Play with the unruly woman is partly a chance for temporary release from the traditional and stable hierarchy; but it is also part of the conflict over efforts to change the basic distribution of power within society.[107]

Russo reclaims the unruly woman of carnival culture more specifically for feminism:

> What would seem to be of great interest at this critical conjuncture ... would be an assessment of how the materials on carnival as historical performance may be configured with the materials on carnival as semiotic performance; in other words, how the relation between the symbolic and cultural constructs of femininity and Womanness and the experience of *women* (as variously identified and subject to multiple determinations) might be brought together toward a dynamic model of a new social subjectivity. ... The figure of the female transgressor as public spectacle is still powerfully resonant, and the possibilities of redeploying this representation as a demystifying or utopian model have not been exhausted.[108]

Given that Russo is willing to stretch "femininity, Womanness, and the experience of *women*" beyond their traditional definitions by noting how they are "variously identified and subject to multiple determinations," I would argue that teenage girls can be unruly figures also. In fact, because adolescence functions as an ambiguous life stage due to its construction as a period of transition, flux, liminality, and mobility, it offers considerable opportunities for female youth to resist the subject positions constructed by the dominant ideals of femininity and adulthood. As Hudson argues, patriarchal society has traditionally constrained adolescent girls' potential unruliness by encouraging their achievement of femininity and relinquishment of adolescence and thus masculinity. Nevertheless, as a result of the development of feminism and other counterhegemonic social movements during the second half of the twentieth century, contemporary girls now have access to a much broader range of ideologies and aesthetics when experimenting with identity. Through their explosive combination of feminist and punk ideologies and aesthetics, grrrl zines are perhaps the best evidence that many contemporary female youth are actively exploring unruly identities that subvert traditional notions of girlhood.

UP FRONT AND IN YOUR FACE: FEMALE UNRULINESS IN GRRRL ZINE TITLES AND COVER ART

As noted above, many female-specific discourses appear in grrrl zines, demonstrating that sex is a primary identity explored by the producers of such texts. Because so many of these sex-specific discourses circulate through such texts, I have limited my analysis here to three: female pride/affirmation; female history and role models; and female beauty standards and body image. Each of these discourses has appeared in numerous grrrl zines in the past decade and, therefore, should be considered among the dominant discourses on which grrrl zinesters rely when exploring identity. Though all of these discourses have been associated with the feminist movement for some time, as I demonstrate, grrrl zinesters often transform them through punk aesthetics and rhetorical strategies so as to explore their relevance to contemporary female youth.

The most evident form of female-specific discourse in grrrl zines involves the affirmation of girls and women, or what might be called "female pride." Indeed, one might argue that this pro-female discourse is so prevalent and structures so many other topics in grrrl zines that it functions as the dominant discourse in grrrl zine culture. Because of grrrl zinesters' privileging of female pride rhetoric, the sites of such discourse are multiple, often occurring outside the zines themselves. For instance, many female youth who make zines demonstrate their allegiance to a pro-female stance by identifying themselves as "grrrl zinesters" and their texts as "grrrl zines." This affirmation of females is practiced also in various female-oriented zine directories that categorize texts produced by females as "grrrl zines," as can be seen in *Action Girl*

Newsletter, Ben Is Dead, and *Grrrl Zine Network.*[109] By gendering themselves and their texts, grrrl zinesters affirm their female identity at the same time that they call attention to the historical marginalization of females in culture, even within arenas where counterhegemonic identities are usually celebrated, such as the zine community. The self-ghettoizing labels of "grrrl zines" and "grrrl zinesters" can be understood in relation to the longer history of cultural feminists' separatist tactics, which have been used to legitimate females, to provide them with a safe discursive space for expression and communication, and thus to form a feminist subaltern public.

At the same time, grrrl zinesters' use of the youth-oriented term "girl" and its common reconfiguration as "grrrl" suggests that their pro-female, feminist perspectives have been influenced by punk culture, which, as noted above, values both youthfulness and a repudiation of conventional meanings through the appropriation and reconfiguration of common words. Thus, through the substitution of two more "r's" for the softer "i," "girl" becomes "grrrl," unconventional, aggressive, and powerful. Moreover, grrrl zinesters' reliance on youth-specific terminology to identify their particular perspective on feminism demonstrates their opposition to the adultism that has long structured feminist culture, politics, and scholarship. Through the labels they assign themselves and their texts, therefore, grrrl zinesters reveal both their influence by and reconfiguration of punk and feminism.

In addition to the female pride demonstrated extra-textually in the labels "grrrl zines" and "grrrl zinesters," the titles and cover art of grrrl zines function as primary textual sites for engagement in pro-female discourse. Although by no means a standardized practice, many grrrl zinesters, especially those creating their first zine, demonstrate their influence by cultural feminism by foregrounding their female pride in their zine titles, as can be seen in *G is for Girl, Sisterfriend, That Girl, The First Tampon, Little Big Sister Zine, Pink DNA, Girlie Jones, Bust, Swing Set Girl, Clitoris, Girl in the Hoodie, Home Economics, Baby Girl, Purse, Looking Glass Girl Zine, Womynfolke, Ragdoll, Girl Swirl Fanzine, Chickfactor, Hey There, Barbie Girl, Girl Wize, Book for Girls,* and *From the Pen of a Liberated Woman.* (Many female-run zine distros, including GERLL Zine Distro, Girl + Distro, Girl on gIRL Productions, Girl Wakes Up, Grrrl Style!, Riot Grrrl Press, Screamqueen, Rebel Grrrl Distro, HousewifeXcore Distro, Girl Gang Distro, Mamas Unidas Distro, BratGrrrl DIY Distro, Chicana Stuff Tiendita, and Papergirl Zine & Music Distro, similarly manifest this pro-female stance in their names.)

Other grrrl zinesters reveal the combined influence of multiple feminist ideologies on their conceptions of female pride. For example, some grrrl zine titles suggest that females are powerful, a position historically associated only with men, and thus evoke a liberal feminist perspective in such titles as *Girl Hero, Call Me Princesa, Sprgrl Conspiracy, Queenzine, Girl Wonder, Venus,*

Hero Grrrl, Queen of the Universe, Girl Infinity, Supergirl, Rocket Queen, Girl Courage, Ms. America, and *Girls Can Do Anything.* In turn, titles like *A-Girl* (short for *Asian Girl*), *Mija, Slant, Esperanza, Bamboo Girl, Mamasita, Blackgirl Stories, Banana Q, La Chica Loca, Hermana, Resist,* and *Korean American Women with Attitude* reveal a pride in femaleness that is integrated with, rather than detached from, racial/ethnic identity (a U.S. third world feminist concept), while titles like *Girl Luv, Bi-Girl World, Lezzie Smut, The Adventures of Baby Dyke,* and *The Making of a Femme* demonstrate the female-centered queer pride of some grrrl zinesters.

The vast majority of grrrl zine titles that have a pro-female stance provocatively reconfigure this cultural feminist perspective via confrontational rhetorical strategies associated with punk, as can be seen in such titles as *Bitch, Girl Germs, Rag Hag, The Bad Girl Club, Fierce Vagina, Girl Fiend, Independent Pussy, Angst Girl, Inner Bitch, Cooties, Annoying Girl, Heartless Bitch, Slut Utopia, Just Like a Girl, Cataclysm Girl, Iron Femme, The Nerdy Grrrl Revolution, Mohawk Pussy, Ladies Homewrecking Journal, This Girl Is Different, Pixxiebitch, Odd Girl Out, Vampira, Not Your Bitch, Girl Frenzy, Bitch Dyke Whore, Pussy Galore, Bitch Slap, Grrrl Trouble, UpSlut, Geek the Girl, Angry Young Woman, The Wrong Girl, Pretty in Punk, Mad Girl, Bitch Rag, Gurlz with Gunz, Pottymouth Girl, Barbie War, Housewife Turned Assassin,* and *Riot Grrrl* (the most-used grrrl zine title to date).[110] Through their appropriation of words and phrases traditionally used to disparage females yet avoided by many earlier feminists (e.g., *bitch, slut, hag, ladies, dyke, whore, just like a girl*), as well as their use of terms that connect females to anger (*mad, bitch, fierce, frenzy*), rebellion (*riot, revolution, war, trouble, mohawk, cataclysm, homewrecking*), alienation (*nerdy, odd, geek, fiend, annoying, wrong*), and the taboo and perverse (*germs, pottymouth, cooties, pussy, rag, vampira*), grrrl zinesters demonstrate the strong influence of punk's unruly and insurgent aesthetics on many young feminists. Indeed, they reveal a willingness to explore identities typically associated with masculinity that is unprecedented in the history of feminism. Nevertheless, by simultaneously foregrounding femaleness in their titles, grrrl zinesters challenge the patriarchy and misogyny that have traditionally structured countercultural communities, such as punk.

Punk's amateurist spirit is evident in many grrrl zine titles also. For instance, the use of alternative spellings (e.g., *luv, wize, grrrl, womyn*) suggests grrrl zinesters' attempts to position themselves and their texts firmly outside the normative standards of middle-class professionalism associated with commercial journalism and academic writing.[111] Moreover, the creators of grrrl zines often do not adhere to the conventional rules of capitalization taught in schools and practiced by journalists and scholars, creating zine titles through lower-case letters only or randomly alternating lower-case and upper-case letters. Such avoidance of the rules of capitalization not only draws attention to such text, but provokes critical awareness of the constructed nature of rules for written discourse. In turn, grrrl zinesters' repeated use of words associated with youth (e.g., *baby, pixxie, pottymouth,* and especially *girl* and *grrrl*) connects punk's amateurist aesthetic with its repudiation of adulthood, at the same time that the gendering of such youthful terms demonstrates a rejection of the adultism found in hegemonic feminist politics and culture. Thus, simply through the titles of their texts, grrrl zinesters reveal their negotiation of and often resistance to the various ideologies impacting both hegemonic and counterhegemonic constructions of female youth.

The covers of grrrl zines are likely the first site through which readers are exposed to a grrrl zinester's explorations of identity. Therefore, it is important to note that such discursive spaces typically bear the mark of several signifying practices other than simply written text. Indeed, just as the rhetorical strategies used to create zine titles reveal much about the ideologies informing their producers' approach to cultural expression, so does the form in which such titles appear. For instance, the titles of many grrrl zines are handwritten, thus revealing a privileging of handcrafted work as a means for authentic expression, a value common in countercultural movements, including punk. In turn, handwritten titles—like the larger handcrafted zine of which they are often a part—suggest a rejection of the design practices valued within the commercial publishing industry yet limited or inaccessible to many youth (e.g., professional typeset print). Other grrrl zinesters demonstrate their opposition to commercial publishing by cutting printed letters from various commercial periodicals and individually reassembling them to form new words. Popularly referred to as the "ransom note" or "cut-up" style, this counterhegemonic practice connects grrrl zinemakers with punks and earlier avant-garde artists who valorized criminals and other disenfranchised individuals over more wholesome members of society. Interestingly, those grrrl zinesters who rely on mechanical print technology typically reconfigure their written text in ways that suggest their rejection of the publishing industry's professional standards and the privileging of more authentic communication styles. For example, many grrrl zinesters use manual typewriters with generic typefaces rather than electronic machinery, while others employ word processing software that produces fonts used in older, manual typewriters, such as Courier.

Many grrrl zinesters demonstrate the strong influence of cultural feminism through the prominent featuring of images of girls or women on the covers of their texts. Indeed, given the personal, autobiographical nature of grrrl zines, it is interesting to note that many covers feature photographs of young women, perhaps the zine creators. With its multiple photographs of a young woman going through her beauty regime, the cover of *Verboslammed #8* is particularly interesting in that it calls attention to femininity's repetitive, laborious construction and thus reveals a poststructuralist approach to gender and feminist ideology (Figure 9).[112] The cover art of some grrrl zines, such as *Bikini Kill #2*, *Doing Maria #1*, and *Girl Germs #4*, reveal the combined influence of feminist and queer ideology in their appropriation and reconfiguration of eroticized female imagery typically associated with heterosexual male pornography.[113] In turn, nonwhite grrrl zinesters often use illustrations of girls or women of color for their covers, as can be seen in various issues of *Slant*, *Aim Your Dick*, *Bamboo Girl*, and *Banana Q*.[114]

Most grrrl zines combine feminist ideologies with punk style in their depictions of female bodies, provocatively attracting the viewer's gaze through unconventional images while also communicating powerful messages about female identity. For example, the cover of *Riot Grrrl NYC #5* includes an illustration of a headless and limbless female torso whose pelvic area appears in the shape of an apple half.[115] *Retail Whore #4* contains a cover photograph of a topless woman looking down at her breasts and squeezing one of her nipples.[116] The cover of *Korespodances #7.1* juxtaposes photographs of female models appropriated from commercial magazines with a photograph of the

Figure 9   Femininity's laborious construction.
Verboslammed #8, 1996. Courtesy of Rebecca Gilbert.

Venus of Willendorf carving.[117] A considerable number of covers foreground a punk stance more explicitly through the use of photographs or illustrations of female youth playing guitars, as can be seen in *Skunk #4* and *Welcome #8*.[118]

Some grrrl zine covers connect the feminist theme of female power with punk's youthful perspective by utilizing images of female characters that have been appropriated from commercial children's culture. For instance, the covers of *Hey There, Barbie Girl* typically utilized images of Mattel's Barbie Doll. The first issue, for example, contains four photographs of a Barbie doll hanging by a noose. Accompanied by the caption, "The Barbie to have when you're not having Barbie," this image reveals the zinemaker's use of *détournement* to signify her rejection of a dominant symbol within commercial girls' culture and perhaps the corporation that has profited from it.[119] Not all covers that use imagery from children's culture are this oppositional, however. For example, the covers of *Ms. America #2* and *Bikini Kill: A Color and Activity Book* (a.k.a. *Bikini Kill #1*) contain images of powerful female characters from the animated television series, *She-Ra, Princess of Power*, while *Nerd Girl #4* contains an image of a Smurfette from *The Smurfs* television series.[120] The use of such images in grrrl zines suggests the considerable degree to which many grrrl zinesters' visual vocabularies, and identity explorations, are influenced by commercial media culture. Thus, while conservative adults fear the ubiquity of commercial media in young people's lives today, grrrl zinesters demonstrate their attempts to gain control over such texts through their recontextualization of images appropriated from media culture. As Hebdige reminds us, punk rhetoric is rooted in the vernacular. In turn, by relying on popular images from media culture to address female and feminist issues, grrrl zinesters make their texts more appealing to girls who may feel alienated by academic feminist discourse. Such efforts speak to bell hooks's call for feminists to "either write in a more accessible manner or write in the manner of their choice and see to it that the piece is made available to others using a style that can be easily understood."[121]

Other grrrl zine covers demonstrate a strict adherence to punk's DIY ethos by featuring handcrafted artwork. Often such drawings reveal the effect of punk aesthetics on feminist ideologies, and vice versa, particularly with regard to the notion of female power. Indeed, in contrast to the more peaceful perspective on femininity valued by many feminist artists during the 1970s, grrrl zines often foreground an aggressive, masculine female identity in their cover art. For example, *Aim Your Dick #1* includes a cover illustration of two female Asian punks standing side-by-side, replete with semishaved heads, work boots, and anarchy and feminist pendants.[122] The cover of *Girl Germs #4* contains a drawing of a young white woman straddling a motorcycle, which bears a license plate of "Evil 69."[123] The cover of *Evolution of a Race Riot* displays one side of a woman's bare torso, her right arm flexed to show her bicep and her hand clenched in a fist.[124] *Slant #5* includes a drawing of a bald white girl holding a handgun next to an Asian girl carrying a baseball bat (Figure 10). Both are wearing baggy, androgynous clothing that covers their female bodies.[125]

The cover art of several other grrrl zines is similarly explicit in its transformation of female power from conventional feminine attributes to those associated with masculinity, thus demonstrating the influence of both cultural and liberal feminism on contemporary female youth. For instance, the cover of *Housewife Turned Assassin #2* includes a drawing of a woman in curlers and a housecoat aiming a gun toward the Supreme Court building,[126] while the cover of *Pixxiebitch #3* contains a drawing of a young girl with a knife in one hand and the head of a doll in the other.[127] Similarly, the cover of *Twat! #2* includes an illustration of a young girl, replete with dress, bloomers, and cornrows, who holds a sickle behind her back.[128] Making the "girl with a gun" theme more literal, the back cover of *Girl Germs #5* contains an image of a woman's hand pointing a handgun at the viewer.[129] As its title suggests, *Gurlz with Guns* regularly depicts females with pistols and rifles on its covers.[130]

The fact that most of these images of aggressive females are hand-drawn demonstrates not only the ability of grrrl zinesters to access such powerful figures through their art, but also the dearth of such imagery in commercial media culture. Moreover, it is important to note that many grrrl zine covers include images of *young* girls empowered by weapons, a provocative aesthetic strategy that likely produces the shock effect theorized by Benjamin, and thus motivates viewers to rethink conventional notions of both girlhood and power. Indeed, these grrrl zine covers demonstrate that the transgressive aesthetics of such countercultural groups as punks, Dadaists, and Situationists can be successfully merged with feminist ideologies to produce a much broader range of unruly young female identities than was available to previous generations of female youth.

BETWEEN THE COVERS: UNRULY FEMALE IDENTITIES IN GRRRL ZINE CONTENTS

Though zine covers serve an important function in being the initial discursive space where creators' ideologies are communicated and identities explored, grrrl zinesters have far more space to experiment with various identities in the multiple pages that appear between their texts' front and back covers. In addition to female pride, several other female-specific discourses appear often in grrrl zines. In the following pages, I analyze grrrl zinesters' explorations of female pride, female history and role models, and female beauty standards and body image in the content of their zines, drawing attention to how the presentation of such topics is informed by both feminist ideologies and punk

Figure 10 Aggressive female power.
Slant #5, 1997. Courtesy of Mimi Thi Nguyen.

aesthetics, which allow for experimentation with counterhegemonic identities as well as opposition to dominant constructions of girlhood.

Reshaping Female Pride as Girl Power

Interestingly, although a pro-female spirit is privileged in the titles and cover art of grrrl zines, this discourse is often presented as pro-feminism within the pages of such texts. Indeed, many grrrl zinesters use their zines to explore their identification as feminist, while also encouraging their readers to do the same. For instance, Kristin Thompson writes in *Riot Grrrl #6*:

The dictionary defines "feminist" as a person who believes in equal rights for both men and women. I am a feminist. So is my dad. And he says so proudly. Don't buy the crap that feminism is dead. Declare that you are one, too, because the more of us who refuse to accept the prescribed stigmas, the less the media and society can use them as tools of oppression.[131]

Similarly assertive about her politics, Marcy writes in *Nerd Girl #4*, "to me, being a feminist is about more than just calling yerself a feminist. it's about action and doing some thing that supports feminism on the whole—no matter what."[132] Given the continued backlash against feminism, some grrrl zinesters use their zines to engage in the various criticisms launched against those who fight to end patriarchy, sexism, and misogyny. For example, *Bikini Kill #2* contains a lengthy rebuttal to many antifeminist statements (what the writer describes as "more subtle ways of discounting and discouraging" females), including "You know, some women manage to 'get beyond' sexism," "You are not *really* a feminist because … ," "But I know a girl who lied about being raped," and "You are exclusionary and alienating to men."[133] Despite the frustration the writer expresses as she refutes each of these statements, the article ends with an illustration of a smiling cheerleader jumping in the air, and the upbeat declaration, "Punk Rock Feminism rules okay."

Some grrrl zines, like *girl~boy/boy~girl* and *grrrl/boi revolutionaries*, reveal their creators' interests in opening lines of communication between males and females about the effects of patriarchy and misogyny; however, other grrrl zine editors use their texts as a safe space to poke fun at men, especially those in power and those who are critical of the feminist movement. Such practices allow female youth to explore a pro-feminist identity specifically through its opposition to anti-feminist perspectives. For example, *Girl Infinity #2* reproduces an email circulated in the mid-1990s that ridicules Pat Robertson's assertions that feminists are organizing in order to subvert all major social institutions and traditional value systems. In her fictional "Feminist Agenda," the writer draws attention to the illogic of Robertson's stance by revealing its foundation in popular stereotypes of feminists and their goals:

8:00–8:15	Introduction, Opening Remarks
8:15–9:15	Plot to Overthrow World Leadership
9:15–9:30	BREAK—Coffee and donuts
9:30–10:30	Undermine World Religions

10:30–12:00 General Attacks on the Institution of the American Family

12:00–1:00 Catered Lunch and Fashion Show

1:00–1:30 Plot to Remove All Men From the World

1:30–2:00 Cake and Champagne

2:00–3:00 Leave Husbands (If Applicable)

3:00–3:30 Kill Children

3:30–5:00 Become Lesbian

5:30–? Evening Mixer; Open Bar.[134]

Ironically, despite the obvious influence of feminism on grrrl zinesters' perspectives, a considerable number of female youth who create zines do not use the terms "feminist" or "feminism" explicitly in their writing. This apparent contradiction is likely due in part to the considerable popularization of feminist ideologies over the past three decades, to the point that such topics as women's equality and sexual harassment, and the people who advocate on behalf of them, are no longer explicitly identified as "feminist." Yet the relative dearth of the words "feminist" and "feminism" in the majority of contemporary grrrl zines is likely due also to the disparagement leveled against feminism for more than a century, particularly during the late twentieth century, the period in which most grrrl zinesters were growing up. As a result of these combined phenomena, many contemporary female youth have absorbed feminist perspectives into their ideological and social frameworks but remain uncomfortable with identifying as feminists for fear of reprisal. Such girls often demonstrate their conflicted identification with feminism through statements that begin with "I'm not a feminist, but ..." At the same time, however, grrrl zinesters' limited use of "feminist" and "feminism" may also be due to their exclusion from dominant forms of feminist politics, culture, and scholarship, and thus identification with other counterhegemonic communities, such as punk. Indeed, riot grrrls' development of a label for their community that does not incorporate the term "feminist" speaks to their alienation from hegemonic forms of feminism.

Thus, despite the residual legacy of various feminist ideologies in grrrl zine culture, it is important to recognize that feminism is often reconfigured in such texts in ways that speak more specifically to the needs and interests of contemporary female youth. "Women's liberation" is not a key phrase or concept deployed here. Moving beyond the victim-oriented discourse of many

1970s' feminists, grrrl zinesters more typically use "girl power" rhetoric to describe their pro-female stance and sociocultural agenda. For example, in *Girl Germs #3*, Jen Smith writes:

> One thing that I am finding a lot of comfort and inspiration from is all these girls, states-wide, that have surfaced. These women are young and down with the kids, down with the revolution. ... And I hear these girls, girls I don't know, girls I have never met. ... They speak to me and I speak to you and I know our time has come ... revolutionary girl soul force ... wow.[135]

Foregrounding the message of Smith's essay, a drawing of two hearts emblazoned with the words "girls rule" appears above it. Like Smith, the other young women who first developed the Riot Grrrl community often drew attention to the political and cultural strength of girls, as can be seen in the "Girl Power" subtitle for *Bikini Kill #2* and the repetition of the Riot Grrrl motto, "Revolution Girl-Style Now!," in numerous zines produced in the early 1990s.

Since Riot Grrrl began promoting girl power, many grrrl zines have included illustrations of female action heroes appropriated from commercial popular culture as a means of signifying this reconfiguration of girlhood and authority. Interestingly, many of these images are from children's media texts and thus promote grrrl zinesters' young feminist perspective while also encouraging it in other girls. The original meanings associated with such images are typically reconfigured with new text, juxtaposed with other images, or placed in a different context in order to suggest a new meaning that is girl-positive. For example, *Housewife Turned Assassin #3* privileges a youthful feminist perspective by including several drawings of Cruella de Vil, the villainess of Disney's *101 Dalmations*,[136] while *Girl Germs #5* includes a publicity photo for the teenpic *Grease*, in which Rizzo, the bad girl character, is featured prominently.[137] Following the inversion strategies associated with punk and carnival culture, these zines place female villains, as opposed to heroines, in the privileged position of feminist role models. Several feminist literary and media theorists have noted that villainess characters allow consumers' to engage in fantasies of power, offering deprivileged females an opportunity to, as Tania Modleski puts it, "achieve, temporarily, the illusion of mastery denied [them] in real life."[138] Although Modleski argues that the female spectator does not identify comfortably with the villainess, since "she not only watches the villainess act out her own hidden wishes, but simultaneously sides with the forces conspiring against fulfillment of those wishes," it is important to note that grrrl zinesters dislocate these female villains from their narrative contexts and thus prevent their textual containment. In doing so, these young female media producers allow for a more comfortable identification with such characters and thereby encourage readers to understand them as powerful role models for girls exploring counterhegemonic identities.

While grrrl zines often include images of powerful women, many grrrl zinesters specifically privilege the rebelliousness of adolescence, thus refashioning women's liberation as girl power. For instance, several of Selena Whang's "Raging Adolescent Girls" illustrations appear in issues of *Girl Germs*. Other zines contain images of teen characters from popular culture, such as Tank Girl, from the independent comic book series by the same name, and Enid and Rebecca from *Ghost World*, an independent comic book series and feature film. Interestingly, many zines that emerged out of the Riot Grrrl movement, such as *Ms. America*, *Nerd Girl*, and *After Sugar Glow*, construct girl power in relation to even younger girls by including illustrations of female children singing, skipping rope, writing letters, and whispering to each other. (These zines also contain various symbols associated with feminine childhood, such as hearts and butterflies.) Other grrrl zinesters reproduce images of eccentric, intelligent, and assertive young female characters appropriated from commercial media culture—including Lisa from *The Simpsons* animated television show, Angelica from Nickelodeon's *Rugrats* series, and Eloise from the popular children's book by the same name—thus refashioning such characters as role models for young girls.

Given the oppositional perspective most zinesters have of dominant society, it is important to note that grrrl zinesters often reconfigure the appearance of images they appropriate from popular culture. Indeed, images taken from commercial media sources typically undergo considerable transformation before appearing in grrrl zines, thus creating new meanings of popular images for viewers. For example, the back cover of *Survival Guide for Her Repellant #3* contains an image of the Japanese manga character, Hello Kitty (a popular girls' accessories line), which has been "punked-up" as "Fuck You Kitty" via a safety pin through her head, an anarchy symbol on her forehead, and the caption, "grrrrrrrr."[139] Meanwhile, *Nerd Girl #4* shows Lucy from the *Peanuts* comic strip wearing a t-shirt emblazoned with a feminist symbol, and a menacing Pippi Longstocking from the Astrid Lindgren novels brandishing a sword and pistol.[140] Several grrrl zines, including *Quarter Inch Squares*, have attempted to expand Mattel's normative construction of young female identity by including a list of "Barbies We Would Like to See," such as Bisexual Barbie, Blue Collar Barbie, Gender Fuck Barbie, Homegirl Barbie, Rebbe Barbie, and Single Mom Barbie.[141]

Other grrrl zinesters demonstrate a DIY approach in their exploration of young female identity by including amateur drawings of unruly girls in their zines. For example, *Girl Germs #4* includes a drawing of two Asian "girl warriors" who are smiling and aiming slingshots at the viewer.[142] Above them appears the caption, "Die white boy!" and below them a second caption, "Action = Life." Attesting to the privileging of handcrafted work in the zine community, a considerable number of grrrl zines contain hand-drawn comic strips that feature assertive and feisty young females. For example, *Ms. America #2* includes a comic strip called "Ninja Girl," about a young female punk who starts a band with her friends after being pushed around by boys at a punk show.[143] Meanwhile, in an attempt to foster the girl power spirit among younger girls, *Nolite te Bastardes Carborundorum #2* includes a drawing of a princess made by the zinemaker's eight-year-old sister (Figure 11).[144]

In her analysis of album-cover artwork for various female-centered bands associated with Riot Grrrl (artwork that is quite similar to that published in grrrl zines), Gayle Wald argues that the use of such girlish images indicates a yearning for "an innocence that was not owned or enjoyed, a grace that was denied."[145] I would argue, however, that grrrl zinesters' use of such imagery is not so much retrospective as it is performed in relation to their present experiences and with an eye toward the future. For in resisting hegemonic forms of feminism developed by adult women, female youth must develop new symbols and role models that better represent their desires and interests. As part of the larger project of punk feminism, grrrl zinesters embrace youthfulness and reconstruct girlhood as a site for new forms of feminist identity and agency.

Unfortunately, despite the counterhegemonic, forward-thinking perspective of most grrrl zinesters, the images of unruly girlhood that appear in their texts are primarily white. This phenomenon is evident in the images appropriated from popular culture as well as the illustrations and photographs of zinesters and friends. Several girls of color have challenged the overwhelming whiteness of grrrl zine culture by foregrounding images of Asian, Latina, and African American females in their texts. For example, most issues of *Slant* and *Aim Your Dick* contain illustrations of their Vietnamese creator, Mimi Nguyen, and her Asian female friends. Similarly, Sabrina Margarita Sandata's *Bamboo Girl* regularly features drawings and photographs of Filipinas and other women of color.

It is important to remember that as much as zines function as a stage for the exploration of unruly girl identities, often the discourse of girl power that permeates grrrl zines is framed by fantasies of independence, self-confidence, and assertiveness driven by as yet unfulfilled desire. In other words, many female youth do *not* feel independent, confident, or assertive. Indeed, one grrrl zinester titled her text *I Dreamed I Was Assertive!* Nevertheless, zines provide a discursive space for girls' experimentations with identities that are neither accessible nor permitted in other aspects of their everyday lives. Although, as noted above, such fantasizing is often initiated via grrrl zinesters' appropriation of powerful female figures from popular culture, as I demonstrate in the following section, grrrl zines also typically include images of and text about *real* women and girls who model the powerful identity these female youth hope to embody one day.

Reconfiguring Feminist History through New Role Models

Much like cultural feminists of the 1970s, grrrl zinesters often combat the patriarchy and misogyny they experience both in dominant society and in counterhegemonic cultures by reconstructing a female-specific history in their texts. This "herstory" not only reclaims girls and women for feminist history, but also works to position grrrl zinesters within a particular historical trajectory and thus mode of identity. Many grrrl zinesters fill their zines with images of and information about female figures of the past who can be

Figure 11 Promoting younger girls' art/work.
Nolite te Bastardes Carborundorum #2, 1997.

looked to as positive feminist role models for girls today. In particular, most grrrl zines contain information about or quotations from well-known feminist activists and writers. For example, *Ms. America #2* devotes a full page to "Riot Grrrandmas,"[146] including Harriet Tubman, Virginia Woolf, Susan B. Anthony, and Anne Sexton, while *Marika #2* contains Sojourner Truth's famous essay, "Ain't I a Woman?"[147] Other grrrl zines participate in the broadening of feminist history (and ideology) by drawing attention to lesser-known females who have bravely forged into male-dominated arenas. For example, *Girlie Jones #2.2* includes a brief editorial congratulating the first four female cadets to successfully complete Hell Week at the Citadel, a military school in South Carolina that until recently admitted only men.[148] Similarly, *Verboslammed #6* is devoted to women and baseball and focuses specifically on the All American Girls' Professional Baseball League and Julie Groteau, the first female player in college baseball.[149]

In addition to identifying certain historical women as feminist role models, many grrrl zines provide lists of books and articles considered important for the development of feminist consciousness, identity, politics, and culture. For example, in a column called "that's all she wrote," the editors of *Girl Germs #2* list such feminist writers as Audre Lorde and bell hooks, and encourage readers to pick up feminist periodicals, like *Lesbian Contradiction* and *The Rude Girl Press*.[150] Similarly, *Fantastic Fanzine #3 1/2* includes "a list of books that you better fucking read," including Trinh T. Minh-ha's *Woman Native Other*, Rita Mae Brown's *Rubyfruit Jungle*, and Susan Faludi's *Backlash*.[151] *Housewife Turned Assassin #3* contains a similar column called "Books We Dig," which includes the endorsement: "all these books touched us in so many ways; helped us see things in a new light & taught us to appreciate different people's circumstances. hope they do the same for you."[152] Included in the editors' list are *The Power of the Image* by Annette Kuhn, and Cherríe Moraga and Gloria Anzaldúa's *This Bridge Called My Back: Writings by Radical Women of Color*.[153] In a bolder gesture, the editors of *Korespondances* have devoted an entire issue of their zine to women's literature.[154] Included in this special issue is a list of "books every [woman] should have," such as *Listen Up: Voices of the Next Feminist Generation* edited by Barbara Findlen, *Sisterhood Is Powerful* edited by Robin Morgan, and *Women's Liberation and the Dialectics of Revolution* by Raya Dunayevskaya.[155]

As these various book lists reveal, grrrl zines play an important role in circulating information about contemporary feminist ideas and role models. Indeed, given that most of the books suggested by grrrl zinesters are taught in college-level women's studies classes, it seems that many young women use their zines to share with younger girls the knowledge they learn in school. Significantly, a large number of these books are independently published, showing zinesters' connections to the larger realm of noncorporate publishing. In addition, many are written by women of color. Although such zines' inclusion of contemporary writings by feminists of color, like their reclamation of historical black feminists, demonstrates grrrl zinesters' influence by U.S. third world feminism, their valorization of such women nevertheless calls attention to the relative absence of African, Latina, and Asian American girls in the overwhelmingly white culture of grrrl zines.

Such inclusions of women of color in the pantheon of feminist role models are obviously well intentioned; yet, they are also safe gestures of racial healing in that they do not require white female youth to interact directly with people of color. As Mimi Nguyen writes in *Evolution of a Race Riot*:

> The race riot has lagged years behind the grrrl one for reasons that should be obvious by now: whiteboy mentality became a legitimate target but whitegirls' racial privilege and discourse went unmarked … except among those of us who were never white. … Zines are full of empty liberal platitudes like "racism is a lack of love," "we're one race—the human race," "I'm colorblind" and we are supposed to be satisfied with these. … Whoop-de-doo: this does shit for me.[156]

Thinking through the difficulties between white women and women of color in the feminist movement, hooks argues:

> Recent focus on the issue of racism has generated discourse but has had little impact on the behavior of white feminists toward black women. … This is not surprising given that frequently [white feminist] discourse is aimed solely in the direction of a white audience and the focus solely on changing attitudes rather than addressing racism in historical and political context. They make us the "objects" of their privileged discourse on race. As "objects," we remain unequals, inferiors.[157]

Addressing white grrrl zinesters directly in *You Might as Well Live #4*, Lauren Martin makes specific suggestions about how they can improve race relations by interacting with, rather than simply reading about, people of color:

> have you examined your own mentality? your white upper-middle class girl mentality? … take all that anger and energy and so something positive, like EDUCATING yourself. acknowledging your privileges … , and taking the time to listen to other people.[158]

To a somewhat greater degree than their reclaiming of historical female figures, grrrl zinesters exhibit their influence by women involved in popular culture, thus stretching the boundaries of traditional feminist history. In true punk spirit, grrrl zinesters often resurrect and reclaim female performers who have been disparaged or silenced as a result of their radical, eccentric, or perverse ideas or behavior, thereby refusing simultaneously both male history and traditional standards for female and feminist identity. Not surprisingly, many of these female performers have been involved in the independent music scene. Sharon Cheslow has made perhaps the most concerted effort in this regard, using her zine, *Interrobang?!*, to publish a list of 200-plus female independent musicians between 1975 and 1980.[159] Other grrrl zinesters reclaim marginalized women musicians in lengthy essays that unpack the relevance of such performers for punk feminism. For example, Tobi Vail asserts in *Bikini Kill #1*:

> You see, part of the revolution (girl style now) is about rescuing our true heroines from obscurity, or in Yoko [Ono]'s case, from disgrace. ... Yoko was so fucking ahead of her time. I mean in a lot of ways she is the first punk rock girl singer ever. ... so let it be known, from now on, that Yoko Ono paved the way, in more ways then one for us angry grrrl rockers.[160]

Connecting Yoko Ono's demonization in the 1970s to a more recent event, Crystal Kile writes angrily in *Girls Can Do Anything #1* about Courtney Love being accused of the death of her husband, Kurt Cobain:

> When I first heard that Kurt Cobain had killed himself, my first thought was, "Man, I hope they don't Yoko Courtney." ... And now, in the wake of Cobain's suicide and Hole bassist Kristin Pfaff's mysterious, possibly heroin-related, death, Courtney Love is being called killer. Black widow.[161]

Rather than participate in such misogynist discourse, Kile lists the various reasons the unruly Love should be seen as a role model for younger feminists:

> Courtney Love had the nerve and the drive to actually, (seemingly) fearlessly live her post-punk rock fantasy to the nth degree while most of us girls stayed home scared, singing into our hairbrushes, doing the groupie thing, or become rock critics or college radio DJs or something while all of the boys started bands. By fucking with the constructedness of "femininity" by (in)articulately mixing sharply smart rage with a carefully unkempt Edie Sedgwick madness, and the opportunities afforded her by her rather privileged, liberal background, she has synthesised the bleached-blonde public persona of the AntiMadonna and the UberCyndiLauper. Sure she's scary, but in a good, amazing, insistent sort of way. I can't hate her for being the heroine she—and a lot of the rest of us "Feminist" and generationally de facto feminist Third Wave babes—wanted for years but couldn't really even imagine ...

Interestingly, since Hanna has become somewhat of a star in the independent music scene via her work with Bikini Kill and Le Tigre, several contemporary grrrl zinesters have used their texts to grapple with her privileged position as a punk feminist role model. For example, *Not Sorry #1* explores rumors about Hanna's postfeminist and transphobic comments. Dismissing such gossip on the lack of evidence, Jenny writes, "it also made me realize that she isn't the perfect being that i always think of her as. it's not fair to her, that people think of her this way."[162]

Many grrrl zines contain lists of favorite contemporary female musicians who serve as important role models for many girls. For example, several early issues of *Ms. America* contained a "Guide to Girl Bands,"[163] and *Housewife Turned Assassin #3* includes a list of "music that keeps us from going nutty."[164] Meanwhile, *The Bad Girl Club* editors created a "cool grrl word find" game that encouraged readers to find the names of various female musicians, like Tobi Vail of Bikini Kill and Lori Barbero of Babes in Toyland.[165] The caption below the game reads, "(its probably rilly easy but I just wanted to honor these girlies somehow!) keep doing cool stuff, ya'all!!" By drawing attention to these various performers' music, these grrrl zinesters represent certain music and musicians as instrumental to young feminist socialization. Indeed, despite their promotion in commercial music magazines, punk feminist bands, like Bikini Kill, Bratmobile, Le Tigre, and Sleater-Kinney, likely receive their broadest promotion via grrrl zines.

In keeping with the traditions of punk fanzines, grrrl zines often include interviews with the members of female-powered rock bands. For example, *Bikini Kill #1* includes an interview with Jean Smith of Mecca Normal, *Girl Germs #4* contains an interview with the all-female band 7 Year Bitch, *Nolite te Bastardes Carborundorum #2* includes an interview with Kathi Wilcox of The Frumpies (and Bikini Kill), and *Suburbia #6* includes an interview with Jeanette of The Chubbies.[166] Some grrrl zines include photographs of female musicians taken at local musical events. For example, *Skunk #4* includes photographs of L7 during a show at Coney Island High School, while *Suburbia #6* includes photographs of various female-powered bands at the Santa Barbara Girls' Convention in 1996, including Foxfire, The Panties, and Sleater-Kinney.[167] Grrrl zinesters' strong emphasis on female rock musicians should not be surprising since, as noted above, grrrl zines developed from punk fanzines in general and lesbian homocore fanzines in particular, both of which privilege musical discourse. Moreover, as Kim France has argued, popular music is one of the primary spaces for feminist expression, communication, and networking today, often speaking to and for a young audience that is alienated by academic feminist rhetoric.[168] In contrast to the independent, folk-oriented performers associated with women's music during the 1970s, many contemporary feminist musicians have worked hard to be legitimated within the male-dominated realm of rock. Such musicians have not only reconfigured the traditional musical styles, lyrics, and performance strategies associated with these genres; they have opened up space for girls' increased participation in music scenes that have long been male-dominated.

At the same time, however, grrrl zinesters' repeated valorization of female rock musicians, most of whom are white, demonstrates their investments in whiteness, while also unconsciously reaffirming the racial politics of rock culture, the zine community, and dominant society. Indeed, in my experience of collecting and studying grrrl zines, *Girl Germs* is one of the few texts created by white female youth that features African American rap performers alongside white punk musicians. In contrast, most grrrl zinesters who are not white make a concerted effort to feature musicians of color in their zines. For example, *Bamboo Girl*'s Sabrina Margarita Sandata frequently uses her zine to promote nonwhite female musicians, like Debbie Smith of Echobelly, Leslie Mah of Tribe 8, and Super Junkey Monkey, a Japanese band. Other nonwhite grrrl zinesters attempt to subvert the white dominance of punk, a music and culture they enjoy, by critiquing white musicians' uncritical reproduction of whiteness and exclusion of people of color. For example, Ani Mukherji of *Split Lip* asserts, "hardcore lyrics target a white audience, which perpetuates the racial make-up of the scene. ... the insert in the Downcast album claimed that hardcore is made of average people like you and me. I simply do not see many other Bengalis in hardcore."[169]

Although female musicians remain the dominant interviewees of grrrl zinesters, several zines contain discussions with other young female artists who have been influential within the punk feminist community and thus also function as role models for girls exploring nonconformist identities. For example, *Girl Germs #2* focuses on Erin Smith, who published the zine, *Teenage Gang Debs*, in the 1990s with her brother Don. Perhaps better known for her membership in Bratmobile, Smith has been a significant role model for grrrl zinesters. Moving beyond the art forms typically associated with punk culture (music and zines), Tina Spangler created *femme flicke* with the express purpose of honoring female filmmakers, and often focused on young feminists working within independent cinema and the punk community, such as Sadie Benning and Lucy Thane. As with the female musicians who are spotlighted in zines made by white girls, the other female artists valorized in such texts tend to be white also. Grrrl zinesters who are Latina, Asian, and African American, however, tend to privilege the work of nonwhite female artists. For example, *Bamboo Girl #9* contains an interview with Korean comedian and actor Margaret Cho.[170]

In an effort to move away from the celebrity discourse that dominates commercial teen magazines (and fanzines), grrrl zines often include interviews with or information about less famous women who have inspired individual zine writers and editors. For example, *Korespondances #6.2* is dedicated to Audrey May, whose women's bookstore, Meristem, was forced to close since it could not compete with corporate bookstore chains, like Borders. Attesting to the broad influence May had in her community, the zine includes testimonials and letters of thanks from many girls and women who have befriended May and visited her store. For instance, Robin writes:

> the first time i heard about meristem was when i was at some hardcore show … when i was 15; i saw a flyer for it on the bulletin board. just the knowledge of the mere PRESENCE of a feminist bookstore totally affected me cos at the time i had not actively feminist friends … and relatively few resources that helped me to develop myself that way.[171]

The combined effect of grrrl zines' essays about and interviews with, as well as lists of books by, influential girls and women is the further development of a female-centric history that continues to be deprivileged in both male-dominated society and youth cultures, like punk. Latina, Asian, and African American grrrl zinesters have diversified this history through their promotion of female artists of color. In turn, by emphasizing the contributions of young female artists, particularly popular musicians, grrrl zinesters legitimate their youthful identity, while also problematizing the adultist herstories developed by older feminist historians. In many ways then, grrrl zines have not only created an archive of punk feminist history, but provided safe discursive spaces where female youth can experiment with unruly identities by learning about other girls and women who have resisted normative feminine roles and behavior.

Refusing Female Beauty Standards through New Body Politics

Since commercial media culture, especially teen magazines, encourages girls to privilege their appearance over their other attributes, it is not surprising that discourse related to female beauty and body image proliferates in grrrl zines. As with the other female-specific discourses circulating in these texts, the prevalence of female beauty/body rhetoric suggests grrrl zinesters' interests in exploring alternate forms of female identity. Yet unlike the discourses of female pride and female history, which grrrl zinesters present positively, the discourse of female beauty and body image is presented primarily in negative terms, suggesting that in order to develop a new body politics for female youth, traditional beauty standards must first be critiqued and rejected.

Many grrrl zinesters reveal a profound disappointment and frustration that their bodies do not measure up to commercial culture's dominant standards of female beauty. For example, May writes in *Marika #2*:

i've been thinking a lot about my body lately and how it affects my self esteem … when i'm under my natural body weight i generally feel more attractive and good about myself in this twisted way even though at the same time I don't feel very confident about my strength and health. … when i think about all the times in my life that i've wasted worrying about the state of my cuteness i feel like i've really cheated myself out of some worthwhile thinking.[172]

More disturbingly, Erika states in *Riot Grrrl #7*, "i hate mirrors. i really do. i can't stand my reflection, my face. … i used to have fantasies about taking a razor and shaving off my face and when it grew back it would be perfect. no flaws, no points of interest whatsoever."[173] Interestingly, many grrrl zinesters connect such feelings of self-loathing directly to commercial media culture's repetitious discourse of self-improvement, as can be seen in this passage from *Revolution Rising #1*:

why do i cry every time that i look in the mirror? why do i look at stupid magazines and wish that i looked like that? why is there so much fucken emphasis placed on looking "pretty"? i am not "pretty" and i dont know that i want to be. i just don't want to hate myself anymore for not being the delicate little flower that im told to be. why does the media try so hard to dictate to us what is and what isnt beautiful. … I am so sick of hating myself. i dont want to cry in the mirror anymore.[174]

Several other grrrl zines, including *Verboslammed #8* and *Korespondances #7.1*, go one step further, discussing the connections between society's standards for female beauty and the girl-dominated disease of anorexia.

Given the oppositional stance most grrrl zinesters have to patriarchy and commercial media culture, traditional standards for female appearance regularly come under attack in grrrl zines. Often such criticism is made explicit in editorials on the cosmetics industry, beauty regimes, and fashion models. For example, *Girlie Jones #2.2* contains an article titled "Role Models, Not Supermodels," which encourages girls to look to mothers and female artists rather than fashion models for inspiration.[175] More often, grrrl zinesters disrupt commercial media messages about female appearance by appropriating images of female beauty regimes and fashion practices from magazines and reconfiguring them in ways that reveal their oppressive characteristics. *Nerd Girl #4*, for instance, has several collages of bra advertisements and fashion images from teen magazines that are juxtaposed with seemingly unrelated captions, like "She thinks high heels are comfortable." As Marcy, the zine's editor notes:

i know that i've talked about this before, but it needs to be repeated over and over again until the issue is taken more seriously. it's about how womyn and their bodies are portrayed in the media. … it makes me sick that only a small percentage of womyn are represented, yet it is sold as a massive culture ideal.[176]

Several grrrl zines draw attention to how clothing and fashion accessories made for females severely contain the body and restrict movement. For example, the editors of *Ms. America #2* make a bold point about the discomfort and lack of balance caused from wearing high-heeled shoes by creating a full-page collage of photographs of such footwear appropriated from a women's catalog.[177] Other grrrl zines also demonstrate their writers' frustrations with female fashion standards. *Meat Hook #4*, for instance, includes an illustration of a naked woman surrounded, paper doll–like, with various items of clothing. The caption reads: "What Shall I Wear? a board game I played as a child is a game I find hard to avoid as an adult so I wear a uniform that is as liberating as it is boring."[178] At the bottom of the picture is a smaller caption which foregrounds girls' frustrations with adhering to dominant fashion standards while attempting to remain comfortably attired: "naturally, none of these clothes fit." Several other grrrl zines include illustrations of female paper dolls with different sets of clothing, a strategy that works to foreground girls' awareness of not only contemporary society's privileged modes of female fashion, but also the performative nature of identity. For example, *Welcome #8* contains six different outfits for paper dolls, including casual attire (jeans and t-shirts), formal attire (dresses below the knee), and "clothes we'll never wear" (tight t-shirts and mini-skirts).[179] (As with their foregrounding of girl characters from commercial media culture, such zinesters' inclusion of board games and paper dolls reveals explorations of youthfulness within grrrl zine culture.)

Attesting to the considerable degree to which female youth in U.S. society are encouraged to think about their appearance, some grrrl zinesters have devoted entire issues of their zines to female body image so as to explore this issue in depth. Indeed, though she discusses her own body image issues, Rebecca Gilbert, the editor of *Verboslammed*, notes the collaborative nature of her zine's eighth issue since "the point of this is to offer as many different viewpoints as possible …"[180] Noting the relationship of female beauty standards (often referred to as "body fascism" in grrrl zines) to other forms of oppression, Terry Moon writes in *Korespondances*'s special body images issue, "we need a revolution whose aim is not merely changing property relationships, but one that aims to create new relationships, including relationships we have to ourselves and our bodies."[181]

Since body image is such a primary discursive theme in female youth culture, it is not surprising to find that many other grrrl zinesters explore issues of weight in their texts. For example, *Housewife Turned Assassin #3* includes an editorial about talk shows that have included segments on children who are embarrassed to be seen with their mothers because they are fat. At a loss for how to respond to such shows (other than writing about it), the author ends with "I cried for those women. It scares me that this attitude is reaching out and grabbing such young minds now."[182] *Bikini Kill #2* reprints a letter from Allison, who reveals the pain and frustration many large girls experience:

> Being fat is one difficult category to be in because you are not only oppressed by sexism, you are oppressed by members of your own sex. They are full of words to shut you up.... Is being a strong and sexy woman the most powerful form of subversion? Maybe the most powerful for those who are born that way but being a strong and "non-beautiful" or "ugly" or "fat" woman and declaring openly that you like the way you are is the most *defiantly powerful* form of subversion. ...

Continuing, she writes with emphasis in bolded text:

> We're not going to starve ourselves
>
> deny ourselves
>
> cut ourselves with knifes
>
> suck out
>
> our fat
>
> our bodies
>
> with vacuums and leave bruises
>
> to satisfy someone else,
>
> to line the pockets of the
>
> billion dollar diet industry.
>
> But we are. We're killing ourselves ... And our sisters our girlfriends are encouraging us to do it *Right Along with us*!!!
>
> No. We are not the rulers of our own waistlines. Not yet. Especially if we think its the only thing we can rule.[183]

Other grrrl zinesters celebrate their fat bodies, recognizing that, in doing so, they resist standards for female beauty perpetuated by the fashion and weight loss industries. For example, Jenny writes in *Not Sorry #1*, "there is so much more to me than fat, but it is definitely an important part of who i am, and i want it to be acknowledged. don't feel sympathy for me, i'm not sorry about who i am ..."[184] More significant perhaps in the battle against female dieting and eating disorders are such zines as *Fat Girl, Fat! So?, Eat Yr*

Heart Out, The Adventures of a Big Girl, and *I'm So Fucking Beautiful,* whose primary purpose is to affirm girls and women whose bodies do not meet the current standard of thinness privileged in commercial fashion magazines and other forms of popular culture. Included in such zines are illustrations, cartoons, and photographs of larger girls and women, reconfigured text about exercise and beauty appropriated from commercial magazines, articles connecting physical insecurity to low self-esteem, and advice on how to appreciate and nurture the body you have. By embracing their nonnormative size and encouraging other large-sized girls to do the same, these grrrl zinesters promote feminist body politics at the same time that they reveal the influence of punk's celebration of abject social phenomena.

Some grrrl zinesters move discourse on female beauty standards and body image beyond issues of gender by reflecting on the difficulties of being nonwhite in a society dominated by white standards of beauty. In her list of "shitty things that have happened or have been said because of my skin color," published in *Evolution of a Race Riot,* Chandra Ray recalls a white boy telling her, "'Black people mixed with white look better, huh?'"[185] Having been immersed in a society where whiteness rules, many nonwhite grrrl zinesters chronicle the effects of white beauty standards on female youth of color. For example, Melissa of *Lucid Nation* writes of a common experience among dark-skinned girls who live in a white-dominated society:

> I learned at an early age to hide the way I had been taught since birth. I stayed out of the sun to make myself even more pale. ... I tried to assimilate every ounce of my Indianness into being white. And people stopped mocking me, but I felt empty and trapped.[186]

Trish Bishon from *Spelling Bee* tells a similar story:

> When I was four, I went to the bathroom and covered myself with powder. I pranced out of the bathroom and told my parents that I had succeeded in my goal of becoming white. I was so proud of myself because in my four-year-old mind, I had reached the ultimate level of being—a white person.[187]

In *Girl Germs #5,* Selena Whang notes the more disturbing effects of racial assimilation by discussing the recent rise in facial reconstruction among Asian females who want to look Caucasian, connecting this phenomenon to the global dissemination of Hollywood movies that feature white actors:

> the japanese invented these quick and easy operations, making folds by cutting slits on yr. eyelids so you look caucasoid, an optical illusion that makes your eyes look bigger. this is called sangkyopul. not

as prevalent but still widespread is breaking yr. nose and raising that bridge, straight and tall. this is called kokosul.[188]

Other grrrl zinesters who are both nonwhite and poor note the pressures they feel with regard to dominant beauty standards, pressures often reinforced by wealthy, white girls. For instance, in an essay called "Whitewash Sin" from *Housewife Turned Assassin #3*, Sisi writes:

> You said you wouldn't judge but you turn around in disgust at my highwaters and torn shoes. Don't you understand that my parents can only afford 1 pair of shoes a year and 2 pairs of jeans. ... You said you want me in your realm of popularity but in the same breath my braids and accent get in your way. ... In two years I have managed to turn my brown hair into a brassy orange mess w/ out braids and w/ bangs. I can hide my brown forehead now. I destroyed myself so much. Constant self denial. Perpetual dissatisfaction. Trying so hard to make a perfect me that people will embrace and not treat differently.[189]

Other nonwhite grrrl zinesters focus positively on their bodies, despite their difference from the white norm. As Mengshin writes in *Sidetracked #8*, for example, "My culture was something I took quite pride in, never regarding it as a relevant cause for ostracism. Mostly, it was something that I just *was*—I just *was* almond-eyed and I just *was* black-haired."[190] By taking pride in their bodies, these girls challenge dominant racial ideologies that are reproduced in part through the self-loathing of people of color.

In addition to celebrating the natural form of their bodies and critiquing dominant female beauty standards, many grrrl zinesters demonstrate their interest in exploring counterhegemonic female identities through nontraditional fashion aesthetics and physical adornment. For example, in *Ms. America #2*, the editors include a column on Wanda Harper, a tattoo artist in their local community.[191] Similarly, *Bamboo Girl #10* contains several photographs by Anh Dao Kolbe that highlight young women's tattoos and piercings.[192] *Skunk #4* has a full-page "make-over" pictorial that shows Vikki, editor of *Psychedelic Wasteland* zine, getting her waist-length hair cut off and her head shaved (Figure 12).[193] In turn, the vast majority of illustrations of female youth that are included in grrrl zines show them adhering to the revolting style of punk culture, replete with tattoos, body piercings, unconventional haircuts, androgynous clothing, and work boots. As these images reveal, many grrrl zinesters demonstrate their interest in developing a new body politics for young feminists that, in its confrontational masculinity, not only reconfigures that advocated by 1970s' feminists, but also moves well beyond the conventional standards of female appearance promoted in commercial teen magazines.

CONCLUSION

In the introduction to her directory of grrrl zines, Darby Romeo of *Ben Is Dead* argues:

> What [the mainstream media] continually lack the insight to mention is the number of zines that are produced by women and how women's participation in the zine world has contributed immensely to the rise of the format. Women continue to bring diversity, creativity, emotion, and energy to zines. They are fresh and deep and inspiring (can you handle that?). They have helped move zines out of the music-only format to encompass a greater variety of topics and issues. ... Grrrl zinesters are truly showing their force.[194]

Figure 12 Nontraditional body politics for noncomformist girls.
Skunk #4, 1995.

As the texts discussed above demonstrate, grrrl zinesters are showing their force not only by moving out of the music-oriented fanzine format, but by foregrounding issues relevant to girls through the privileging of female-centric discourses from a youthful perspective. In turn, these zinesters are expanding girls' written culture through their provocative combination of punk and feminist ideologies, rhetoric, and aesthetics, thus continuing while also reconfiguring the discursive and representational practices long associated with countercultural formations.

Moreover, by merging these various practices in their texts, grrrl zinesters are able to explore unruly identities that they may not be able to perform publicly in their everyday lives. Chief among the nonconformist identities explored in grrrl zines is that of the punk feminist, a subject position that radically challenges not only the ideologies of gender dominant within society and punk culture, but also the generational dynamics traditionally associated with the feminist movement. As indicated by the various zines discussed here, the vast number of grrrl zinesters exploring this particular identity suggests that it is constructed in both individual and collective ways. Whether the effects of these multiple performances of young female unruliness will be temporary or long term—a debate that continues among scholars of carnival culture—only time will tell. Nevertheless, it seems clear that within contemporary U.S. society, new forms of girlhood are being imagined that seriously challenge conventional power structures based on sex and gender, as well as age and generation. Even if occurring only at the textual level, grrrl zinesters' performances of unruliness indicate that the repetitive cycle by which traditional girlhood is produced and normalized is being actively resisted by a considerable number of contemporary American female youth.

In the next chapter, I continue my examination of girl-made media texts by analyzing various films and videos created by female youth during the past decade. Although few of these texts are as counterhegemonic as grrrl zines, they, too, reveal their producers' attempts to explore nonconformist identities while also negotiating the traditional ideologies of gender and generation circulating in commercial media culture.

5

Developing the Girl's Gaze
Female Youth and Film Production

To me the great hope is that now [that] these little 8mm video recorders
are around, and people who normally wouldn't make movies are going
to be making them. And suddenly, one day some little fat girl in Ohio
is going to be the new Mozart and make a beautiful film with her
father's camcorder, and for once the so-called professionalism about
movies will be destroyed forever, and it will really become an art form.

—Francis Ford Coppola[1]

We didn't need Hollywood; we were Hollywood.

—Sadie Benning[2]

In the early 1990s, Sadie Benning rose to much acclaim in the U.S. art world
after releasing several videos about her female adolescence, including *If Every
Girl Had a Diary, A Place Called Lovely,* and the Riot Grrrl–inspired *Girl
Power.*[3] Living at that time with her mother in Milwaukee, Wisconsin, and
producing videos on a Fisher-Price Pixelvision camera bought for her by her
father, she effectively became the Midwestern girl director whom Francis Ford
Coppola predicted would materialize as a result of the camcorder's wide dis-

persion. Benning's early videos, most of which she created in her bedroom, are clearly from a teenager's perspective, yet debunk the stereotypical notion of girls' bedroom culture as a cheerful space of heterosexual awakening and passive media consumption. Instead, Benning presents herself as both a lesbian and a filmmaker who is anxious about the alienating and often violent society in which she lives. Similar to Riot Grrrl zines, her autobiographical and inexpensively produced videos freely appropriate materials from commercial media culture, relocating and reconfiguring them in order to tell her own story of growing up lesbian. Benning's videos began to be screened publicly in 1990, and in less than a year she was being hyped by art critics as the "auteur of adolescence."[4]

Benning was not the only American girl engaging actively in filmmaking in the United States during the 1990s, however. Alyssa Buecker received considerable attention for her videos during this same period, though from a different audience. Having made her first film, *Hazel, the Guinea Pig's Package*,[5] in 1996 at the age of eleven and directed two more movies in the series by 2000, Buecker was commissioned by HBO Family to create yet another guinea-pig drama, *Carrot Wars*, a *Star Wars* parody. In addition, she filmed a spoof of Nickelodeon's *Figure It Out*, called *Figure It Out, Guinea Pig Style*, for the children's cable network in 1999.[6] Buecker has won several awards for her films, runs her own film company (Milbo Productions), and plans to have a career in filmmaking. Also gaining media attention in the 1990s, teen sisters Ashli and Callie Pfeiffer joined forces in 1998 with their best friends, twins Maggie and Sabrina Kelley, to produce their first film, *Benny*, which won an award at the National Children's Film Festival.[7] The team has since formed their own company (YaYa Productions) to create other films, and was commissioned by HBO Family in 2000 to produce a film for its youth media program, *30 x 30 Kid Flicks*.[8] The most contemporary teenage girl to receive such public attention for her film work is twelve-year-old Emily Hagins, whose zombie movie, *Pathogen*, is scheduled for release during the spring of 2006. Hagins is the first teenage girl in the United States to direct a feature-length film.[9]

Like Benning, Hagins, Buecker, and the YaYa sisters are helping to erode the stereotype of cinematically unproductive girls that the Independent Film Channel exploited in its first promotional campaign, "Break the Rules."[10] Yet, these girls' success did not come easily in a world of filmmaking still dominated by adult males. Indeed, although the number of female youth engaged in filmmaking in the United States has risen substantially since the early 1990s, girl directors are still anomalies in both film culture and girls' culture.

In order to understand better the reasons that female youth are not drawn to filmmaking, the first part of this chapter analyzes the various barriers that have prevented girls from using film as a means for communication and creative expression. In particular, I explore the masculinization of filmmaking roles, technology, and education. These gendered structures are still largely in place at the turn of the twenty-first century; however, various social transformations—including the diffusion of feminist ideology, the increased accessibility of inexpensive video technology, and the introduction of more media education programs for youth—have allowed contemporary girls to gain more access to and attention within the world of filmmaking. As a result, the number of girls producing movies today is on the rise. The remainder of this chapter consists of close textual analyses of numerous U.S. girls' films created during the late 1990s and early 2000s, examining in particular the various themes and perspectives that are common across this body of texts.[11]

THE BOYS' CLUB: PATRIARCHY AND SEXISM IN COMMERCIAL FILMMAKING

As discussed in Chapter 1, female youth have used writing as a form of communication and creative expression for over two centuries. By comparison, very few girls have been involved in filmmaking until quite recently. The reasons for this situation are many and deserve greater attention by those of us committed to subverting the hegemonic structures of cultural production and developing a truly democratic system of communication.

The first and most obvious explanation for girls' minimal engagement in filmmaking is that the equipment needed for such practices was, until recently, quite expensive for the vast majority of youth, their parents, and their schools. Thus, most girls (and boys) were not involved in filmmaking prior to the late twentieth century simply as a result of their minimal level of disposable income and minimal access to filmmaking technologies. This problem has been lessened somewhat in recent years by both the introduction of relatively inexpensive filmmaking equipment, as well as an increase in school- and community-based media education programs that teach young people film production skills. At the same time, however, if we look closer at the group of contemporary youth who have their own filmmaking equipment, a significant difference between the sexes is evident. From my studies of young directors over the past six years, I have found that boys tend to outnumber girls 10 to 1 in owning their own film or video cameras. Such an imbalance mirrors that of mixed-sex media education classes and workshops, which enroll a disproportionate number of boys in comparison to girls. Economics alone, therefore, cannot explain the relatively low number of girls who are actively involved in making movies.

Andrea Richards, author of *Girl Director*, a guidebook for girls' filmmakers, points us in the right direction for finding an explanation for this phenomenon when she states, "I think it honestly doesn't occur to girls that they can be a film director—the possibility has never even been planted in their heads, because it's so off limits through cultural and gender stereotypes."[12] In order to explore how this thinking has retained such power, despite the widespread diffusion of feminist sentiment in the past three decades, it is useful to examine the primary realm of its (re)production: the film industry.

Patriarchal ideology, whose hegemony has long relied on a sexual division of labor, has sustained the male domination of, and female marginalization within, commercial filmmaking for decades. Indeed, as has been the case since the first motion picture camera was invented, men far outnumber women in virtually all sectors of contemporary film production. Such male dominance puts interested females at a severe disadvantage, as the primary roles involved in film production, especially director and cinematographer, have been naturalized as male. As Christine Spines notes in a recent article on gender in the contemporary film industry:

> One of the biggest obstacles faced by aspiring women directors—and the toughest to overcome—is the problem of perception. Since the days of John Huston and John Ford, Hollywood's romantic notion of the director has been mythologized as a commanding, Hemmingwayesque frontiersman or an all-powerful warlord.[13]

In turn, Michelle Citron, a feminist filmmaker and media scholar, has noted how the common perception of the film director as male has led to the masculinization of the director's role and hence film production as a cultural practice:

> I've always thought of ... film as more "masculine." ... When you direct a movie, you are directing a small army. It's about taking authority. It's about possibly firing people and about saying, "Not today," and "Give me this shot," and "I have no time for this now."[14]

Like Citron, several other successful women directors have spoken out about their experiences within the historically male-dominated realm of film production. Though anecdotal, their comments provide considerable insight into the gender dynamics at play within the film industry, particularly in light of the few studies conducted on this topic. For example, when interviewed by Janis Cole and Holly Dale for their book *Calling the Shots: Profiles of Women Filmmakers*, independent director Jill Godmilow, perhaps best known for her documentary *Antonia: Portrait of a Woman*, suggests that it is the traditional patterns of gender socialization that put women at a disadvantage in the world of filmmaking:

> Is it hard being a woman filmmaker? Yes, it is. But the problems have to do with being raised in this culture. Feeling legitimate giving orders. Feeling legitimate believing in your bizarre way of doing it up against the critical expertise and talent of people who have done it

twenty-five times more than you, and who say you can't do it that way. Those are the problems of being a woman filmmaker. Feeling entitled, feeling legitimate, trusting yourself, asking for what you want.[15]

But the masculine qualities associated with the role of director are not the only gendered barriers to aspiring female filmmakers. Martha Coolidge, director of several commercially successful films and acclaimed television programs, recalls that when she arrived in Hollywood in the early 1980s, sexist attitudes toward aspiring female directors were the norm:

> I can't even describe to you what it was like when I first got here. [It] was unbelievable. I ... went for my first jobs and said, "I really want to be a director." And they said, "Don't tell anybody you want to be a director! My God, just tell them you're dying to be a production assistant. You really want to be a film editor some day maybe. And whatever you do, get a manicure, wear eyelashes, and more make-up."[16]

Andi Ruane, a grip[17] who has worked on such films as *Daredevil*, *Punch Drunk Love*, and *House of Sand and Fog*, argues that sexism remains quite strong in the film industry today, despite the dramatic increase in women's involvement at all levels of the business since the 1970s: "I know a few people (in the industry) who openly say they will not hire a woman. They don't think that women can do the job. They also think that they are distracting."[18] Film and television director Karen Arthur connects this sexism to the patriarchal apprentice system historically associated with filmmaking and other trades:

> It's like any other craft. People have been around for a long time, and what they've been doing from the beginning ... is handing the jobs down—father son, father son, father son. And that still happens. Great producers would hand it down to their sons. Writers would hand it down to their sons. Directors to their sons, and there was a community that was built out of that.[19]

In this male-dominated system, women directors are typically seen as anomalies and are often criticized by male colleagues for their attempted entrance into a historically homosocial world. Some female filmmakers attribute such dynamics to antiquated views on sex and gender held by men in power within the industry. For example, Sandy Wilson, director of *American Boyfriends* and *My American Cousin*, argues:

> [A] lot of the power, and the money, and the control [in Hollywood] is watched over by men. And a lot of those men don't yet feel comfortable in dealing with a woman on an equal footing. They're far more used to having women as ... actresses, or secretaries, or wives. People

they can either dismiss or divorce. ... So in that regard it's a little difficult to find men who enjoy working with women ...[20]

As a result of the historical patriarchy and sexism that have structured film production, few women have received enough attention to be considered acclaimed filmmakers, much less role models for aspiring directors. In Alexandra Juhasz's collection *Women of Vision*, several women who became involved in filmmaking in the 1960s and 1970s recall the dearth of female filmmakers at that time, despite the increasing presence of women in other professional jobs and realms of public life during that period. For example, Barbara Hammer, acclaimed lesbian director of such films as *Dyketactics* and *Women I Love*, remembers that as a film student she was not "aware of any other women's cinema ... besides Maya Deren."[21] Julia Reichert, who began producing and directing films in the early 1970s, connects the relative absence of female filmmakers during that period to the larger problem of women's limited training in cinema: "I'm a member of a generation without mentors. No one showed me the ropes as I do regularly for women now."[22] Several of the women filmmakers interviewed for *Calling the Shots* similarly note the lack of female mentorship in their lives. As Randa Haines, director of *Children of a Lesser God*, recalls:

> When I was a script supervisor I don't think I ever met a woman director. People would come up to me and say, "You should be a director." I'd think, "Gee, that's a great idea, but how do I do it?" I didn't have any role models or anyone to focus on. I can remember thinking at the time, "There aren't any women making films." I'm sure it affected my waiting [to become a director].[23]

Amy Heckerling, well known today for her commercially successful and feminist-inflected teenpics *Clueless* and *Fast Times at Ridgemont High*, recalls:

> When I was going to film school, my father would always say, "Yeah right, a woman director." He'd never heard of such a thing. And when I'd try to say, "Well what about Elaine May?" he'd say, "Who else?" And I couldn't think of anyone else.[24]

Many contemporary female directors consider the financial and critical success of Susan Seidelman's *Desperately Seeking Susan* in 1985 as a positive turning point for women in the commercial film industry. Nevertheless, Seidelman herself seems skeptical that any real systemic change has occurred since that time: "When you look at the statistics of how many women are actually directing feature films, it's pretty horrendous. Let's face it, Hollywood is still run by men."[25] Joan Tewkesbury, who has written and directed several television movies and programs, agrees, suggesting some of the ways this gender imbalance might change:

> [U]ntil a woman owns a film studio, until a woman comes with a hundred million dollars in her repertoire, I don't think it's going to be much easier [for women filmmakers] at all. Because really, in this town, money is power. You have all these [male] heads of studios and you have all these jobs that women have been slotted into, and they don't mean anything.[26]

Yet, as the popular actor-cum-director Jodie Foster argues, sexism is not the only barrier keeping women filmmakers from gaining more work in the industry. Economic factors are given much more consideration by those most invested in the commercial aspects of filmmaking:

> It's about the globalization of the film business. Making a quality film is just not a studio's biggest priority when what they make money doing is [an action film like] *Independence Day*. The movie industry has fallen into the same rut that most big corporate structures have.[27]

Sharing this view, Seidelman puts it more bluntly: "Hollywood is a business and if monkeys were directing movies that were commercially successful, Hollywood would have monkeys directing movies."[28]

Capitalism alone cannot explain women directors' marginalization in the film industry, however. Patriarchy works alongside profit motives to shape not only the types of filmmakers who get the most work, but also the types of films that get made. Wanting to take full financial advantage of the synergistic, multimedia conglomerates of which they are a part, the contemporary film studios privilege those movies that consistently perform well with their coveted eighteen- to thirty-four-year-old male audience: male-centered action/adventure blockbusters. Antonia Bird, director of such commercial films as *Priest* and *Mad Love*, draws attention to this current trend in Hollywood and its effects on female filmmakers, who often have different interests, goals, and audiences in mind: "I'm aware that the types of films getting made are much more of what I call boys' films. It's this school boy humor that's suddenly become very fashionable. ... [O]bviously they're not going to ask the likes of me to direct those kinds of films."[29]

As Bird suggests, film content and genres are also significant components in the persistent masculinization of commercial filmmaking and marginalization of women directors. Spines concurs: "Subject matter has been the biggest stumbling block for women..."[30] While "men's films," particularly those in the larger action/adventure genre (e.g., western, gangster, detective, spy films), have long been privileged by the movie industry and celebrated by critics, "women's films," especially romantic and family melodramas, have more often been disparaged despite their popularity and commercial potential. As a result, many men in the industry have discouraged women who aspire to be directors because they believe that these newcomers will necessarily focus on "women's issues" and can bring only a feminine or feminist perspective to their work. As Godmilow explains:

> You see, women's cinema is still marginal, or cinema that has a decidedly feminist point of view, or that treats the subject of women in a way that's not voyeuristic. Those films don't make as much money. I think that's the essence of [the film industry's] feminist phobia. I don't think it's ideological. I think it's financial.[31]

Filmmaker Lizzie Borden agrees: "It's hard because if you're a woman very often what you're trying to do is things that are more marginal and therefore you're censored by whatever economic systems occur in this culture that say, 'No that's not an economically viable idea.'"[32] Thus, capitalism and patriarchy seem to work together in privileging male content, male spectators, and male directors.

OTHER BOYS' CLUBS: INDEPENDENT AND AMATEUR FILMMAKING

Given women's limited access to jobs in the commercial film industry, many aspiring female directors have found a more welcoming and supportive environment in the world of independent cinema. Women's access to this realm increased considerably in the 1960s with the diffusion of feminist sentiments, as well as the expansion of arts funding and introduction of new sync-sound 16mm cameras that required less expertise to operate. As Julia Lesage and Annette Kuhn have demonstrated independently, the development of such technology was extremely significant to the rise of feminist cinema, for 16mm equipment helped women to create a new form of documentary filmmaking in the late 1960s that was grounded in feminist ideologies of collective production, politicizing the personal, and nonhierarchical decision making.[33] As more women gained entrance to film schools and were exposed to film theory in the 1970s, women's experimental/avant-garde filmmaking increased considerably, eventually replacing documentary as the privileged feminist form. The 1980s saw the further expansion of feminist filmmaking practices as a result of advancements in video technology.

Women's independent cinema flourished in the late 1970s and early 1980s; however, severe funding cuts and a changed political environment significantly transformed this realm during mid-1980s, especially for women. While a number of male filmmakers, such as Spike Lee, achieved considerable success in the independent arena during this period, the infrastructure supporting independent women directors, especially those who were outwardly feminist or queer, underwent drastic changes. As lesbian filmmaker Hammer recalls:

> I felt that the '80s were a very repressive period in the United States. I couldn't get a show in the art establishment. ... It was very difficult; I hadn't received a grant at that time. For ten years, the works were all funded out of my pocket. ... I decided that if I took women out of the frame, the films couldn't be objected to ...[34]

Arguing for a reconceptualization of women's cinema in light of these changes, feminist filmmaker Citron wrote in 1988:

> The context has changed since the 1970s, so those of us working within it must also change. On the simplest level, we have lost our audiences as previously defined (for example, the large network of broad-based women's centres has greatly diminished). ... Only two distributors of women's films remain in the United States: New Day Films ... and Women Make Movies. Other films are occasionally picked up by broader independent distributors. ... But no matter who distributes "alternative" films, there are fewer companies handling fewer films and exhibiting to smaller audiences.[35]

As Citron describes, the conservative sociopolitical climate of the 1980s left many independent female filmmakers without a broad, supportive network and scrambling to compete with men. Margaret Caples of Chicago's Community Film Workshop agrees:

> It's a male-dominated field, even in the independent area. When I think about it, most of the administrators of media arts centers are women. Does that say anything? ... [M]ost of the people who use our centers are men. ... [In 1996,] with our Build Illinois Grant we gave out twelve grants, and we only had one woman.[36]

Male dominance of film production also exists in the primary sphere of contemporary girls' film production—amateur filmmaking. But this was not always the case. As Patricia Zimmerman's research demonstrates, women were active amateur filmmakers during the first decades of the twentieth century, documenting their homes and children and thus extending the practices of home photography that had begun in the late 1880s.[37] (Women's involvement in commercial filmmaking was substantial during this period also.) By the 1950s, however, home movie production had become dominated by men. Indeed, a Bell and Howell report from 1961 indicates that fathers were producing twice as many films as mothers at that time.[38] Like the other technology-centered domestic hobbies in which men of the postwar era were encouraged to immerse themselves, home moviemaking became a means by which middle-class males could both construct their masculinity and affirm their authority within what was increasingly understood as a feminized social space. Describing one 8mm home movie from 1956, Zimmerman notes:

> The angle of the camera, its mobility, and its control over representation unfurl patriarchal prerogative. ... The father is absent from all of these images. ... Yet the camera imprints his presence and control over the actors. It traces his leisure, his time away from work, his experiments with family and technology.[39]

In *Home Movies and Other Necessary Fictions*, Citron similarly points to the patriarchal character of home movies:

> Most often it is the father who holds the camera and peers through the lens. ... Dad has near total control. With film in particular, positioned behind the lens, constrained by a roll of celluloid that lasts only three minutes, Dad must edit in the camera, constantly making choices of what to film. ... Technology, as we all know, is historically the province of men.[40]

Though neither Zimmerman nor Citron analyzes the masculinization of home moviemaking in relation to the specific sociohistorical context of its emergence, it is important to note that popular discourse during the post World War II era actively promoted a domestic form of patriarchal authority by privileging the middle-class breadwinning father, thus helping to reintegrate men into the family circle after World War II. In contrast, the housewife—a role that isolated women from the public sphere except with regard to consumerism—was promoted as the ideal for all women.[41]

Just as a waning economy and the diffusion of feminist sensibilities since the 1970s has encouraged more women to seek work outside the domestic sphere, the introduction of video camcorders in the 1980s and even smaller digital video cameras in the 1990s has promised to make the world of home moviemaking more accessible to women. Nevertheless, recent reports indicate that men continue to purchase and use home video cameras to a far greater extent than women. For example, a Consumer Electronics Association (CEA) survey from 2000 found that although the gap between male and female general use of electronic technology seems to be narrowing, "[m]en still have the possessive edge when it comes to 'interactive' devices like computers, video games, and camcorders."[42] Indeed, CEA found the biggest discrepancy between the sexes in video camera use: 44 percent of men surveyed used such technology on a regular basis compared to only 33 percent of women. A more recent Good Housekeeping survey similarly found sex-related discrepancies in the use of consumer electronics, reporting that women today are most comfortable with homecare appliances, such as microwave ovens and vacuum cleaners, and least comfortable with media technology, like computers and video camcorders.[43] Such reports reveal that the domestic sphere, the realm of many young people's initial filmmaking adventures, continues to be male-dominated. Thus, the gender dynamics of home moviemaking work alongside those of commercial and independent film production to construct girls' understanding of filmmaking as an activity dominated by men and off limits to members of their sex.

THE TECHNOPHALLIC CINEMATIC APPARATUS: THE GENDERING OF FILM TECHNOLOGY AND TRAINING

Given the historical male domination of amateur, independent, and commercial film production, female youth interested in making movies have had few women role models to emulate. Nevertheless, as Mary Ann Clawson argues, the dearth of female role models is not by itself an adequate explanation for the minimal number of girls involved in forms of cultural production traditionally dominated by men.[44] We must look elsewhere, therefore, to locate and understand additional barriers to girls' participation in such realms. For example, in addition to filmmaking roles and film production at large, we need to consider how the technologies involved in this cultural practice have been gendered to such an extent that female youth feel excluded from using them, for as Claire Johnston has argued, "The tools and techniques of cinema themselves, as part of reality, are an expression of the prevailing ideology: they are not neutral ..."[45] Even though women have gained greater access to filmmaking since the 1970s, as recent reports from CEA and Good Housekeeping indicate, women today still tend to use such equipment far less than men. It is likely, therefore, that such technology has been naturalized as masculine and that, as a result, women and girls understand it as not for them.

Since the 1970s, feminist scholars in numerous disciplines have been examining the relationship of technology and gender. Unfortunately, very few have discussed how the equipment used in film production is gendered. Laura Mulvey's theory of the camera's "male gaze" seems the closest any feminist film scholar has come to exploring further Johnston's assertion about the sexism governing the movie camera's development.[46] Almost initiating what could have been a substantial theoretical exploration of the gendered construction of filmmaking technology and its relation to the traditional place of females in film production (in front of the camera, not behind it), Mulvey turned away from the movie-making apparatus and toward the screen, examining in detail the way that Hollywood's traditional forms of editing, narrative, and cinematography relate to, and reproduce, traditional ideologies of gender. Since the publication of her groundbreaking essay, "Visual Pleasure in

Narrative Cinema," many other feminist film scholars have followed her lead, ignoring the material aspects of film production to focus on issues of representation and spectatorship. Nevertheless, Mulvey's essay can help to initiate a critical discussion of filmmaking technology, and I want to return to it here in order to explore further girls' historical avoidance of film production.

Though Mulvey does not elaborate on it, the idea that men control the cinematic apparatus (or at least did so at the time her essay was written) is the keystone to her theory of the male gaze. (E. Ann Kaplan helped to clarify this point by noting that "while technically neutral, [the camera's] look ... is inherently voyeuristic and usually 'male' in the sense that a man is generally doing the filming.")[47] Significantly, Mulvey relates the masculinizing of the camera's perspective to the gender dynamics involved in the practice of looking, thus contextualizing the male gaze as an effect of patriarchy:

> In a world ordered by sexual imbalance, pleasure in looking has been split between active/male and passive/female. The determining male gaze projects its phantasy on to the female figure which is styled accordingly. In their traditional exhibitionist role women are simultaneously looked at and displayed, with their appearance coded for strong visual and erotic impact so that they can be said to connote *to-be-looked-at-ness*.[48]

Interestingly, Mulvey connects looking not only to males but also to the realm of action here, thus echoing John Berger, who had argued a few years earlier that "*men act* and *women appear*."[49] Elaborating on this point, Berger notes that while women in patriarchal societies are encouraged to be spectacles for the male gaze, "[a] man's presence is dependent upon the promise of power which he embodies [and is suggestive of] what he is capable of doing to you or for you."[50] In other words, a man's identity is specifically related to his ability to act, and through such actions, his ability to display power. In her analysis of Mulvey's theory, Kaplan reiterates this point when she notes, "[M]en do not simply look; their gaze carries with it the power of action and of possession which is lacking in the female gaze."[51]

Tracing the philosophical roots of the male = active/female = passive binary, Susan Bordo notes that Aristotle theorized human conception as requiring the "effective and active" element of male sperm and the "passive" contribution of female ova.[52] As Bordo demonstrates, this erroneous understanding of sperm as energetically striving for contact with a passively waiting ovum is still popular today, helping to reaffirm the naturalized opposition of the sexes in other realms of discourse. Through Bordo then we can better understand the masculinizing of film technology as related not only to the gendered practice of looking, but also to the broader gendering of action and productivity as male-specific qualities.

In her analysis of the gendering of musical instruments, Mavis Bayton goes somewhat further than Mulvey in relating electronic media technologies to men's attempts to bolster their masculinity and power. She notes, for example:

> The electric guitar, as situated within the masculinist discourse of rock, is virtually seen as an extension of the male body. This is always implicit and sometimes explicit, as when men mime masturbating with their "axes." ... (Male) musical skills become synonymous with (male) sexual skills.[53]

Though Bayton does not state so explicitly, this particular gendering and sexualizing of the electric guitar is associated primarily with hard rock, a musical style whose sonic and performative aesthetics of power were developed in the late 1960s by such male guitarists as Jimi Hendrix and Jimmy Page. Interestingly, because of these guitarists' frequent masturbatory use of their instruments—not to mention their musical accompaniment by vocalists singing sexually explicit lyrics, as well as their social accompaniment by young women with whom they had primarily sexual relationships—the musical style they helped to create is often referred to as "cock rock."

Applying Bayton's argument about the phallic power of the electric guitar to the world of cinema, I would argue that the movie camera often serves a similar purpose, extending the male body beyond its physiological boundaries, and thus increasing the power, sexual and otherwise, that is symbolically affiliated with that body. In other words, the camera operates as what Steve Waksman (in relation to the electric guitar) has labeled a "technophallus," a device that multiplies the power of the male gaze and reaffirms men's traditional role as those in control of the recording and representation of others, particularly females.[54] Masculinity is further confirmed on movie cameras, like other technologies produced for men, through additional components, such as lenses, that make them, as Zimmerman notes, "infinitely extensible—there's always more to add, to buy, to build—linkages to 'do-it-yourself' frontierism."[55] Pushing her point even further, Zimmerman asks rhetorically, "Might one profanely suggest that these extensible machines evoke multiplicity, plurality, and are endless texts which demand endless mastery?"

The heavy weight of most film and video cameras made prior to the late 1990s contributed to the masculinization of this technology and the dearth of female cinematographers, since the lifting and carrying of heavy equipment has historically been connected with the (working-class) male body. It is disturbing, therefore, that despite reductions in the size of cameras, the masculinization of film technology has continued unabated to this day. Reproducing the historical connection between masculinity and movie cameras, while also broadening it to include film equipment produced for youth, Danish toy maker Lego released a filmmaking kit in 2000 called the Steven Spielberg

MovieMaker Set. The specific marketing of this kit to male youth is not just evident in its title, however, for its packaging design relies on dark and primary colors, as well as images of jeeps, dinosaurs, and male figures wearing hard hats.

An extension of the gendering of camera equipment, filmmaking technical discourse is male-dominated and masculine also. In order to understand this phenomenon, I turn again to feminist theorists of popular music for assistance, since to my knowledge no film scholars have studied it. As Bayton argues, for example, "technical language is often used [by men in rock scenes] as a power strategy in a mystifying way in order to exclude women."[56] Bayton's observation is confirmed by Sara Cohen, who, in her study of Liverpool's rock scene, found that "[t]he conversation within the scene's male networks … is frequently 'insider-ish,' involving nicknames, in-jokes and jargon that discourage women newcomers from joining in."[57] In other words, men maintain their control of such scenes by deploying specific cultural capital to which few women have access. Clawson's research on the formation of rock bands helps to explain such exclusionary tactics: "[T]he composition of rock bands mirrors the sex-segregated organisation of pre-teen and early adolescent social life. By using peer networks to become musicians, [boys] necessarily rely on structures of acquaintanceship that show extensive gender separation."[58] Boys maintain their authority over these homosocial groups through various tactics that reinforce their masculine identity, such as their wielding of technical jargon, as well as their performance of loud music, valorization of skill, and adoption of band names that connote power and aggression. As Bayton's and Cohen's research demonstrates, many male musicians continue to rely on these tactics well into their adult years, thus unconsciously excluding women performers from their homosocial networks.

Similar discursive and behavioral patterns occur in the various shops that rent and sell filmmaking equipment. Indeed, such stores typically are owned, managed, and operated by men, many of whom use their technical knowledge and jargon to reinforce their masculinity, bond with other men, and exclude females. This masculinization of film-oriented shops mirrors that of stores selling other technical gear, such as musical equipment. As Bayton notes, for example:

> Guitar shops are [a] "male" terrain: they rarely employ women as assistants, and the customers are overwhelmingly male. Thus boys tend to feel at home there. In any of these shops you can observe the assertive way in which young men try out the equipment.[59]

Given such an overwhelmingly male environment, girls and women often feel like trespassers in these tech-oriented spaces, as Bayton notes:

[N]early every one of my [female] interviewees said that guitar shops felt like alien territory. … Novice guitarists … reported that trying out the equipment was akin to being on trial; they were scared of showing themselves up and being "put down" by the assistants or laughed at, whilst experienced players related tales of condescension or of simply being ignored.[60]

Both Bayton and Cohen demonstrate that the exclusionary discourse used by men within male-dominated rock scenes extends to the various commercial publications that focus on the technical side of musical production. For instance, in her analysis of guitar magazines published during the late 1980s and 1990s, Bayton found that "the overwhelming majority of photos, features, and news were of male guitarists: women's presence has been absolutely minimal. … [A]ll the technical advice pages and playing advice were by men. All the covers depicted male guitarists."[61] Similarly, Cohen concludes that "trade magazines and journals … discussing the music and the technicalities of its production [are produced] for a predominantly male readership."[62]

Trade publications for filmmakers similarly masculinize the roles, technology, and practices associated with filmmaking for their predominantly male readership. A quick perusal of *American Cinematographer*'s contents over the past decade, for example, reveals the relative absence of women, except in photographs from films featuring female actors. In contrast, male cinematographers, such as Vilmos Zsigmond, Michael Chapman, and Pawel Edelman, are regularly celebrated, and camera equipment consistently fetishized. The magazine's accompanying website is similarly male-dominated.

The discursive construction of filmmakers as male and film production as masculine continues well beyond trade magazines, however. Most commercial newspapers and magazines present filmmaking from a masculinist perspective regardless of which sector of this cultural realm is discussed. For instance, despite the rise of girl directors in the 1990s, the press ignored the film and video work of most female youth during this period, while boy filmmakers received considerable attention from journalists and media critics, as well as commercial enterprises interested in capitalizing on youth-made media. For example, the press heavily promoted Harmony Korine (*Gummo*) and Matty Rich (*Straight Out of Brooklyn*) in the early 1990s, and many journalists highlighted their significance to cinema culture by presenting them as the first teenagers to write and direct feature-length films.[63] Sadie Benning was the only teenage girl to receive such notoriety during this period, yet most interest in her came from the art world, not film critics.

Journalists' construction of youth filmmaking as male-dominated has continued to manifest itself in contemporary popular discourse, despite the dramatic increase in girl directors in recent years. For example, in a 1999 article for the *Austin Chronicle* on the increase of young filmmakers, Marc Savlov focuses primarily on two twelve-year-old boy directors and constructs all young filmmakers as male through his referral to "budding Cormans and Spielbergs," a gendered discursive strategy also used by Paul Wisenthal in his *USA Today* article, "Pint-Size Producers Get Focused, Mini-Spielbergs Bloom."[64] Similarly, Jack Hitt's male bias with regard to filmmaking, as well as other cultural activities, is clear throughout his article "Film at 11 (or 12, or 13)," published in the *New York Times Magazine* in 2000: "Normally when you meet two 12-year-olds, fooling around after school with a JVC videocam, you would expect a few weeks later to discover that they had graduated to skateboards, girls or computer hacking."[65] Although skateboarding and computer hacking are not activities in which only boys participate, Hitt nevertheless relies on the stereotypical gendering of these activities as masculine, and reproduces it by mentioning "girls," thus reaffirming by association filmmaking's popular construction as a male-dominated activity. Chris Garcia of the *Austin American-Statesman* mentions several teenage girls in a 2002 article on youth filmmaking classes in Central Texas. Yet he, too, resorts to gender stereotypes when discussing young people's desires to take up filmmaking:

> With inspirations like Steven Spielberg, who shot lavish war films as a child, and local do-it-yourselfers Richard Linklater and Robert Rodriguez, plus the sudden accessibility of cameras that run as low as $400, it's less a question of "if" than "when."[66]

Echoing Savlov and Wisenthal, Garcia's (or perhaps his editor's) male perspective on youth filmmaking appears also in the secondary title of his article: "Directors: The Next Spielberg or Lucas?"

Although it may seem a stretch to connect the masculinization of youth filmmaking and young filmmakers to the male sex of the few journalists who write about these topics, it is interesting to note that the reporters who acknowledge the presence of girl directors are primarily women. Indeed, in keeping with the traditional gender dynamics of journalism, magazine and newspaper editors have typically assigned women reporters to articles about girls' media education, likely because this topic is understood to be of concern to females only.[67] In contrast to articles dealing with the larger arena of youth media education, most of articles about girls' programs not only focus on female students, but also depict these young girls in accompanying photographs, as can be seen in Julie Bourbon's "School Producing Young Filmmakers" for the *Washington Post*.[68] While such girl-centered articles make female youth in media production visible, the number of such texts still pales in comparison to those that center on boy filmmakers, a situation that leaves many girls, and their parents, with an understanding that the world of film production, even at the most amateur level, is not female-friendly.

As Bourbon's focus on the training of girl directors suggests, a final and crucial component of the gendering of filmmaking that needs further attention is the male dominance of media education both by students and instructors. As the above recollections of many women directors reveal, young women were typically discouraged from pursuing training in filmmaking prior to the late 1970s. The American Film Institute did not introduce its Directors' Workshop for Women until 1975, and many college- and graduate-level film production programs did not actively encourage female applicants until the 1980s. Indeed, film director Coolidge recalls, "When I applied to film school they told me I couldn't be a director because I was a woman."[69] More females today attend film production programs than two decades ago. Nevertheless, a recent report indicates that at the top five U.S. schools for film training—American Film Institute, Columbia University, New York University, the University of California, Los Angeles, and the University of Southern California—women comprised only 36 percent of all incoming students on average.[70] Moreover, as Anne Orwin and Adrianne Carageorge note in their study of college-level film production programs, because of the "pervasive attitude that men come to ... school already knowing how to use equipment ... [t]he isolation of women occurs fairly early in this process."[71] Since few young women were formally trained in film production prior to the 1980s, the number of older female professors who might help young women negotiate the patriarchy and sexism associated with this cultural realm is minimal at best.

Though classes in film production are offered in many U.S. public high schools today, most young people interested in filmmaking initially learn such practices on their own or with friends. From my discussions with young filmmakers over the past six years, I have noted that a considerable number of male youth take up filmmaking just as they might playing a musical instrument or joining a band, that is, through what Clawson calls "structures of acquaintanceship."[72] In other words, boys who are interested in filmmaking often seek out friends who have similar interests and equipment to share, collectively learning film technology and production practices and collaborating on each other's projects. Since such social structures often are sex segregated, particularly during early adolescence, boys' strategies for developing and maintaining such informal film training networks may unconsciously work to exclude members of the opposite sex. In turn, girls who seek out help in learning film practices from friends and family members often meet with considerable resistance. Reporting on one such young woman, journalist Katie Dean writes:

> Andi Ruane spent about a year pestering her friend's uncle, a special effects technician in the film industry, to let her "sweep his floors" so she could start learning the trade. He eventually let her work for free,

then hired her as an apprentice.... After working for him for a while, Ruane asked him why he resisted teaching her for so long. "He said it was because he didn't think a girl could do the job," said Ruane, who has worked in the film industry for the past seven years. "I proved him wrong."[73]

As administrators of schools and community centers increasingly recognize the need for contemporary youth to be visually literate, a considerable number of young people have been given the opportunity to learn filmmaking in academic and noncurricular settings. Nevertheless, these programs still tend to be dominated by male teachers and students. From my observations of mixed-sex media workshops for youth, the ratio of boys to girls is typically unbalanced, with male youth, particularly those in their mid- to late teens, dominating such programs. As discussed in Chapter 3, several media educators confirm such observations, noting that boys tend to control film technology and dominate privileged crew positions more than girls. This male domination of media education has contributed to the further naturalization of filmmaking as a masculine practice.

The historical male dominance and thus masculinizing of filmmaking roles, technology, spaces, discourse, and training have resulted in many girls having minimal desire to engage in this form of communication and creative expression. As filmmaker Allison Anders recalls, "[W]hen I was a girl I didn't know I could be a film director. In fact, I only vaguely knew what a director was. And when I did, it never occurred to me that a girl could be one."[74] Yet the reasons that many female youth do not see film as a viable format for their cultural expression entail more than the patriarchal dynamics of film production. As discussed in the Introduction, a just as significant barrier to girls' involvement in film production is their socialization as females in a society still largely structured by traditional ideologies of gender. Thus, we cannot absent from this scenario the degree to which patriarchal societies, where sex and gender continue to be conflated, encourage girls to privilege feminine attributes and female activities over all other components of identity and modes of behavior.

It is not surprising then that few commercial entities targeting female youth address this market as potential filmmakers, despite the rising number of girl directors in recent years. For example, teen magazines, the primary medium addressed specifically to girls, typically do not include articles and advertisements related to film production, though they often feature young female actors, like Brandy Norwood and Natalie Portman, as celebrity models. Advertisements for the New York Film Academy appear in recent issues of *YM* magazine; however, the only young filmmakers included in the magazine's articles about film production are male.[75] Even *Sassy*, which regularly highlighted young female zinemakers and musicians during its hey-day in the 1990s, tended to ignore filmmaking as an activity in which girls engage. An article from April 1996 featuring Miranda July's Big Miss Moviola project is one of the magazine's very few instances of acknowledging girls' filmmaking.[76] Fortunately, several local newspapers in the United States have focused on girls' media education programs and girl filmmakers in recent years; however, the extent to which young females read these articles and are inspired by them is questionable given their primary address to a middle-class adult readership.[77]

SEEN AND HEARD: THE RISE OF GIRL FILMMAKERS IN CONTEXT

Despite the numerous barriers that have historically prevented most female youth from being interested in filmmaking, recent transformations in technology, education, ideology, and youth culture have resulted in a considerable number of contemporary girls gaining access to and successfully negotiating the male-dominated world of film production. The introduction of the video camcorder in the early 1980s was enormously significant in this regard, for it freed filmmakers from many of the expensive technologies and onerous practices traditionally involved in producing movies. In addition to offering filmmakers greater mobility, video cameras do not require extensive lighting systems, and, more significantly, eliminate the need for and cost of developing film. Furthermore, video editing is less complicated and costly than film editing. Because of these unique features, camcorders replaced Super 8 film cameras as the primary filmmaking technology within most middle-class homes and film training programs by the early 1990s. As a result of recent advancements in digital technology, most contemporary video cameras are small and light enough to be easily operated by young children. Moreover, both image and sound editing can now be performed on personal computers, thus allowing young people to engage in postproduction activities for relatively minimal expense.

Another factor in the rise of girl filmmakers at the turn of the twenty-first century is the recent reconfiguration of school-based media literacy curricula into programs that combine media analysis with training in film production, as discussed in Chapter 3. A renaissance in community-based media production workshops has occurred recently also, as private sponsors, such as the John D. and Catherine T. MacArthur Foundation, and governmental agencies, like the U.S. Department of Education's Arts in Education Program, have invested in extracurricular programs designed to help bridge the "media divide." As a result of growth in these two sectors of media education, American youth today have far more access to, training in, and sustained engagement with the tools and techniques of filmmaking than ever before.

The rise of youth film production that was inspired by the introduction of the camcorder and the growth and reconfiguration of media education programs has in turn had several related effects that, because they have occurred simultaneously, have helped the development of a supportive infrastructure for young filmmakers. For example, several video cameras for children, such as Fisher-Price's Pixelvision camera and the Steven Spielberg MovieMaker Set, have been introduced in the past decade, thus helping younger children to see filmmaking as a fun hobby. Guidebooks for aspiring directors, such as Kaye Black's *Kid Vid*, have been published recently also, thereby providing youth, especially those without access to the Internet and media education programs, instructions in basic filmmaking skills.[78] In addition, a considerable number of film festivals for youth-made movies have emerged in the past decade, including Youth Media Jam, the Backyard National Children's Film Festival, the Loud and Clear Teen Film Festival, the Tower of Youth Film Festival, and the Do It Your Own Damn Self!! National Youth Video and Film Festival. In turn, several larger, adult-oriented festivals, such as the Chicago International Film Festival and the Cinematexas International Short Film Festival (via Cinemakids), now include screenings of movies made by young people. Many films shown at these festivals are picked up by the HBO Family channel, which features youth-made movies on *30 x 30: Kid Flicks*, and by the Corporation for Public Broadcasting, which screens such films on PBS's *Zoom*.

In addition to these developments in media education and youth filmmaking, the recent rise in girls' filmmaking has been greatly facilitated by transformations in sex and gender ideologies, which have in turn impacted contemporary girlhood. As discussed in the Introduction, Angela McRobbie attributes such changes to a "new *habitus* of gender relations" that has developed as a result of feminism.[79] Though many contemporary American girls continue to privilege traditional femininity, most female youth are resistant to conservative ideologies of gender that limit their options for identity and activity to the feminine realm. Since young females are now encouraged to develop qualities traditionally associated with masculinity in order to be successful in school and work, girls' interests in historically male-dominated activities are no longer seen as abnormal or at risk of subverting their female identity. In turn, the homosociality traditionally associated with early adolescent activities has begun to break down, providing girls with greater access to those structures of acquaintanceship that facilitate the development of technical knowledge and skills.

Recognizing these transformations in girls' identities and activities, several manufacturers have recently introduced products that capitalize on girls' heightened interest and engagement in filmmaking. For example, Mattel recently released the Barbie Wireless Video Camera, which works primarily as a karaoke machine. Clearly designed with stereotypical ideas about girls' tastes and cultural activities in mind, this "pink technology" is meant to lessen girls' alienation from electronic equipment by encouraging them to adopt the position of pop singer alongside that of filmmaker. The likely purchasers of such cameras, however, are parents who are socializing their daughters according to traditional ideologies of gender and thus have some anxiety over the recent expansion of girls' cultural interests into historically male-dominated activities.

Transformations in youth culture have contributed to the recent rise in girls' filmmaking also. The Riot Grrrl community has reconfigured the practices associated with girls' culture by encouraging young females to be politically and culturally active through various forms of media production. Although riot grrrls have tended to privilege music and zines as the primary means for girls' cultural expression, as demonstrated in Chapter 2, they also have inspired many female youth to pick up film and video cameras, document their lives, and tell their own stories of contemporary girlhood. Indeed, Sadie Benning, the best-known girl director to date, has indicated that her early filmmaking practices were enormously inspired by the "girl power" message spread by the Riot Grrrl movement.

The various sociocultural changes noted above have played major roles in increasing the number of contemporary girls interested in filmmaking. Yet because female youth are at the very least doubly disenfranchised as a result of their sex and age, the development of a broad support system has been necessary to sustain their girls' interest and engagement in film production. Of primary importance to this infrastructure are the many girl-centered filmmaking workshops and programs that have been introduced recently, such as Reel Grrls, Girls Film School, It's a She Shoot, and Girls Make Headlines. As discussed in Chapter 3, the development of such programs can be linked not only to the growth of the media education and grrrl power movements during the 1990s, but also, and perhaps more significantly, to the growing number of young women who have been formally trained in film production and thus understand the special needs female youth have when learning to use film technology. One particular need addressed by the women who have launched girls' media education programs is the presence of supportive mentors. Although not all girl filmmakers are trained in such programs, many female youth credit women teachers of coed programs for lighting, and keeping lit, their creative spark. For example, Alyssa Buecker, the acclaimed director of the guinea pig film series, credits Karen Dillon, her teacher at Lawrence Arts Center in Kansas, with inspiring her to make movies.[80]

The infrastructure for girls' film production has been further expanded and solidified by the young women who have attempted to inspire girl filmmakers outside the classroom. For example, Andrea Richards wrote the guidebook *Girl Director* in an effort to get more female youth to see film production as a fun, creative, and enlightening experience. Written and illustrated in a casual, spunky style, Richards's book is filled with helpful hints on filmmaking from successful women directors. The publication of this female-written and -centered book demonstrates a shift in the predominantly male-dominated realm of guidebooks in media production. As film director and producer Yvonne Welbon suggests:

> [h]aving the information out there helps to create the possibility for young girls to think about being filmmakers. ... This will hopefully make it possible for a young girl to think about being a director of photography or a gaffer or a writer or a producer.[81]

Like many of the young women who are involved in girls' media education, Richards believes that learning about women directors, being educated in the tools and practices of filmmaking, and making movies can substantially enrich girls' lives:

> Part of what I wanted to do with the book was to demystify the process of filmmaking in general, to make it extremely accessible by encouraging girls to make films by any means necessary. ... Filmmaking doesn't have to be a huge production that is limited to an elite group of artists or Hollywood moguls. It can be just as easy as putting out a zine. Which led me to wonder why girls aren't doing more of it ... especially today's girls, who are far more comfortable with technology and have easier access to tools ... than girls of my generation did. So from the beginning, the book was about empowering girls to pick up cameras and have both the know-how and the confidence to call the shots.[82]

In true girl power spirit, Richards acknowledges that her writing of *Girl Director* was about taking direct action and encouraging girls to do the same. As the introduction to her book states:

> Yeah, you ought to be in pictures—making them, that is. ... So are you going to be a couch potato your whole life, watching other people's stories, or are you ready to take charge and put something of your own on the screen? By making a movie, you can show your perspective on a story, a song, an idea, the world, whatever. So, girl director, why not take your place on the set? We're all waiting.[83]

In contrast to their commercial counterparts, several alternative teen magazines have attempted to inspire girls' interest in filmmaking also. For example, *New Moon*, a teen-produced girls' magazine, published an interview in its May–June 1999 issue with independent filmmaker Julie Dash (*Illusions*, *Daughters of the Dust*) that includes tips for aspiring screenwriters.[84] The magazine's November–December 2002 issue features a story by members of the girl-run editorial board about their trip to Hollywood.[85] Though their tour largely focused on commercial television production and visits with female actors, the girls also met with producer Jane Hartwell and were able to share their views on cinematic representations of girlhood.

Another important component of the infrastructure that supports young female directors is girl-centered film festivals. In 2003, the San Diego Women Film Foundation launched the first all-girls' film festival in history: the San Diego Girl Film Festival. Though this festival does not screen films made only by female youth, it is girl-centered. As stated in the festival's promotional literature:

> Through an all girl film festival featuring films about young women created by women of all ages, we will provide many opportunities for the women film producers and directors to act as mentors helping guide the next generation of female youth into leadership roles. The film festival helps young filmmakers gain exposure and experience within their field, propelling their careers forward.[86]

To my knowledge, only two adult-oriented film festivals have included programs devoted specifically to girls' movies. Women in the Director's Chair, a Chicago-based annual festival, regularly packages girls' films in its Media Girls Tour, a traveling program that has been screened in cities across the United States. The DocSide Short Film Festival included a special girl program in 2000.[87] The fifteen documentaries included in that program are now available in a compilation video, *Smashing the Myth (or Not Just White, Rich, and Dangerously Thin)*, which is distributed by Listen Up!, a national network of youth media organizations.[88] Featured at the Sundance Institute's Gen-Y Studio in 2001, this compilation has brought much recognition to the girl directors whose films are included in it.

In addition to Listen Up!, other enterprises have emerged with the specific goal of distributing girls' movies beyond their creators' small circle of friends and family members. Founded in 2001, SheFilms.org was developed to be a continuous online short film festival showcasing films directed by female youth. According to its executive director, Kettia Ming, the organization's goal was to encourage girls to see filmmaking as an option: "We know that teenage girls can do more than apply make-up and idolize celebrities. ... SheFilms.org provides girls with a venue to tap into the depth of creativity and intelligence that they're more than capable of."[89] Now defunct, SheFilms.org once offered via its website filmmaking tips and information on women directors for aspiring young female filmmakers.

As discussed in more detail in Chapter 2, Big Miss Moviola (now Joanie 4 Jackie) is an independent distribution service for female-produced films that was created in 1995 by filmmaker and performance artist Miranda July.

To date, Big Miss Moviola has distributed over one hundred films made by teenage girls and young women on twelve different compilation tapes. The project's website serves as an alternate marketplace for the selling of the tapes, as well as a public forum for communication between its featured filmmakers and other female youth interested in media production.[90]

These various initiatives, which were specifically designed to increase young females' interest and involvement in filmmaking, have contributed to more girls producing movies than at any other point in U.S. history. Inspired and sustained by a broad and stable infrastructure that supports and promotes their work, many contemporary girl directors have won prizes at film festivals, formed their own production companies, and received contracts for future work from powerful entertainment enterprises. Given such success and the fact that most of these girls have expressed a strong interest in having a career in film production, a study of the movies made while they were young seems in order. Moreover, close analyses of these films help to shed light on girl directors' interests, pleasures, and fears, as well as their relationship to the commercial media industries whose portrayals of girlhood have dominated the American cultural landscape for many decades.

AN UNFORMED FIELD: STUDYING GIRLS' FILMS

The burgeoning field of girl-made movies presents several problems for scholars wanting to study such texts. Most significantly, despite the recent increase in girl directors, filmmaking is not yet practiced by as great a number of female youth as other forms of media production, such as zinemaking. As a result, the current pool of girls' films is not large enough to make arguments about such texts' common narrative and aesthetic styles, if indeed such similarities exist. Nevertheless, some tentative comments about girls' movies can be made that might help us to begin a critical study of this unique group of cultural texts.

Girls' films appear in all forms that currently define the larger field of cinema, including narrative, documentary, and experimental, as well as live action and animation. In turn, many female youth have experimented with televisual forms, particularly the music video, news magazine, and public service announcement (PSA). With the exception of 35mm and 16mm film, which are far too expensive and unwieldy for most young filmmakers, girls' movies have been made in virtually all cinematic formats currently available: Super 8 film; VHS, Hi8, and digital video; and computer animation. Since contemporary female youth have the most access to analog and digital video, most girls' films currently in circulation appear in one of these formats. Some older female adolescents have produced films that are fifteen to thirty minutes long; however, most girl-made movies are under five minutes in length. The short duration of the majority of girls' films is primarily due to their creators' minimal filmmaking experience, access to resources, and disposable time. In addition, the privileging of the PSA as a pedagogic and social tool by media educators and funding agencies has lead to the dominance of girls' film culture by these extremely short texts, which are usually thirty to sixty seconds long.

The form a girl's film takes is often linked to her socioeconomic status, and thus the material conditions of her media education and filmmaking practices. For example, middle-class and older female youth typically learn about media production in schools or in workshops paid for by their parents, and often have access to their parents' or their own filmmaking equipment. These girls tend to work individually or in very small groups that privilege the role of the director, a situation that mirrors the traditional class-based stereotype of the autonomous artist, as well as the hierarchical structure of commercial filmmaking. The girls mentioned at the beginning of this chapter—Sadie Benning, Alyssa Buecker, Emily Hagins, and the YaYa Productions team—are good examples of young female filmmakers in this category.

In contrast, most working-class and younger girls tend to learn about filmmaking in free or low-cost community-based media workshops, like as Project Chrysalis and Skyline Youth Producers, since their parents cannot afford, do not want to finance, or do not feel their daughters are fully committed to fee-based programs. In turn, schools in poor districts often do not provide training in filmmaking, particularly at the elementary and middle-school levels. Girl directors in this second category typically share filmmaking equipment and work collaboratively with each other, as evidenced by the multiple individuals who are credited for the same crew role (e.g., director, cinematographer, editor) in their films. These different conditions of media education and filmmaking often result in poor and younger girls creating films that involve a large ensemble of actors or real subjects, and middle-class and older girls producing films that contain very few characters.

Class-based tastes seem to impact the style and content of girls' movies also. For instance, many media programs designed for middle-class youth, such as Center for Young Cinema, tend to steer their students toward narrative and experimental films, thus continuing the individualist perspective and formalist approach historically privileged in upper-class culture and the fine arts. In contrast, community-based workshops for disadvantaged youth, such as Educational Video Center, encourage students to represent themselves and their communities as authentically as possible so as to counter media stereotypes. Girls in these latter workshops typically coproduce documentaries and, to a lesser extent, narrative films informed by social realism, and thus reinforce the collective perspective and realist aesthetic privileged in working-class culture and activist media.[91] (It is important to note that none of the characteristics mentioned to this point is specific to films produced by girls;

rather they define youth-made movies in general. In other words, sex and gender do not play a role in these various traits.)

Girls' movies, while generally categorizable as documentary, narrative, or experimental, have yet to evolve and subdivide into discernible genres. Despite the difficulty this phenomenon poses to the study of girls' films, one possible starting point for determining how such films differ from those made by women (with whom girls share a sex category) and those made by boys (with whom girls share an age category) is the relationship of such texts to their creators' identities. The discursive approach to identity and authorship advocated by Richard Dyer (discussed in detail in Chapter 4) is useful in this regard.[92] Moreover, by combining Dyer's theory with that of Wendy Hollway,[93] we can argue that girl filmmakers have the most access to and investment in those discourses made available to them "on account of who they are."[94] Girl directors have multiple identities in which they can invest, and not all are related to demographic categories, like age and race. Nevertheless, many girl directors seem interested in using their films to explore sex and gender, even if they do not do so explicitly. In other words, "girl" is the discursive location from which these young filmmakers feel they have the most authority to express and represent themselves. Not surprisingly, a recent increase in the number of girls of color and young lesbians who make movies has resulted in a concurrent rise in the number of girls' films that specifically address the construction of gender and generation in relation to race, ethnicity, and sexuality. It is interesting to note, therefore, how strongly girlhood is foregrounded in the movies made by these young directors who typically do not have the privilege of isolating sex and gender from the other components of their identity.

Just as Dyer notes that queer filmmakers have access to a specific set of discourses as a result of their involvement in gay and lesbian cultures, girls' films reveal young females' access to particular discourses in relation to the social formation that most solicits their engagement: commercial girls' culture. Yet most girl directors are not interested in reproducing the media stereotype of female youth as boy-obsessed, appearance-oriented shopaholics, and thus indicate their resistance to, if not subversion of, this cliché in their texts. In fact, girl directors often radically reconfigure the formulaic discourses and representational strategies relied upon by the entertainment industries to represent girlhood. Thus, another approach that scholars can use to study girls' movies is examining how these texts form a dialogic relationship with, and often a critique of, media texts produced for girls by the commercial media industries, especially teen magazines and movies. Before engaging in such a study, however, we must first consider the common narrative tropes and discursive strategies used to represent girlhood in commercial media, for they can help to explain the particular images and issues female youth attempt to negotiate in their own films.

Reacting largely to the American public's fascination with teenage girls during World War II, the U.S. film industry first produced a large number of girl-centered movies during the 1940s. Films like *Janie, Junior Miss, Kiss and Tell, A Date with Judy,* and *Miss Annie Rooney* introduced many of the narrative and representational conventions now associated with Hollywood's female teenpics: a white, heterosexual, upper-middle-class high-school-age female protagonist in a comedic "coming-of-age" plot that revolves around the girl's pursuit of an intimate relationship as well as her involvement in some scheme that causes both domestic disruption and romantic conflict.[95] These early female teenpics depicted girl protagonists and their friends wearing trendy fashions and hairstyles, mouthing the latest teenage jargon, and engaging in activities newly associated with teenage girls, yet still strongly affiliated with femininity, such as babysitting and gossiping on the telephone. In keeping with the sociocultural climate in which they were made, such films also reproduced traditional ideologies of female subjectivity by commenting continuously on girls' future roles as wives and mothers.

Despite the broad diffusion of feminist ideologies since the early 1970s, many contemporary girl-centered films produced by Hollywood continue to construct teenage girls according to these conventions. Commercial teen magazines, the primary media texts targeting female youth, have followed suit. Still shaped by patriarchal capitalist ideologies, such periodicals consistently privilege feminine appearance, encouraging girls to surveil their bodies, find imperfections, and purchase products to overcome these problems, all with the goal of attracting heterosexual male attention. Historically, white female youth performing an upper-middle-class heterosexual identity have dominated these texts. Since the early 1990s, teen magazine publishers and the advertisers that support them have attempted to attract more Latina, Asian, and African American readers by featuring darker skinned girls of ambiguous racial identity. At the same time, however, lesbian and working-class female youth continue to be marginalized, if not ignored, in these texts.

As a result of the popularity of *Sassy*'s feminist address among teenage girls in the late 1980s and early 1990s, several alternative teen magazines were introduced in the mid- to late 1990s, including *Teen Voices, Empowered,* and *blue jean magazine.* Together with girls' zines, these periodicals have helped to expand the discursive and representational strategies used to portray girlhood, primarily by depriviliging beauty and heterosexual romance while also featuring girls of different races, classes, and sexualities. Somewhat concurrent with the introduction of alternative magazines for female youth, the number of independent films about nonconformist teenage girls rose substantially, likely due to an increase in female and feminist screenwriters, directors, and producers since the mid-1980s. *Foxfire, All Over Me, Girls Town,* and *The Incredibly True Story of Two Girls in Love,* for example, all subordinate boys and romance, foregrounding instead girls' development of same-sex friendships.[96] Such films reveal a significant transformation in the world of girl-centered cinema. Though typically featuring white girls as protagonists, by including young lesbians, girls of color, and working-class female youth, these films have helped to expand the representation of girlhood far beyond its traditional boundaries. Since many of these films (and their directors) have been featured in girls' zines and teen magazines, their widespread promotion has helped to inspire female youth who resist traditional representations of girlhood to pick up cameras and tell their own stories.

ESTABLISHING THE GIRL'S GAZE: EXPLORING IDENTITY IN GIRL-MADE MOVIES

Female Beauty Standards and Body Image

Given the overwhelming amount of attention paid to physical appearance in commercial media texts targeting female youth, it is not surprising that the primary topics framing a considerable number of girls' films are female beauty standards and body image problems. Lillian Ripley's *What if Barbie Had a Voice?* innovatively uses a Barbie doll to foreground these issues.[97] The film begins with a white teenage girl considering her reflection in a full-length mirror. Disgusted with herself for obsessing about her appearance, the girl throws her white, blonde-haired Barbie in a trash can. In the animated sequence that follows, the naked Barbie climbs out of the can and similarly surveils herself in the mirror. After donning jeans and a t-shirt, she covers her conventional makeup with a black marker and cuts her mouth open with a pair of scissors so that she can unleash her voice. Ending with the question, "Would Barbie reject herself?" the film cleverly draws attention to the connections between commercial girls' culture, female beauty standards, and girls' difficulties with assertiveness.

Barbie, by Anna Bulley and Katie McCord, also critiques Mattel's popular doll.[98] This short film begins with a traditionally attired blonde Barbie telling viewers that a dangerous epidemic of girls' high self-esteem must be stopped. Her mission?: To remind girls that "life will go easier if you just conform." The film then shows in quick succession multiple Barbies that subvert the doll's conventional feminine image: Butch Barbie, who plays basketball and wears a pair of cut-off shorts and a t-shirt bearing a purple triangle (a symbol associated with gay and lesbian pride); Greenpeace Barbie, who watches dolphins at the beach; Gothic Barbie, who appears sullen in her black attire; and Rave Rat Barbie, who has wild hair and colorful clothing and dances passionately.[99] By putting Mattel's dolls through several unconventional makeovers, the filmmakers demonstrate their rejection of commercial girls' culture and conventional beauty standards, as well as their interest in exploring alternate identities.

Several other girl-made movies similarly connect girls' negative opinions about themselves to dominant female beauty standards, while also encouraging female youth to reject the idealized images offered them in commercial popular culture. For example, both Kat Bauman's *Barbie Resized*[100] and Project Chrysalis's *Fight Girl Poisoning*[101] use animated images cut from teen magazines to demonstrate the inhuman body dimensions of Barbie dolls and fashion models. Similarly, participants in the Girls Making Headlines 2000 workshop created an animation sequence for their larger news magazine that demonstrates the young filmmakers' resistance to Britney Spears, a white pop star who was promoted heavily during the late 1990s and early 2000s, especially in commercial media texts directed toward girls.[102] Spears is critiqued also in *Silicone Bone*, which was made by a group of students at the Girls Film School.[103] This film features a montage of celebrity and fashion model photographs from commercial magazines that are juxtaposed with live-action scenes of a girl rubbing her stomach, shaving her legs, curling her eyelashes, brushing her hair, and trying to put on tight jeans (Figure 13). It ends with "[T]hanks to Britney Spears for giving us all something to compare ourselves to," thus calling out the pop star for her investment in and uncritical reproduction of beauty standards that the majority of girls can never hope to achieve.

In addition to girls' magazines, dolls, and pop stars, other forms of commercial media culture are actively critiqued in films produced by female youth. For example, in a parody of the television series, *Baywatch*, Emily Vissette

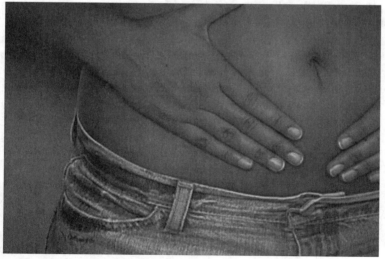

Figure 13 Critiquing female beauty culture.
Silicone Bone, 2004. Courtesy of Girls Film School™.

explicitly comments on the sexual objectification of young female bodies in prime-time television. Reconfiguring the primary text's title as *Baywatch Babes ... or Not*, Vissette's video depicts her racially diverse group of friends playfully striking fashion model poses on a beach.[104] Avoiding the conventions of the television show, however, the film's presentation of the girls' bodies does not suggest their passive fetishization for male spectators. Instead, it highlights their agency and assertiveness, ending with a bold address to female youth at large: "Be Great, Be Strong, and Be You." By appropriating and reconfiguring a popular media text for her film's content, Vissette challenges viewers familiar with *Baywatch* to reflect critically on the sexualized young women who are privileged in U.S. commercial culture.

Several girls' films specifically critique commercial teen magazines for reproducing unhealthy beauty standards for female youth. In *Listen to Your Angel*, a short film made by Leah Ruthrauff and Miquela Suazo, two white adolescent girls are shown perusing a teen magazine.[105] After looking through its pages, one girl states that she thinks she needs to diet, while her friend insists that she looks fine. In order to display how female youth are conflicted over this issue, the filmmakers insert into this image small frames of an angel who suggests the girl looks fine as she is and a devil who suggests she should lose weight. By using this conventional filmmaking strategy to represent the struggle between good and evil, the directors allow viewers to quickly associate girls' problems with their body image with commercial popular culture. Moreover, by foregrounding the relationship between girlfriends, *Listen to Your Angel* suggests that female youth should turn to people, specifically other females, rather than media texts for support and affirmation.

Body Rhapsody, made by Sina Gedlu, Louisa Jackson, Marianne Maksirisombat, and Emily Zisette, reworks the lyrics and music video images of Queen's "Bohemian Rhapsody" to comment directly on commercial magazines' repetitive messages of self-surveillance and weight loss.[106] The video begins with an image of a white adolescent girl reading a fashion magazine on her bed. On the soundtrack, a girl sings, "Mama, just weighed myself / Wanna put a gun against my head / *Cosmo* says I'm overfed / Mama, diet's just begun / And now I've got to get off all this weight." After perusing the magazine's images of beautiful women, the girl evaluates herself in the mirror and is disgusted by what she sees. This scene is followed by a quadruply split-screen image of three girls singing to the first vocalist, mimicking directly a shot in the music video produced to promote Queen's song: "Too bad you feel this way / Sends shivers down my spine / Watching your body weight decline." As if hearing and responding to the other voices, the girl who surveils her figure picks up a hammer and shatters the mirror. Adding to the power of this image, the first vocalist sings, "Goodbye, body image / You've got to go / Gotta leave that all behind / And face the truth." The film ends with the smashed mirror's reflection of the girl flexing her arm, an image meant to signify her recovered power. It is important to note that the girl's increased sense of self-worth and agency are reinforced in this video through Queen's hard rock sound, Brian May's loud, distorted guitar chords redeployed here as a metaphor for girl power.

I Am Beautiful, by Jennifer Sugg, also explores the connection of commercial magazines and girls' negative body image.[107] In this movie, a white teenage girl is shown cutting out images of models from a fashion magazine, which she then pastes to her mirror for ease of comparison with her own body. Intercut between these images are close-ups of a scale and the girl jogging, as Marilyn Manson's rock song, "Beautiful People," plays loudly on the soundtrack: "Hey you, what do ya see? / Something beautiful, something free?"[108] Though it ends much like Body Rhapsody, with the girl smashing the mirror, I Am Beautiful goes one step further in showing a girl destroying her cosmetics, thus highlighting the relationship of the commercial publishing and beauty industries and sending a message that female youth should reject both.

Several other films made by female youth comment on girls' body image problems and critique commercial beauty culture without direct references to specific media texts or celebrities. For example, in Mirror, a PSA made by Alix Brown, a white teenage girl is depicted applying makeup to her face, while at the bottom of the screen, a caption reads, "The feminine mystique has succeeded in burying millions of women alive. What are you getting ready for?"[109] Drawing a connection between being obliterated ("buried alive") and applying excessive cosmetics, this short film also comments on how girls' beautification projects are motivated by the desire to attract heterosexual male attention. Beauty Marks, by Tess Jubran, also foregrounds the dangers of female beauty standards.[110] The film begins as a fictional television talk show featuring a white young female host who shares her beauty secrets with viewers. As the host comments on applying makeup, brushing hair, taking care of her body, finding appropriate clothes, and improving her self-confidence, her statements are subverted through scenes of a white teenage girl accidentally sticking an eyeliner pencil in her eye, pulling out hair with her brush, bingeing on fast food, trying on different pairs of tight jeans, and throwing up in a toilet. Jubran foregrounds the superficiality of the host's statements by shooting her scenes in color, while the more realistic scenarios depicting the hazards of beauty regimes are shot in black and white. Playing off the joke about beauty trends suggested in its title, the film ends with the caption, "Beauty should not leave permanent marks."

Girl Power, made by students in Project Chrysalis, is a compilation of short animations, many of which address girls' troubled body image and rejection of commercial beauty culture.[111] For example, a simple hand-drawn animation sequence shows a girl standing in front of a mirror. As the girl criticizes her appearance—"You're too fat," "Your eyes are too small," and "You have a big nose"—her reflection grows larger and more distorted. Eventually, the girl shouts, "No!" and the mirror cracks into pieces that fall on the floor, thereby suggesting her freedom from the body surveillance required by beauty culture. Another animated sequence in *Girl Power* begins with an illustration of a voluptuous blonde woman in a tight red bikini. As the image recedes into the background, an illustration of a white teenage girl with short hair wearing a sweat suit appears. Looking at the woman's image, the girl says, "Is that supposed to be me? Yeah, right!"

Far less positive about these issues, Ilana Urbach's *Prufrock and Me* comments on the alienation some teenage girls feel as a result of their appearance.[112] This narrative film focuses on a white adolescent girl who is disappointed in her large body size and its effects on her interpersonal relationships. Interestingly, scenes depicting the girl's everyday reality of loneliness and self-loathing are shot in black and white, while segments representing the girl's daydreams about what her life would be like if she were thin (e.g., having a boyfriend and several girlfriends) are shot in color. Through its realistic depiction of the difficulties faced by larger-sized female youth in a fat-phobic society, as well as its use of fantasy sequences to explore desires to be popular and physically appealing, *Prufrock and Me* poignantly demonstrates girls' struggles with the ideals of heterosexual femininity and their effects on self-worth and happiness.

Body Image, by Mieko Krell, uses the conventions of documentary filmmaking to raise awareness about girls' different relations to and strategies for negotiating dominant beauty standards.[113] For example, a white, thin girl who admits to weighing only 101 pounds discusses how she began dieting at a very young age due to her involvement in ballet, as well as her investment in popular culture messages about being thin. This segment is poignantly juxtaposed with an interview of a medium-sized African American girl who comments on how the commercial media reproduce the female ideal as white, blonde, and thin, and how girls like her are virtually invisible because of their race and body shape. In a provocative scene that suggests her self-confidence and power, this girl is shown walking assertively down a school hallway. By focusing on female youth of different races and sizes, *Body Image* refuses to generalize girls and their difficulties, foregrounding instead the relationship of identity and culture to girls' self-esteem and cultural visibility. As one of the very few girls' films to address how beauty standards and body image problems are racially specific, *Body Image* is a significant contribution to the growing body of girl-made movies.

Given that participants in girls-only media education programs are often encouraged by their instructors to critically assess the representation of girls and women in commercial media culture, the fact that so many girl directors use their films to explore topics like beauty standards and body image is not surprising. As noted in Chapter 3, the women educators who teach such programs intentionally facilitate their students' development of critical viewing skills so that they can better understand commercial media texts targeting their demographic and be more discerning in their entertainment choices. As the Reel Grrls website states, "As media play such an influential role in our global society, we believe that if women and girls are to achieve equality and advancement in today's world they must be taught to be media literate."[114] Diane Zander of Girls Making Headlines notes similar goals for the program she helped to design:

> We talked [with students] about what it means to be a girl: how the media treats girls, what challenges and conflicts there are. We talked a lot about these ideas because the content of this class was foremost—that the girls emerge with a critical sense of what their identity as a girl means for themselves personally and for the culture in general.[115]

More significantly perhaps, these programs facilitate their students' movement from media analysis to media production, often using the same girl-centered materials (e.g., teen magazines, Barbie dolls) to engage female youth in both processes. As the promotional discourse for Reel Grrls states, "We believe that it is important to give young women the skills to critically evaluate the media they are exposed to and then to empower them to produce their own media."[116] Similarly, Zander recalls:

> We wanted [the girls'] projects to reflect the content issues we had discussed in the classes. We encouraged reflection on how girls are represented now and how these girls want to be represented. This manifested itself in a number of ways with each group: appropriating traditional images and making them into subversive images in the animation, going out on the street to ask questions, finding girls who are making alternative media, and representing their own process of creating something different. This felt like a natural outgrowth of the class, rather than something being imposed on them.[117]

As the objectives of both Reel Grrls and Girls Making Headlines reveal, many of the young women who have organized girls-only media education programs consider reflection on female identity and media representation a crucial step in the development of girls' critical consciousness about both gender and commercial media culture, and encourage their students to continue this process in their creative practices. These single-sex programs provide a safe space for girls to reflect critically on their relationship to female beauty

culture, while also offering a supportive environment for creatively expressing the negative emotions and social consequences they experience when they
fail to achieve the standards set by that culture.

Sex and Gender Identity

Though many girl directors use the topics of beauty standards and body image
to critically assess what it means to be female in contemporary U.S. society,
others use different discursive frameworks when exploring their sex and
gender identity. For instance, some young female filmmakers demonstrate
a strong interest in celebrating women and female-specific activities. *Video
Icons*, a collection of short films about powerful women produced by students
in the 2003 Reel Grrls program, is a good example.[118] Interestingly, these films
focus on a wide variety of such women, including female artists, such as the
poet Sappho and artist Frida Kahlo, female spiritual figures, like the goddesses
Isis and Demeter, and contemporary female celebrities, such as basketball star
Sheryl Swoopes and singer Aaliyah Dana Haughton. By claiming these various
women as role models, the filmmakers demonstrate their interest in connecting female identity with talent, power, and expressive creativity. Another film
celebrating female power is Theresa Benkman and Leela Townsley's *What if
Men Menstruated?*[119] Rather than foregrounding strong women, however, this
humorous short film features male action figures engaging in various male-
dominated activities, such as football, wrestling, and military combat, while
menstruating. By connecting this sex-specific condition with activities and
dolls that connote strength and courage, the filmmakers subvert the conventional constructions of females as weak and vulnerable and of menstruation
as a condition that precludes physical activity.

In contrast to *Video Icons* and *What if Men Menstruated?*, most girls'
films that explore females in U.S. society reveal a somewhat negative perspective. For example, Ryan Davis's short film, *Girls*, uses the strategy of *détournement* to comment upon advertising culture's perpetuation of traditional
feminine behavior.[120] Juxtaposing documentary images of women's domestic
behavior in the 1950s with contemporary television commercials showing
women grocery shopping, housecleaning, and caring for children, Davis's film
makes a poignant statement on how advertising continues to privilege wom-
en's domesticity above their other activities and identities. Driving this point
home further, the film incorporates the Beastie Boys' song, "Girls" ("Girls—to
do the dishes / Girls—to clean up my room / Girls—to do the laundry"), yet
purposely distorts the sound of the male singer's voice, thereby suggesting the
filmmaker's resistance to and power over such discourse.[121]

Several girls' films have focused specifically on the behavior expected of
females in traditional heterosexual relationships to comment on patriarchal

ideologies of gender. Tricia Grashaw's *The Ultimate Guide to Flirting*, for example, uses parody to illustrate the ludicrous gender display girls are encouraged to adopt in heterosexual dating rituals.[122] In this silent film, two white adolescent girls happen upon a guide for flirting in a commercial teen magazine, and begin practicing the techniques described in order to improve their attractiveness to the opposite sex. When the girls eventually try out their new flirting skills on a group of white teenage boys, they are immediately rejected as annoying. The parodic, exaggerated, and somewhat unruly facial expressions and body movements of the two female characters, not to mention the nonnormative appearance of the actors playing them, demonstrate the filmmaker's active resistance to the heterosexualized discourse of teen magazines that encourages girls to manipulate their bodies and behavior in order to attract boys.

Another girls' film that critiques the feminine behavior female youth are encouraged to exhibit to attract male attention is *Tomboygirl* by Candice Yoo.[123] Created in Japanese anime style, this short animation tells the tale of a girl who exhibits masculine qualities when socializing with her girlfriends. At a coed party, however, one of her friends hears the "tomboy" giggling like a little girl, trying to gain the attention of the boys in the room (Figure 14). In foregrounding the friend's surprise at this radical transformation, *Tomboygirl* draws attention to the painful period many adolescent girls experience as they

Figure 14   Losing girlfriends to boys and feminine display.
Tomboygirl, 2002. Courtesy of Reach LA.

are encouraged to withdraw from their girlfriends and to do all they can to attract members of the opposite sex.

Other girl filmmakers explore what it means to be female in U.S. society by focusing on how sexism and misogyny affect the lives of many girls and women. For example, a considerable number of PSAs produced by girls are about date rape and sexual abuse, as can be seen in *Love Shouldn't Hurt* by Tamara Garcia, *It's Never OK* by Arielle Davis, and *No More Silence* by Cassie Reeder, Kim Phillips, Natalie Camavati, and Kelly Rolfes.[124] A more humorous take on sexism, Natasha Norton's *Now You Know How We Feel* uses role reversal to demonstrate the negative effects of sexual harassment. In this film, several white girls use cat calls and bodily groping to sexually objectify a white teenage boy, thus encouraging male viewers to identify with the victim and to consider their own role in perpetuating the mistreatment of females.[125] Tenzin Tingkhye's *What Would Your Family Do?* moves sexual abuse discourse beyond its conventional framework of males versus females by including ethnicity and intergenerational dynamics in the discussion.[126] Focusing on several Asian girls, the film foregrounds the difficulty such female youth have telling socially conservative parents about their experiences of sexual harassment and violence.

In *Pushing Back the Limits*, Ashli and Callie Pfeiffer and Maggie and Sabrina Kelley explore how female roles in patriarchal society have changed over time.[127] The film's central character is a nineteenth-century white immigrant girl who is alienated from her family, exiled from her community, and eventually killed as a result of her interests in writing. Commenting on the positive effects of the feminist movement, the film ends with a scene of a contemporary white girl perusing a bookstore and finding many texts written by women. The filmmakers' most poignant message about transformations in girlhood over the past hundred years, however, is their creation of the film itself, a message that is driven home in the credits, which include multiple images of the girl directors in action.

Focusing on the complexity of gender identity for contemporary girls and women, Lauren Dowdall's *Femininity*[128] is a visual portrait of Bruno Bettelheim's theory of how girls are "raised in contradiction."[129] Noting how patriarchal ideologies of gender encourage females to be weak, passive, vulnerable, and "impossibly beautiful," Dowdall explores the daily struggle she faces in trying to balance those feminine attributes with her desire to be strong, in control, a leader, and athletic. As she argues, her desires and goals are often subverted by others' expectations for her to be fully feminine. For example, her strength is questioned when others expect her to show weakness. Though *Femininity* does not explore it, this balancing act is one that is perhaps experienced most by middle-class female youth, who are encouraged to display characteristics long associated with masculinity in order to be successful in the male-dominated public sphere, while also being expected to perfect a feminine appearance so as not to be too threatening.

Although Dowdall's film helps to expand girl directors' exploration of female gender identity beyond traditional femininity, several other young female filmmakers have produced movies that reveal a much stronger interest in exploring girls' performances of masculinity and engagement in male-dominated activities. For example, *Pick Me*, a short animation by Stephanie Dunn, focuses on her experiences of playing on a co-ed soccer team, and relates the difficulties girls have in being seen as legitimate and worthy when competing with boys in sports.[130] The last player picked for her local soccer team, Stephanie recalls how she amazed her male teammates by kicking a goal: "All the boys are like, 'Man, she can do *so* good at soccer.'" Rather than presenting her achievement in this male-dominated game as problematic for her identity as a girl, Stephanie's film includes a photograph of her smiling broadly while in voiceover she basks in her success: "I'm the bomb. ... I felt so incredibly happy about myself."

Several films made by young lesbians have focused more explicitly on girls' displays of masculinity outside the public realms that legitimize such behavior, like sports. *Are You a Boy or a Girl?*, by Taizet Hernandez, is one of the few girl-made films that explores the real life gender-bending of a young female.[131] In this short documentary, Hernandez discusses in first person the various social spaces where her sex is questioned because of her male attire and masculine traits, particularly sex-specific spaces, like women's restrooms and locker rooms. In turn, she describes the discomfort her masculine appearance and behavior cause her family, and the regret she feels as a result of not interacting with her dying grandfather because of her gender-bent identity.

Ana Lopez's *Looks Like a Girl* is another girls' film that raises the visibility of young lesbians while also exploring their nonconformist gender performances.[132] Focusing specifically on the differences between what she calls "fem" and "stud" identities in young lesbian culture, Lopez highlights the ways in which these girls negotiate the traditional connotations of masculinity and femininity. In fact, the documentary's young lesbians reveal their awareness of how their gender identity can be misinterpreted as reinscribing oppressive gender roles, even by members of the queer community.

Unlike these young lesbian documentarists, most heterosexual girl directors explore masculinity only through the realm of fantasy, often using sex-based role reversals as a means of presenting girls' masculine displays in a familiar, and thus less threatening, way. Such films do not comment directly on conventional representations of female youth; nevertheless, they implicitly critique the commercial film industry, whose products repeatedly suggest that girls and women are not powerful and must be saved by men. For example, by reversing the sex of the victim and the psychokiller in its short horror narrative,

Emily Vissette's *Scary Movie Spot* overturns the cinematic stereotype of passive female youth, particularly in the slasher genre.[133] Similarly, Cesy Urbina's *I Popped His Cherry* makes a comment on the conventional gender roles of teenpics in its reversal of the typical female virgin/male "player" dynamic.[134] Placing a girl in the position of the aggressive sexual hunter, the film critiques the double standard of promiscuous male sexuality and virginal girlhood commonly reproduced in commercial media texts. Ginny Habereder's film, *Paybax*, explores the reversal of gender norms by focusing on a small and nonaggressive teenage boy who is harassed by other male youth until he finds a girlfriend who is stronger than all of them.[135] Rather than entertain girls' physical displays of masculinity, as Urbina's, Vissette's, and Habereder's films do, *The Sensible Girl*, by Elizabeth Mims, locates such gender performance in communication practices.[136] A short narrative film about an overly assertive, sometimes aggressive, young woman named Mary, *The Sensible Girl* uses comedy and melodramatic performances to explore the power struggles in an unconventionally gendered heterosexual relationship. Though spectators are encouraged to empathize with Mary's passive, do-gooder boyfriend, in light of the many negative depictions of female youth in commercial cinema, it is likely that many girl viewers find this self-confident young female character refreshing.

A Story of Hope, by Meghan Baker, Adriana Medine, Kimani Nagurski, and Julia Wells, combines themes in both *Paybax* and *Scary Movie Spot* in a parody of early twentieth-century melodramas and contemporary superhero blockbusters.[137] Silent and shot primarily in black and white, the film centers on three girls who encounter an evil Irish prairie dog during a walk in the country. The girls are initially feminized in the film through their costuming and names (Iris, Grace, and Petunia), and the viewer is led to believe that the dog will easily kill them. At the last minute, however, the girls transform into superheroes, replete with black t-shirts emblazoned with the symbols of Spiderman, Superman, and Batman, and save themselves and others by killing the dog. Like many other girls' films that employ fantasy narratives, the conclusion appears in color. As narrative texts, *Paybax*, *Scary Movie Spot*, *I Popped His Cherry*, *The Sensible Girl*, and *A Story of Hope* demonstrate that, given the dearth of images of powerful female youth in commercial media culture, heterosexual girl directors must often resort to fiction and placing girls in roles and activities historically dominated by males in order to represent girl power. By featuring young female characters who are more powerful than male peers and monsters, these fictional films reveal their creators' desire to explore forms of agency perhaps not available to them in their everyday lives. Meanwhile, movies made by young lesbians, such as *Are You a Boy or a Girl?* and *Looks Like a Girl*, provide poignant, real-life stories of queer youth struggling with heterosexual gender norms, thus helping to expand the spectrum of girls' media representations and American girlhood beyond their conventional boundaries.

Interpersonal Relationships

As both *Paybax* and *I Popped His Cherry* demonstrate, a considerable number of girls' films, especially those by older teens, focus on sexual relationships. The popularity of this theme in movies made by female youth is not surprising given that girls are encouraged to privilege interpersonal relations, and the emergence of a sexualized identity is one of the most significant markers of adolescence. At first glance, girls' films that focus on heterosexual dating appear at risk of reproducing traditional sexual and gender politics; however, few of these movies mimic the "happily-ever-after" romance narratives produced for girls by the commercial culture industries. Instead, such films demonstrate an active negotiation of and, at times, resistance to both heterosexual and patriarchal ideologies. For example, *A Party*, by Kimberly Po, pulls in the viewer through a story about what appears to be a typical heterosexual dating experience; yet, the film's main objective is to explore the controversial issue of date rape, not romance.[138]

Although Po uses melodramatic conventions to portray and then complicate a romance narrative, other girl directors have used humor to poke fun at heterosexual dating and gender roles. For example, Carley Steiner's *The Nightcrawlers* first appears to be a conventional story about a girl obsessed with finding a boyfriend.[139] Yet, Steiner's use of comedic editing strategies, which show in quick succession the many potential boyfriends who come knocking at her door (mimicking a scene from *The Commitments*), demonstrates her belief that a pursuit of the perfect mate is an impossible, if not ridiculous, task.[140] Ultimately, *The Nightcrawlers* serves as a critical comment on the frustration that ensues when girls follow the advice of commercial media culture and make heterosexual romance their primary criterion for happiness.

Several young lesbians' movies have challenged the heterosexual themes privileged in commercial media texts by offering an alternative perspective on interpersonal relationships. For example, as discussed at the beginning of this chapter, the majority of Sadie Benning's early videos focus on the development of her young lesbian identity.[141] In turn, Ana Lopez's *Gay Girls on the PL* and *Looks Like a Girl* both document the dating experiences of young Latina lesbians.[142] *Double Consciousness*, by Amber Friedlander, similarly subverts the heterosexual framework of adolescence presented by the commercial media industries.[143] In this film, the lead character is caught between her conservative parents and her developing lesbian sexuality, and thus is forced to lead a bifurcated life in a homophobic environment.

Taizet Hernandez's *We Love Our Lesbian Daughters* similarly explores young lesbians' coming out experiences.[144] In this short documentary, several parents recall the emotions they experienced when hearing for the first time that their daughters are gay. While some parents demonstrate their acceptance of their daughters' sexuality, others recall the pain they felt when their daughters' came out to them. These confessional scenes are balanced by interviews with the girls themselves, who relate their confused emotions—a mix of pride, happiness, shame, and fear—when talking to their parents about their sexuality. A rare glimpse into the lives of queer young Latinas, *We Love Our Lesbian Daughters* does not explore how racial and cultural differences impact the coming out experiences of girls of color, choosing instead to foreground sexual identity over ethnic identity.

Love Knows No Gender, by Zoe Euster, takes a more humorous approach in its portrayal of young lesbianism.[145] In this narrative film, a young woman is shown preparing for a date, while on the soundtrack family members make various comments that lead listeners to believe that she has been partnerless for some time: "At least now I know I'll have grandchildren." Viewers are encouraged to understand the woman's date as male; however, heterosexual readings of the film are subverted at the conclusion when the woman passionately kisses her female partner. Using a similar narrative strategy, *Coming Out*, by Kali Snowden, Tina Huang, and Dharma Sa, reverses the discursive conventions of heterocentrism and homophobia.[146] By focusing on a teenage girl coming out as heterosexual in a queer-dominated society, the filmmakers

Figure 15 Heterophobia in a homocentric world. *Coming Out*, 2004. Courtesy of Reel Grrls.

create a comical but poignant film about the abuse young lesbians often face upon publicizing their sexuality (Figure 15).

In contrast to most films made by heterosexual girls, movies made by young lesbians often privilege the theme of same-sex friendships. For example, Lopez's *Gay Girls on the PL* and its companion piece, *Looks Like a Girl*, explore the filmmaker's dating life and its close relationship to her female friendships. In the first documentary, viewers witness Lopez conversing with other young lesbians on a queer telephone "party line." As the director notes, "drama" ensues when she discovers her ex-girlfriend, who is now just a friend, chatting with her current girlfriend. At the conclusion of *Gay Girls on the PL*, Lopez tells viewers she is going into "party line rehab," breaking up with her girlfriend in order to be alone for a while, which is where we find her at the start of *Looks Like a Girl*. The sequel focuses on Lopez using the Internet to find other young lesbians of color. Yet, in contrast to the earlier film, *Looks Like a Girl* is primarily concerned with the friendships the director develops via a queer chat room. In contrast to films like *Tomboygirl*, which reveal the difficult time straight girls have bridging the gulf between their homosocial and heterosexual worlds, Lopez's two movies point to the very thin boundary that often exists between friends and lovers in the queer community.

Unfortunately, as *A Story of Hope*, *Prufrock and Me*, and *The Ultimate Guide to Flirting* suggest, very few films made by heterosexual girls focus on female friendships without the involvement of males in the narrative. Gina Podesta's *3 Bitches* is another example of this narrative trend in films made by heterosexual female youth.[147] Though the film concludes with the bonding of two nonconformist white girls, the majority of its plot focuses on three popular white girls' relationships with their boyfriends. Indeed, one of the primary reasons the two outsiders become friends is because one of them has been abused by her boyfriend. It is difficult to determine the reasons why so many straight young female directors fail to focus solely on girls' friendships; however, I would argue that since girls' movies about heterosexual dating are typically made by older teens, such texts reveal their creators' negotiation of the often dramatic shift in social relations that is encouraged when girls enter adolescence, a theme foregrounded in *Tomboygirl*. Once bound tightly to their girlfriends, female youth are encouraged to disidentify and separate from their female friends in order to establish relationships with boys. At the same time, girls' films that show female friendships emerging from the demise of heterosexual relationships, such as *3 Bitches*, may demonstrate their creators' awakening consciousness of and resistance to heterosexual patriarchy.

Although few girls' films made in the 1990s focus solely on female friendships, this pattern seems to be changing in recent years, and not just because of the rising number of young lesbian directors. For example, *First Impressions from Seven Friends*, made by Tomekeh Porter (Watkins), Tiffany Spence,

Tiffany Webb, and Shara Williams, explores how seven African American girls met and initially formed opinions about each other.[148] A few girls form negative impressions of others (e.g., a girl displaying too much attitude); however, *First Impressions* is ultimately a celebration of the close friendships formed by these seven female youth—outside the presence of boys. Indeed, no boys are mentioned in the film, a strategy that allows the filmmakers to avoid altogether the criticism of "male bashing" that is often attributed to pro-female discourse. In turn, several recent girl-made movies have explored the end of female friendships by means other than one girl's involvement in a heterosexual relationship. *Skipping Rope*, by Katie Long, focuses on two white best friends whose relationship is finally brought to a sudden end when one of the girls commits suicide.[149] Through dichotomous costuming (conservative versus punk), the film subtly suggests that the two girls have grown apart over the years, slowing decreasing the regular communication and interaction that kept them aware of each other's feelings.

One of the few girls' movies to explore female siblings' relationships, Linzi Silverman's *Sisters* is an examination of the disturbing thoughts that can go through a girl's head when she is jealous of her sister.[150] The black and white film begins by showing two white sisters as playful and loving with each other. When the older sister goes to sleep, however, a nightmare begins with the girl watching her parents shower attention on her younger sister. In a jealous rage (signified through a reddening of the film footage), the older sister chases her younger sibling, eventually stabbing and killing her. Though *Sisters* concludes with a black and white scene showing the older sister asleep, thereby suggesting that what viewers just witnessed was a dream, the film's ending (and meaning) is made ambiguous by depicting the younger sister next to the bed, still dressed in bloody clothes.

Race, Ethnicity, and Disability

Most of the films discussed to this point were created by white, Anglo girls and fail to address race and ethnicity directly. Instead, these filmmakers, having the privilege to ignore issues of race and ethnicity due to their dominant position within U.S. social hierarchy, explore identity primarily through the lenses of sex and gender. Such girls' lack of attention to race and ethnicity likely goes unnoticed by most white, Anglo viewers, who share a similar privilege of nonreflexivity about their privileged social status. Nevertheless, it is important to note that by not addressing the specificity of their racial and ethnic position, white, Anglo girl directors are unconsciously reproducing those identities as normative. In other words, within the world of girl-made movies, only female youth of color and non-Anglo girls have the burden of racial and ethnic representation.

Movies made by African, Latina, Asian, Arab, and Native American female youth often focus explicitly on the intersections between sex, gender, race, and ethnicity by featuring girls of color and exploring their multiple identities. As noted above, for example, *Body Image* expands girl directors' discourse about female beauty standards and cultural visibility by discussing their relation to racial identity; *What Would Your Family Do?* draws attention to how race and ethnicity affect girls' experiences of sharing experiences of sexual abuse; *Looks Like a Girl* broadens young lesbian representations beyond white, Anglo culture; and *First Impressions of Seven Friends* refocuses girls' friendship narratives through an African American lens. By foregrounding race and ethnicity as significant modes of identity that affect girls' private and public lives, each of these films helps both to diversify girls' film culture and to complicate the commercial media industries' conventional constructions of girlhood. Moreover, they expose and call into question the absence of racial and ethnic themes in films made by white, Anglo girls.

Several other films by girls of color and non-Anglo female youth make race and ethnicity primary topics in their films also. For example, *La Gazelle: The Wilma Rudolph Story*, an animation by Amina Jones, foregrounds the personal tragedies this African American woman overcame to achieve success as an Olympian athlete.[151] In privileging Rudolph's African American heritage alongside her female subjectivity, *La Gazelle* affirms the multiple identities of girls of color while also contributing to the reconstruction of the traditionally marginalized history of black women. In addition, the film helps to expand the group of powerful women who serve as girls' role models beyond its conventional white boundaries. Relying on more personal experiences, Hollie Jenkins's short documentary, *Baking Bread at Santa Clara Pueblo*, focuses on a group of Native American girls who learn bread-baking from their older female relatives.[152] By focusing on Native American girls learning and embracing their ethnic heritage, this film not only challenges white-dominated mainstream depictions of girlhood, which are usually devoid of such themes, but critiques the male-dominated portrayals of Native Americans circulating in commercial popular culture. Interestingly, both of these films demonstrate their creators' search outside their generational group for role models, thus commenting on the importance of intergenerational relationships within these two communities.

Several other girl-made movies explore forms of racial and ethnic identity that are either marginalized within or ignored by commercial girls' culture. For example, Astrid Maldonado's *Mi Nombre*, inspired by a passage from Sandra Cisneros's novel, *House on Mango Street*, entails a poetic bilingual video performance by four Mexican American girls that celebrates the beauty, power, and diversity of young Latinas, as well as the Spanish language.[153] By including four different girls in her film, Maldonado is able to convey differences among Mexican American girls while also challenging one-dimensional stereotypes of young Latinas. Another film that affirms and complicates girls' ethnic identity is Ramalah Yusufzai's *Share Our World*, a documentary about three Pakistani American girls growing up in New York City.[154] Refusing to homogenize the experiences of these girls, the film shows how their relationships to faith and culture differ radically. For example, one girl lives a modern, secular, "Americanized" life, while another tries to keep true to the daily rituals of her Muslim faith. *B.A.M. (Black As Me)*, by Triniti Eberhardt-Corbin, Rachel Johnson, and Jomiah Price-Simpson, similarly documents the lives of three African Americans girls in order to portray the complexity of their identities and refute the commercial media's homogenization of members of their race, sex, and age.[155]

Some girl-made movies take a far less celebratory approach to race and ethnicity, typically by exploring the conflicts girls of color and non-Anglo female youth experience when trying to merge their multiracial or multiethnic identities. For example, Miyo Ann Tubridy's *Name* focuses on the difficulty she had coming to grips with her Japanese mother's assimilationist perspective, which led to the privileging of her daughter's Anglo middle name.[156] At the end of her film, the director boldly writes her name on a chalkboard as "Miyo Tubridy," reclaiming the Japanese half of her identity by excluding her middle name. A similar conflict is represented in Komal Herkishnami's *Seventeen*, which explores the different experiences the filmmaker has had as a result of her multicultural identity both in her parents' home country and in the United States, where she was raised.[157] A first-generation Indian American somewhat out of place in both societies, she struggles to find legitimization for her identity within the predominantly white and Western culture with which she is most familiar, asserting, "I never saw anyone like me in a *Seventeen* magazine." Similarly, Skyline Youth Producers' *Latinas Proving Themselves* centers on the conflicts young Latina Americans face as they try to balance traditional Latino family values with American ideals of achievement and individualism.[158] In this documentary, girls talk with older Latinas about the difficulties of leaving home, entering college, and attempting to balance work and family life. By focusing on this intergenerational group, the filmmakers affirm a community-based perspective that is often subordinated or ignored in commercial media culture, as well as films produced by white, wealthy girls.

As these films demonstrate, media production can serve as a powerful medium for girls who are marginalized in society and stereotyped within commercial media culture not only because of their sex and age, but also as a result of their racial and ethnic identities. The films these female youth produce are a direct response to such disenfranchisement, as they demand a right to self-representation and carve out a place for such girls within the larger public sphere. As an African American girl director asserted when interviewed about her film on HBO Family's *30 x 30 Kid Flicks*:

> We wanted to write about something that related to us. Most shows on TV have these high rich white kids [who] live in big houses and all that. We live in New York in apartments or houses or whatever, and it's not all gravy for us. So we wanted to do something that related to us.[159]

This objective echoes that of women of color who have become filmmakers so as to represent members of their community who are often stereotyped or ignored by the commercial media industries. For many nonwhite directors living within a predominantly white society that objective is formed at a very young age. For example, Euzhan Palcy, the Afro Caribbean director of *A Dry White Season* and first black woman to direct a Hollywood feature film, recalls:

> When I was ten years old, I decided to become a filmmaker because on the TV, and in theaters too, every time I had a chance to see a black actor in the movies ... they had black parts, very stupid parts. I made a kind of wish. I said, I have to be a filmmaker. I have to talk about my people. I have to show what black actors can play, and to give the real image of us, not stereotype us like that. The idea worked in my mind for many years.[160]

My Name Is Ruth is perhaps the best example of how film can make visible those girls who are explicitly ignored by the commercial media industries and given minimal space in public society.[161] In this documentary, director Ruth Smith explores a disease that marred her appearance and crippled her physical abilities at an early age. By turning the camera on herself, Smith reveals not only the considerable number of difficulties she faces as a disabled person, but the many ingenious methods developed by individuals with physical handicaps in an effort to surmount the barriers that might keep them from participating fully in life. Moreover, by placing herself at the center of her film's narrative, she provocatively challenges viewers to gaze upon the socially invisible body of a disfigured girl and to recognize that individuals like her also are part of the spectrum of contemporary female youth, as well as contemporary media producers.

Generation

Many movies made by female youth reveal their creators' active negotiations of discourses of sex, gender, and sexuality, and, to a lesser extent, race, ethnicity, and disability. In comparison, few girls' films reveal such levels of engagement with discourses of age and generation. This avoidance of explicit generational discourse by many girl filmmakers can be understood in part as a result of the traditional ideologies of gender and generation that discourage girls, especially those most invested in heterosexual patriarchy, from fully occupying their generational identity.[162]

Nevertheless, some girl filmmakers reveal their negotiations of age and generational identity in a subtle manner that is worth exploring further. For example, *Barbie, Barbie Resized, Fight Girl Poisoning*, and *What if Barbie Had a Voice?* all use popular toys marketed specifically to girls to comment on the dangerous effects of female beauty standards on girls. Meanwhile, *What if Men Menstruated?* demonstrates its unique generational perspective by employing male action figures. Thus, all of these films reveal their producers' negotiations of popular culture texts that are on hand, as Dyer argues, "on account of who they are"—youth. In turn, *Listen to Your Angel, Body Rhapsody, I Am Beautiful*, and *Baywatch Babes ... or Not* specifically connect adolescent girls' negative body image and low self-esteem to teen magazines, those female-centered periodicals specifically marketed to youth. *Mirror, Beauty Marks*, and *Prufrock and Me* focus on how teenage girls manipulate their appearance in order to attract the attention of male youth, thus foregrounding a practice that has long been used to socialize female adolescents as feminine and heterosexual. Indeed, a considerable number of girls' films demonstrate a reconfiguration of gender-specific discourse, specifically female appearance, according to their creators' unique generational perspective.

Interestingly, many films produced by adolescent girls suggest their creators' investments in and negotiations of generational identity through their incorporation of particular music. For instance, *Girls, Body Rhapsody*, and *I Am Beautiful* all have soundtracks that rely on rock or rap songs, musical styles conventionally associated with young people. Meanwhile, one of the filmmakers in the *Video Icons* compilation celebrates pop singer Aaliyah as a positive role model for African American girls, while the directors of *Girls Making Headlines* reject pop star Britney Spears because of her negative influence on young female beauty standards. This rejection of Spears might also indicate such girls' transition from commercial preteen culture, which is pop-oriented, to teen culture, which privileges less conformist musical styles and performers.

Some girl-made movies subtly comment on their filmmakers' generational identity by showing characters' engagement in age-specific activities. For example, *Pick Me* focuses on a girl in a children's soccer league, while *I Popped His Cherry* centers on the experience of losing one's virginity. (Interestingly, though a considerable number of girls' films involve the world of dating, few of these movies foreground the unique experiences of the first date or first kiss, a convention of girl-centered teenpics, such as *Sixteen Candles*.) By featuring female friends, films like *3 Bitches, Skipping Rope*, and *First Impressions of Seven Friends* suggest a type of female homosociality that is typically linked to adolescence not adulthood. *My Name Is Ruth* examines youth development from a different perspective, revealing the unique challenges disabled girls face as they grow older and enter into new social situations.

As the titles *Girls, Girl Power, Tomboygirl, Fight Girl Poisoning, Gay Girls on the PL, Looks Like a Girl,* and *Are You a Boy or a Girl?* suggest, some young female directors subtly assert their generational identity by foregrounding their identity as girls rather than women, a strategy employed by grrrl zinesters also. Other girl directors reveal a strong interest in their youthful identity, foregrounding the rebelliousness associated with childhood and adolescence as a means of resisting traditional gender roles and behaviors. This theme is playfully handled in *Gimme Cookies,* by the Pfeiffer and Kelley sisters.[163] In this film, a young girl makes several attempts to reach a cookie jar that sits on top of her family's refrigerator. Humorously suggesting the limits of youthful rebellion, the film shows the mother walking into the room just as the girl gets the jar.

Exploring a slightly older generational identity, Erica Shapiro's *Twin Tales* uses the clever doubling of her sound and image tracks to connect teenage girls' rebelliousness directly to the emergence of feminist consciousness.[164] On the soundtrack, a young woman talks about her early experiences in ballet class, a traditional sphere of feminine socialization for wealthy girls, yet one that is potentially subverted by the homosociality of the environment and, in this specific case, risqué stories of sex and cigarette smoking told by older girls. As the narrator continues her tale, a young woman is shown running down the street away from a possible stalker. Later, this same woman is depicted in her room, absorbed in Simone de Beauvoir's *The Second Sex* and several other influential feminist texts. Thus, while the film's images explore the girl's growing awareness of patriarchy and misogyny, the soundtrack suggests her understanding of the greater need for both female independence and female solidarity in the face of such difficulties.

Other girls' films also suggest that growing up is a problematic experience, though take this theme in a different direction by exploring child-parent relations. This project is explicit in *Zerzura* by Natalie Neptune, a documentary in which three teenage girls, through direct address, reveal their experiences of growing up female (Figure 16).[165] Interestingly, each of the girls focuses specifically on her mother's behavior in order to explain her own personality. One girl in particular discusses the painful relationship she has with her mother as a result of her interest in joining the military, noting, "No, *she's* not different. She's stayed the same for forty-eight years. *I'm* the one who's different. I'm rebelling against everything she knows." This theme of a girl's rebellion against her mother in the process of forming identity is evident in *Name* also.

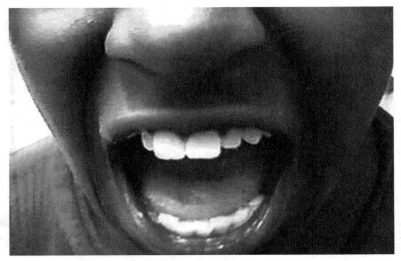

Figure 16 The trials and tribulations of growing up female.
Zerzura, 2000. Courtesy of Downtown Community Television Center, Inc.

The theme of generational identity as constructed through opposition to one's elders is also raised in *We Love Our Lesbian Daughters*. Indeed, though some of the first-generation Mexican American parents in this documentary discuss their loving acceptance of their lesbian daughters, several reveal the fear, shame, and disappointment they felt upon learning that their daughters are gay. In turn, the young lesbians in the film, all second-generation Latinas, discuss the conflicted emotions of happiness and sadness they had when coming out. Unlike the subjects in *Zerzura*, however, the girls in *We Love Our Lesbian Daughters* are never fully oppositional to their mothers and fathers. In fact, the final image in the film shows a girl playing cards with her parents and siblings, thereby foregrounding the importance of family in Latino culture. The theme of intergenerational respect and community is evident in several other films by girls of color, including *Latinas Proving Themselves* and *Baking Bread at Santa Clara Pueblo*. Nevertheless, these films, like both *What Would Your Family Do?* and *We Love Our Lesbian Daughters*, also reveal the unique experiences girls in these communities have as a result of their attempts to balance their cultural heritage and values with those of contemporary American society.

CONCLUSION

More American girls are taking classes in filmmaking and producing their own movies than many adults imagine. The vast majority of films created by these female youth reveal their creators' active engagement with commercial popular culture, especially girls' culture and the extent to which it informs their explorations of identity. Yet, rather than mimicking the representational practices of the film industry, these young female directors are developing the "girl's gaze" by challenging the ideologies of gender, generation, sexuality, race, ethnicity, and disability prevalent in U.S. society and commercial film culture. We have yet to see a "girl Mozart" whose films destroy the professionalism privileged in the commercial film industry, as Francis Ford Coppola once dreamed would happen as a result of the wide availability of inexpensive video camcorders. Nevertheless, those girls who are using film and video cameras to record their stories, experiences, dreams, and fears are, at the very least, transforming girlhood and female youth culture. For, by using a form of media that makes visible the unseen and audible the unheard, these directors are expanding considerably girls' public representation, complicating the stories associated with their demographic group, and challenging stereotypes of female youth as technically ignorant and culturally unproductive.

6
Cybergurls
Female Youth, Digital Fluencies, and Web Design

We have to teach our younger generation of women that they are free to explore computers in their own way and to draw their own conclusions about the usefulness of these machines. And we start it all with a simple thought that could be the beginning of a revolution: How hard can it be?

—Karen Coyle[1]

Using the Web as a showcase for my work gives me an opportunity for feedback and refining it. Despite the fact that the Net often inspires a feeling of reclusiveness, it's been my salvation, an alternative to a reality that isn't always all that attractive.

—Heather Susan Reddy[2]

It is not an overstatement to say that the world, U.S. society, and my home are all different places than when I began this book project over a decade ago. Personal computers and CD players, digital still and video cameras, DVD and

MP3 players have been purchased by so many individuals and at such a rapid rate that a considerable number of Americans now consider these appliances to be as essential to their everyday lives as televisions and telephones. In fact, even those relics of "old" media are being transformed via digital technology. Given the radical social changes initiated by such technologies over the past ten years, it seems the traditional divisions of Western history, "Before Christ" and "Anno Domini," might soon be renamed "Before Computers" and "After Digital."

Clearly, digital technologies have significantly altered American media consumption. But digital technologies have transformed the spheres of media production also, allowing for greater ease in those processes than ever before. No longer dependent on numerous expensive, technically sophisticated apparatuses that require specialized training, media producers can now rely on personal computers (PCs) and software packages that offer quick, easy, and efficient methods for creating near-professional texts. The integration of digital technologies in the creation of films, print media, and musical recordings over the past decade has radically altered the production of contemporary popular culture. The digital technology that has changed the world of media production most dramatically, however, is the Internet. Combining the creation, distribution, and exhibition of media texts in one apparatus, the Internet's other unique features are its interactive capabilities, its virtually infinite storage capacity, and its ability to link users to multiple sites as well as other Internet users quickly and simultaneously, a feature commonly referred to as the World Wide Web.

The Internet has grown exponentially since its introduction in the late 1960s, now supporting nearly ten million websites created by individuals from around the world.[3] The number of Internet users worldwide surpassed one billion in 2005, and that figure is expected to double by 2011. One notable, though little acknowledged, result of this digital revolution is its transformation of youth media production. Digital technologies, like computers and the Web, have not simply improved earlier forms of youth media, such as zine-making, they have also initiated new ways for young people to creatively express themselves and communicate with others. As Julian Sefton-Green and Vivienne Reiss argue:

> [T]he increasing accessibility of [digital] technologies has created significant opportunities for young people to become cultural producers, rather than mere consumers. Using equipment that is now much more easily available, not just in their own homes or peer groups but also in formal and informal education, young people participate much more readily in activities such as music production, image manipulation, design, and desktop or web-site publishing.[4]

Even girls, historically stereotyped as technophobic and technically incompetent, are employing digital technologies to produce their own media, as the epigraph above from fifteen-year-old web designer Heather Susan Reddy attests. This chapter focuses on girls' active participation in the construction of cyberspace through their practices of web design.

DIGITAL REVOLUTION, DIGITAL DIVIDE: YOUNG PEOPLE'S ACCESS TO COMPUTERS AND THE INTERNET

The digital revolution that resulted from the quick and broad proliferation of personal computers and the Internet during the mid- to late 1990s has significantly affected the lives of young people in the United States, directly impacting their experiences at home, in school, and in their communities. For instance, in 1984, only 27 percent of students from preschool through college used PCs at school. By 1997, that rate had risen to 69 percent.[5] With regard to Internet access, only 3 percent of public school classrooms, labs, and libraries were wired in 1994; yet, that figure had risen to 93 percent by 2003.[6] This dramatic increase in schools with Internet access is largely the result of various government, industry, and advocacy initiatives that emerged in the wake of the U.S. Department of Commerce's 1995 report, *Falling through the Net.*[7] Indeed, within only seven years, the same department released its *A Nation Online* report, which argued that the "digital divide" it brought to public awareness had now closed.[8]

Though schools remain the primary location for most young people's interaction with digital technologies, many American youth have access to computers and Internet service at home also. By 2004, 65.1 percent of U.S. households had Internet access at home.[9] As this figure suggests, the percentage of home computers and Internet access has not risen as substantially as it has for those in public schools. This phenomenon is directly related to class disparities. For example, in 2001, 51.7 percent of young people 3 to 17 years of age with family incomes of $75,000 or more had Internet access at home. Not surprisingly, the rate for families with household incomes between $20,000 and $25,000 was substantially lower: only 15 percent.[10] In addition to income differences, racial disparities exist in young people's home computer and Internet use. Recent statistics show that more than a third of young white and Asian Americans use the Internet at home, while only 15 percent of African American and 13 percent of Latino youth have access to wired computers at home.[11]

Although a digital divide has long existed between the poor and the affluent, a new gap has grown between homes, schools, libraries, and workplaces that rely on traditional telephone modems to access the Internet and those with broadband access. Indeed, while household broadband subscriptions rose some 300 percent between 2000 and 2004, this increase was experienced primarily among high-income families.[12] The difference in speed between telephone and broadband connections has a direct impact on Internet use and thus web usability and digital productivity. Because it provides faster connection to as well as speed on the Internet, broadband increases users' productive capabilities. In contrast, Internet access through telephone modems is quite slow, often resulting in a frustrating experience of uploading and downloading information. At the time of this book's publication, a new divide was emerging between homes, schools, libraries, and workplaces with wireless Internet access ("wi-fi") and those dependent on wired technology. Here the difference in usability is not so much speed as mobility, with wi-fi networking systems on laptops allowing users to access the Internet without being directly wired into and thus physically close to a modem.

The digital divide that exists among American youth today, therefore, means that the young people who are online most frequently tend to be those who are upper-middle-class. Unlike their less wealthy peers, these privileged youth have computers, as well as broadband access to the Internet, at both school and home. Moreover, these young computer users have considerable disposable/leisure time that allows them to have frequent, long-term engagements with such technologies. This situation directly impacts their quick development of computing skills and facilitates a broad range of activities in which they can participate when online.

WIRED YOUTH: YOUNG PEOPLE'S ONLINE ENGAGEMENT AND ACTIVITIES

Despite the economically based digital divide that persists today in the United States, in comparison to ten years ago, a considerable number of American youth are online in some way, either at school, at home, or in a public setting, such as a library. In fact, recent findings from the Pew Internet and American Life Project show that 81 percent of teenagers between the ages of 12 and 17 are now online, and a Media Metrix report indicates that members of this demographic group spend an average of 303 minutes per month wired to the Internet.[13] Other research organizations have tracked over time the number of young frequent online users, and their data similarly reveal a significant rise in recent years in both the number of youth online and the amount of time such youth spend in cyberspace. For example, a 2005 study by the Kaiser Family Foundation shows that the amount of all Americans between the ages of 8 and 18 who are online for more than an hour per day almost doubled between 1999 and 2004, rising from 15 to 27 percent.[14]

This recent Kaiser study also suggests, however, that for those young people who have access to the Internet at home, their amount of online time is significantly affected by their age and where their computer is located. For instance, although children ages 8 to 11 use computers on average of only 37 minutes each day, teenagers 15 to 18 have an average daily use of 82 minutes.[15] In turn, of the 8 to 18 year olds studied, those without a computer in their bedroom reported only 47 minutes of daily computer use on average compared to 90 minutes for those with a computer in their bedroom.[16]

Differences in time spent online are related to sex also. Girls, like women, were slower to adapt to the Internet during the mid- to late 1990s than boys and men. Yet, a 2000 study conducted for Media Metrix and Jupiter Communications reported that girls between 12 and 17 years old were the fastest growing group of Internet users.[17] That same year, a report from the U.S. Department of Commerce indicated online parity among boys and girls ages 3 to 17.[18] A more recent survey by the National School Boards Foundation (NSBF) found that by 2003, girls between 9 and 17 had surpassed their male peers in Internet use.[19]

Determining the number of wired youth today and the amount of time they spend in cyberspace provides important benchmarks for factoring transformations in young people's computing experiences; but equally important to discern is how these youth spend their time when online. Kaiser's most recent study notes that from 1999 to 2004, young people's daily online time that was not spent on homework more than doubled, from 27 to 62 minutes, thus suggesting an increase related specifically to recreation rather than education.[20] Of the 8 to 18 year olds surveyed for that study, the dominant use of the computer was for playing games, while the Internet was most used for instant messaging (66%), followed by downloading music (64%), surfing the Web for information (50%), listening to the radio (48%), shopping (38%), and creating websites (32%).[21]

Other researchers have found distinct differences between the uses and interests of wired male and female youth. For example, the NSBF survey indicates that while twice as many boys than girls between the ages of 9 and 17 report going online to play games, considerably more female than male youth report using the Web for schoolwork, information gathering, and communicating with others via email.[22] The study also found that girls from the age of 2 to 12 are twice as likely to use email as boys are. Indeed, 68 percent of the study's young female respondents reported using email at least once a week, while 30 percent of the boys indicated that they never engage in this activity. Girls are also more likely to participate in online chat rooms and message boards than are male youth.

Although the NSBF study shows that fewer girls than boys in the 9 to 17 age group use the Internet for entertainment purposes at least once a week (45 compared to 65 percent), many female youth clearly surf the Web often. Again, *how* girls surf is an important question to consider if we are to understand more fully girls' Internet experience. A 1999 study conducted by the Kaiser Family Foundation shows that female youth between the ages of 8 and 18 are more likely to visit websites related to popular entertainment than those related to sports, the sites most frequented by boys.[23] Unfortunately, few recent studies have been conducted to examine the specific websites girls visit, how they interact with those sites, and how much time they spend during those engagements.

In turn, I have been unable to find any statistical data showing what percentage of girls is currently engaged in advanced forms of online activity, such as web design. Kaiser's most recent study of youth media practices reports that 32 percent of youth have created websites; however, this figure is not broken down further by sex. Nevertheless, the general consensus among those who study gender and cyberculture is that, as with adults, more male than female youth are engaged in web design, as well as other advanced computing practices. The reasons for this gender disparity are complex and deserve closer analysis, particularly if strategies are to be developed that can correct this imbalance.

ANOTHER BOYS' CLUB: THE MALE AND MASCULINE WORLD OF COMPUTER CULTURE

As noted above, disparity in income level is the dominant reason for the divide between the wired and the unwired. Yet many feminist scholars and female information technology (IT) professionals remind us that sex is a significant factor also in an individual's level of access to, interest in, confidence with, training in, and engagement with computing technologies. Indeed, despite dramatic increases in the sale and use of personal computers since the mid-1990s, research continues to show considerable differences in how males and females interact with such technology in their everyday lives. For instance, although recent data reveal virtual parity between U.S. males and females in terms of Internet use, a digital divide between the two sexes persists within the educational and professional fields of IT and computer science (CS). In fact, women still comprise less than 25 percent of IT professionals, only 8 percent of IT engineers, and 5 percent of IT management, despite women's significant gains in most other professions since the 1970s.[24] Given these low figures of general female involvement, it is not surprising that the number of women of color working in the IT field is notably lower than that of white women, who typically have more education and access to professional fields.

Scholars have produced different explanations for the minimal number of women IT professionals. For instance, Tracy Camp argues that this phenomenon is an effect of the "incredibly shrinking pipeline" of women in computer science training programs.[25] In fact, in 1999, girls represented only 17 percent of the computer science advanced placement test-takers in the U.S. despite comprising almost 50 percent of high school classes in this field.[26] Race seems to be a significant factor in teenage girls' computer training. Indeed, the extremely low number of African American girls and young Latinas taking such exams contrasts dramatically with their representation in the larger U.S. population.

The pipeline shrinks more significantly as women progress further in their education. As Camp, Keith Miller, and Vanessa Davies note, data from the mid-1990s demonstrated a disturbing trend with regard to women's training for the IT field:

> The proportion of bachelor degrees awarded to women in all disciplines has increased almost every year for decades, to a high of 55.2% in 1995–96. This increasing percentage of women earning college degrees has had a positive effect on the percentage of women earning degrees in all science and engineering fields, except CS. In CS, the percentage of bachelor's degrees awarded to women decreased almost every year from 1983–84 (37.1%) to 1995–96 (27.5%).[27]

These statistics represent almost a 26 percent decrease over just 12 years, and as a result many feminist scholars and women IT professionals had great fears during the late 1990s that such figures would decline further with the new millennium, despite the increasing proliferation of digital technologies.

Valerie Clarke's explanation of young women's low level of interest in pursuing CS degrees is that "unquestioned values, beliefs, and expectations" are embedded in the frameworks that structure popular discourse of gender and computing.[28] One barrier explored by Clarke and other feminist researchers is that female youth have been presented with a computing world that is both institutionally and symbolically patriarchal and masculinist. Several feminist scholars have pointed to the historic domination of the IT field by men, and thus the naturalized masculinization of computer discourse and environments over the past several decades. For example, in 1984, Sherry Turkle explored the gendered construction of computing culture by focusing on the activities and discourses privileged by different groups of computer users. Hackers, she argued, are perhaps the most invested in patriarchal masculinity, and thus create a culture off-limits to females: "Though hackers would deny that theirs is a macho culture, the preoccupation with winning and of subjecting oneself to increasingly violent tests make their world peculiarly male in spirit, peculiarly unfriendly to women."[29] In 1985, Sara Kiesler, Lee Sproull, and Jacquelynne Eccles demonstrated that computer games, educational software, and computer and information science (CIS) curricula are often produced with a male bias, a phenomenon Eileen Green, Jenny Owen, and Den Pain subsequently labeled "gendered by design."[30] Liesbet Van Zoonen has argued more recently that "[t]he so-called 'actor network' of human and technical actors involved in the development of the Internet as a technology is almost 100 percent male."[31]

Patriarchy and sexism exist outside the realms of computer hardware and software development, however. For example, teachers and professors of computer science have traditionally been male, a phenomenon that is both the cause and the effect of few women pursuing CS degrees.[32] According to a Taulbee Survey by the Computing Research Association, women comprised only 15.8 percent of assistant professors, 12.3 percent of associate professors, and 8.6 percent of full professors in computer science programs during the 2002–3 academic year.[33] Moreover, many CS classrooms reproduce patriarchal ideologies that subjugate girls. A 1999 study found, for example, that students in an 11th-grade computer science class reported that girls had greater teacher support and self-confidence in single-sex environments than either males or females in mixed-sex classes.[34] Although some girls engaged in formal computer training have reported little overt discrimination from teachers,[35] other female youth note that their male classmates or computer club mates can be intimidating, compromising girls' confidence and thus involvement in such activities. For example, as teenager Susannah Camic reports:

> In middle and high school, I have often been the one girl in a computer lab with 30 to 40 boys. In middle school, I was often told simply to go away by boys who had logged into illegal sites and thought I might tell the teacher what they were up to. ... Sometimes there was a chance to "chat" on America Online, but the boys would refuse to let us [girls] near the keyboard, and we could only look on as they typed in sexual remarks and jokes.[36]

Though the realms of education and work remain primary in scholarship on gender and computing, males and patriarchal ideologies similarly dominate other sites within cyberculture. For example, stores that sell and repair digital technologies, such as CompUSA, Circuit City, and Fryes Electronics, are staffed by young, mostly white men who, like clerks in film and musician shops, wield technical knowledge as a means of bolstering their masculinity and power over customers and other clerks. In turn, popular culture has traditionally reinforced the patriarchy of computer culture many girls and women experience in their everyday lives. Clarke drew attention to this phenomenon in 1990 by demonstrating that males have traditionally occupied the role of computer users in popular films, videos, television, and magazines.[37] The number of real-life female computer users has grown substantially since Clarke's study; however, contemporary popular discourse continues to present men as the typical computer user. For instance, although *Wired*, the most popular computing magazine in the United States, has women on its writing staff and management team, the periodical consistently uses discourse that privileges hypermasculine manhood while marginalizing women according to gender stereotypes. Melanie Stewart Millar theorizes that such use of patriarchal and sexist discourse is meant to appeal to *Wired*'s target market of young heterosexual men who see themselves as pioneers in the digital frontier.[38] Much like periodicals targeting filmmakers and musicians, computing magazines consistently construct a male homosocial world where men and masculinity are affirmed, and women and femininity are subordinated, if not excluded outright. Matthew Weinstein's work suggests that such gendered patterns of representing computer users are also evident in print advertisements for digital technology.[39]

Given the institutional and symbolic structures that reproduce the patriarchy of computer culture, it is not surprising that, as Judy Wajcman argues, "[i]n our society the computer has become socially constructed as a male domain: children learn from an early age to associate computers with boys and men."[40] Indeed, girls have been actively encouraged to understand this sphere of activity as off-limits to members of their sex category. As several studies have shown, parents often contribute to this perception by buying more computers and enrollments in computer camps for their sons than their daughters.[41]

And, yet, the masculine construction of computer culture is only half the story here. As discussed in the Introduction, girls' fears of failure, which are exacerbated by commercial discourse that encourages them to scrutinize their bodies and find imperfection, often prevent them from engaging in activities that are unfamiliar. Such anxieties seem particularly heightened around practices that exist outside the conventional realm of females and femininity, such as computing. As the founder of the girls-only Lilith Computer Club,[42] Susannah Camic, notes: "One of the things that's difficult for girls is that you can't use a computer very long without getting some kind of error. When girls encounter that they start to think, 'I can't do it,' and they back off. The boys tend to be more confident and just keep plowing ahead."[43]

One of the computing practices noted by scholars and computing professionals as essential for developing digital fluency is "tinkering," experimenting with different aspects of computer hardware and software.[44] Yet, because tinkering with technology has historically been connected with men and thus is socially constructed as masculine, few girls are encouraged to engage in it. Moreover, because computer tinkering often leads to error, as Camic suggests, and thus possible suggestions of the user's lack of skill, girls anxious about appearing imperfect, especially in the company of males, can be quite resistant to participating in this activity. Using her own computer class as an example of how this phenomenon develops, Camic reports:

> In my middle school computer lab, the teacher was famous for outbursts at students who made mistakes and caused difficulties in the

computer network. As a result, whenever I sat down at a computer next to a girl who was a beginning computer user and suggested that we experiment with a new command or program, her response was always: "Let's not do it. I don't want to screw anything up."[45]

Thus, as Judy McClain, a philanthropist who has helped fund girls' computer workshops, argues, "[I]f there's no support system for [girls], they start lessening their expectations of what they can accomplish."[46]

TOWARD A TECH-SAVVY GIRLHOOD: RESOLVING GIRLS' COMPUTATIONAL RETICENCE

Much of the feminist research on computing during the 1980s focused on adult women. Yet, since the early 1990s, a considerable number of scholars have launched studies to determine not only the barriers to girls' interests and involvement in computing, but also the strategies that might eliminate those deterrents. For example, in 1990, the National Educational Computing Conference (NECC) held a preconference workshop titled "In Search of Gender-Free Paradigms for Computer Science Education."[47] The workshop was organized around the premise that the substantial decline in young women's pursuit of CS degrees during the late 1980s was attributable to male bias in the field. Clarke substantiated this assumption, noting that in addition to the male domination of the computing field and the masculinization of digital technologies, twelve common beliefs limit girls' interest and participation in CS coursework: girls are no good at computing or computer science; boys have more computing experience; girls are not interested in computers or computer science; teachers favor boys' in computer-based instruction; teachers are not aware of or open to sex differences in learning strategies; parents demonstrate sex-specific expectations of and behavior toward their children with regard to computers and computing; sex-based differences exist with regard to uses of computer technology; it's women's responsibility to change their attitudes toward computers and computing; the isolationist image of the computer hacker is unappealing to females; computing is inherently technological; women's timetables often conflict with the scheduling and work required for CS classes; and teachers and counselors do not prepare female students with regard to course prerequisites.[48]

Tasked to develop recommendations to alter such beliefs and encourage more girls to take interest in computing, the workshop attendees' suggestions included: a nationwide initiative at the middle school level to design educational programs in computing that appeal to girls; the development of nationwide computer-oriented parent education and teacher development programs; increased digital resources in schools and colleges; a reward structure for CS professors; and more mentoring programs, guest lectures, and financial aid for college and graduate students.[49]

Since the publication of the NECC workshop report in 1992, researchers from many different disciplines, including education, computer science, and media studies, have explored various aspects of girls' computing.[50] Grounding such studies are not only statistics showing women's declining pursuit of computer-oriented degrees and jobs, but also the assumption that a lack of involvement with computers diminishes girls' educational experiences, prevents them from developing particular cognitive abilities, limits their capacity for communication, makes them ill-equipped to compete in the twenty-first-century workforce, and thus decreases their ability to participate actively in civic matters.

Motivated by and building on the work of such scholars, several nonprofit organizations have recently initiated their own research projects to explore in more detail the reasons behind girls' minimal computing interest and engagement, what Turkle labels "computer reticence," as well as to determine possible solutions to this problem.[51] Though the findings from these studies were introduced long after feminist scholars initiated research on the gender dynamics of computer culture, these reports have received far more public attention than most studies published in academic texts, and thus have helped to facilitate the development of many new programs and organizations dedicated to improving girls' relationships with computers.

Perhaps the most influential study in this regard is *Tech-Savvy: Educating Girls in the New Computer Age*, by the American Association of University Women (AAUW).[52] Published in 2000, *Tech-Savvy* delved deeper into some of the findings produced from AAUW's earlier study, *Gender Gaps: Where Schools Still Fail Our Children*, including the low participation of female youth in CS courses, girls' infrequent use of computers outside school, girls' minimal confidence and perceived lack of ability with regard to using computers, and the reinforcement of gender biases in computer software.[53] *Tech-Savvy* is the culmination of two years of research by AAUW's Educational Foundation Commission on Technology, Gender, and Teacher Education. Cochaired by Sherry Turkle and Patricia Diaz Dennis, the commission was comprised of women researchers, educators, journalists, and entrepreneurs actively involved in cyberculture and education.

Tech-Savvy's study moved the discussion of girls' computational reticence in new directions by involving focus groups with 70 middle and high school girls with diverse racial identities, as well as email surveys with 892 teachers.[54] The commission's key findings include: girls think computer programming classes are dull and tedious; girls are uninspired by career options in computing; girls find computer games violent and boring; gender equity in computing is measured only quantitatively; and teachers' computer training emphasizes the technical properties of computing hardware rather than applications and uses.[55] With these findings in mind, the commission's primary recommendations include: cultivating girls' interests in IT jobs; changing the gender dynamics of computing in popular culture; transforming software design; setting new standards for measuring computer literacy; preparing tech-savvy teachers; and giving girls a "boost" into the pipeline of computer science.[56]

As AAUW's *Tech-Savvy* report makes clear, only a minimal number of contemporary female youth are interested in taking computer science classes and participating in computer clubs, much less pursuing a CS degree or a career in the IT field. In fact, the study found that many girls have a "we can, but we don't want to" attitude, which suggests their ambivalence toward and disenchantment with cyberculture rather than a lack of access to or aptitude in it.[57] The AAUW's commissioners, like many other feminist scholars in this field, see this attitude as problematically limiting girls' future educational and career options. It is important to be mindful, however, of the biases that structure such concerns. Indeed, most research on girls' computing seems based on the middle-class assumption that all girls will go to college and pursue careers, and thus will be better prepared to handle both if they develop fluency in digital technologies at a young age. Yet clearly these options are not available to all female youth. Moreover, many girls with class privilege yet disaffected attitudes toward dominant society eventually opt out of the traditional lifestyle in which their parents invest. For these female youth, much like poor girls, computing has a different meaning and can be put to different uses. In consideration of these other female youth—those whose needs, interests, and goals are largely absent from most studies on girls' computing—it is necessary to think through the other, noncurricular methods by and spaces in which young females gain interests in and develop long-term, sustained engagements with digital technologies.

As the *Tech-Savvy* commissioners argue, "Different children will encounter different entry points into computing—some through art, for example, some through design, some through mathematics. These multiple entry points need to be respected and encouraged."[58] (Note that "through recreation" is not one of the entry points noted here.) Yet, in only two other places in their report do the commissioners reiterate this argument: "[T]here are likely to be multiple paths to [computing] competence, aside from the attainment of a degree with a formal computer science major," and "[I]t is … desirable for more women to feel comfortable in the culture of computing, no matter what their eventual occupational, social, or family roles may be."[59] Although the likelihood of the first phenomena and the hope for the second seem to have encouraged the commissioners to recommend that the metaphor of a "pipeline" into computer culture be substituted by a "web" or "net," *Tech-Savvy*, like many other studies of girls' computing to date, ultimately pays little attention to the noncurricular spaces in which female youth engage with digital technologies.[60] As Nancy Kaplan and Eva Farrell point out:

> Focusing predominantly on communications practices in two sites— among professional women or in school settings, both elementary and secondary—most studies have yet to take into account the entrance of young women into electronic discourse especially when their participation occurs outside of formal educational settings.[61]

Clearly, the AAUW commission's emphasis on improving girls' computing in school is related to the organization's overall goal to ameliorate girls' and women's education and, by extension, other aspects of their lives. In turn, many feminist scholars share a concern about girls' school-based computer training as a result of their affiliation with the fields of education and computer science, as well as their commitment to expanding women's job opportunities and social power. Nevertheless, if improving girls' computing experiences and transforming cyberculture in the process are primary goals,[62] it seems short-sighted for researchers to focus on only one, and one of the most formal and institutionalized, of the multiple spaces in which female youth engage with digital technologies. As Turkle notes, many computing classes emphasize a heavily structured learning style that is not appropriate for all students, and thus does not facilitate their full engagement with such technology. Instead, she argues for training

> [i]n relatively unconstrained settings, [where] the computer facilitates a new basis for engagement in technical and mathematical thinking, one that allows for [students'] appropriation through a "close encounter" with an interactive, reactive "psychological machine" and with computational objects that can be experienced as tactile and physical. It is a style that emphasizes negotiation rather than command of computational objects, a style that suggests a conversation rather than a monologue. This is a port of entry into a world of formal systems for many people who have always kept a distance from them. It is a port of entry with particular significance for women.[63]

Paul Willis similarly argues that scholars must look outside the formal institutions that structure and contain young people's experiences, for they do not provide the only, or even the best, training grounds for development:

> The informal realm of "leisure" is of vital and increasing importance for the operation of symbolic work as identity-making. There is simply decreasing room for creativity in the necessary symbolic work of most paid work, so its impetus is thrown increasingly on to,

or develops more in, leisure activities. ... [M]ost of the jobs which young people occupy simply cannot offer the intrinsic satisfaction of skill in the making of useful things well. ... [T]he reality is that many, if not most, young people feel more themselves in leisure than they do at work. Though only "fun" and apparently inconsequential, it's actually where their creative symbolic activities are most at play.[64]

Inspired by these perspectives, I want to help expand scholarship on girls' computing into the noncurricular arena by analyzing girls' informal training and practices in web design within their own homes.

In addition to paying attention to girls' unstructured, noncurricular computing activities, more consideration must be given to how girls make use of digital technologies *as youth*, rather than simply to how their current engagements with computers and the Internet might impact their opportunities as adults. Some girls' activities in cyberspace will likely help them to be better prepared for adult tasks and responsibilities, such as college and careers. Yet many female youth have already begun engaging actively in cyberspace, an arena that is quickly becoming the primary site of communication, business, and information gathering in our society, public realms of life from which young people were once but are no longer excluded. With this in mind, I am interested in exploring how girls' efforts to stake a claim in cyberspace during their youth through practices like web design might be indicative of transformations in not only girls' culture, but also commerce and media culture.

CYBERGURLS: STUDYING FEMALE YOUTH AND WEB CULTURE

Recent reports demonstrate that the number of girls using computers and the Internet in the United States has increased exponentially over the past decade. Yet clearly not all American girls have the same web skills, nor do all engage in the same online activities. As with other demographic groups, girls' interactions with the Web are diverse, encompassing a wide spectrum of practices ranging from those that involve minimal technical skill, like playing games and surfing the Web, to those that require specialized knowledge, such as web design. In between these two poles are a variety of other online activities that require at least some skill in reading, writing, and typing, including emailing, instant messaging, and participating in chat rooms and message boards.

Not surprisingly, most girls who are online regularly from a young age develop skills that progress somewhat easily from web surfing and game play to emailing and other forms of online communication. Because computers have been incorporated into most U.S. classrooms as primary learning tools, and the Web is utilized by both students and teachers alike as an information resource, schools have functioned as a primary site for nurturing girls' elementary computer-based skills, especially those that involve pointing, click-ing, dragging, dropping, and, for older students, typing. As recent studies of home Internet use suggest, these basic computing skills are further reinforced for female youth whose families have wired computers, as girls typically use these specific skills at home to communicate with others and gather informa-tion for school projects.

Unfortunately, web surfing, game play, and emailing comprise the entirety of most contemporary girls' online practices, just as pointing, clicking, drag-ging, dropping, and typing encompass the extent of their web-based skills. Though some teachers facilitate student training in web design, often these lessons and thus students' skill development are compromised by the minimal amount of time allotted for most class sessions. In turn, since few teachers have advanced computer skills, those who facilitate web design instruction often rely on free web authoring programs that typically require only mouse skills, such as those available via Lycos Angelfire and Yahoo! Geocities. Though some students have longer engagement with computers after school as a result of their involvement in computer clubs, the percentage of female youth who participate in such extracurricular computing activities remains quite low in comparison to boys. As a result of these various factors, schools are rarely the location where female youth develop advanced technical skills, such as HTML (hypertext markup language), and progress to complex computing activities, such as web design.

In order to help determine the various factors that lead girls to move beyond basic web activities and become active in constructing cyberspace, the remainder of this chapter discusses findings from my recent ethnographic study of a particular group of young female web designers—online distro owners—and the development of their web-based skills. Distros are small, independent distribution companies that sell handcrafted goods, such as zines, buttons, and stickers. Before the proliferation of digital technologies, distros were primarily mail-order companies; many now exist online. Most of these companies are run by individuals in their late teens and early twen-ties, and cater primarily to a market of young people interested in consuming media texts and other commodities that have been produced independent of corporate culture.

Several other scholars have studied girls' web design, including Kimberley Gregson, Sharon Mazzarella, Claudia Mitchell, Jacqueline Reid-Walsh, and Susannah Stern.[65] These researchers have primarily used content and dis-course analyses to explore how adolescent girls' websites function in relation to self-expression, community building, and girls' culture. In turn, Pamela Takayoshi has conducted an ethnographic study with two young female web designers, Emily and Meghan Huot, which explores their online writ-ing, assertions of voice, and constructions of identity.[66] Meanwhile, Michelle

Comstock and Marion Leonard have examined girls' websites in their larger studies of grrrl zines, Elke Zobl has analyzed female-run zine distros as part of her analysis of the international grrrl zine community, and Doreen Piano has explored such distros alongside women's zine catalogs and compilation zines in her study of young feminists' subcultural production.[67]

Unfortunately, because most scholars studying girls' web design are primarily interested in issues of identity and community rather than aesthetics or skill development, very few have considered the formal components of girls' websites.[68] Moreover, to my knowledge, none has examined in depth how female youth develop their web skills and activities over time.[69] Given the disparities among female youth in terms of access to, training in, and sustained engagements with wired computers, however, we cannot assume that web design, an advanced computing activity, is an obvious or easy next step for female youth who began their online ventures through emailing, instant messaging, and web surfing. Nevertheless, as Kaplan and Farrell argue:

> [S]ome women persist [in their engagement with digital technologies] despite the barriers to entry and the problems they find. ... We need to know more about what attracts women to electronic environments and what features of the activities we engage in sustain us in these new spaces. And we need to find out what might account for the presence of some adolescent women, a "next generation" of electronic communicators: how do those adolescents who gravitate to electronic spaces and seem to thrive there come into the subculture and find pleasure, amusement, and interest there?[70]

It is my hope that by studying in depth female youth who are active, long-term participants in web culture and the websites they create, we can understand better how some girls are able to overcome the various hurdles young females face with regard to developing advanced computing skills and investing in the construction of cyberspace.

FROM EMAILING TO DISTROING: THE DEVELOPMENT OF YOUNG FEMALE WEB DESIGNERS

With the objective of expanding scholarship on girls' web design in new directions, my study investigates how female youth become interested in web design and develop the advanced computing skills required for the creation and maintenance of websites. Using information collected from an ethnographic study of twelve young female distro owners, I explore such girls' autodidactic, noncurricular training in web design, as well as the various phases of web-based activity through which they moved before creating their own websites.

Online distro owners were chosen as the focus of this study because their web skills and participation in digital culture are quite high in comparison to other young female web users. In addition to creating online businesses, which require regular maintenance, these teenage girls and young women are active in web culture via email, instant messaging, message boards, and online journals (also known as "web logs" or, more commonly, "blogs"). Another reason I am interested in studying this specific group of young female web designers is because the particular type of websites they develop—online distros— allows them to merge, and thus blur the distinctions between, several practices essential to media culture: *consumption* (most of these girls read zines and have created a mechanism by which other zine readers can obtain such texts); *production* (most create zines and have produced at least one website, their distro); *entrepreneurship* (all are business owners, even if they rarely make a profit or a living from this work); *community development* (most encourage communication with their customers, and all participate in groups related to micro media).[71]

In my survey, I asked these young female distro owners to provide the following information: their birth year, race, and past and present socioeconomic status; the various forms of digital technology they have used since first going online; their involvement in various web-based activities, such as emailing, surfing, journaling, and participating in message boards; their history of producing zines, websites, and distros; their reasons for starting a distro; the factors that were most influential on their interest in producing websites; the factors that were most useful to training in web design; the authoring tools they use to produce websites; their least and most favorite aspects of web design; and those aspects of design that they feel are most essential for a successful website and distro.

Of the initial 26 distro owners selected for this study, the resulting pool of research subjects was comprised of 9 white females and 3 Latinas.[72] At the time of my study, the respondents were between the ages of 18 and 29. The average age of respondents was 22.2, and most were in their early 20s. Although this book focuses primarily on girls' media production, I included several young women in this study in order to better assess how online skills and activities of young females transform over time. Despite their current age, therefore, all subjects began their online ventures, including web design, sometime between the ages of 8 and 21. The average length of time for their participation in web culture to date is 7.1 years, with the longest amount of time online to date for any one participant being 10 years and the shortest only 1.

Most of the distro owners in this study are currently high school and college students. (Only one is pursuing a degree related to computing.) In turn, several are stay-at-home mothers or part-time employees. Thus, all subjects have a somewhat flexible schedule that allows for their regular participation in the various practices related to web design and distro ownership. Interestingly, the vast majority of subjects who are no longer financially supported by their parents have much lower household incomes than when they were youth, perhaps as a result of their commitment to radical politics and the micro media community (discussed in more detail below). Nevertheless, all subjects have their own computers and, with one exception, access the Internet through broadband cable modems, suggesting their frequent and lengthy daily computer use, as well as considerable commitment to cyberculture. In turn, several have purchased an Internet domain for their distros.

In an effort to broaden the methodologies used to study girls' web design, the final section of this chapter includes formal analyses of the subjects' distros, including their aesthetic and structural components. The twelve female-run distros examined here are C/S Distro, Dreamer's Distro, Fork 'n Spoon Mail Order, HousewifeXcore Distro, Ladymen Distro, Mad People Distro, MY MY Distro, Neon Pavement Distro, Spy Kids Distro, Supernova Distro, Wingless Zine Distro, and Wrong Number Distro.[73] Unfortunately, comparative analyses of current and older versions of each of these sites, and thus individual designers' development in web design, are virtually impossible. Most of the older versions of these distros have not been archived on the Internet.[74] Moreover, of those distros whose earlier iterations are archived, usually only a few pages have been saved, which results in an incomplete picture of the distro. In turn, the original source code of archived sites typically cannot be viewed, which makes discerning a designer's web skills at the moment she wrote such code quite difficult. Of the twelve distros in this study only one, Supernova, has enough (three) archived versions with viewable source code to allow for some comparative analyses of the same designer's web skills over more than one year. Thus, I primarily make comparative analyses of the skills exhibited currently by all twelve distro owners in their websites.

GOING ONLINE: GIRLS' INITIAL ADVENTURES IN WEB CULTURE

The average age of my survey subjects' initial experiences with the Internet and World Wide Web was 14.8 years old, with the youngest being 8 and the oldest 21. Although two respondents had gone online only in the past two years, all other respondents have been online since the mid- to late 1990s, a period of considerable expansion of the Internet into various sectors of U.S. society. Several research subjects' responses indicate that their first computing experiences occurred simultaneously with their initial online experiences, thus suggesting their access to a wired computer either at home or at school. As noted above, most public schools were wired over the course of the 1990s, while the number of homes with Internet access lagged behind during this period. Indeed, the largest group of families with home computers and Internet access at that time were those who were white with household incomes of $75,000 and up. Half of this study's participants fit within that group, reporting that as teenagers their families' income was between $55,000 and $150,000 per year. Though the other half reported household incomes in the $18,000 to $54,000 range, some of these subjects also had wired computers in their homes when they were youth. Yet several recall experiencing some curtailment of their online activities as a result of the relatively high cost of Internet subscriptions at that time. For example, one respondent remembers devising innovative ways to participate in online culture while also keeping her families' Internet bills low:

> When I first started making websites we had an AOL [America On Line] account & back then it was still charged by the hour. I was living with my Dad & he wasn't all about me spending too much time online so I would compose it in some sort of text editor & then copy & paste it once I signed on, I had to do that with emails too to avoid using too much time.[75]

Other respondents, likely as a result of their household's low income or the lack of Internet accessibility in their community, report that their experiences in cyberculture as youth were postponed by the absence of a computer or modem at home. For example, one respondent notes, "I think [I went online in] 1999. I didn't have internet though til the summer of 2000, when my parents could afford a computer. When I was first introduced to the internet it was through a required class I took at my junior high."[76] Another recalls, "I started going online at school in late 1998 or early 1999. My home finally had internet access in the late spring of 1999."[77] These responses are in keeping with reports that most American youth have more access to the Internet at school than at home. Other respondents without access to a wired computer at home or school when they were young recall developing alternative strategies for getting online. For example, one respondent recalls, "We didn't have the internet until we moved to California in 1995. My mom's best friend had it at their house, and her daughter was sort of my big sister figure. We'd go online together all the time."[78]

Much like the female youth in other recent studies of home Internet use, the vast majority of subjects in my study indicated that once they got online, emailing and participating in chat rooms and message boards were their primary activities. For example, one respondent recalls, "I first went online when I was a sophomore in high school which was 1996. ... I would spend hours chatting in the AOL riot grrrl chat room or posting to message boards, like Chainsaw."[79] Another respondent notes, "We had AOL and I spent most of my online time in chat rooms or instant messenger conversations, emailing, and surfing the web."[80] These findings are in keeping with various studies that demonstrate that girls' online activities are primarily related to communication.[81] Yet the respondents' reported high level of involvement in chat rooms and message boards is also suggestive of a greater interest in and commitment to web culture than that normally found in female youth. Indeed, the respondents' regular engagement in these activities and committed investment in the communities such practices produce likely contributed to their web-skill confidence and their advanced uses of digital technologies. As Ann Locke Davidson and Janet Ward Schofield found in an earlier study of girls' collaborative online activities, "[T]he presence of socially similar others was helpful for promoting active participation as well as lessened anxiety about technical learning. This, in turn, likely contributed to increased technological learning more generally."[82]

Also significant in this regard is the fact that many of the message boards and chat rooms in which my study's respondents participated as teenagers were launched by other girls and women. Such message board creators or moderators seem to have served a role-modeling function in these subjects' lives, encouraging many of them to take a more active role in developing a female-centered cyberculture. As Davidson and Schofield noted in their study, "[G]irls derived comfort and confidence from their observations with a technically proficient female teacher."[83] It is also important to note that all of the subjects in my study reported being actively involved in zine culture (e.g., reading zines, making zines, tabling[84] at zine conventions) at the time of their initial online engagements. Their commitment to this actively discursive community seems to have encouraged their regular participation in message boards, as well as their interest in other web-based forms of communication.

Several respondents reported that surfing the Web was also important to their early adventures in cyberspace, as it allowed them to gather information and discover interesting sites. For example, one respondent who first went online at school recalls, "We were not allowed to surf unless we were looking for content or images for our pages. But I surfed anyway to look at zines and take down distro addresses for mail order catalogs and such."[85] Another notes, "I went online in about 1997 and all I did was print out pictures of 80s nostalgia. Eventually and thankfully, I got around to chatting and web design about two years later."[86] Another subject recalls surfing for recipes.[87] Unfortunately, few other respondents remember specifically the types of websites they frequented as teenagers. Nonetheless, it is likely that the subjects' regular engagement in web surfing helped expose them to a wide variety of websites, thus providing them with some elementary forms of knowledge about web design even before they began to construct their own sites. Indeed, one subject relates her learning of HTML directly to her early surfing activities.[88] As discussed below, viewing websites' source code is the primary means by which the subjects in this study learned web design, and familiarity with and interest in particular websites is a necessary step before source code viewing can take place.[89] Thus, surfing is an essential step in developing more advanced web-based computer skills.

WEBGURLS: INITIAL FORAYS INTO WEB DESIGN

The span of time between going online and creating websites can be quite short for some female youth committed to cyberculture. Among the participants in my study, the average length of time between initially going online and creating a website was 1.3 years, with the shortest span being only a few months and the longest 3 years. Such movement from one digital activity to another, often within a short period of time, is supported by other research on young people's web skill acquisition. For example, in his study of male adolescents who are active in cyberculture, Chris Abbott found that several felt "pressure to move on to 'the next thing' [after exploring bulletin boards], in this case a web page."[90] Differences in the length of time between respondents' initial engagement in online culture and creating a website do not appear to be related directly to their age, as younger and older females alike demonstrated both quick and slow adaptation to new web skills. The youngest age at which a subject created her first website was 8 years old, while the oldest was 22 for an average age of 15.4 among all respondents. Ten of the respondents, however, created their first website by the age of 17.

When asked to select factors that most inspired their interest in producing websites, the majority of respondents reported owning a computer, surfing the Web, playing video games, and participating in online message boards.[91] Some respondents also noted less primary influences, such as reading Internet guidebooks, being encouraged by a parent, friend, or partner, and liking computer-savvy female characters in popular culture, such as Willow in *Buffy the Vampire Slayer*. Interestingly, only one respondent noted that taking a computer class inspired her desire to become involved in web design, a finding that suggests that other researchers' recommendations to focus primarily on schools and teacher training in order to improve girls' relationships with computer culture need to be reexamined.[92]

The research subjects were also asked to identify which factors were most useful in developing their knowledge about web design, and respondents indicated overwhelmingly that their web training was informal, largely autodidactic, and comprised primarily of viewing the source pages of well-liked websites. A typical response in this regard was, "I was 17 when I designed my first website, but I was never satisfied with it. If I saw something nifty on a site, I would view the source of the page and dig through the code to see how they did whatever it was that I liked."[93] Another respondent noted,

"Practice, practice, and more" when asked how she developed her knowledge in web design.[94] Such responses suggest that these young female computer users became increasingly confident in the tinkering activities seen by the AAUW commissioners and other researchers as essential to the development of fluency with digital technologies.[95]

Many respondents noted that chatting online with other bloggers, web designers, and entrepreneurs on such sites as Live Journal, Laundromatic, and The Switchboards was only slightly less significant in their web training than viewing source code.[96] For example, one respondent recalls:

> I loved the internet, so I was online all the time and eventually discovered the whole teen personal site craze through message boards. I thought the stuff those girls were doing was awesome, so I would view the sources of their sites and make my own from altering their HTML.[97]

In turn, visiting online guides in web design was identified as a significant component in these girls' skill development. As one respondent notes, "I was never taught by a class or book, but I still use lissaexplainsitall.com all the time. It's so useful!"[98] Similarly, another respondent notes, "I taught myself all of my own web-design skills. I used the Webmonkey tutorials … and Google searches to help me figure out everything I needed to know."[99]

Secondary influences on the development of respondents' web skills include print guidebooks and supportive parents, teachers, friends, and partners. One interesting finding is that not one respondent noted that a sibling inspired them to go online or influenced their training in web design. This finding may be the result of many subjects' status as an only child, or the sister of siblings who are either much older or much younger than they are. In other words, even respondents who were not the only child appear to have been generationally isolated within their families, which might suggest a reason for their interests in physically solitary recreational activities, such as computing. In turn, only two respondents indicated that a computer class was useful for developing their web skills, yet neither ranked this activity as highly useful. Again, this finding suggests that other researchers' recommendations for improving girls' school-based computing need to be rethought in relation to female youth who develop an interest in such skills and activities elsewhere.

Several subjects indicated that they used free web authoring programs, such as those provided by AOL, Geocities, Freewebs, and Angelfire, when they began their initial forays into web design. This strategy seems to have been employed primarily by those girls who began making websites during their preteen and early teenage years. For example, the youngest respondent in the study recalls, "I started designing web pages when I was 8 using the regular Geocities or Angelfire templates."[100] A teenage respondent who was asked why she does not create the HTML code for her distro replied, "freewebs.com already had different backgrounds you could choose from."[101] Similarly, another teenage respondent reported, "I used Angelfire. It basically did everything for me."[102] As discussed in further detail below, such web authoring programs do not require much skill in web design, as they create HTML code as users select from an array of layout designs, colors, fonts, and images by pointing and clicking.

Nine of the twelve respondents reported training themselves in HTML either after or instead of using web authoring programs. Such self-training in HTML primarily involved perusing the source code of other websites or referencing online guides or print guidebooks. Typical responses in this regard include, "A friend of mine helped me get started and I have been figuring it out by myself ever since then, sometimes with the help of tutorial websites."[103] Some respondents demonstrate pride in their autodidacticism:

> When I was around fifteen or sixteen … , my mother and I both wanted our own websites so we started teaching ourselves HTML and various coding. I was self-taught in all my HTML knowledge (no classes, just searches), Photoshop, scripting, and dHTML. It actually prompted my interest in high school to take programming classes.[104]

(Interestingly, this girl's experiences in computer training occurred in reverse order to the typical scenario feminist scholars of computing typically imagine, with female youth receiving training in digital technologies in school before expanding into the noncurricular arena.) Similarly, another responded reports:

> All I know now I've taught myself. I basically draw a picture in my sketchbook, then reference how to do all that through tutorials or what I've learned through customizing my livejournal. When I tell distro owners I hand code all my html, they shudder and tell me to invest in Dreamweaver or something.[105]

Other subjects were less positive when describing the development of their coding skills. For example, one respondent noted: "I am self-taught but my skills are so out-of-date. I write everything by hand in some sort of crude fashion that most browsers don't even read properly although I am slowly learning more about html 4.0. It's all a process!"[106]

Some subjects reveal pride in their early ventures in web design, suggesting how their first websites allowed them to assert themselves publicly and to construct their own place within cyberspace. For example, one respondent notes:

> I … taught myself how to do a little bit of html approx[imately] two years before I started the distro. I used to create little websites about really whatever because I enjoyed to write and thought it was such a neat thing, being able to create a space that's all yours on the web.[107]

Other subjects, however, were self-deprecating when describing their initial web designs. For example, one respondent who began web design as a teenager and was asked to recall her first website states:

> My jr. high website? We either had to make a page about us ... or like a fan site, and I did mine about punk rock ... OMG [Oh, my God] this is so embarrassing!!!!!! ... That website later changed into my distro. ... It was BAD. I've tried to erase those from my memory.[108]

Another subject recalls, "I made a personal website using AOL's site builder. It consisted of one page, lots of scrolling and even more photos of Courtney Love. It was horrid."[109] Asked to describe this website in more detail, she elaborates:

> My first AOL website was created pretty much because I could. As in, they offered the space so I figured I should use it and use it I did. I posted my riot grrrl-esque rants about sexism along with photos of Courtney Love and my other rockstar crushes. I linked to other AOL websites my friends were making, which were usually just as awful as mine, but it was something new and we were excited.[110]

Though such subjects' negative recollections of their early websites seem to be used to distance themselves from their initial, amateur endeavors at web design, such recollections also construct these designers' current skills as advanced and polished. Indeed, the subject who built the AOL-supported site as a teenager has gone on to design numerous websites, both for herself and others. Because her design skills have developed considerably over time and with experience, she is able to see clearly how her old websites do not measure up to her current standards.

DISTROGURLS: DEMONSTRATING FURTHER COMMITMENT TO CYBERCULTURE

Among the subjects in my study, the average age for creating an online distro was 19.3 years old, with the oldest age being 27 and the youngest 13. Nine of twelve respondents were 21 or younger when they started their distro, and four were 18 or under. The average length of time between the respondents' design of their first website and the introduction of their distro was 3.2 years, over twice as long as the average amount of time they took from first going online to creating a website. The shortest span between creating a website and starting a distro was less than a year, and the longest was 10 years. Again, differences with regard to the length of time between respondents' initial engagement in these advanced web activities do not appear to be related to age, as teenage girls and young women alike demonstrated both quick and slow commitment to starting a distro. Instead, the long period of time it took these teenage girls and young women to launch their distros seems primarily related to the need for advanced web skills in creating and maintaining not just these websites, but the businesses they support.

Most subjects revealed that they decided to start an online distro only after they felt confident in their web design skills and had established a strong commitment to micro media culture, especially the zine community. Indeed, while the respondents provided a variety of answers when asked their primary reason for creating an online distro, a reoccurring response was that they had a desire to participate more actively in zine culture and to help distribute zines and other independently produced goods to a wider audience. For example:

I just wanted to be a part of the zine community in a bigger way.[111]

I wanted to be able to distribute zines that I enjoyed and that had impacted me in some way.[112]

I wanted to help spread zines that I love to a wider audience. I figured the best way to do that would be to start a distro.[113]

[I wanted] to spread independent literature and music.[114]

I wanted to help support the underground scene.[115]

I absolutely adore the DIY scene and this is my subtle way of being a vein in the community. A slight way of giving back & helping others get the word out of their project(s).[116]

At the time I started there were not many distros around. So I started mine to help out the community as well as to show off zines that I loved.[117]

Some subjects connect their commitment to zine culture with more specific personal reasons for starting an online distro also. For example, the owner of C/S Distro, who identifies as Chicana, reports that she wanted to "try to have a place where one can get more Chicana and POC [People of Color] zines."[118] Supernova's owner notes that her young age was a significant factor in starting a distro:

At 13 I was on the lower end of the age spectrum [when I started my distro], but I knew there were other young teenagers out there who were into zines too, and maybe feeling a bit intimidated by distros run by older people. So by being someone who was more their age, I hope to get rid of that intimidation.[119]

In turn, the owner of Fork 'n Spoon reports, "I love food zines and food-themed crafts, but I couldn't find many distros that carried much of either, so I started my own."[120] Meanwhile, some distro owners note that online distribution businesses are easier and less expensive to run than those use print catalogs. For instance, Wingless Zine Distro's owner states:

> I'm also addicted to the Internet and I love that I can keep everything up-to-date in a flash, as opposed to printing up catalogs and going out of stock. I also like the low start-up fee (all I have to pay for is the zines because my [web] hosting is free, to do a catalog I'd have to pay to make copies of it and also the postage of distributing it).[121]

Creating and maintaining an online distro involves many activities in addition to web design, including having in-depth knowledge of the products to be sold, soliciting and selecting goods for sale, promoting products, bookkeeping, communicating with customers, and packaging and mailing purchases. Running a distro, therefore, entails considerable effort, time, expense, and commitment, a point made repeatedly when I asked respondents if they had any advice for young females interested in this activity:

> Starting your own distro is much, much harder then you may think, so the advice I have is to think about it, love zines, and be prepared to not make any money, even lose money. Working hard and being courteous does pay off, it just takes time.[122]

> Read up on distros—there's several zines and websites dedicated to this. ... Take into account the TIME involved, that often it'll be fruitless for some ... single parenting + having a distro = hard stuff![123]

> Listen to everyone when they say it is hard 'cause it is!!! It's hours and hours at the post office, answering submissions (yes or no), packing orders, updating websites, looking for zines to distro, planning tabling, PayPal-ing and paying people, keeping records making flyers, etc. and you don't get paid for any of this![124]

> Running a distro is a LOT of hard work that I don't think many of us took into consideration before starting one. It requires quite a bit of time and money to start it up, you have to build up a reputation among the zine community, and promotion is so important![125]

> Distros are hard work. Be sure that you can manage your site effectively before setting it up to be a distro. You need lots of time and energy to keep people updated and to be responsible about orders. People depend on you to communicate with them. They send you their hard-earned money and you have to respect that and respect

them. It takes time to build up a reputation and a few small mistakes can destroy it.[126]

Some young females interested in running a distro collaborate with others in order to accomplish all of the activities required for the successful operation of such a business. For example, MY MY Distro is corun by two sisters, and the Ladymen and Wrong Number distros are both managed by a small group of friends. Given the numerous activities involved in creating and maintaining an online distro, it is not surprising that many of these web-based businesses go on hiatus periodically or cease operations permanently. In fact, approximately 10 percent of the female-run distros considered for inclusion in this study were either temporarily or permanently closed.

DISTROS, CYBERGURL STYLE!: DEVELOPING SKILL IN WEB DESIGN

A survey of young female distro owners can elicit useful information about such individuals' computer training, web skills, and online experiences. Yet formal analyses of the websites such owners create can provide further information about the level of skill they have achieved in design and coding. In the remainder of this chapter, therefore, I closely examine the aesthetic and structural components of the twelve distros in this study, with the hope of expanding our understanding of the various decisions girls make when creating websites.

Given the numerous possibilities available to web designers in terms of words, images, typography, colors, page layout, site organization, and navigational tools, it is not surprise that the distros analyzed for this project are quite different from each other in terms of not only appearance but structure, lending them each a unique character. As Susannah Stern argues:

> Mediated presentations oblige their creators to make choices about what to include and omit, and how to present and re-present information. Such decisions signal creators' attitudes about what is more or less important to them. Girls who design home pages likewise make decisions that affect how their page will look and what their audience will learn about them.[127]

In one of her early studies of home pages, Stern discusses the significance of aesthetic decisions to girl web designers' expressions of "tone," by which she means "the various components of girls' pages (such as word choice, site organization, colour, images, and the actual content) that work together to exude an overall demeanour."[128] Although the online distros included in my project are less personal in theme and objective than the home pages examined by

Stern, these sites were nevertheless created through particular aesthetic and architectural decisions that communicate specific messages about the distros themselves, their owners, and the goods they sell. As I will demonstrate, these websites express at least two distinct tones, one associated primarily with the professional arena of commerce, and one more closely affiliated with the informal world of friendship and community. That distro owners are able to successfully merge these two somewhat contradictory tones in their websites demonstrates not only their considerable skill in web design, but also their savvy about these two cultures and the means by which they can be brought together in one medium.

Building Distros: Web Authoring Programs and HTML

As mentioned previously, several of the distro owners in this study used free web authoring programs provided online by such companies as AOL and Yahoo! Geocities when they started making websites.[129] Because these programs require minimal knowledge of and experience with coding, they are quite useful to individuals who are unfamiliar or less skilled in HTML. Simply by pointing and clicking, users can select particular design components for their sites, including layout, color, fonts, and images. As users do so, the web authoring program writes HTML code into a browser window facsimile that users can eventually publish online as a website. Such authoring programs vastly reduce the amount of work involved in positioning and aligning text, images, and graphics, practices that are quite laborious and time consuming when designers write code themselves.

At the same time, however, web authoring programs, particularly those that are available for free online, are quite limited with regard to different options users have for fonts, colors, images, and layout, which can be a detriment to those attempting to create unique sites. For example, the owner of Wingless Zine Distro reports, "I used some of the templates on Geocities and Homestead before I knew much about HTML. I ran screaming from those pre-packaged sites when I saw a terrible site that had the exact same template as mine."[130] Nevertheless, some of these authoring programs allow designers, typically for a cost, to edit the HTML codes they create, thus providing a mechanism to further customize the generic sites generated by such programs' basic software.

Of the twelve distros in this study, only three—Spy Kids Distro, Neon Pavement Distro, and Fork 'n Spoon Mail Order—were produced via web authoring programs. Each distro owner's decision to utilize a free authoring program was likely due to the short amount of time she had spent online and creating websites before deciding to launch her own distro. As the owner of Fork 'n Spoon states:

> I use a Blogger blog [for my distro] that I've modified by embedding links and adding my logo. I do this because my html skills are really limited and the blog enables me to update my distro often and I can add new items and pictures without having to know much html.[131]

An analysis of these three sites helps to elucidate the types of distros created by female youth who have minimal HTML skill, as well as the advantages and disadvantages of web authoring programs.

The website for Spy Kids Distro is very simple in design.[132] Built from a web authoring template available for free on Lycos Angelfire, the contents of the site's home page consists of the distro name and logo, a short message with product updates, a navigation menu, and an image of Bubbles from the animated cartoon series *The Power Puff Girls*. The distro's logo is oval shaped, and includes a black-on-white illustration of a teenage girl with short hair peeking around a wall and holding a zine in one hand. With the exception of the distro name and logo, which are centered on the page, all of the information on the Spy Kids' site is flush left, a typical layout for Angelfire templates. The background color of all pages is black, and most of the site's text is white, except for the internal links on the navigation menu, which are turquoise blue. These links, appearing in text form (e.g., "The Catalog"), take users to the site's various pages,[133] including a guestbook, a message board, a page with the distro's products, a page for potential submitters, a page that provides information on the distro owner, a link to join the Spy Kids mailing list, a page on the Spy Kids "Street Team" (organized to promote the distro), and a FAQ (Frequently Asked Questions) page. The navigation menu does not appear on pages other than the home page, requiring users to return to the home page to navigate the site. A review of archived older versions of the Spy Kids site reveals no significant updates in layout or design over a four-year period, only in product details.

The current Neon Pavement Distro website is minimalist and professional in appearance.[134] In fact, the Freewebs template the designer used for this site is titled "Sleek." Each page, including the home page, includes a dark gray background that is subdivided into smaller royal blue, light gray, and white blocks. The title of the distro appears at the top of each page in white, lowercase letters. The site's navigation menu appears on the left and is comprised of text-based links. Currently on the home page, beneath the distro's name and to the right, is a special announcement: "buy five or more zines, receive one zine free of your choice and all orders over $10 will receive free shipping until may 31!" Below this announcement and to the right are two identical black and white photographs of train tracks. These images are stacked vertically. At the very bottom of the home page is a counter that calculates the number of visitors to the site.

The other pages of the Neon Pavement distro include two product pages, identified as "zines a-m" and "zines n-z," an "order/submit" page for customers and zinemakers, an "about/contact" page, which provides information about the distro owner and her postal and email addresses, an "order tracking/updates" page, which includes tracking information, product updates, and a linked guestbook, and a "links" page, which connects users to other distros and zines. With the exception of the "order tracking/updates" page, which has a white background and separate horizontal rectangles in dark and light gray for each order and update, all other Neon Pavement pages are similar in layout and color to the home page. The different appearance of the "order tracking/updates" page is likely due to its construction via another web authoring program provided online by Live Journal.

The website for Fork 'n Spoon Mail Order is considerably different in appearance and tone from those for the Spy Kids and Neon Pavement distros.[135] Most obviously, the design for Fork 'n Spoon is less serious, which is largely the result of its busier appearance and privileging of the color pink. It is less minimalist in design than Neon Pavement Distro, but more professional than Spy Kids Distro. As noted above, Fork 'n Spoon's owner utilized a free web authoring program from Blogger to create her distro site. The particular template she chose, "Son of Moto," produces a home page, which is white and bordered by one color (pink, in this case) (Figure 17). The title of the distro appears in white lettering in the upper left-hand corner, and is separated by a simple, white and pink cross-stitch border. The rest of the home page's content is divided into two very long vertical columns, the screen length of which is normative for blogs but atypical for other websites, because of the tendency for users to become easily distracted by too much information or annoyed by the slow download time of long pages. In the left column are the most recent product updates, some of which include photographs, followed by several logos from other zine distros and independent entrepreneurs that are externally linked to those sites, and then by older product updates. (These other sites are also hyperlinked on Fork 'n Spoon's "links" page.) In the right column is a short "about me" section, which is linked to the owner's blogger profile, the navigation menu (titled "Our Stuff"), the distro's logo, a section titled "Previous Posts," a section titled "Archives," a logo for blogger.com, and an interactive component from notifylist.com that allows users to sign up for email updates from the distro's owner.

The other sections of the Fork 'n Spoon distro include eight pages devoted to different products (zines, poetry books, stationary, accessories, soap, kitchen gear, vintage items, and buttons), an order form page, a submissions page, an "about" page, and an external links page. As is the case for most other distros and well-designed websites, all other Fork 'n Spoon pages are similar in layout and color as the home page, with the exception that the distro title appears in a

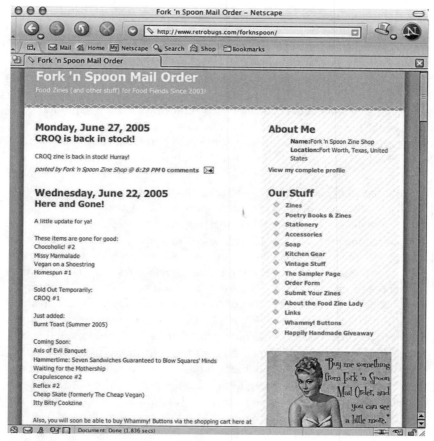

Figure 17 A template produced website.
Fork 'n Spoon Mail Order, 2005. Courtesy of Stephanie Scarborough.

darker pink hue on subsequent pages. While the right side of these other pages continues to show the same information as on the home page, the content that appears on the left side of each page is specific to the theme of that page (e.g., zines, or ordering).

As is clear from an analysis of these three sites, distro owners who utilize free authoring programs to build websites do not demonstrate similar uses of such software, nor construct sites with similar styles. In fact, each of these three owners was able to create a unique tone for her distro in spite of the limited range of style templates offered by the web-authoring program they used. Although the owner of Spy Kids has a "bare bones" distro style that has changed little over the course of the site's existence, Fork 'n Spoon and Neon Pavement have more elaborate websites that likely demanded more time, labor, and skill to develop despite their owners' use of templates and minimal design experience.

This range of tone and design complexity is also noticeable within the eight distros created through HTML, though web designers who use hand coding are able to produce more uniquely individual sites. The use of HTML coding alone suggests that distro owners have intermediate to advanced web skills, for they are not dependent on web authoring software to produce sites for them. Though HTML is not difficult to learn, its acquisition is based on text rather than sound, reading and writing rather than hearing and speaking. Therefore, it is a language somewhat difficult for younger children without such skills to acquire. In turn, HTML requires strong attention to detail as well as extensive practice to be used efficiently and appropriately, thus demanding a considerable amount of focused time spent on a computer.

As the distro owners revealed in their responses to my survey, very few have formal training in HTML; most have learned this language by viewing the source code of other websites. In addition, these owners have supplemented their training in web design via both print and online guidebooks. This autodidactism should not be misinterpreted as contributing to unformed knowledge or unpolished skills, however. Most of the distros are visually appealing and, perhaps more importantly, easily navigated, which suggests that their designers have spent considerable time and effort in choosing the aesthetic components and fine-tuning the structural elements of their sites. A comparative analysis of these distros' stylistic and architectural components, however, reveals different levels of skill among this small group of young female web designers, which in turn suggests different amounts of online experience, as well as different levels of commitment to professional web design and the communicative aspects of cyberculture.

Site Organization

One of the first decisions that a designer must make when creating a website is how its information will be presented structurally. Page length, typically expressed by computer users in terms of the number of computer screens it takes to view all information for a specific page, is a primary consideration here. As web instructor Margaret Batschelet notes, the presentation of text in digital media is quite different from that of print media:

> Web usability studies have indicated that many readers, particularly casual ones, prefer short pages. Usability specialist Jakob Nielsen has pointed out that reading from a computer screen is around 25 percent slower than reading from a [print] page; moreover, readers have reported that they feel uncomfortable reading long pages of text on screen. ... [R]eaders need more accessible chunks of information onscreen so that they can assimilate the material quickly and move on.[136]

As a result of these findings, web instructors and guidebooks typically suggest that designers divide the content of their websites into several short pages, preferably only one computer screen in length. This web page structure does not require the reader to wait for long pages to download, a prospect that is especially frustrating for those with only a telephone modem, nor to scroll through lengthy pages with multiple paragraphs on a variety of topics.

The vast majority of distros in this study adhere to the short page length recommended by web instructors and guidebooks and practiced by professional web designers. Most distro pages are only one screen in length and thus provide minimal information on a specific topic that can be accessed quickly by users. In general, the only distro pages that exceeded this one-page rule were those devoted to products and external links, which suggests that users are more willing to linger on such pages, browsing information at their own speed. Of the twelve distros in this study, the two notable exceptions to the short page-length rule are Ladymen Distro and Fork 'n Spoon Mail Order, whose sites are comprised of pages that are two to five computer screens in length. As noted above, the lengthy pages that comprise the Fork 'n Spoon site are likely the result of the blogging template used by the owner. Ladymen Distro's excessive page length may be the result of a designer who has less developed web skills, less exposure to professional web design, or less frustration with downloading similarly structured sites.

All of the distros included in this study also conform to the multi-page norm for user-friendly web design. In addition to a home page, which typically contains the distro name, a welcome message, and product updates, each distro site has separate pages devoted to products, ordering, and submissions. Zines are the primary goods sold by distros. In order to provide information about each zine but not frustrate customers with one long page that includes all the titles for sale, most distros' zine catalogs are subdivided into several different pages based on the first letters of zine titles (e.g., A–F, G–M, N–S, T–Z). Most distros sell a few other types of handcrafted goods also, such as buttons and music, and have separate pages for those products. While many distros allow for both mail and online order, several in this study, including Fork 'n Spoon, HousewifeXcore, MY MY, and Wrong Number, have more advanced customer services, such as order tracking and shopping cart viewing.[137] The addition of these particular commercial components suggests such owners' considerable commitment to customer service and perhaps advanced web skills, since these components require additional hyperlinks and association with other online entities, such as PayPal. At the same time, however, other distro owners distance themselves from corporate ventures and capitalist structures and thus rely solely on cash payments and mail-order purchases.

Layout

Website layout entails the positioning and alignment of text, images, and graphics for each page, and thus is of extreme importance in producing an effective, easy-to-use site that communicates professionalism and commitment to users. Of all the various activities involved in web design, layout requires perhaps the most advanced knowledge of and skill with HTML, as Batschelet notes:

> Unfortunately, HTML wasn't devised as a design medium; it was originally thought of simply as a way to convey text. Thus, many of the techniques that designers have come up with to make Web page design more effective are essentially workarounds, ways of making data devices such as tables substitute for design grids.[138]

In order to avoid overlapping and other layout mishaps and thus to produce a website design that looks professional, web designers must learn to write HTML tables. This type of coding allows designers to subdivide web page content into different cells, and then to manipulate the positioning and alignment of text, images, and graphics within those cells. Obviously, the more cells a designer creates through tables, the more complex the site's layout. Of the twelve distros in this study, six employed multiple tables in their web page layouts, which suggests that their designers have moved beyond elementary HTML coding skills.

More advanced web designers employ frames in order to manipulate text, images, and graphics in page layouts. Like tables, frames allow a designer to divide web pages into various sections that can be worked on independently. Yet, unlike tables, frames are independent HTML files that are connected in a master HTML file called a frameset. Frames allow for particular features to appear on each page of a website, such as a distro name or navigation bar, despite other information that may change from page to page, such as product descriptions. As Batschelet notes:

> Frames offer many advantages for layout: they're very good for making comparisons between items because you can have items side-by-side in the frames. They can break your page into interesting segments that you can treat individually: you can put a banner in a frame, for example, without having it influence the material in the other frames, as it would if you placed it on the page without a grid. Frames also allow your reader to have some interaction with your page; as the reader clicks a link, a frame on the page shows the changes.[139]

Unfortunately, one of the main disadvantages of using multiple frames to construct a web page is that they typically require more download time and thus often inspire user frustration, especially for those who access the Internet via a telephone modem.

Most of the distros in this study that were constructed through HTML coding used frames, which suggests that their designers have developed somewhat advanced skills in web design. Indeed, an analysis of the tags, tables, and frames used to construct various iterations of these sites reveals that their designers have moved from intermediate to advanced web design skills over the course of their work on these distros. For example, source code for a 2002 version of Supernova Distro indicates that the designer used only tags and tables, whereas code for a 2003 iteration shows her use of frames also.[140] Moreover, the code for both of these versions of Supernova demonstrates that their designer was already well versed in the use of Cascading Style Sheets by 2002. Such sheets were introduced to web designers in 1997 in order to provide features found lacking in earlier versions of HTML, but were not compliant with most web browsers and thus not used by many web designers until a few years ago.[141] Despite her young age, therefore, Supernova's teenage designer demonstrates considerable skill in some of the most advanced web coding strategies currently available.

Navigation Tools

The layout of sites is a crucial factor in attracting users and keeping their attention. Yet when the distro owners in this study were asked what component of web design they think is most important to the success of their sites, most answered "navigation tools":

> I guess the most important aspect to me is a site that is easy to navigate. I don't like getting lost within a web page & not being able to find my way out.[142]

> I think navigation [is among] the most important. First off, I have had people say they were confused about a site I used to have ... and I've seen people, or even myself, complain about the same thing with various websites.[143]

> I need my sites to be easily navigated. I hate sites with pages that require the use of my browser's back button. I prefer simplicity and ease of use, I try not to clutter things up or make them confusing.[144]

> Navigation is ... a big element because I want my customers to be able to flow through the shop without any worries of where or how to go next.[145]

> I think navigation is most important. If people can't easily find your items, you lose business.[146]

> I love websites that have hidden pages and creative navigation sys-
> tems but I think for a site like mine, you have to make it easy to find
> your way around and get what you're looking for![147]

Distros cannot afford to have their clients get lost or frustrated in the process of browsing, ordering, or submitting products. While profit is not a primary goal for most distro owners, they are conscious that they provide a unique service to the micro media community, and risk annoying members of it, as well as earning a bad reputation, if their distros have poor usability.

As noted above, one of the primary techniques used to make a website user-friendly is to divide its content into multiple pages. This practice orga-nizes a site's information into small, manageable sections, and thus contrib-utes to the ease with which users access and navigate such information. One of the primary components in a website's usability is its internal links, which connect individual pages of a site to one another. Written in HTML code, yet signified on screen either by text or icons, the internal links of a website appear on its navigation menu. When a user clicks one of the links, a differ-ent Internet address or URL[148] is accessed, taking the user to a new web page within the site.

Of the twelve distros in this study, nine had text-based navigation menus, which, as a result of the use of frames, appeared on each page, so as to not require clients to use their browser's back button to return to the home page in order to access other pages. Only one distro, Ladymen, did not include the same navigation menu on all its pages. In turn, the navigation bar for Dreamer's Distro is a pull-down menu that appears in different locations on the site's various pages and requires users to scroll down a list, thus adding more time and potential frustration to their online experience. Moreover, Dreamer's pull-down menu does not permit users to view the site's various links at all times. Thus, newcomers to this site must perform extra work in order to familiarize themselves with the distro's contents.

In addition to the links that connect a website's various pages to the home page, most sites contain internal links for images that appear on those pages. Numerous illustrations and photographs are accessible on the Web and thus are easily added to sites simply by typing such images' URLs in the source code. Nevertheless, the inclusion of image files in websites typically requires extra time and energy spent designing page layout, and thus is more typical in sites created by intermediate or advanced designers than in those produced by designers with little HTML experience. Moreover, many designers who possess advanced web skills include images in their websites that have been scanned via an apparatus external to their computer or manipulated through image editing software, processes that require both skill and expensive equip-ment. The majority of online distros in this study include images. However, because graphics files are much larger in size and thus take more time to download than text files, most owners avoid user frustration by limiting the number of image files linked to their site to a bare minimum, often only one. As the owner of C/S Distro notes, using "low images for those that are on dialup [modems]" is one of the design elements most important to her.[149] In contrast to this common practice among distro designers, the websites for Ladymen and Fork 'n Spoon contain numerous images on each page. (The types of images linked to these distros are discussed in more detail below.)

In addition to the internal links that allow users to navigate a website's various pages and graphic files, most web designers include external links that enable users to connect to other individuals via email, as well as to other websites. As commercial sites that require communication between owners and clients, most distros have external links to their owners' email addresses, typically on a "contact" page. Of the numerous external links to other websites that are linked to distros in this study, most are for other distros, zinemakers, and other individuals or organizations associated with the micro media community. With the exception of Ladymen Distro, which uses both icons and text for external links, the distros employ text-based links so as to shorten the download time for the various pages associated with their sites. Only one of the sites in this study, Dreamer's Distro, did not have a page devoted to links or an external link to the owner's email address, which suggests her lack of familiarity with or concern about norms for professional websites and online customer service.

Style

In addition to a website's organized layout and user-friendly navigation tools, simplicity in design or style is highly valued among web designers and web users. As web instructor Batschelet argues:

> In general, you want your Web design to create a sense of unity and context for your message. Because it's so easy for your readers to slip from your site to another … , your readers should never be confused about whether they're still at your site. A consistent design, with some of the same elements on every page, … will send a clear message that each page belongs to the same site.[150]

The distro owners in my study agree that simplicity and consistency in web design are of utmost importance. For example, MY MY's owner asserts, "I appreciate a clean design,"[151] while the owner of Neon Pavement Distro notes that she likes her site to look "neat and put together."[152] In turn, the owner of Mad People Distro reports, "Whenever I create a new layout for the distro, I focus on two things—accessibility and aesthetics. I try to come up with simple yet 'pretty' layouts."[153] Wrong Number's designer argues that "appeal" is one of the most important aspects of web design: "I make sure the image is appropriate, is pleasing to the eye, and ties into the theme."[154] Though few of these distro owners report having been formally trained in web design, their appreciation and employment of a clean, professional style is likely the result of the informal education they have gained during years of surfing the Web and viewing other websites.

As mentioned previously, the distros analyzed for this project are quite different from each other in terms of appearance. Yet, of all the distros in this study, the vast majority had a simple, yet professional style. Most distro owners achieved this look not only through the use of tables or frames, which neatly organize and align site content, but also through a minimal amount of information on each page. As noted above, for most distros in this study, each page can be seen via only one computer screen, which means that users spend very little time scrolling down pages and waiting for information to download. With the exception of the product pages, the web pages associated with these sites typically contain only one image and at most two short paragraphs of text, which results in a considerable amount of empty, "white" space and a

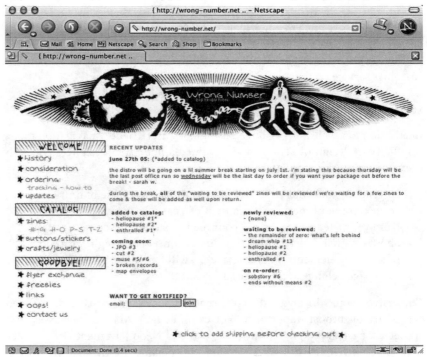

Figure 18 Clean, professional web design.
Wrong Number Distro, 2005. Courtesy of Sarah Lynne Wells.

minimalist feel (Figure 18). Moreover, all but one of the distros have the same layout for all of their pages so that users can find information easily and navigate quickly when they change pages.

In contrast to the other eleven distros in this study, Ladymen has a somewhat unpolished style, which is largely the result of long pages with inconsistent layouts, and many blinking and pop-up full-color advertisements that result from being produced through and hosted by Freeservers, a commercially supported website. In fact, Ladymen is the only distro in this study that includes corporate advertisements, which are considered anathema by most distro owners and other individuals within the micro media community because of such ads' relationship to capitalist commerce. Web designers who do not have easy access to free web space must rely on hosting sites that in turn are often advertiser-supported. In turn, as Abbott noted in his study of young web authors, "Making it look different is not a concern for many young people in the early stages of their involvement with web design."[155] Indeed, for some inexperienced web designers, creating a site that includes advertisements might help them think they have "arrived," since the vast majority of contemporary websites contain ads. Nevertheless, within the smaller world of online distros, Ladymen's choice to utilize an advertiser-supported site seems quite odd, particularly given its owners' commitment to radical media and its designer's reported four years of web design experience.[156] Moreover, many free web authoring and hosting sites exist today that do not require clients to incorporate advertisements into their websites, including Freewebs, Yahoo! Geocities, and Lycos Tripod.

Batschelet argues that unity of information is an essential component of effective web design style. Some distro owners establish such unity by selecting a name for their distro that suggests the type of products sold. For example, the owner of Fork 'n Spoon Mail Order, asserts that "my distro focuses mostly on food-themed zines and crafts, so I wanted to give it a name that reflected that."[157] Interestingly, while most distro owners participate actively in the zine community, only one subject in my study has a distro whose name is related directly to the zine she creates: The owner of Wingless Zine Distro has a zine titled "Flying without Wings."

As discussed in Chapter 4 in relation to grrrl zines, many female distro owners produce a feminist perspective for their sites by incorporating gendered terms in their distro names, such as Beer for Girls, BratGrrrl DIY, Chicana stuff Tiendita (now C/S Distro), ComuFEM, Girl + Distro, Girl Gang Distro, Grrrl Style!, Poor Girl's Dreams, Rebel Grrrl Distro, Screamqueen, Mamas Unidas Distro, and Starfire Witch Distro. Interestingly, only two of the twelve distros in this study have gendered names: Ladymen Distro and HousewifeXcore Distro. Nevertheless, both of these names suggest a feminist or queer perspective on gender. One of the co-owners of Ladymen Distro explains her distro name choice by noting, "I am a big fan of the song 'Ballad of a Ladyman' by Sleater-Kinney, and I also think that it is important to fight gender roles." [158] In addition to the name's connection to punk feminism via this song, "Ladymen" troubles traditional gender norms by merging a conventional term for adult males with a somewhat archaic label for rich women that has been recently reappropriated by some punk feminists. "HousewifeXcore" suggests a more ironic stance through its convergence of a moniker for traditional middle-class femininity with a term typically used to signify straight-edge punks.[159] As the owner notes, she "decided to have a focus, feminism ..., a theme, the 1950s, and HousewifeXcore was born."[160]

Although most distro designers also create consistency in their websites by maintaining the same layout design for each page, when surveyed, few mentioned specifically that creating a visual theme is part of their web design strategy. Yet, as the owner of Supernova Distro suggests, a distro's overall character is communicated through its graphics, particularly those that appear on a site's splash or home page, because they are one of the easiest forms of website information to read and process:

> I always had my distros layout centered around a theme. The last layout, that I kept up forever, was really summery. I used photos from a photo album I bought at a thrift store that were from the 60's and were beautiful. I literally think one of the reasons why people liked my distro was for that layout![161]

The images that the owner included in this version of Supernova are, indeed, visually appealing, as well as consistent in theme, thus attesting to her interest in both attracting users' attention and providing a pleasurable, unified site for their perusal (Figure 19). Over the years, Supernova's owner has created several different themes for her distro based around particular images of girls and women, such as Elizabeth Taylor, Bettie Page, Alla Nazimova, and Stormy, a young female action hero from the television cartoon series, *Rainbow Brite*.[162] One site's theme was centered around 1940s' photobooth pictures of an anonymous woman in a cowboy hat. As Supernova's owner remarks, her selection of these images was directly related to her taste preferences at different ages:

> Each image I used generally had to do with aesthetics or what I was into at the time. I really liked the cartoony pop art type stuff when I was in my early teens, so I used the Liz Taylor/Rainbow Brite images to reflect that. Then I started getting into pinups and silent film actresses (Bettie Page, Alla Nazimova), and then vintage snapshots (cowboy girl, the 60's photo album)! So the images I chose

Figure 19 Creating a consistent website theme.
Supernova Distro, 2003–2005. Courtesy of Meredith Wallace.

pretty much reflected what I thought was aesthetically pleasing at the time.[163]

As Supernova's owner suggests, the number of images web designers have to choose from to establish the tone of their sites is almost infinite, particularly since, like colors and fonts, so many illustrations and photographs are available on the Web. Nonetheless, the distro owners in this study reveal some common interests in their choice of site graphics that in turn suggest their commitment to particular communities and activities. For instance, five of the twelve distros in this study employed illustrations or photographs of women and girls, and many designers, such as that of Supernova, consistently used images of females in each new version of their site. (Also suggestive of a female-positive tone, the primary photograph on the HousewifeXcore home page is of a pink range, an appliance typically associated with women.) Interestingly, the two youngest owners in the study, those who run the Spy Kids and Supernova distros, are the only subjects to have images of girls on their sites. More specifically, they have both included images of young female action heroes from animated cartoon series, specifically Bubbles from *The Power Puff Girls* and Stormy from *Rainbow Brite*, which suggests their investment in commercial popular culture, as well as fictional imagery that portrays female youth as powerful figures. In contrast to these brightly colored, pop images, the illustrations and photographs of women that appear on other distros are typically not as aggressive or contemporary in appearance. For example, the home page of Dreamer's Distro contains an illustration of a woman typing, while the woman who appears in Fork 'n Spoon's logo looks like a pin-up model. Though different in tone, the style of drawing in these two latter images is associated with a much earlier time period, perhaps the 1940s, suggesting the designers' ironic redeployment of prefeminist images for contemporary purposes.

The use of female imagery in these distros suggests their owners' attempts both to attract female users to their distros and to quickly communicate the feminist values associated with them. Only second to images of girls and women are images related to communication. For example, in keeping with its name, both the current and first iterations of Wrong Number Distro's home page include an image of a telephone. For several other distros, the themes of females and communication appear in the same image. For instance, the logo for Spy Kids Distro includes an image of a teenage girl holding a zine, the woman in Fork 'n Spoon's logo speaks directly to the distro's visitors, and, as mentioned above, the woman on the home page for Dreamer's Distro is typing.

Another design element that contributes to the style of websites is typography. Indeed, the font chosen for written text is quite significant to a site's overall theme or mood, for each font has distinct characteristics that communicate a specific character. For instance, serif fonts, which have short extensions at the ends of letters, and thus are more complex in design, suggest formality and tradition, largely because of their traditional use in literature and professional documents. In contrast, sans-serif fonts are simple and "clean," and have a casual, modern feel.

Interestingly, despite her minimal time online and as a web designer, the owner of Neon Pavement Distro is the only distro owner in this study to mention typography when asked to state her top priorities in web design: "Having a[n] easy to read font that stays the same throughout the website ... , so it looks like my distro is neat and put together."[164] The main text of her site appears in Times New Roman (i.e., i started this distro), and special announcements appear in italicized Georgia (i.e., *buy five or more zines*). Meanwhile, the primary text for the site—that is the text that users will see first and pay the most attention to, such as the distro name, navigation bar, and section titles—all appear in Arial, a sans-serif font that is simple, yet professional in appearance (e.g., ordering information).

Other distro owners did not specify typography as a primary component of good web design; however, it is clear that most of them are aware of the expressive tone of fonts and thus take special care in choosing their site's typography. For instance, the vast majority of designers in this study employ a sans-serif font (e.g., Arial, Comic Sans, Geneva, Helvetica, Verdana) for their primary text, which contributes to a casual and simple tone for their sites. Only three—Dreamer's, Ladymen, and Spy Kids—use serif fonts for their title banners, a design component that contrasts somewhat with the informal tone suggested by the owners' word choices for their sites' written text, as well as the handcrafted nature of their distros' products.

Several distro owners have chosen less common fonts for their sites, which suggests their access to a larger bank of type fonts, as well as their awareness of the importance of uniqueness in capturing and holding a web user's attention. For example, one of the early designs for Supernova Distro utilized an outlined, bolded font in white, which was suggestive of 1960s' pop typography and worked well alongside the Andy Warhol painting that appears on the site's splash page.[165] Other distro designers have used more embellished fonts for their distro names, section titles, or navigation menus in order to suggest their site's uniqueness and their own creativity. For example, the title and main navigation text on HousewifeXcore Distro appears in a sans-serif font with each letter appearing inside a heart shape, much like Valentine candy hearts.

One final design element contributes to the simple, yet professional style of most distros in this study: color. In response to a survey question about what elements of design they believe are most important for their sites, several distro owners reported that color was primary:

I want everything to be … eye pleasingly colorful.[166]

I hate bright colors & stick to pastels which is rather amusing since I wouldn't be caught dead wearing half the colors I use on sites.[167]

Color is … key, because you want something appealing to the viewer, and color downloads [are] easier than some big graphic if you have dial up [Internet access].[168]

Color [is] also important. If your website is drab and dull people may not be as interested in it.[169]

In keeping with the clean, professional style advocated by most web instructors, the color palette of most of these distros is consistent from page to page, a strategy that helps users acclimate quickly to new pages without feeling that they have strayed into another website.

Also contributing to the professional style associated with commercial websites, the number of colors on distro site is usually kept to a minimum, and many designers use only two colors for contrast. Ladymen Distro is the exception here, utilizing over four colors for its fonts alone. Four out of twelve distros utilize white as a background color, while three have a pink background, one has a yellow background, one has a black background, and another is gray. Dreamer's is the only one of the twelve distros that includes a background pattern, a visual component that, though sophisticated in appearance, is typically avoided by web designers who want their sites to load quickly so as to not frustrate users, especially those with dial-up Internet access.

Interestingly, despite the lack of gender in most names of distros in this study, femininity is often expressed in these female-run websites through the color pink. Two distro designers, those for Fork 'n Spoon and HousewifeXcore, use pink as a primary color in their sites, while several other designers maintain a pastel palette throughout their sites by using pink alongside pale yellow, blue, or green, as can be seen in the MY MY and Wingless distros. Although the use of pink is clearly common in female distro design, not all owners privilege this color or the gender it signifies. For example, several distro owners, including those for C/S, Dreamer's, Spy Kids, and Wrong Number, have created a serious or somber tone, and thus more masculine mood, for their sites by employing black as their primary color. Still other designers create a genderless feel for their distros by using primary or gender-neutral colors, as can be seen in Mad People and Neon Pavement.

Several distro owners have created logos for their websites, a design component that also contributes to their professional style. Since the creation of a logo takes much effort and time, their existence suggests an designer's considerable commitment to cyberculture and e-commerce. Of all the distros that have logos, none employs any other image on its home page, thus encouraging users to identify solely with the message conveyed by the logo. The logos are used on multiple pages and do not change despite transformations in the distro's layout, thus lending a consistent style and mood to the site. These logos include both the distro's name and thematic images. For example, the logo for Wingless Zine Distro has an art deco appearance, its name appearing in a bold, outlined deco font, with each letter separated from the next by a period. The distro's name is underlined five times in alternating stripes of pink and purple, which are suggestive of wings. Spy Kids' logo, which, as noted above, includes a black-on-white illustration of a girl holding a zine in one hand and peeking around a wall, contains the name of the distro in an italicized font. The only other logo containing an image of a female, that for Fork 'n Spoon, has the appearance of a 1940s' advertisement. Comprising most of the logo is an illustration of a white, blonde-haired young woman holding the hem of her white, strapless evening gown up on one thigh in order to expose her legs. Most of her legs and feet, however, are concealed via a pink banner that contains the name of the distro. To the right of the woman's head is a suggestive tag line, which reads, "Buy me something from Fork 'n Spoon Mail Order, and you can see a little more." At the bottom of the logo is another pink banner containing the distro's web address. The logo for Wrong Number Distro is complex in both design and message. Constructed in an overall oval shape, the logo's left side includes an image of the globe that is connected by a telephone cord to an image on the right of a man in a suit sitting on a large telephone receiver. Several small stars appear on the left and right sides also. Overall, the logo is black and white, except for the distro's name, which appears in light blue at the upper center of the image.

Obviously, distro owners must carefully design their websites in such a way as to attract both the right consumers and the right producers. Yet sometimes a site's users do not correctly interpret its designer's intention in creating a specific theme, as the owner of HousewifeXcore notes:

> My design is supposed to be ironic. At first it was supposed to be sorta 1950s, like secret subversive feminist suburban housewives. But the design kinda went out on its own and became this pink stove and candy hearts. I want to change it to something else. … I've been getting all these zines that don't really fit my mission statement.[170]

At other times, it is the designer herself who is the cause for the design update. As the owner of MY MY Distro notes on her site's current home page, "I got totally sick of the last design because I felt it looked like every 're-design' I do."[171] Not surprisingly, therefore, distro owners often change their website design, retooling particular components so as to make their distros more appealing, easier to navigate, or more in tune with their objectives. Updating, like maintaining, websites suggests a designer's commitment to both web users and cyberculture. On a more practical level, it strengthens designers' web skills by encouraging them to tinker with new aesthetic and structural components.

Dual Purposes: Commerce and Communication

As noted above, distros are primarily commercial entities: their purpose is to acquire and sell merchandise. Because of this, developing and maintaining a professional style—that is, one that privileges organization, consistency, and usability—is essential if a distro owner wants to attract customers, establish good working relationships, and meet her commercial objectives.

Nevertheless, most distros contain other types of content that suggest that these websites are not only, or even primarily, commercial in nature. For example, of the twelve distros included in this study, nine have an "about" page that gives background information on the distro or distro owner, including her name and her purpose in running a distro. In turn, four distros have a separate "contact" page that typically includes the distro owner's email address and, less often, her instant messaging and online journal nicknames. Four distros have email update lists, three have guestbooks, three have an FAQ page, and one has an events page. The inclusion of this type of information is strong evidence of distro owners' attempts to facilitate communication with other individuals and thus to build and maintain community. As Doreen Piano argues, therefore:

> [Distros] convey a dual function: they sell and distribute "goods" that are produced and consumed by women which may not be readily available at Rite-Aid or Barnes and Noble, and they act as congregating spaces for women who produce and consume these goods.[172]

In this regard, online distros seem to serve similar purposes as the feminist bookstores that were introduced in the 1970s.[173] As Linda Steiner notes about this development:

> [C]onventional sales outlets are unlikely to stock feminist media in the ways they carry *Time* or *Newsweek*. ... A variety of alternative distribution networks have emerged as crucial. ... Feminist bookstores, of which 88 operated in the United States in 1985 ... , often issue newsletters or organize other events—poetry readings or lectures, for example—to provide continuing support for and critique of the movement.[174]

In the context of feminist bookstores' quick decline over the 1990s as a result of the success of both large bookstore chains, like Borders, and online bookstores, such as Amazon, it seems that female-run distros are taking up this community-building function. Yet, as Piano argues, distro owners represent not only a new generation of feminist media distributors, but also a unique type because of their commitment to cyberculture:

> [Distro owners'] use of electronic technologies facilitates an alternative Net-economy by galvanizing a subculture in ways that traditional distribution methods could not, and also by making the distribution and consumption of feminist goods available to a broader market, thus helping to create feminist pockets or zones in cyberspace. … In having distros go electronic, women's subcultural production broadens its sphere, making geographic location less pertinent to sustaining the community.[175]

As demonstrated above, the commercial function of distros is typically supported through a professional, user-friendly design. Their communication and community-building function, however, requires a different tone, one of informality and friendliness. Perhaps the best place to begin a formal analysis of this tone is with the written text that appears on these sites, particularly the text that appears on a distro's home page, for this is the first page users interact with and thus the one that must attract and maintain their interest for the site to be effective. With this in mind, many distros have a "welcome message" on their home page. For example, Dreamer's home page reads:

> Welcome to Dreamer's Distro! Hope you like the new layout. Here you'll find a wide variety of zines and some comics as well as custom 1" buttons. In the future more fun treats will be here. Any questions feel free to ask them via the contact page. Get custom buttons in small amounts or wholesale. Up to you on the design, quantity, etc. Made to be original just for you. Want your zine distributed here? Check out the get distroed page.[176]

Addressing the user directly, this welcome message contains useful information for consumers and producers alike: the distro's name, the site's new design, the types of products for sale, and which pages contain information about how to contact the owner and how to make submissions ("get distroed"). The exclamation mark in the first sentence suggests enthusiasm, and the minimalist structure of the other sentences, often produced through the absence of subjects (e.g., "Hope you like the new layout," "Made to be original just for you"), creates a direct yet casual and conversational tone. The owner's statement that she is welcoming of communication from users contributes to the friendliness suggested by the rest of the message. Moreover, by noting the distro's new layout, the owner communicates the historical nature and thus commercial success of the site, which, in conjunction with the casual, friendly tone, likely eases whatever anxiety potential submitters may have, while also encouraging users to become consumers and part of the distro's regular clientele.

This direct, informal, and conversational tone is common to the text in other distros' welcome messages also. And, as Stern might argue, this "spirited" tone is like that found in many other girl-made websites: "Overall, spirited site authors [portray] their world as a mostly happy place, in which adversity can be overcome and the future is bright."[177] Stern understands girls' use this tone as either their attempt to present themselves as "good girls," or a demonstration of their ability to "navigat[e] relatively easily and happily through adolescence." Yet, given Piano's point that distros have dual purposes, it is interesting to note that the spirited tone used in distro welcome messages has both commercial and communication functions, for it encourages users to feel comfortable and thus purchase some products, while also implying a potential connection with the owner and thus motivating communication and building community.

Interestingly, many owners whose distros have been online for several months or more use their home pages to highlight product updates, forgoing a welcome message and relocating information about the distro's history to an "about" or "information" page. This practice suggests the user's previous visits to and thus familiarity with the distro, its owner, or other distro sites, contributing to the user's sense of insider knowledge and thus community, even if that is not the reality. Indeed, often the language used on this type of distro home page suggests that a conversation is in process between the owner and her customers. For example, a recent version of MY MY's home page reads:

> welcome back!
>
> So here's the deal. I got totally sick of the last design because I felt it looked like every "re-design" I do. So, you old schoolers will remember this photo from a previous Girl Swirl design but it's such a great shot & since (sadly) Veronica is no longer helping out at MY MY (with school ending & work she just doesn't have the time) I felt like this was a good way to see her go!
>
> Like I promised, there are new items in the shop. I also recategorized the shop to make it easier to shop. The images are better & larger, things just look better (I think). I hope you like it.
>
> xo taryn[178]

The language used for this distro home page lends a sense of intimacy not necessarily evoked in other welcome messages, which tend to imply users' lack of familiarity with a site.

Another form of distro writing that suggests owners' commitment to community building appears in the about pages or mission statements many owners attach to their sites.[179] Such statements clearly announce their owners' membership in not only the zine and "do it yourself" (DIY) media communities, but larger political communities as well. For example, Neon Pavement Distro's "about" page reads: "I started this distro up in June of 2004 with the hopes of being able to spread of my love of zines to the rest of the world. Being able to distribute zines that impact me is the best part of having a distro."[180] The about page for Wrong Number Distro notes a similar love of zines: "Our main goal, in bringing about this distro, is to connect diverse zines, crafts, (& more!) into one central spot for distribution. To give back to all the zinesters that fed our souls with wonderful material!"[181] The website for Mad People Distro reveals:

> I originally started the distro ... with the intent of carrying projects based out of Southern California. Soon after, I shot that idea to hell— simply because I realized that with that intention, I'd be excluding a plethora of amazing zines, books, music, etc. ... I realized that I wanted the distro to be about supporting all forms of independent media, no matter where it's from, and distributing to people who will and do care about it.[182]

The owner of HousewifeXcore boldly states her distro's purpose in the website's title bar—"cuz ladies need revolution too"—a radical theme that she continues below on the home page:

> HousewifeXcore Distro loves carrying DIY skillshare zines, zines with an anarcha-feminist slant that inspire creative resistance, DIY and alternative health zines that share information and document experiences, zines by queer and trans people, and zines that contribute positively to the radical community. Our goal is to empower female, queer, and trans identified people through zines and take back their self representation while encouraging acceptance and community in the zine underground.[183]

Other owners include similarly politicized statements about products they like to sell in their distro. For instance, Dreamer's website states, "Dreamer's Distro welcomes all sorts of zines, comics, and anything else that's creative. Nothing that could be offensive such as racism, sexism, homophobia, etc. That is not tolerated here."[184] Ladymen Distro announces its connection to a larger progressive community via its home page: "Ladymen is now working in conjunction with NJ Infoshop and NJ Anarcha-Feminists. This means we will sometimes be tabling with the infoshop and choosing certain titles from our catalog to table on behalf of the anarcha-feminists."[185] A similarly politicized message appears when users click on the "Why" link that appears on C/S Distro's home page: "Small Press: A publishing effort to put out more diverse zines."[186] Meanwhile, the owner of C/S notes her connection to the larger community of radical people of color on her distro's about page:

> I was reminded of my original mission statement when I was reading an article of an old issue of Broken Pencil, written by Leah Lakshmi Piepzna-Samarasinha, "Brown Star Kids: Zinemakers of Colour Shake Things Up." That's what it was all about. And every time I get discouraged by lack of chicano zinesters or zines by people of color, or support or what have you–I tell myself–if I leave, then what? Yes, life gets in the way–(but it makes for interesting zine material!)–kids are had, rent must be paid, dreams are put on shelves-but we still fight right? A pen, a can of spray paint, words, we fight to connect.

> *The only distro of its kind dedicated to having people of color's voices heard and projects seen. We are trans friendly, political, activist, mamas, theorists, cooks, poor, students, writers ... striving to find the voices of writers that get lost on the white page.*[187]

Attesting to the owner's commitment to this cause, C/S is the only distro in this study whose site contains both English and Spanish.

Perhaps the most significant indicator of distro owners' attempts to facilitate communication and build community is their sites' numerous external links. As Piano notes, "once a distro is accessed, other distros and DIY sites are easy to find through ... links. These citation practices act to unify disparate feminist sites in cyberspace."[188] As noted above, eleven out of the twelve distros in this study have a "links" page that connects users to other websites. Several distros have so many external links that they are listed by category. For example, HousewifeXcore Distro separates its external links into ten major categories: local stuff, zinesters, zine resources, USA distros, Canadian distros, international distros, buy and make shit, activism, cunt health, and online journal communities. As this list of links suggests, the vast majority of distros' external links are for other distros, zinesters, and individuals and organizations related to the radical media community.[189] The linking of distros to other distros is by itself evidence that these sites are not solely commercial ventures, for rarely do profit-oriented businesses advertise their competitors. As the owner of HousewifeXcore states on her distro's links page: "I am listing the distros by region so you can contact them to see if they do tabling at local shows/events, distribute local zines, and to support your local zine community."[190] The one website to be most linked to distros in this study is Pander Zine Distro.[191] Begun as a mail order zine catalog by Ericka Lyn Bailie-Byrne in 1995, Pander's online version was launched in 1997. As one of the oldest and most successful distros on the Web, it is considered by many female distro owners to be a model for their own websites. One of the unique components of Pander that is shared by only a few of the distros in this study is its message board, Pander Forums.[192] Though not a female-exclusive space, Pander Forums facilitates communication and community among zinesters and distro owners around the world, including the vast majority of the owners in this study. Indeed, the Pander Forums seem to have a policing function for distro design, as one of their ongoing topics is "Your experiences with distros, which ones were good/bad?"

In addition to Pander Forums, several of the distro owners in this study are members of and have external links to Zinesters.net, a discussion-based mailing list for zinemakers hosted by Yahoo! Groups, as well as Grrrlzines.net, a message board that is part of the larger Grrrl Zine Network.[193] Another message board more recently introduced to the Web and more specific to distro owners is Distrokids, an online community that is connected to LiveJournal.com and thus demonstrates the strong connections between the zine, distro, and journal community.[194]

As these various external links demonstrate, many of the teenage girls and young women who own distros are committed to far more than making money from the goods they sell. In fact, most do not expect to realize profits from their distribution efforts. Instead, as Piano argues, they "intervene in corporate consumerism by promoting subcultural production that distinguishes itself from mainstream marketing through stylistic, political, and economic deviations."[195] Moreover, by privileging the goals of communication and community development over capital gains, these young female distro owners have found a way to maintain and promote their political convictions while also participating in commerce. Yet this is not just a matter of balancing capitalism and radical politics, for in selling handcrafted goods made by female youth similar to themselves via the Internet, these distro owners are helping to produce a different economy, one that utilizes the skills, technologies, and even design practices of industry but values communication, community, and disenfranchised individuals over traditional commercial and patriarchal objectives.

CONCLUSION

Many of the female youth who design websites today have not received computer training in school settings. Nor have they been influenced to develop advanced computing skills by teachers and parents. Moreover, few have received the sorts of gender-specific "boosts" advocated by AAUW and other organizations in order to improve young females' interests and interactions with digital technologies. Rather, these girls' web training is largely autodidactic and occurs primarily within their own homes. Pragmatic entrepreneurs, they teach themselves how to create websites primarily by surfing the Web and perusing the source code of sites they like. Inspired to express themselves, facilitate communication, and build relationships, they have appropriated new electronic technologies in order to extend and improve the communicative practices in which they are already engaging. Thus, their innovative uses of digital technologies and active participation in cyberculture begins not as a result of their pursuit of college degrees in computer science or careers in information technology, but rather out of a commitment to progressive politics and counterhegemonic media.

Although my study's findings are based on only a small group of young female distro owners, and thus are not generalizable to all girl web designers or to all young female computer users, they nevertheless reveal some of the ways that female youth develop interest, training, and experience in computing outside academic settings. It is my hope that the results of this study will encourage other feminist scholars interested in girls' cyberculture to question their assumptions about the places where and reasons why young females interact with digital technologies. As AAUW's *Tech-Savvy* argues, calculating the number of female youth enrolled in computer science classes might produce an easy benchmark by which to evaluate girls' participation in cyberculture, but it is not the only or even the best means to do so.[196] By studying girls' computing only within school settings, we risk limiting considerably our understanding of girls' relationships with such technologies and the various ways they participate in building cyberculture. Instead, we must consider the multiple ways girls' fluency with digital technologies is manifested, and, to do that, we must look to the multiple sites of girls' everyday lives, including their bedrooms. As Julian Sefton-Green and Vivienne Reiss argue, the practices of wired youth, such as the distro owners in my study, "reflect a more general trend towards the home as a key site ... of cultural production," which in turn should encourage researchers to pay more attention to "young people's 'informal' cultural competencies."[197]

Moving quickly from emailing and web surfing to message boards and chat rooms to web authoring programs and HTML coding over the span of a few short years, an ever increasing number of contemporary female youth are helping to erode the patriarchal construction of computer users and the stereotype of technophobic girls, while also transforming girls' bedroom culture and capitalist conceptions of the Web. The innovative uses to which today's female youth are putting computers and the Internet should make those of us committed to social change hopeful for what girls of future generations might be able to do with the various technologies that define their worlds.

Conclusion
No Small Thing

We don't listen to what you say
Girls get busy not in the way
Girls make music, we're here to stay
Hey! Hey! Hey!

—Bratmobile[1]

Since I began research for this book in the early 1990s, the world of U.S. girls' media production has expanded in ways I could not even imagine, despite my hope that more female youth would recognize the power of self-representation, self-publishing, and self-distribution. Indeed, very few of the girl-made media texts analyzed here had been produced when I started this project, and even fewer were in circulation beyond their creators' immediate communities. At that time, most young female media producers were making zines, though few individuals outside the micro media community had ever seen one. The Riot Grrrl community and the bands that helped form it were just beginning to receive public attention, as were several young female rappers. The film community had one prominent girl director, Sadie Benning, and the Internet had yet to revolutionize U.S. society. Given the history of race and class relations in the field of media production, it is not surprising that most girl media producers at that time were white and upper-middle-class.

In the ten-plus years since I read my first grrrl zine, my home has become a virtual museum of media texts produced by female youth, thus attesting to the considerable growth of girl-made media over that period. My book shelves are lined with girls' movies; my stereo cabinet holds girls' tapes, records, and CDs; my closet contains boxes of girls' zines; and my web browser's bookmarks page is loaded with links to girls' websites. The expansion of girls' media culture can be seen well beyond my house and such texts, however, particularly in the numerous media production guidebooks, workshops, and technologies introduced for female youth over the course of the past decade. In my wildest dreams, I never imagined when I began research for this project that something like Girls Film School would exist, nor did I think manufacturers would deign to produce camcorders and computers specifically for female youth. Yet now we have numerous girl-centered media education programs across the country, and Barbie Video Cams and Disney Princess Laptops are available in toy stores nationwide and online. Moreover, I never thought girls themselves would be the ones who seized control over the merchandizing and distribution of their own media texts. (After all, the commercial culture industries have proven for several generations now how adept they are at expropriating and capitalizing on youth-made media.) But now we have online distros run by girls as young as thirteen who, as a result of their "do it yourself" (DIY) ethos and feminist politics, are transforming e-commerce and traditional distribution practices. Perhaps the greatest achievement in the realm of girls' media has been the increase in young female media producers of color, as evidenced by zines like *Evolution of a Race Riot*, films like *Share Our World*, and websites like C/S Distro.

This is a different girl culture than the one I experienced when growing up, and it makes me envious I didn't have the same opportunities. Nevertheless, the realm of girls' media is not as rosy as it seems from my description above, despite that being a somewhat appropriate color choice. As noted in this book's Introduction, very few individuals who aren't a girl zinemaker, filmmaker, musician, or web designer—or the friend, parent, sibling, or teacher of one—are aware that girl-made media texts even exist. Thus, stereotypes persist in our society of female youth as culturally unproductive and of media production as a realm occupied only by adults. When I've told new acquaintances that I was writing a book about girls' media, they assumed that I meant texts produced by adults *about* girls, like *Clueless* and *That's So Raven*, not those created *by* girls themselves. And when I clarified that I'm interested in young female media producers, many respond with, "Oh, you mean like Britney Spears?" Well, actually, *no*, NOT like her. Clearly, there's still some educating to do.

A rosy presentation of girls' media production is compromised in other ways as well. Most significantly, there continue to be relatively few girls of color and poor female youth involved in media production, despite the considerable efforts of various media educators and community activists. Thus, contemporary girls' media is being shaped primarily by those with consider-able social privilege and power, a situation that mirrors the history of race and class relations in the commercial publishing, broadcasting, and filmmak-ing industries. In turn, considerably uneven development is evident in the different sectors that make up the larger sphere of girls' media. Zinemaking continues to remain the dominant form of media production among female youth, largely as a result of its accessibility and connection to girls' written culture. In fact, thousands of girls' zines have been produced by female youth over the past ten years, helping to give rise to a large, supportive infrastruc-ture maintained in part by female-run catalogs, online distros, and message boards. Currently challenging zines' privileged place in girls' media produc-tion are websites made by female youth. Encompassing a broad range of digital media, from one-off, one-screen home pages to regularly updated, multi-page online businesses, the "girl wide web" is expanding exponentially every day.

Far less growth can be seen, however, in the realm of girls' film. Although girls-only media production programs, like Reel Grrls, and girl-oriented film guidebooks, like *Girl Director*, are helping to increase the number of female youth who interact with film and video cameras, on average only one-tenth of the movies submitted to and screened at youth film festivals each year are cre-ated by girls.[2] Meanwhile, the one area of girls' media production that seemed to have the greatest potential when I started this project—girls' music—has proven to be the most disappointing for me. In the early 1990s, young female punks, like the members of Bikini Kill, Bratmobile, and Heavens to Betsy, and rappers, like Queen Latifah, Lauryn Hill, and Salt'n'Pepa, were receiving considerable public attention in girl-oriented magazines like *Sassy*, and in the process encouraging millions of female youth nationwide to see music-mak-ing as a culturally and politically significant practice. At Riot Grrrl conven-tions, girls with little to no music experience were picking up drumsticks and guitars, grabbing the mic, singing, and screaming, as if their lives depended on it. In the hip-hop community, girls were largely confined to the conventional female role of fan. Yet a few brave girls challenged the male-dominated aspects of this culture by rapping and scratching. Girls were seizing the stage!

But just when girl rock and rap seemed to have finally come into their own, most of the bands affiliated with Riot Grrrl broke up, MTV began promoting gangsta style more rigorously, and female youth from five on up were being encouraged to invest in the Spice Girls. As feminist musician Ani DiFranco recalls, it seemed as if the Apocalypse had happened.[3] A pop group comprised of five young women who did not sing their own lyrics, play their own instruments, or manage their own careers, the Spice Girls have been fol-lowed in recent years by a string of young female pop singers, such as Britney Spears, Mandy Moore, and Hilary Duff, who similarly invest in the traditional gender and sexual dynamics of that position and its role in the patriarchal, heterosexual marketplace. As a result, the number of female youth interested in expressing themselves through writing songs, playing instruments, and recording music dropped off considerably over the course of the 1990s, and this book doesn't have a chapter on the one sector of girls' media production I initially had the greatest exposure to, interest in, and hope for.

I don't have room here to explore how the decline of girls' music in the 1990s is related to the recording industry's decreasing interest in promoting women-made music. (Suffice it to say, U.S. society has been experiencing a strong backlash against feminism and other radical politics since the late 1990s as a result of the rise of social conservatives and religious fundamentalists.) Nevertheless, I do think it is enlightening to consider why there aren't as many female youth playing and recording music today as writing zines, designing websites, and shooting movies, for this phenomenon clearly attests to the fact that gender dynamics are not the same across all forms of media production.

Certainly, there's an economic factor involved in the relative dearth of girls' music in American popular culture. The various practices and technologies involved in musical production have traditionally been more expensive than those required of zinemaking, filmmaking, or web design. In turn, a crucial factor to remember here is that the amount of activity in a particular sector of media production is typically determined by its output of texts. Yet, while zine, film, and web production all result in material products, music-making usually does not. It is primarily a performative medium. In other words, when musicians play, the sounds they produce typically are not recorded, as the technology they use in such instances is meant only for sound production and amplification. Producing a tape, record, or CD, therefore, involves leasing recording space and equipment, paying sound engineers, reproducing the recording, packaging the product, contracting with a distributor, and promoting that music via the media. Even when friends accomplish such nonperformative practices, there is usually some sort of expense involved, even if only in the form of in-kind service. In contrast, zines require little equipment and expense to reproduce, promote, and distribute; in fact, most zinesters accomplish each of these practices on their own. Websites don't require reproduction or distribution, so the primary costs involved in this form of media production are computing equipment and Internet access, considerable costs, for sure, but when it comes to young web designers, these expenses are often covered by parents, schools, or community centers. Though films require some money to reproduce, distribute, and exhibit, the declining prices of DV cameras and editing software have made filmmaking another relatively inexpensive form of media production for youth.

If economics were the only factor limiting girls' engagement in musical production, other individuals without much capital, including boys, would have a difficult time producing music also. Yet, a quick perusal of *Spin* or

Vibe magazine shows that's obviously not the case. Plenty of male youth are rocking and jamming, which suggests that, if an equal number of girls are not, gender is at play here. As scholars such as Mavis Bayton, Sara Cohen, Mary Ann Clawson, Tricia Rose, and Robin D. G. Kelley have demonstrated, females are marginalized in popular music production because of the hetero-sexual patriarchy invested in by the majority of individuals affiliated with this cultural realm, including many females. Indeed, as Cohen argues:

> Within Euro-American cultures there tends to be a general assump-tion that rock music is male culture comprising male activities and styles. Women, meanwhile, tend to be associated with a marginal, decorative or less creative role, hence the common stereotype of glamorous women who act as backing singers for male groups or fea-ture on their videos or other merchandise, and girls as adoring fans who scream at male performers.[4]

The same gender dynamics Cohen describes are clearly operative within hip-hop and most other forms of popular music.

Yet patriarchy is not inherent to music cultures; it is socially constructed within them. As Cohen argues, "rock is produced as male through the every-day activities that comprise the scene; through the sensual, emotional aspects of the scene; and through the system of ideas that inform the scene."[5] The various sites of musical scenes where such gender dynamics are in play include musician roles (vocalists and instrumentalists), instruments and amplifica-tion equipment, musical training, band formation, sound, lyrics, genre, visual representation (album covers, music videos, promotional photos, and films), performance style, gigging culture, touring, sound engineering, musical con-sumerism, the recording industry, trade magazines, and popular and aca-demic music criticism.

The main barriers for females attempting to become musicians are those they face in their initial years of performance. As Cohen suggests, the only musician role in which girls are encouraged to engage is singing. Lucy Green explains the common adoption of this role by females by demonstrating that in using the voice as an instrument, avoiding technology (except for amplifi-cation), and privileging the body as spectacle, female vocalists reaffirm their feminine subjectivity and thus do not compromise the patriarchy of the music culture in which they participate.[6] As Bayton puts it, "The status 'woman' seems to obscure that of 'musician.'"[7] This theory alone helps to explain why so many female musicians, particularly those who are young and meet con-ventional beauty standards, are vocalists.

Nonetheless, Green's theory does not fully explain why so few female musicians, especially girls, are instrumentalists, though her discussion of the masculinization of musical technology moves us in the right direction for understanding this phenomenon.[8] Here again, the social reproduction of heterosexual patriarchy is a primary factor limiting girls' musical opportunities. If female youth demonstrate an interest in learning to perform music, more often than not they are encouraged to invest in the instruments associated with classical music rather than the electronic instruments used to produce popular music. The terms used to describe the sounds produced by these different instruments—quiet, soft, and harmonious versus loud, hard, and discordant—are strongly bifurcated along feminine and masculine lines, thus contributing to the overall gendering of musical sound. In most school bands, therefore, teachers encourage girls to play small woodwind or string instruments, such as flutes and violins, while boys dominate larger and louder instruments, particularly horns and drums.[9] Many middle-class parents contribute to this dichotomized gender socialization by paying for their daughters' piano lessons and buying their sons guitars.

At the same time, however, many young people get access to and learn instruments, especially those used to produce popular music, outside educational institutions, and it is in this noncurricular arena of instrument and skill acquisition that girls' participation seems most discouraged. As Bayton argues, for example, "Guitar shops are ... 'male' terrain: they rarely employ women as assistants, and the customers are overwhelmingly male."[10] Noting that "boys tend to feel at home there," she demonstrates through interviews with female musicians that girls rarely do. Similarly, as Carol Jennings found in her study of young female musicians:

> Their encounters with sales assistants in music shops demonstrate how a woman who wants to buy an instrument, strings, or other equipment is likely to be either harassed or ignored. ... [W]omen often feel alien, judged, or mocked [in such stores], which seriously undermines their self-confidence and sense of entitlement.[11]

Bayton demonstrates how the patriarchy and sexism that contribute to girls feeling alien in equipment stores is continued in the discursive sites associated with popular music scenes, particularly trade magazines,[12] while David Uskovich reveals their prevalence in online message boards devoted to gear culture.[13]

As Uskovich, Green, and Bayton all note, in addition to the problem of sexism perpetuated in the physical and discursive spaces of popular music culture, girls face barriers to playing electronic instruments because of their association with males and masculinity. As Bayton explains in relation to the electric guitar, for example:

> Rock is associated with technology, which is itself strongly categorized as "masculine." "Femininity" involves a socially manu-

factured physical, mechanical and technical helplessness, whilst "masculinity" involves a display of technical competence. ... Thus young women may be drawn towards the electric guitar but are put off by the multitude of electronic and electrical components, which are a basic requirement for a rock performance: leads, plugs, amplifiers, plug-boards, etc. ... Moreover, technical language is often used as a power strategy in a mystifying way in order to exclude women. This can happen informally amongst groups of male musicians, by sound crews at gigs, by technicians in recording studios and so on.[14]

In his study of hip-hop culture, whose primary musical instruments—turntables and samplers—are also electronic, Kelley found similar gender dynamics in play: "Young men often discouraged or ridiculed women emcees; such women were often denied access to technology, ignored, or pressured by gender conventions to stay out of a cultural form identified as rough, profane, and male."[15] But the connection of technology to males and masculinity only partially explains girls' discomfort with engaging with electronic instruments. As Bayton notes, "The very first steps in learning the electric guitar force a young woman to break with one of the norms of traditional 'femininity'; long, manicured, polished fingernails must be cut down."[16] In turn, playing drums typically results in sweat and large biceps, neither of which is coded as feminine.

All of these factors contribute greatly to girls' lack of interest in playing electronic instruments, so many don't even try. Those who do find it hard to enter into the networks that would encourage their regular practice and development of their skill, such as rock bands or rap crews. As Clawson explains, "In contrast to a classical orchestra or a marching band, the rock group is initially organized around existing friendship networks rather than through the initiative of an adult authority."[17] Noting that "American childhood is organised around a gender separation which promotes the social articulation and maintenance of difference," Clawson argues that the vast majority of musicians' first rock bands are comprised of male youth who had preexisting friendships.[18]

Since gender dynamics have transformed since the time Clawson's survey respondents were youth (i.e., the early 1960s), particularly for girls, her explanation for the male-dominance of youthful rock bands as related to preteen gender segregation seems problematic today. Nevertheless, she makes a convincing argument for how such bands operate as cultural sites where boys' masculinity is strongly reaffirmed, primarily through the appropriation of "power" band names, the perfection of forceful, space-occupying performance styles, and the playing of loud, discordant music. Cohen adds to this explanation by noting that male band members perpetuate their close-knit affiliations by "refer[ring] to each other by nicknames, us[ing] technical and in-house jargon and shar[ing] the jokes and jibes, the myths, hype and bravado surrounding bands and band-related activity."[19] In other words, rock is a male-exclusive discursive world to which few girls have access, and, as Kelley's work demonstrates, similar practices are privileged by many males in rap scenes. Clawson notes that all of these practices are available to and taken up by male band members "long before they develop music skills,"[20] thus helping to produce a sphere of activity that bolsters their masculinity while also discouraging most girls' participation. Bayton agrees, noting that "teenage women are not often welcomed in male music-making cliques and thus do not generally get the insider information and tips which are routinely traded within them. Male musicians tend to be possessive about such technical information."[21] Male exchanges of cultural capital seem particularly gender exclusive when musicians are inexperienced (which typically coincides with their youth), for as Will Straw argues, such forms of connoisseurship serve to bolster the semblance of male power.[22] As one of the young women in Jennings's survey recalls of her entrance into playing rock music:

> You know, it's just like anything else. It seems like it's harder [for girls] to get started. Because I know when I started ... it was ... all guys playing all the time and I didn't know if they'd take us seriously. And they, I don't know if they did at first, but definitely by the end, you know, they even felt us as a threat.[23]

Yet this focus on boys' behavior tells only half the story behind girls' reticence at playing instruments and joining bands and crews associated with popular music, for, as discussed in the Introduction, female youth are encouraged to privilege the gender associated with members of their sex category over all other components of identity. Thus, while boys affirm their masculinity through such activities as bands and sports, their female peers are taught to focus on improving their appearance so as to garner the attention of males. Moreover, as Bayton argues:

> Compared to boys, teenage women lack money, time, space, transport and access to equipment. They are pressurized (by commercial teen culture and their schoolfriends) to get a boyfriend. The search for romance can devour their time, better preparing them for the role of fan than for that of musician.[24]

Clearly, there are many girls who do not ascribe to traditional gender norms, and those female youth seem to have a somewhat easier time learning to play popular music instruments and joining bands and crews. Yet, as Clawson found in her study:

[M]any girls showed a pattern of experimentation with instruments that did not evolve directly into their incorporation into a self-defined band. In contrast to the men's almost teleological accounts of their early musical activities, women offered narratives of devaluation. They were dismissive, assigning little value to efforts they carefully defined as "not serious," "not real," or as necessarily subordinated to other more important concerns. ... Girls lacked access to an entitlement that seemed to be assumed by boys: the cultural authority to initiate band formation.[25]

Given the processes of gender socialization that are heightened during adolescence and leave many female youth with decreased levels of self-worth and increased ambitions of perfection, it is not surprising that Clawson's survey revealed that many female musicians do not commit to bands until they are in their early twenties.[26]

Jennings found similar results in her ethnography of young female musicians. Focusing in particular on the gender dynamics of high school rock bands, she notes that several of her research subjects reported discomfort with their local "battle of the bands" event, during which various young rock groups attempt to outperform each other. For example, one young woman recalled:

[T]here would just be a bunch of boys getting up there and making a lot of noise, and it was just great fun, ... and it would be cool, no matter what, no matter how awful it sounded, it didn't matter. But if you get a group of girls up there, okay, or even just one girl in one band, it's either, "Oh, Gosh, they're awful," or ... everyone's just gonna stare directly at them.[27]

As a result of the ridicule heaped upon other inexperienced female performers, this respondent reported that she was inspired to play an instrument only after she saw Kim Gordon play with Sonic Youth: "[W]hen you go to a show and there's a woman, forget it, you're excited. ... You know deep inside that you can do it. ... It just kind of drives it home when you see other women do it."[28] Although Clawson is dubious about the primacy of female role models in facilitating girls' desire to learn to play instruments,[29] Jennings's young female respondents make clear that experiencing another women's musical success is a significant factor in increasing a girl's confidence in playing.

These various gendered barriers help to explain the minimal amount of girls' music circulating in contemporary popular culture. For if female youth are discouraged from liking loud, hard music, playing electronic instruments, buying equipment, developing friendships with boys, joining bands and crews, and obtaining and exchanging music-based cultural capital, how in the world do they get up the nerve to perform publicly, much less make a record? As Bayton's in-depth ethnographic study of women rock musicians, *Frock Rock*, makes clear, patriarchy and sexism are still rampant in the various practices related to musical performance and recording, including gigging, touring, recording, and promotion, thus helping to sustain a cultural environment that is often intimidating, if not hostile, to females.[30] Though women's music culture has inspired, supported, and promoted female performers for three decades now through female-centered music festivals, record labels, and sound engineering companies, most girls are unaware that this alternate music culture exists.[31] Indeed, little effort has been made in this community with regard to female youth as a result of the feminist and lesbian communities' historical focus on adult women.

While female youth interested in zinemaking, filmmaking, and web design now have a solid infrastructure in place to help them overcome the barriers posed by the traditional gendering of electronic technologies and media production, a complete support system for aspiring girl musicians does not yet exist in the United States. This absence has contributed to girls' lack of engagement as musical performers, especially instrumentalists. As discussed in Chapter 2, riot grrrls helped to form a support system for young female musicians in the early 1990s that was largely devoted to getting records made, distributed, and promoted. Listening to the music of assertive, talented female musicians, or reading about them in zines, however, is usually not enough to motivate a girl to learn an instrument, write music, and form a band.

Girls' historical lack of interest, confidence, and participation in making and recording music is currently motivating a new generation of young women to help female youth gain greater access to and training in electronic instruments and the musical cultures of which they are a part. Much like initiatives for improving girls' filmmaking and computing, these girl-centered music projects have been designed with the understanding that female youth are doubly disadvantaged in our society as a result of their sex and age, and thus need a "leg up" to become interested and engaged in media production. The women who developed such projects are also aware that girls have a difficult time taking interest in and using the instruments and technology traditionally associated with popular music, and thus need supportive spaces and mentors that can facilitate their confidence with such equipment.

Misty McElroy designed the Rock'n'Roll Camp for Girls in 2000 as part of her community service and senior thesis requirement at Portland State University in Oregon (Figure 20).[32] She indicates that her idea to create the camp was inspired largely by her first-hand experience of males having an obvious "edge" in rock music culture, as well as the success of other women-led grassroots initiatives, such as battered women's shelters and Ladyfest conventions. Seeing rock as "a genre of rebellion and expression," McElroy notes that the objectives of the Rock'n'Roll Camp for Girls are "to establish an early

Figure 20 Facilitating girls' engagement with electronic music technology. Rock'n'Roll Camp for Girls, 2002. Photo by Jodi Kansagor. Courtesy of Misty McElroy.

foundation and interest in rock music" for younger girls, to provide "advanced instruction" for more experienced campers, and to offer "a variety of hands-on music projects that encourage self-expression and self-reliance."[33] Promotional discourse for the camp also notes other goals, such as "to impart basic knowledge about developing musical projects, provide opportunities for question and answer sessions with female role models, and provide a forum for peers to discuss a wide range of musical and socially/culturally relevant topics."[34]

In addition to learning musical techniques and technologies, the campers participate in confidence-building skills, such as self-defense classes and public performances. Echoing several other girl media educators' perceptions of the gender dynamics involved in youth media production, McElroy notes:

> [Y]oung girls [don't] care if boys are around while they discover/ explore music -- but by a certain age socialization sets in and girls become self-conscious, inhibited, watched, judged, and sexualized ... by boys. [T]his has a striking effect on the level of girls' confidence and willingness to explore their own forms of expression. ... Girls shouldn't have to deal with that when they're just discovering their sense of power and entitlement.[35]

In addition to facilitating a form of creative expression rarely allowed in traditional educational institutions, therefore, the Rock'n'Roll Camp for

Girls attempts to provide a single-sex environment where girls "feel freer to experiment with different ideas and activities, because they don't feel as constrained by compulsory heterosexuality."[36] As McElroy argues, "[G]irls are still going out on a limb to play rock music. ... Such power is rarely offered to girls. And that power threatens the patriarchy, even the young, developing patriarchy." Interestingly, despite her interest in girls-only education, McElroy explicitly distances herself and the camp from the girls' advocacy movement, noting: "I don't relate to that. I'm not empowering them. The girls create it themselves."[37]

Started as a week-long summer-time venture, the camp's success over its first three years inspired McElroy and her staff to launch the Girls Rock Institute, which provides year-round classes and private lessons in rock musicianship for female youth ages ten to eighteen. The institute also rents out practice space and equipment and hosts periodic workshops on such topics as producing music videos so as to improve girls' cultural capital and confidence. To date, middle-class white girls have comprised the majority of campers and students, primarily due to their greater amount of disposable income and leisure time in comparison with poor girls. In addition, McElroy reports that she has a more difficult time getting racially and economically disadvantaged girls interested in performing rock music. As she sees it, in addition to such girls perceiving rock as "white," their parents don't think of their daughters as "entitled" to such forms of cultural expression. Nevertheless, through short rock workshops in schools located in poor neighborhoods, many of which are dominated by young people of color, McElroy continues her mission to put electric guitars in all girls' hands so that they can feel the power of noise and learn to wield it.

Since the Rock'n'Roll Camp for Girls opened, several other girls-only music workshops and camps have sprung up around the country, including the Southern Girls Rock'n'Roll Camp, which was introduced in 2003 in Murfreesboro, Tennessee.[38] In 2004, the Institute for Musical Arts, a nonprofit organization formed in 1987 to supporting women musicians, introduced its first Rock & Roll Girls Camp in Northampton, Massachusetts.[39] In 2005, the East Coast version of the Portland-based Rock'n'Roll Camp for Girls was launched in New York City.[40] Titled the Willie Mae Rock'n'Roll Camp for Girls, the camp is named after "Big Mama" Thornton, an African American blues singer, songwriter, and instrumentalist. Not surprisingly, middle-class white girls have comprised the majority of participants at these various single-sex camps and programs, likely as a result of the greater amount of disposable income and leisure time they have in comparison to poor girls, as well as differences in musical tastes based on race and ethnicity. Unfortunately, I know of no similar musical camps for girls developed within the hip-hop community.

In addition to girl-specific rock camps, musical instrument manufacturers and guidebook publishers have contributed to the burgeoning infrastructure facilitating girls' interest and involvement in musical production. For example, Tish Ciravolo founded Daisy Rock Guitars in 2000 in order to attract more female youth to rock instruments. According to the company's website, Ciravolo's dream is that "every girl who wants to play guitar is welcomed and inspired to do so."[41] Daisy Rock's catalog includes acoustic, acoustic-electric, and electric guitars, as well as basses, in a variety of girl-friendly colors and styles, including the Daisy, Pixie, Stardust, Butterfly, Heartbreaker, and Rock Candy series. Not to be shut out of potential guitar sales, Fender, one of the oldest manufacturers in the business, teamed with Sanrio in 2005 to produce a pink Hello Kitty Stratocaster. That same year, Daisy Rock expanded its goals of inspiring female youth to play guitar by publishing guidebooks for girls on basic guitar and bass methods.[42] Meanwhile, Rock House and Amsco Publishing introduced a DVD titled *Guitar for Girls*, the first audiovisual guitar guide created specifically for female youth.[43] Attesting to girls' growing interest in playing this instrument, *Guitar for Girls* is now in its second printing. Gearing its products toward younger children, Mattel has worked with such toy manufacturers as Kids Station and Kids Direct to create Barbie guitars, pianos, and drum sets for girls. Seemingly wary of producing electronic equipment for younger females, Disney has recently introduced a line of musical instruments manufactured by Manley called Disney Princess Music Magic, which includes the Chirp N Chime Flute, the Dance N Spin Harp, the Play Along Violin, the Bloomin' Tunes Keyboard, and the Royal Rhythm 5-Piece Percussion Set.

The most recent technological innovation to facilitate girls' musical production was not developed specifically with female youth in mind, however. The introduction of inexpensive, PC-based music composition programs, particularly Apple's GarageBand, which was first marketed in 2004, has allowed girls who are familiar with computing technologies but perhaps lack access to, capital for, or training in traditional instruments to develop their musical skills digitally. These programs are not just sophisticated karaoke machines, but rather encourage female youth to move beyond the feminized role of singer via engagement with a broad range of musical instruments, all manipulable through a PC keyboard and mouse. Moreover, if money permits, girls can make music by themselves within their own homes, thus avoiding the male-dominated networks, spaces, and jargon typically affiliated with popular music production. If girls are interested in having others listen to their compositions, they can easily email them or upload them to the Web via MP3 files. Only time will tell if "soft synth" music production programs like GarageBand will revolutionize girls' bedroom culture as much as PCs, the Internet, and video cameras did a decade ago.

Since most of the initiatives launched to help female youth overcome the hurdles they face in accessing musical equipment, training, and support have been introduced only in the past five years, we have yet to see any demonstrable effects on girls' music-making. Nevertheless, as this infrastructure becomes more stable and expands further, I believe we will witness the recording of numerous young female musicians whose presence within this realm of popular culture will hopefully subvert the patriarchy and sexism historically associated with it. In the meantime, more feminist scholars need to undertake research in this area, for without critical attention to the numerous dynamics at play in limiting girls' musicianship, the infrastructure devoted to improving it will lack complete efficacy.

The stakes of girls' media production are roughly the same as those for members of other disadvantaged groups who are engaged in this cultural practice. As Walter Benjamin's theory of radical media praxis suggests, the expansion of female youth culture beyond media consumption, a practice that reaffirms their femininity and thus patriarchal systems of power, to media production, a practice traditionally dominated by adult men, can and does effect transformations in the larger arenas of culture and society.[44] For when girls invest in the role of media producer, they simultaneously engage in the politics of representation and thus in the dynamics of social power. In turn, their practices of self-representation, which not only negotiate but often subvert representations of girlhood produced by the commercial media industries, help to expand and transform popular culture, and in so doing contribute to the formation of the democratic media system that is intrinsic to a progressive society.

Though I have attempted throughout this book to consider girls as *girls* and not as future women, the stakes of girls' media production are necessarily connected to those of women's culture. Though not all girl zinemakers, filmmakers, musicians, and web designers will enroll in college programs and participate in professions related to media culture, some girls' high level of interest and involvement in producing media today suggests that their commitment to this practice will continue into their adult years, thus expanding and transforming the world of women's media. There is some evidence that this change is already occurring. For instance, many of the female youth originally associated with the Riot Grrrl movement in the early 1990s have continued to remain active within the realm of punk feminist media. In turn, several graduates of Reel Grrls and Girls Film School have enrolled in college-level film production programs or are already working in that field professionally. Meanwhile, a considerable number of grrrl zinesters have taken their commitment to this media form and its larger community to new heights via their creation and management of distros. Again, girls' development as musicians does not seem as promising, as the vast majority of female youth who become involved in musical performance today are investing fully in the sexed-up, commercially oriented pop star role, thus perpetuating rather than subverting the heterosexual patriarchy long rampant in the recording industry. Hopefully, initiatives like the Rock'n'Roll Camp for Girls will inspire more female youth to write their own music, play their own instruments, manage their own careers, and start their own recording labels.

Though I don't want to privilege the realm of work over that of leisure, since recreation is essential to our identity formation, social development, and general well-being, I am hopeful that girls' involvement in media production at a young age will encourage them to see this practice as a potential option for future jobs and careers. Although women have made some in-roads in the various U.S. media industries since the 1970s, recent reports demonstrate that such institutions are still overwhelmingly dominated and controlled by males. Indeed, a study by the University of Pennsylvania's Annenberg Public Policy Center indicates that in 2002 women comprised only 13 percent of the top executive positions and 8 percent of board members at eleven major entertainment companies.[45] Statistics from the Director's Guild of America are more grim, indicating that women directed only 9 of the 145 films released in the year ending April 2002.[46] In turn, of all primetime programs broadcast during the 1999–2000 season by the six television networks (ABC, CBS, NBC, FOX, UPN, and the WB), only 18 percent had executive producers, coexecutive producers, and creators who were female.[47] Recent studies of the print and broadcast news industries are similarly dismal, having found that women make up only 20.2 percent of news directors at TV stations, 21.9 percent at radio stations, and 34 percent at major newspapers.[48] Meanwhile, a study by the Media Management Center at Northwestern University revealed that the top editor positions held by women at major newspapers declined from 25 percent to 20 percent between 2000 and 2002.[49] In turn, a *Billboard* survey noted that women hold only 24 percent of executive positions at the major recording labels.[50] And despite the phenomenal expansion of the Internet and web-based businesses in the past decade, only 16 percent of executives in the largest e-companies are women.[51] While no Fortune 500 communication company has a majority of women executives and board members, publishing companies have traditionally hired the largest number of females for leadership positions. Indeed, the only executive positions related to media production in which women have consistently outnumbered men is as editors of women's and girls' magazines.[52]

Of course, the number of female media industry executives does not translate directly into the number of women writers, musicians, reporters, directors, and web designers working in these various fields, nor does it translate into the number of women who choose to create media outside the dominant commercial context. Nevertheless, these statistics affirm what many girls and women know too well: a disproportionate number of men continue to drive and control U.S. media culture. The rise in girls' involvement in media production is, therefore, quite significant, for it suggests that U.S. popular culture and society may soon change in fairly dramatic ways. If we look closely, we can see those transformations already beginning, for the growth of girls' media since the early 1990s indicates that a considerable number of contemporary female youth have the confidence to stand up, speak out, and be publicly present in ways that most women of my generation can only marvel at and envy. Maybe I'm still wearing rose-colored glasses, but, in my book, this girl power is no small thing.

Notes

PREFACE

1. Angela McRobbie and Jenny Garber, "Girls and Subcultures," *Resistance through Rituals: Youth Subcultures in Post-War Britain*, Stuart Hall and Tony Jefferson, eds. (London: Harper Collins Academic, 1976) 209–22.

INTRODUCTION

1. X-ray Spex, "Oh Bondage Up Yours!" *Germ Free Adolescents*, Virgin Records, 1977.
2. Rainbow Media produced this commercial in Feb. 1998.
3. "Zinesters" is the common name for individuals who make zines, small, hand-made publications produced for pleasure not profit.
4. Although the rise in girls' media production is evident in the increasing number of girl-made media texts in public circulation since the 1990s, it is extremely difficult to calculate how many girls are involved in media production today, given that some female youth participate only one time in media projects, while others are producing continuously. In addition, it is difficult to calculate the approximate number of girl-produced media texts at any given time, given that there is no single distribution organization that disseminates such texts.
5. To a lesser extent, the introduction and expansion of infrastructures for non-commercial media production and distribution, the rise of cable television and web-based enterprises in need of inexpensive content, and the commercial exploitation of youth as cultural producers have contributed to this phenomenon also.

6. Gladys D. Ganley, *The Exploding Political Power of Personal Media* (Norwood: Ablex Publishing, 1992) 2, 3.

7. For example, see Gerry Bloustien, *Girl Making: A Cross-Cultural Ethnography on the Processes of Growing Up Female* (New York: Berghahn Books, 2003); Carol Jennings, "Girls Make Music: Polyphony and Identity in Teenage Rock Bands," *Growing Up Girls: Popular Culture and the Construction of Identity*, Sharon R. Mazzarella and Norma Odom Pecora, eds. (New York: Peter Lang, 2001) 175–92; Marion Leonard, "Paper Planes: Traveling the New Grrrl Geographies," *Cool Places: Geographies of Youth Cultures*, Tracey Skelton and Gill Valentine, eds. (New York: Routledge, 1998) 101–18; Susannah Stern, "Adolescent Girls' Expression on Web Home Pages: Spirited, Sombre and Self-Conscious Sites," *Convergence* 5.4 (Winter 1999) 22–41.

8. Angela McRobbie and Jenny Garber, "Girls and Subcultures," *Resistance through Rituals: Youth Subcultures in Post-War Britain*, Stuart Hall and Tony Jefferson, eds. (London: Harper Collins Academic, 1976) 209–22.

9. See Mary Celeste Kearney, "Producing Girls: Rethinking the Study of Female Youth Culture," *Delinquents and Debutantes: Twentieth-Century American Girls' Cultures*, Sherrie A. Inness, ed. (New York: New York University Press, 1998) 285–310.

10. For example, see Susan Murray, "Saving Our So-Called Lives: Girl Fandom, Adolescent Subjectivity, and *My So-Called Life*," *Kids' Media Culture*, Marsha Kinder, ed. (Durham: Duke University Press, 1999) 221-35; and Dawn H. Currie, *Girl Talk: Adolescent Magazines and Their Readers* (Toronto: University of Toronto Press, 1995).

11. For example, see Sheryl Garratt, "All of Us, All of You," *Signed, Sealed, and Delivered: True Life Stories of Women in Pop*, Sue Steward and Sheryl Garratt, eds. (Boston: South End Press, 1984) 138–51; and Lisa A. Lewis, *Gender Politics and MTV: Voicing the Difference* (Philadelphia: Temple University Press, 1990).

12. It is often difficult, however, to discern the age of girl media producers from the texts they create, since they typically do not explicitly identify their age.

13. Joseph F. Kett, *Rites of Passage: Adolescence in America, 1790 to the Present* (New York: Basic Books, 1977) 14–31.

14. Barbara Hudson, "Femininity and Adolescence," *Gender and Generation*, Angela McRobbie and Mica Nava, eds. (London: Macmillan, 1984) 31. It is important to be mindful of historical context: Since adolescence was not recognized as a unique lifestage until the end of the nineteenth century, young females prior to that period may not have experienced the conundrum of feminine adolescence theorized by Hudson.

15. G. Stanley Hall is credited with first theorizing about adolescence as a unique life-stage. See *Adolescence: Its Psychology and Its Relation to Physiology, Anthropology, Sociology, Sex, Crime, Religion and Education*, 2 vols. (New York: D. Appleton and Co., 1904).

16. Hudson 35.

17. Hudson 37.

18. Hudson 51. Simone de Beauvoir, *The Second Sex*, H. M. Parshley, trans. (1949; New York, Vintage, 1989).

19. Gayle Rubin, "The Traffic of Women: Notes on the Political Economy of Sex," *Toward an Anthropology of Women*, Rayna R. Reiter, ed. (New York: Monthly Review Press, 1975) 157–210.

20. Hudson 35.

21. Judith Halberstam, *Female Masculinity* (Durham: Duke University Press, 1998) 267.

22. Halberstam 193.

23. Gayle S. Rubin, "Thinking Sex: Notes for a Radical Theory of the Politics of Sexuality," *The Lesbian and Gay Studies Reader*, Henry Abelove, Michele Aina Barale, and David M. Halperin, eds. (New York: Routledge, 1993) 13.

24. Mavis Bayton, "Women and the Electric Guitar," *Sexing the Groove: Popular Music and Gender*, Sheila Whiteley, ed. (New York: Routledge, 1997) 39.

25. Sue Curry Jansen, "Gender and the Information Society: A Socially Structured Silence," *Journal of Communication 39.3* (Summer 1989) 196–97.

26. Cynthia Cockburn, *Machinery of Dominance: Women, Men, and Technical Know-How* (London: Pluto, 1985) 12.

27. Angela McRobbie, "Just Like a *Jackie* Story," *Feminism for Girls: An Adventure Story*, Angela McRobbie and Trisha McCabe, eds. (London: Routledge and Kegan Paul, 1981) 127–28.

28. Angela McRobbie, "*Jackie* Magazine: Romantic Individualism and the Teenage Girl," *Feminism and Female Youth Culture: From* Jackie *to* Just Seventeen (Boston: Unwin Hyman, 1991) 127.

29. Iris Young, *Throwing Like a Girl and Other Essays on Feminist Philosophy and Social Theory* (Bloomington: Indiana University Press, 1990); Lyn Mikel Brown, "Telling a Girl's Life: Self-Authorization as a Form of Resistance," *Women, Girls, and Psychotherapy: Reframing Resistance*, Carol Gilligan, Annie G. Rogers, and Deborah L. Tolman, eds. (New York: Harrington Park, 1991) 71–86.

30. Beauvoir 267.

31. Beauvoir 280, 282, 298.

32. Beauvoir 291.

33. Kelly Schrum, "Some Wore Bobby Sox: The Emergence of Teenage Girls' Culture in the United States, 1920-1950," disseration, Johns Hopkins University, 2000, 203.

34. Joan Jacobs Brumberg, *The Body Project: An Intimate History of American Girls* (New York: Random House, 1997).

35. Alison E. Field, Lilian Cheung, Anne M. Wolf, David B. Herzog, Steven L. Gortmaker, and Graham A. Colditz, "Exposure to Mass Media and Weight Concerns Among Girls," *Pediatrics* 103.3 (1999) e36.

36. Ellen McCracken, *Decoding Women's Magazines: From Mademoiselle to Ms.* (New York: St. Martin's Press, 1993) 147.

37. For example, see Michel Foucault, *Discipline and Punish: The Birth of the Prison*, Alan Sheridan, trans. (New York: Pantheon Books, 1977).

38. Angela McRobbie, "*Jackie* and *Just Seventeen*: Girls' Comics and Magazines in the 1980s," *Feminism and Youth Culture: From* Jackie *to* Just Seventeen (Boston: Unwin Hyman, 1991) 163.

39. Mary Polce-Lynch, Barbara J. Myers, Wendy Kliewer, and Christopher Kilmartin, "Adolescent Self-Esteem and Gender: Exploring Relations to Sexual Harassment,

Body Image, Media Influence, and Emotional Expression," *Journal of Youth and Adolescence* 30.2 (2001) 225–44.

40. Hudson 31.

41. Mary Ann Clawson, "Masculinity and Skill Acquisition in the Adolescent Rock Band," *Popular Music* 18.1 (1999) 105–6.

42. Lyn Mikel Brown, *Raising Their Voices: The Politics of Girls' Anger* (Cambridge: Harvard University Press, 1998) 124.

43. Angela McRobbie, "Shut Up and Dance: Youth Culture and Changing Modes of Femininity," *Cultural Studies* 7.3 (Oct. 1993) 408. McRobbie borrows the term "habitus" from Pierre Bourdieu, who, in prying it free from its conventional medical meaning, uses it to describe the structured and structuring structure that generates each individual's practices, tastes, and ideological dispositions. See *Distinction: A Social Critique of the Judgment of Taste*, Richard Nice, trans. (Cambridge: Harvard University Press, 1984), especially Chapter 3.

44. Brown 7.

45. Beverley Skeggs, *Formations of Class and Gender: Becoming Respectable* (Thousand Oaks: Sage, 1997) 18.

46. Poor women need few inducements like "liberation" to seek jobs outside the domestic sphere given the harsh economic realities of their lives.

47. For analyses of mid-twentieth-century girls' culture, see McRobbie and Garber; and Simon Frith, *Sound Effects: Youth, Leisure, and the Politics of Rock 'n' Roll* (New York: Pantheon, 1981) 225–34.

48. Kathleen Kent Rowe, "Roseanne: Unruly Woman as Domestic Goddess," *Screen* 31.4 (Winter 1990) 410.

49. Clemencia Rodriguez, *Fissures in the Mediascape: An International Study of Citizens' Media* (Creskill: Hampton Press, 2001) 3.

50. Donna Haraway, "A Manifesto for Cyborgs: Science, Technology, and Socialist Feminism in the 1980s," *Socialist Review* 80 (1985) 65–108.

51. *Détournement* (literally, the diversion of footsteps) involves appropriating something from its original context and placing it in a different context to produce meaning.

52. bell hooks, "Talking Back," *Out There: Marginalization and Contemporary Cultures*, Russell Ferguson, Martha Gever, Trinh T. Minh-ha, and Cornel West, eds. (New York: New Museum of Contemporary Art and MIT, 1990) 340.

53. Lisa Dodson and Jillian Dickert, "Girls' Family Labor in Low-Income Households: A Decade of Qualitative Research," *Journal of Marriage and the Family* 66.2 (May 2004) 318–33.

54. Roger Sabin, "'I Won't Let that Dago By': Rethinking Punk and Racism," *Punk Rock: So What?: The Cultural Legacy of Punk*, Roger Sabin, ed. (New York: Routledge, 1999) 199–218; Mimi Nguyen, "Tales of an Asiatic Geek Girl: *Slant* from Paper to Pixels," *Technicolor: Race, Technology, and Everyday Life*, Alondra Nelson and Thuy Linh N. Tu with Alicia Headlam Hines, eds. (New York: New York University Press, 2001) 177–90.

55. Imani Perry, "Who(se) Am I?: The Identity and Image of Women in Hip-Hop," *Gender, Race, and Class in Media: A Text-Reader*, 2nd ed., Gail Dines and Jean M. Humez, eds. (Thousand Oaks: Sage, 2003) 136–48.

56. Kimberlé Williams Crenshaw is credited with describing this approach to identity as intersectional. See "Demarginalizing the Intersection of Race and Sex: A Black Feminist Critique of Antidiscrimination Doctrine, Feminist Theory and Antiracist Politics," *University of Chicago Legal Forum* (1989) 139–67.

57. Trinh T. Minh-ha, *Reassemblage* (Women Make Movies, 1982).

CHAPTER 1

1. Lina Beard and Adelia B. Beard, *Indoor and Outdoor Handicraft and Recreation for Girls* (New York: Scribner's, 1904) iv.

2. Sadie Benning, "19 Years Old," *Visions* (Fall 1992) 54.

3. Lina Beard and Adelia B. Beard, *The American Girls Handy Book: How to Amuse Yourself and Others* (New York: Scribner's, 1887); *New Ideas for Work and Play: What a Girl Can Make and Do* (New York: Scribner's, 1902). See note 1 also.

4. Daniel Carter Beard, *The American Boys Handy Book: What to Do and How to Do It* (New York: Scribner's, 1882).

5. For an examination of the Victorian era's conservative gender dynamics, see Barbara Welter, "The Cult of True Womanhood: 1820–1950," *American Quarterly* 17.2 (Summer 1966) 151–73.

6. Raymond Williams, *Marxism and Literature* (London: Oxford University Press, 1977) 124.

7. Angela McRobbie and Jenny Garber, "Girls and Subcultures," *Resistance through Rituals: Youth Subcultures in Post-War Britain*, Stuart Hall and Tony Jefferson, eds. (London: Harper Collins Academic, 1976) 209–22.

8. McRobbie and Garber 211.

9. McRobbie and Garber 219.

10. McRobbie and Garber 211.

11. McRobbie and Garber 213.

12. McRobbie and Garber 213.

13. Kelly Schrum, "Some Wore Bobby Sox: The Emergence of Teenage Girls' Culture in the United States, 1920-1950," dissertation, Johns Hopkins University, 2000.

14. McRobbie and Garber 213.

15. McRobbie and Garber 221.

16. Angela McRobbie and Jenny Garber, "Girls and Subcultures," *Feminism and Youth Culture: From Jackie to Just Seventeen* (Boston: Unwin Hyman, 1991) 13–14.

17. Erica Carter, "Alice in Consumer Wonderland: West German Case Studies in Gender and Consumer Culture," *Gender and Generation*, Angela McRobbie and Mica Nava, eds. (London: Macmillan, 1984) 188.

18. Kathy Peiss, *Cheap Amusements: Working Women and Leisure in Turn-of-the-Century New York* (Philadelphia: Temple University Press, 1986) 5, 23.

19. Joseph M. Hawes, "The Strange History of Female Adolescence in the United States," *Journal of Psychohistory* 13.1 (Summer 1985) 53.

20. Carroll Smith-Rosenberg, "The Female World of Love and Ritual: Relations Between Women in Nineteenth Century America," *Signs: Journal of Women in Culture and Society* 1.1 (1975) 9.

21. Smith-Rosenberg 16.

22. See Miriam Forman-Brunell, "Work," *Girlhood in America: An Encyclopedia*, Vol. 2, Miriam Forman-Brunell, ed. (Santa Barbara: ABC-CLIO, 2001) 682–83.

23. Patricia J. Cooper and Norma Bradley Allen, *The Quilters: Women and Domestic Art* (New York: Doubleday, 1977) 76.

24. Carla Bittel, "Arts and Crafts," *Girlhood in America: An Encyclopedia*, Vol. 1, Miriam Forman-Brunell, ed. (Santa Barbara: ABC-CLIO, 2001) 43.

25. Cooper and Bradley Allen 17.

26. Jacqueline Tobin and Raymond G. Dobard, *Hidden in Plain View: The Secret Story of Quilts and the Underground Railroad* (New York: Doubleday, 1999).

27. Anita Reznicek, "Education of Girls," *Girlhood in America: An Encyclopedia*, Vol.1, Miriam Forman-Brunell, ed. (Santa Barbara: ABC-CLIO, 2001) 251.

28. Mary Jaene Edmonds, *Samplers and Samplermakers: An American Schoolgirl Art*, 1700–1850 (New York: Rizzoli, 1991) 13.

29. Catherine E. Beecher, *A Treatise on Domestic Economy* (New York: Source Book Press, 1841).

30. See Christine Frederick, *The New Housekeeping: Efficiency Studies in Home Management* (Garden City: Doubleday, 1913).

31. Samplermaking was a lost art by the mid-1800s (Edmonds 154).

32. Dinah Maria Mulock, "A Woman's Thoughts about Women: Something to Do," *Chamber's Journal of Popular Literature, Science and the Arts* 7 (2 May 1857) 274.

33. Thayer quoted in Jane Hunter, "Inscribing the Self in the Heart of the Family: Diaries and Girlhood in Late-Victorian America," *American Quarterly* 44.1 (Mar. 1992) 55.

34. Foster Rhea Dulles, *America Learns to Play: A History of Popular Recreation, 1607–1940* (New York: D. Appleton-Century, 1940) 86.

35. Sally Mitchell, "Girls' Culture: At Work," *The Girl's Own: Cultural Histories of the Anglo-American Girl, 1830-1915*, Claudia Nelson and Lynne Vallone, eds. (Athens: University of Georgia Press, 1994) 255–56.

36. See note 3.

37. Dulles 202.

38. The Girl Scouts, for example, introduced a merit badge in photography in 1917. Beginning in 1929, Kodak manufactured several cameras specifically for scouts. See the Kodak Girl Collection website, 20 Nov. 2004 <http://www.kodakgirl.com>, and the Vintage Girl Scout Camp Museum website, 20 Nov. 2004 <http://www.pages.ivillage.com/campnurse/id5.html>.

39. Virginia Woolf, *A Room of One's Own* (1929; New York: Harcourt Brace Jovanovich, 1981).

40. Woolf quoted in Mary Gordon, "Foreword," *A Room of One's Own*, xiv.

41. Gordon viii.

42. Kristine M. McCusker, "Communication," *Girlhood in America: An Encyclopedia*, Vol. 1, Miriam Forman-Brunell, ed. (Santa Barbara: ABC-CLIO, 2001) 147.

43. Mrs. John Farrar (Eliza Ware), *The Youth's Letter-Writer* (New York: Bartlett and Raynor, 1834).

44. McCusker 147.

45. Hunter 65.

46. Hunter 56.

47. Hunter 56.
48. McCusker 147.
49. Hunter 67–68.
50. Jane Greer and Miriam Forman-Brunell, "Diaries," *Girlhood in America: An Encyclopedia*, Vol. 1, Miriam Forman-Brunell, ed. (Santa Barbara: ABC-CLIO, 2001) 209–10.
51. Greer and Forman-Brunell 210.
52. Schrum 383.
53. Schrum 9–10.
54. Joseph F. Kett, *Rites of Passage: Adolescence in America, 1790 to the Present* (New York: Basic Books, 1977) 144.
55. Kett 95-96.
56. Peiss 34-45.
57.. Kett 14-31.
58. Peiss 47.
59. Peiss 152.
60. Peiss; Schrum; Georganne Scheiner, *Signifying Female Adolescence : Film Representations and Fans, 1920–1950* (Westport: Praeger, 2000); Melvyn Stokes, "Female Audiences of the 1920s and Early 1930s," *Identifying Hollywood's Audiences: Cultural Identity and the Movies*, Melvyn Stokes and Richard Maltby, eds. (London: BFI Publishing, 1999) 42–60.
61. Schrum 368.
62. Scheiner 15–16.
63. Schrum 435.
64. Schrum 281–82, 289, 307.
65. Schrum 273–74.
66. Arnold Shaw, "Sinatrauma: The Proclamation of a New Era," *The Frank Sinatra Reader*, Steven Petkov and Leonard Mustazza, eds. (New York: Oxford University Press, 1995) 18–29.
67. Scheiner 86.
68. Leo C. Rosten, *Hollywood: The Movie Colony, The Movie Makers* (New York: Harcourt, Brace and Company, 1941) 409.
69. Scheiner 85–86.
70. Scheiner 124.
71. Henry Jenkins, *Textual Poachers: Television Fans and Participatory Culture* (New York: Routledge, 1992) 45.
72. Michel de Certeau, *The Practice of Everyday Life*, Steven Rendall, trans. (Berkeley: University of California Press, 1984).
73. Jenkins 49.
74. Pierre Bourdieu, *Distinction: A Social Critique of the Judgment of Taste*, Richard Nice, trans. (Cambridge: Harvard University Press, 1984).
75. John Fiske, "The Cultural Economy of Fandom," *The Adoring Audience: Fan Culture and Popular Media*, Lisa A. Lewis, ed. (New York: Routledge, 1992) 30.
76. Scheiner 133.
77. McRobbie and Garber 13–14. See also Sheryl Garratt, "All of Us, All of You," *Signed, Sealed, and Delivered: True Life Stories of Women in Pop*, Sue Steward and Sheryl Garratt, eds. (Boston: South End Press, 1984) 138–51; Barbara Ehrenreich,

Elizabeth Hess, and Gloria Jacobs, "Beatlemania: Girls Just Want to Have Fun," *The Adoring Audience: Fan Culture and Popular Media*, Lisa A. Lewis, ed. (New York: Routledge, 1992) 84–106.

78. Lizabeth Cohen, *A Consumer's Republic: The Politics of Mass Consumption in Postwar America* (New York: Knopf, 2003).

79. Elaine Tyler May, *Homeward Bound: American Families in the Cold War Era* (New York: Basic Books, 1988).

80. Lori Twersky, "Devils or Angels? The Female Teenage Audience Examined," *Trouser Press* (Apr. 1981) 28.

81. Cheryl Cline, "Essays from Bitch: The Women's Rock Newsletter with Bite," *The Adoring Audience: Fan Culture and Popular Media*, Lisa A. Lewis, ed. (New York: Routledge, 1992) 74. Originally published as "David Lee Roth—Threat or Menace?" *Bitch: The Women's Rock Mag with Bite* (Mar. 1986).

82. Lucy O'Brien, "The Woman Punk Made Me," *Punk Rock: So What?: The Cultural Legacy of Punk*, Roger Sabin, ed. (London: Routledge, 1999) 188, 197.

83. Angela McRobbie, "Second-Hand Dresses and the Role of the Ragmarket," *Zoot Suits and Second-Hand Dresses: An Anthology of Fashion and Music*, Angela McRobbie, ed. (Boston: Unwin Hyman, 1988) 38.

84. Vermilion quoted in *Search and Destroy #1–6: The Complete Reprint*, V. Vale, ed. (San Francisco: V/Search Publications, 1996) 6.

85. Bertei quoted in Jon Savage, *England's Dreaming: Anarchy, Sex Pistols, Punk Rock and Beyond* (New York: St. Martin's Press, 1992) 442.

86. For more information on female punk musicians of the 1970s and early 1980s, see "Women in Punk 1975–1980, Part 1," *Interrobang?! #2*, ed. Sharon Cheslow (Washington, D.C.: self-published, 1994); and "Women in Punk 1975–1980, Part 2," *Interrobang?! #3*, ed. Sharon Cheslow (Washington, D.C.: self-published, 1996–1997), 23 Oct. 2004 <http://www.mindspring.com/~acheslow/AuntMary/bang/wip.html>.

87. Helen Reddington, "'Lady' Punks in Bands: A Subculturette?" *The Post-Subcultures Reader*, David Muggleton and Rupert Weinzierl, eds. (New York: Berg, 2003) 248.

88. Dave Laing, *One Chord Wonders: Power and Meaning in Punk Rock* (Milton Keynes: Open University Press, 1985) 125.

89. Sharon Cheslow, Interview for Riot Grrrl Collection, Experience Music Project (Dec. 1999).

90. Reddington 242.

91. Savage 202.

92. Most histories of punk culture ignore female participation in zinemaking (not to mention other cultural practices) during the 1970s and 1980s. An exception to this male bias is David James's "Poetry/Punk/Production: Some Recent Writing in LA," *Postmodernism and Its Discontents: Theories, Practices*, E. Ann Kaplan, ed. (New York: Verso, 1988) 163–86.

93. Nancy Guevara, "Women Writin' Rappin' Breakin'," *The Year Left 2: An American Socialist Yearbook*, Mike Davis, Manning Marable, Fred Pfeil, and Michael Sprinker, eds. (Stonybrook: Verso: 1987) 172, 174.

94. Guevara 170, 169.

95. Guevara 163.

96. Robin D. G. Kelley, *Yo' Mama's Disfunktional!: Fighting the Culture Wars in Urban America* (Boston: Beacon, 1997) 69.

97. Kelley 71–74.

98. Tricia Rose, *Black Noise: Rap Music and Black Culture in Contemporary America* (Hanover: Wesleyan University Press, 1994) 57.

99. Murray Forman, "'Movin' Closer to an Independent Funk': Black Feminist Theory, Standpoint, and Women in Rap," *Women's Studies* 23 (1994) 41–42.

100. Rose 170.

101. Rose 176.

102. Forman 45.

103. Imani Perry, "It's My Thang and I'll Swing It the Way That I Feel!: Sexuality and Black Women Rappers," *Gender, Race, and Class in Media: A Text-Reader*, Gail Dines and Jean M. Humez, eds. (Thousand Oaks: Sage, 1995) 529, 528.

104. Michael Brake, *Comparative Youth Culture: The Sociology of Youth Culture and Youth Subcultures in America, Britain and Canada* (London: Routledge & Kegan Paul, 1985) 179.

105. Kelley 69–70.

106. Rose 57–58.

107. O'Brien 194.

108. O'Brien 193, 194.

109. O'Brien 193.

110. O'Brien 195.

111. Angela McRobbie, "Settling Accounts with Subcultures: A Feminist Critique," *On Record: Rock, Pop, and the Written Word*, Simon Frith and Andrew Goodwin, eds. (New York: Pantheon Books, 1990) 80.

112. Angela McRobbie, "Shut Up and Dance: Youth Culture and Changing Modes of Femininity," *Cultural Studies* 7.3 (Oct. 1993) 408.

CHAPTER 2

1. Reinstein quoted in V. Vale, ed., *Zines!*, Vol. 1 (San Francisco: V/Search Publication, 1996) 169. Originally published in *Fantastic Fanzine*.

2. *RIGHT NOW. RIOT GRRRL* quoted in Vale 165.

3. Since most contemporary riot grrrls are teenagers and women in their early twenties, and since Riot Grrrl activism is specifically oriented toward the social position of girlhood, I typically refer to members of this community as "girls" and "female youth."

4. Mary Celeste Kearney, "The Missing Links: Riot Grrrl—Feminism—Lesbian Culture," *Sexing the Groove: Gender and Popular Music*, Sheila Whiteley, ed. (New York: Routledge, 1997) 207–29.

5. Mary Celeste Kearney, "'Don't Need You': Rethinking Identity Politics and Separatism from a Grrrl Perspective," *Youth Culture: Identity in a Postmodern World*, Jonathon S. Epstein, ed. (Malden: Blackwell, 1998) 148–88.

6. Dick Hebdige, *Subculture: The Meaning of Style* (1979; London: Routledge, 1991); *Resistance through Rituals: Youth Subcultures in Post-War Britain*, Stuart Hall and Tony Jefferson, eds. (London: HarperCollins Academic, 1976).

7. For example, see John Clarke, Stuart Hall, Tony Jefferson, and Brian Roberts, "Subcultures, Cultures, and Class," *Resistance through Rituals*, 9–74.

8. Hebdige 101, 111.

9. Angela McRobbie, "Shut Up and Dance: Youth Culture and Changing Modes of Femininity," *Cultural Studies* 7.3 (Oct. 1993) 411.

10. See *The Post-Subcultures Reader*, David Muggleton and Rupert Weinzierl, eds. (New York: Berg, 2003).

11. Gilbert Ryle, "Thinking and Reflecting," *Collected Papers*, Vol. 2 (London: Hutchinson, 1971) 465–79; Clifford Geertz, *The Interpretation of Cultures* (New York: Basic Books, 1973).

12. McRobbie 412.

13. Sadie Plant, *The Most Radical Gesture: The Situationist International in a Postmodern Age* (New York: Routledge, 1992).

14. Walter Benjamin, "The Author as Producer," *Walter Benjamin: Selected Writings, Vol. 2, 1927–1934*, Rodney Livingstone, trans., Michael W. Jennings, Howard Eiland, and Gary Smith, eds. (Cambridge: Harvard University Press, 1999) 768–82.

15. Paul Willis, *Common Culture: Symbolic Work at Play in the Everyday Cultures of the Young* (Buckingham: Open University Press, 1990) 17.

16. McRobbie 410.

17. Lucy O'Brien, "The Woman Punk Made Me," *Punk Rock: So What?: The Cultural Legacy of Punk*, Roger Sabin, ed. (London: Routledge, 1999) 186–98; Angela McRobbie, "Second-Hand Dresses and the Role of the Ragmarket," *Zoot Suits and Second-Hand Dresses: An Anthology of Fashion and Music*, Angela McRobbie, ed. (Boston: Unwin Hyman, 1988) 23–49; Helen Reddington, "'Lady' Punks in Bands: A Subculturette?" *The Post-Subcultures Reader*, David Muggleton and Rupert Weinzierl, eds. (New York: Berg, 2003) 239–51; Nancy Guevara, "Women Writin' Rappin' Breakin'," *The Year Left 2: An American Socialist Yearbook*, Mike Davis, Manning Marable, Fred Pfeil, and Michael Sprinker, eds. (Stonybrook: Verso: 1987) 160–75; and Tricia Rose, *Black Noise: Rap Music and Black Culture in Contemporary America* (Hanover: Wesleyan University Press, 1994).

18. Imani Perry, "Who(se) Am I?: The Identity and Image of Women in Hip-Hop," *Gender, Race, and Class in Media: A Text-Reader*, 2nd ed., Gail Dines and Jean M. Humez, eds. (Thousand Oaks: Sage, 2003) 136–48.

19. Gayle Wald, "One of the Boys? Whiteness, Gender, and Popular Music Studies," *Whiteness: A Critical Reader*, Mike Hill, ed. (New York: New York University Press, 1997) 153.

20. Donna Gaines, *Teenage Wasteland: Suburbia's Dead End Kids* (New York: Harper Perennial, 1991) 198.

21. Connolly quoted in Steven Blush, *American Hardcore: A Tribal History* (Los Angeles: Feral House, 2001) 35.

22. Maffeo quoted in Andrea Juno, *Angry Women in Rock*, Vol. 1 (New York: Juno Books, 1996) 124.

23. For histories of Riot Grrrl's early years, see Juno 82–103 and 120–33; Mark Andersen and Mark Jenkins, *Dance of Days: Two Decades of Punk in the Nation's Capital* (New York: Soft Skull Press, 2001); Experience Music Project website,

"Riot Grrrl Retrospective," 23 Feb. 2003 <http://www.emplive.com/explore/riot_grrrl/index.asp>.

24. Neuman quoted in Andersen and Jenkins 315.

25. Juno 100.

26. *Revolution Girl Style Now* was the title of Bikini Kill's first cassette recording (K Records and Simple Machines, 1991).

27. Hanna quoted in Val C. Phoenix, "From Womyn to Grrrls: Finding Sisterhood in Girl Style Revolution," *Deneuve* (Jan.–Feb. 1994) 41.

28. Heavens to Betsy, "Terrorist," *Calculated*, Kill Rock Stars, 1993.

29. Bratmobile, "and i live in a town where the boys amputate their hearts," *The Real Janelle*, Kill Rock Stars, 1993.

30. Bikini Kill, "Double Dare Ya," Bikini Kill, *Kill Rock Stars*, 1992.

31. Bikini Kill, "New Radio," single, *Kill Rock Stars*, 1993.

32. Hanna quoted in Gina Arnold, "Bikini Kill: 'Revolution Girl-Style,'" *Option* 44 (May–June 1992) 44–45.

33. Smith quoted in, Experience Music Project.

34. Neuman quoted in, Experience Music Project.

35. *Bikini Kill: A Color and Activity Book*, Kathleen Hanna, ed. (Olympia: self-published, 1991) n.p. Note: Bibliographic information for zines is often incomplete due to the absence of information about editors, geographic location, and publication date within such documents.

36. *Riot Grrrl* #8 (Washington, D.C.: self-published, Aug. 1993) n.p.

37. Juno 99. Emily White, "Revolution Girl Style Now," *LA Weekly* (10 July 1992) 20–28.

38. Erin Smith of Bratmobile, *Sassy's* "Washington Bureau Chief" in the early 1990s, likely initiated this effort.

39. Joanne Gottlieb and Gayle Wald, "Smells Like Teen Spirit: Riot Grrrls, Revolution and Women in Independent Rock," *Microphone Fiends: Youth Music and Youth Culture*, Andrew Ross and Tricia Rose, eds. (New York: Routledge, 1994) 265.

40. Jessica Rosenberg and Gitana Garofalo, "Riot Grrrl: Revolutions from Within," *Signs: Journal of Women in Culture and Society* 23.3 (1998) 810.

41. Lea Thompson, "Media-Grrrl vs. Riot Grrrl" (1997), 23 Feb. 2003 <http://cerebro.cs.xu.edu/~tankgirl/twelvelittlegrrrls/papers/mediagrrrl.html>.

42. Vail quoted in Experience Music Project.

43. For a description of the convention, see Melissa Klein, "Riot Grrrls Go-Go," *off our backs* 23.2 (Feb. 1993) 6–12.

44. Benedict Anderson, *Imagined Communities: Reflections on the Origin and Spread of Nationalism* (London: Verso, 1991).

45. See Virginia Woolf, *A Room of One's Own* (1929; New York: Harcourt Brace Jovanovich, 1981).

46. Gottlieb and Wald.

47. Tucker quoted in Experience Music Project.

48. Misty quoted in Hillary Carlip, *Girl Power: Young Women Speak Out!* (New York: Warner, 1995) 58.

49. Bragin quoted in Rosenberg and Garofalo 817–18.

50. Rosenberg and Garofalo 811.

51. Barbara Hudson, "Femininity and Adolescence," *Gender and Generation*, Angela McRobbie and Mica Nava, eds. (London: Macmillan, 1984) 31–53.

52. Wald.

53. McRobbie, "Shut Up" 408.

54. Angela McRobbie, "Settling Accounts with Subcultures: A Feminist Critique," *On Record: Rock, Pop, and the Written Word*, Simon Frith and Andrew Goodwin, eds. (New York: Pantheon Books, 1990) 80. Originally published in *Screen Education* 34 (Spring 1980) 37-49.

55. Angela McRobbie and Jenny Garber, "Girls and Subcultures," *Resistance through Rituals* 219.

56. Angela McRobbie and Jenny Garber, "Girls and Subcultures," *Feminism and Youth Culture: From* Jackie *to* Just Seventeen (Boston: Unwin Hyman, 1991) 13.

57. McCarley quoted in Rosenberg and Garofalo 823–24.

58. Benjamin 777.

59. *Bikini Kill #1* n.p.

60. *Bikini Kill #2*, Kathleen Hanna, ed. (Washington, D.C.: self-published, 1991) n.p.

61. *Bikini Kill #2* n.p.

62. Spirit, "What Is a Riot Grrrl Anyway?" 6 Jan. 1995 <http://www.columbia.edu/~rli3/music_html/bikini_kill/girl.html>.

63. Xyerra quoted in Doreen Piano, "Congregating Women: Reading 3rd Wave Feminist Practices in Subcultural Production," *Rhizomes* 4 (Spring 2002), 15 July 2002 <http://www.rhizomes.net/issue4/piano.html>.

64. Witknee, "(Closing) Comments on Zines and Whatnot," *A Girl's Guide to Taking Over the World: Writings from the Girl Zine Revolution*, Karen Green and Tristan Taormino, eds. (New York: St. Martin's Press, 1997) 141. Originally published in *Alien*.

65. Renee quoted in Carlip 38. Originally published in *Stumble*.

66. *Bikini Kill #1* n.p.

67. This traditional connotation of "network" is deployed in several analyses of Riot Grrrl's media practices, especially Marion Leonard's "'Rebel Girl, You Are the Queen of My World': Feminism, 'Subculture' and Grrrl Power," *Sexing the Groove: Popular Music and Gender*, Sheila Whiteley, ed. (New York: Routledge, 1997) 230–55.

68. My expanded conception of networking here is somewhat in line with Ednie Kaeh Garrison's theory of feminist networking as involving a "technologic"; however, I do not see riot grrrls' or other young feminists' forms of networking through media technology as innovative or unique to contemporary feminism. See Garrison's "U.S. Feminism—Grrrl Style!: Youth (Sub)cultures and the Technologics of the Third Wave," *Feminist Studies* 26.1 (Spring 2000) 141–70.

69. For example, see Paul Du Gay, ed., *Production of Culture/Cultures of Production* (Thousand Oaks: Sage, 1997).

70. Despite the common use of "alternative" to describe forms of media not produced by the commercial culture industries, I refrain from using this term, given its nonspecificity and, in some cases, inaccuracy. Additionally, I avoid using "independent" as it is similarly nonspecific and inaccurate, as well as "underground," since it fails to acknowledge such media's interactions with the "overground" sectors of commercial and governmental cultural production. "Micro media" is

a more appropriate umbrella term for this type of media, particularly since it suggests the minimal amount of capital invested in and output created by media producers not associated with corporate culture.

71. In differentiating between the micro, commercial, and government sectors, I do not mean to suggest that commercial objectives and practices exist in only one of these realms. Rather I want to draw attention to the unique privileging of commerce in the sector commonly referred to as "mainstream culture."

72. Each of these activities is actually composed of a variety of sub-activities. For example, the production of a recorded song entails both the creation of its lyrics and sound, as well as the many practices involved in the recording process.

73. For a description of *la perruque*, see Michel de Certeau, *The Practice of Everyday Life*, Steven Rendall, trans. (Berkeley: University of California Press, 1984) 25–26.

74. Hanna quoted in Juno 98.

75. Tobi Vail, *Jigsaw #5* (Olympia: self-published, Summer 1992) n.p.

76. For example, see Laurel Gilbert and Crystal Kile, *Surfergrrrls: Look Ethel! An Internet Guide for Us!* (Seattle: Seal Press, 1995); and Karen Green and Tristan Taormino, eds., *A Girl's Guide to Taking Over the World: Writings from the Girl Zine Revolution* (New York: St. Martin's Press, 1997).

77. Tony Grajeda, "The 'Feminization' of Rock," *Rock Over the Edge: Transformations in Popular Music Culture*, Roger Beebe, Denise Fulbrook, and Ben Saunders, eds. (Durham: Duke University Press, 2002) 233–54.

78. See the Conclusion, as well as Sara Cohen, "Men Making a Scene: Rock Music and the Production of Gender," *Sexing the Groove: Popular Music and Gender*, Sheila Whiteley, ed. (New York: Routledge, 1997) 17–36.

79. Juno 103.

80. *RIGHT NOW. RIOT GRRRL* quoted in Vale 165.

81. Maffeo quoted in Juno 129–30.

82. Mavis Bayton, "Feminist Musical Practice: Problems and Contradictions," *Rock and Popular Music: Politics, Policies, Institutions*, Tony Bennett, Simon Frith, Lawrence Grossberg, John Shepherd, and Graeme Turner, eds. (London: Routledge, 1993) 177–92.

83. Tinuviel, "Villa Villakula," 29 Aug. 2002 <http://www.sprintmail.com/~misstinuviel/vvk.html>.

84. Tinuviel.

85. Tinuviel.

86. Christina Kelly, *Sassy* music editor, quoted in Arnold 46.

87. Kristin Thompson and Jenny Toomey, *An Introductory Mechanics Guide to Putting Out Records, Cassettes and CD's*, 6th ed. (Arlington: Simple Machines, 1999), 10 Oct. 2004 < http://www.indiecentre.com/info/guide.cfm>.

88. Benning quoted in Phoenix 41–42.

89. Benning quoted in Mark Ewert, "Sadie Benning," *Mirage* 4 (Aug. 1992) 3.

90. Ewert 3; Sadie Benning, "19 Years Old," *Visions* (Fall 1992) 54.

91. Benning quoted in Vail n.p.

92. Benning quoted in Vail n.p.

93. Tina Spangler, "Grrrls on Film," *femme flicke #5* (Brooklyn: self-published, 1996) n.p.

94. Delayen quoted in *femme flicke #7*, Tina Spangler, ed. (Brooklyn: self-published, 1997) n.p.

95. Jacobson quoted in Tara Mateik, "Surveying the Scene: Excerpts from the D.I.Y. Distro Resource Guide," *Felix* 2.2 (2000) 13, 23 Feb. 2003 <http://www.e-felix. org/issue5/mateik.html>.

96. July quoted in "She's Way Sassy!" *Sassy* (Apr. 1996) 24.

97. Miranda July, *Velvet Chainletter* directory (Portland: Big Miss Moviola, Apr. 1996) n.p.

98. Miranda, July, *U-Matic Chainletter* directory (Portland: Big Miss Moviola, July 1997) n.p.

99. July, *Velvet Chainletter* directory n.p.

100. Joanie for Jackie website, 29 Aug. 2002 <http://www. joanie4jackie.com>.

101. July, *Velvet Chainletter* directory n.p.

102. Miranda July, *Underwater Chainletter* directory (Portland: Big Miss Moviola, Oct. 1996) n.p.

103. July, *Velvet Chainletter* directory n.p.

104. July, *Underwater Chainletter* directory n.p.

105. Nina Malkin, "It's a Grrrl Thing," *Seventeen* (May 1993) 81.

106. Ann Japenga, "Grunge 'R' Us: Exploiting, Co-Opting and Neutralizing the Counterculture," *Los Angeles Times Magazine* (14 Nov. 1993) 26.

107. Lorraine Ali, "The Grrls Fight Back," *Los Angeles Times* (27 July 1995) F11.

108. Spivey quoted in Rosenberg and Garofalo 829.

109. See "Grrrl Maxi-Info Pad," (self-published and circulated via the Internet) 26 Jan. 1995; and Riot Grrrl Directory, 3rd ed. (2003–2004), 10 Oct. 2004 <http://members.tripod.com/~yoodle/rg.html>.

110. Bragin quoted in Rosenberg and Garofalo 839.

111. The next chapter contains a historical overview of the U.S. girls' advocacy movement.

112. McCarley quoted in Rosenberg and Garofalo 837.

113. Toomey quoted in Andersen and Jenkins 318.

114. Nguyen quoted in V. Vale, ed., *Zines!*, Vol. 2 (San Francisco: V/Search Publication, 1997) 61.

115. Nguyen quoted in Vale, *Zines!*, Vol. 2, 61.

116. Nguyen quoted in Vale, *Zines!*, Vol. 2, 63.

117. Jen Smith, "Doin' It for the Ladies—Youth Feminism: Cultural Productions/ Cultural Activism," *Third Wave Agenda: Being Feminist, Doing Feminism*, Leslie Heywood and Jennifer Drake, eds. (Minneapolis: University of Minnesota Press, 1997) 229.

118. Smith 229–30.

119. Smith 230.

120. Blyele quoted in Ali F1 and F11.

121. For information on other Riot Grrrl–inspired conventions, see the Ladyfest website <http://www.ladyfest.org> and Southern Girls Convention website <http// www. southerngirlsconvention.org>.

122. Fritz Hahn, "Bartender of the Month: August 2002: Lili Kotlyarov-Montoya," 23 Oct. 2003 <http//www.washingtonpost.com/wp-srv/entertainment/new_features/barsclubs/bartender080.htm>.

123. Although Bikini Kill and Heavens to Betsy disbanded in the mid-1990s, the members of Bratmobile merely took a hiatus, relaunching their band in 1999.

124. Carland quoted in *femme flicke #7* 32.

125. Carland quoted in *femme flicke #7* 31.

126. Carland quoted in *femme flicke #7* 31.

127. Piano ¶18.

128. Benjamin 777.

129. Mimi Nguyen, *Slanderous* (16 May 2000), 29 Aug. 2002 <http://www.worsethanqueer.com/slander/51600.html>.

CHAPTER 3

1. Girls, Women + Media Project website, "What Can I Do? (Glad You Asked): Media Activism 101," 31 Jan. 2003 <http://www.mediaandwomen.org/whatcani.html>.

2. Caples quoted in Alexandra Juhasz, ed., *Women of Vision: Histories in Feminist Film and Video* (Minneapolis: University of Minnesota Press, 2001) 115.

3. Girls Inc. website, "Girls Get the Message: A Media Literacy Program" (Jan. 2001), 8 Aug. 2002 <http://www.girlsinc.org/ic/page.php?id=1.2.3>.

4. Girls Inc. website, "Facts: Girls and Media" (Feb. 2002) 8 Aug. 2002 <http://www.girlsinc.org/ic/page.php?id=3.1.12>.

5. Girls Inc., "Girls Re-Cast TV Action Kit," 8 Aug. 2002 <http://www.girlsinc.org/PROGRAMS.html>.

6. Girls Inc. website, "Girls Get the Message."

7. David Buckingham, *Media Education: Literacy, Learning and Contemporary Culture* (Malden: Blackwell, 2003) 44–45.

8. See Sharon Smith, "The Image of Women in Film: Some Suggestions for Future Research," *Women and Film* 1 (1972) 13–21.

9. Girls Inc.'s promotional literature indicates that the Girls Get the Message program will enable girls "to appropriate the power of media by expressing themselves through various media forms"; however, I found no evidence of a practical component in other literature on this program. See Girls Inc., *Annotated Bibliography* (New York: Girls Inc., 2002) 7.

10. Girls. Inc. website, "Bold Girls: Examine, Experiment, Explore," 8 Aug. 2002 <http://www. girlsinc.org/gc/page.php?id=3.4.17>.

11. I participated in these events as both an instructor and an observer.

12. Girl Scouts of the U.S.A., *Media Know-How for Cadette and Senior Girl Scouts* (New York: Girl Scouts of the U.S.A., 1999).

13. Girl Scouts of the U.S.A. 20.

14. Girls, Women + Media Project website.

15. "Media education" is often used both as an umbrella term for the various approaches to teaching young people about and through media, and for those curricula specifically focused on media production. To avoid confusion, I use the term "media pedagogy" when discussing the broader field. I use "media literacy" when referencing curricula that primarily facilitate students' critical media analysis.

16. Steve Goodman outlines three similar approaches in media pedagogy: technology integration, media literacy, and community media arts. See *Teaching Youth*

Media: A Critical Guide to Literacy, Video Production, and Social Change (New York: Teachers College Press, 2003) 10–18.

17. Melvyn Stokes, "Female Audiences of the 1920s and Early 1930s," *Identifying Hollywood's Audiences: Cultural Identity and the Movies*, Melvyn Stokes and Richard Maltby, eds. (London: BFI Publishing, 1999) 42–60.

18. Fredric Wertham, *The Seduction of the Innocent* (New York: Rinehart, 1954).

19. Phillip Marchand, *Marshall McLuhan: The Medium and the Messenger* (New York: Ticknor & Fields, 1989) 136–38.

20. Surgeon General's Scientific Advisory Committee on Television and Social Behavior, *Television and Growing Up: The Impact of Televised Violence* (Washington, D.C.: U.S. Public Health Service and U.S. Government Printing Office, 1972).

21. Ford Foundation, *Television and Children: Priorities for Research* (Reston: Ford Foundation, 1975).

22. Kathleen Tyner, *Literacy in a Digital World: Teaching and Learning in the Age of Information* (Mahwah: Lawrence Erlbaum Associates, 1998) 134–35.

23. Lucinda Furlong, "Media Literacy Moves a Step Ahead," *The Independent: Film and Video Monthly* (June 2001) 28.

24. Roy Stafford, "Redefining Creativity: Extended Project Work in GCSE Media Studies," *Watching Media Learning: Making Sense of Media Education*, David Buckingham, ed. (Bristol: Taylor & Francis, 1990) 81–100.

25. David Buckingham, "Media Education: From Pedagogy to Practice," *Watching Media Learning: Making Sense of Media Education*, David Buckingham, ed. (Bristol: Taylor & Francis, 1990) 3–5.

26. Wendy Ewald and Alexandra Lightfoot, *I Wanna Take Me a Picture: Teaching Photography and Writing to Children* (Boston: Beacon Press, 2001) 7.

27. Tyner 140–48.

28. Max Horkheimer and Theodor W. Adorno, *Dialectic of Enlightenment*, John Cumming, trans. (1944; New York: Continuum, 1993).

29. Neil Postman, *Amusing Ourselves to Death: Public Discourse in the Age of Show Business* (New York: Viking, 1985).

30. Tyner 136.

31. Roger Desmond, "Media Literacy in the Home: Acquisition vs. Deficit Models," *Media Literacy in the Information Age*, Robert Kubey, ed. (New Brunswick: Transaction Books, 1997) 338.

32. Tyner 147.

33. David Sholle and Stan Denski, "Critical Media Literacy: Reading, Remapping, Rewriting," *Rethinking Media Literacy: A Critical Pedagogy of Representation*, Peter McLaren, Rhonda Hammer, David Sholle, and Susan Smith Reilly, eds. (New York: Peter Lang, 1995) 13.

34. Henry Jenkins, *Textual Poachers: Television Fans and Participatory Culture* (New York: Routledge, 1992).

35. John Ehrenreich and Barbara Ehrenreich, "The Professional Managerial Class," *Between Labor and Capital*, Pat Walker, ed. (Boston: South End Press, 1979) 17.

36. Laurie Ouellette, "TV Viewing as Good Citizenship?: Political Rationality, Enlightened Democracy and PBS," *Cultural Studies* 13.1 (1999) 69.

37. Pierre Bourdieu, *Distinction: A Social Critique of the Judgment of Taste*, Richard Nice, trans. (Cambridge: Harvard University Press, 1984).

38. Buckingham, *Media Education* 11–12.

39. David Sholle and Stan Denski, *Media Education and the (Re)Production of Culture* (Westport: Bergin & Garvey, 1994) 116.

40. Gloria DeGaetano and Kathleen Bander, *Screen Smarts: A Family Guide to Media Literacy* (Boston: Houghton Mifflin, 1996).

41. Nancy Cott, *The Grounding of Modern Feminism* (New Haven: Yale University Press, 1987) 16.

42. Barbara Ryan, *Feminism and the Women's Movement: Dynamics of Change in Social Movement, Ideology, and Activism* (New York: Routledge, 1992) 11.

43. Ryan 12.

44. Ryan 11.

45. For example, Sarah Grand, "The Modern Girl," *North American Review* 158 (June 1894) 706–14.

46. Joseph M. Hawes, "The Strange History of Female Adolescence in the United States," *Journal of Psychohistory* 13.1 (Summer 1985) 55.

47. Barbara Welter, "The Cult of True Womanhood: 1820–1950," *American Quarterly* 17.2 (Summer 1966) 151–73.

48. Hawes 55.

49. G. Stanley Hall, *Adolescence: Its Psychology and Its Relation to Physiology, Anthropology, Sociology, Sex, Crime, Religion and Education*, 2 vols. (New York: D. Appleton, 1904).

50. Kathy Peiss, *Cheap Amusements: Working Women and Leisure in Turn-of-the-Century New York* (Philadelphia: Temple University Press, 1986) 165–66.

51. Peiss 166.

52. Peiss 175.

53. Peiss 184.

54. Peiss 186.

55. Paula Fass, *The Damned and the Beautiful: American Youth in the 1920's* (New York: Oxford University Press, 1977) 25.

56. Charlotte Perkins Gilman, "Vanguard, Rear-guard, and Mud-guard," *Century Magazine* 104 (1922) 351–53.

57. Fass 23.

58. Mary Rothschild and Georganne Scheiner, "Girl Scouts," *Girlhood in America: An Encyclopedia*, Vol. 1, Miriam Forman-Brunell, ed. (Santa Barbara: ABC-CLIO, 2001) 317.

59. Erin McMurray, "Camp Fire Girls," *Girlhood in America: An Encyclopedia*, Vol. 1, Miriam Forman-Brunell, ed. (Santa Barbara: ABC-CLIO, 2001) 88.

60. Janis S. Bohan, "Age and Sex Differences in Self-Concept," *Adolescence* 8.3 (Fall 1973) 379–84.

61. Carol Gilligan, *In a Different Voice: Psychological Theory and Women's Development* (1982; Cambridge: Harvard University Press, 1993).

62. Carol Gilligan, Nona Lyons, and Trudy J. Hammer, *Making Connections: The Relational Worlds of Adolescent Girls at Emma Willard School* (Cambridge: Harvard University Press, 1990); Carol Gilligan and Annie G. Rogers, *Translating the Language of Adolescent Girls: Themes of Moral Voice and Stages of Ego*

Development (Cambridge: Harvard University, 1988); Carol Gilligan, Annie G. Rogers, and Deborah L. Tolman, eds., *Women, Girls and Psychotherapy: Reframing Resistance* (New York: Harrington Park Press, 1991).

63. American Association of University Women, *Shortchanging Girls, Shortchanging America* (Washington, D.C.: AAUW Education Foundation, 1991); Myra Sadker and David Sadker, *Failing at Fairness: How Our Schools Cheat Girls* (New York: Touchstone, 1994); Peggy Orenstein, *SchoolGirls: Young Women, Self-Esteem and the Confidence Gap* (New York: Anchor, 1994); Mary Pipher, *Reviving Ophelia: Saving the Selves of Adolescent Girls* (New York: Pantheon, 1994).

64. For example, see American Association of University Women, *Separated by Sex: A Critical Look at Single-Sex Education for Girls* (Washington, D.C.: AAUW Education Foundation, 1998).

65. Lyn Mikel Brown, *Raising Their Voices: The Politics of Girls' Anger* (Cambridge: Harvard University Press, 1998) vii.

66. Fine and Macpherson quoted in Michelle Fine, *Disruptive Voices* (Albany: State University of New York Press, 1992) 178.

67. Joan Jacobs Brumberg, *The Body Project: An Intimate History of American Girls* (New York: Random House, 1997) 211.

68. Brumberg 197.

69. Brumberg 207.

70. Brumberg 211.

71. Pipher 12–13.

72. Orenstein's *SchoolGirls* and Brown's *Raising Their Voices* are notable exceptions. See also Jill McLean Taylor, Carol Gilligan, and Amy M. Sullivan, *Between Voice and Silence: Women and Girls, Race and Relationship* (Cambridge: Harvard University Press, 1995).

73. Julie Bettie, "Women without Class: Chicas, Cholas, Trash, and the Presence/ Absence of Class Identity," *Signs: Journal of Women in Culture and Society* 26.1 (Autumn 2000) 2.

74. Rachel Orviro, "I am a Girl," 8 Aug. 2002 <http://www.voiceofwomen.com/articles/girl.html>.

75. Mary E. Odem, *Delinquent Daughters: Protecting and Policing Adolescent Female Sexuality in the United States, 1885–1920* (Chapel Hill: University of North Carolina Press, 1995).

76. Girls Inc., "Strong, Smart, Bold," promotional brochure (New York: Girls Inc., 2002) 5.

77. Girl Scouts of the U.S.A. website, "About Girl Scouts of the U.S.A," 23 Aug. 2003 <http://www.girlscouts.org/about/>.

78. Andrea Johnston's Girls Speak Out program was later reworked as a book: *Girls Speak Out: Finding Your True Self* (New York: Scholastic, 1997).

79. Originally titled the Ophelia Educational Fund, the organization changed its name to GENaustin in 2001.

80. "HHS Girl Power! Fact Sheet," *Girl Power! Backgrounder* (Washington, D.C.: U.S. Department of Health and Human Services, 1997) 3.

81. Information about bradford and It's a She Shoot was obtained through a formal interview on 3 Oct. 2002, as well as several informal conversations with the author.

82. k. bradford, email announcement for It's a She Shoot (15 Sept. 2002).

83. Information about Graham and Reel Grrls was obtained through a telephone interview on 26 July 2002 and subsequent email correspondence on 8 Oct. 2002 with the author, as well as through the Reel Grrls website (http://reelgrrls.org/), and articles about the program: Candy Hatcher, "Girls' Film Shatters Old Images of Women," *Seattle Post-Intelligencer* (20 June 2001), 15 Oct. 2002 <http://seat-tlepi.nwsource.com/hat.cher/28188_candy20.shtml>; Elisabeth Keating, "Seattle Teens Combine Filmmaking, Activism," *Women's eNews* (17 July 2002), 10 Aug. 2002 <http//www.womensenews.com/article.cfm/dyn/aid/616/context/archive>; Hannah Levin, "Yer Critique," *The Stranger.com* (7 June 2001) 10 Aug. 2002 <http://www.thestranger.com/2001-06-07/film2.html>.

84. Reel Grrls website.

85. The Guerilla Girls is a feminist activist group that advocates on behalf of women in the arts.

86. Graham quoted in Levin.

87. Information about Fort and the Girls Film School was obtained through a telephone interview on 24 July 2002, as well as through email correspondence on 12 Feb. 2003 with Tanya Doriss, the school's assistant director. Information was obtained also via the Girls Film School website (http://girlsfilmschool.csf.edu/program.html) and articles about the program: Deborah Baker, "Girls Get Touch of Celluloid Life," *Albuquerque Journal* (22 June 2002), 11 Aug. 2002 <http://girls-filmschool.csf.edu/gfspress/2002/ABQjournalN6-22-02.html>; Robin Clark, "Girl Behind the Camera," *Santa Fe New Mexican* (23 June 2000), 11 Aug. 2002 <http://www.girlsfilmschool.csf.edu/gfspress/SFNewMex-6-23-00.html>; Diana Heil, "College Combines Entertainment, Education," *Albuquerque Journal* (26 June 2000), 8 Aug. 2002 <http://girlsfilmschool.csf.edu/gfspress/ABQJournalN-6-26-00.html>; "iMovie and Macs Help Girls Go to Hollywood," 11 Aug. 2002 <http://www.apple.com/education/hed/macsinaction/girlsfilmschool/>; Heidi Utz, "Boys on the Side: Fostering Future Female Filmmakers," *Santa Fe Reporter* (3 July 2001), 11 Aug. 2002 <http://girlsfilmschool.csf.edu/gfspress/reporter7-3-01.html>.; Katie Dean, "Film School for Girls' Eyes Only," *Wired News* (17 June 2002), 11 Aug. 2002 <http://www.wired.com/news/print/0,1294,53171,00.html>.

88. Girls Film School website.

89. Fort quoted in "iMovie."

90. Fort quoted in Clark.

91. Fort quoted in Utz.

92. Claire Johnston, "Women's Cinema as Counter-Cinema," *Notes on Women's Cinema*, Claire Johnston, ed. (London: Society for Education in Film and Television, 1973) 24–31.

93. Adrianne McCurrach quoted in Dean.

94. Street-Level Youth Media, "Girls Only Pilot Program," 10 Nov. 2004 <http://www.streetlevel.iit.edu/outhprojects/chikweb/Programs/o.html>.

95. Street-Level Youth Media, "Girls Group," 10 Nov. 2004 <http://streetlevel.iit.edu/girlsg.html>.

96. San Diego Women Film Foundation, "Divas Direct," 15 Oct. 2004 <http://sdgff.org/ywfp.htm>.

97. Amanda Lotz and Sharon Ross developed Girls Making Headlines in Spring 2000. Upon Lotz's relocation, Diane Zander stepped in as the workshop's coinstructor for the Summer 2000 class. Elizabeth Sikes taught the class by herself in summer 2001. Clarissa Moore served as the teaching assistant both years. In addition to the author's observation of Girls Making Headlines classes in 2000 and 2001, information about this program was obtained through email questionnaires and informal conversations with the cofounders and instructors. Lotz responded to the author's questionnaire via email on 21 Jun. 2001; Moore responded on 22 Apr. 2001; Ross on 30 Apr. 2001 and 30 Sept. 2002; Zander on 20 Apr. 2001 and 22 Sept. 2002.

98. Ross, email, 30 Apr. 2001.

99. Information on Latinitas was obtained through Laura Donnelly's responses to the author's email questionnaire on 2 Feb. 2005, as well as several informal conversations with Donnelly and Alicia Rascon.

100. Latinitas, "What People Are Saying about Latinitas," promotional flyer (Austin: self-published, 2004).

101. Donnelly, email, 2 Feb. 2005.

102. Desmond 338–39.

103. Ladislaus M. Semali, *Literacy in Multimedia America: Integrating Media Education across the Curriculum* (New York: Falmer Press, 2000) 81–86.

104. Paolo Freire, *Pedagogy of the Oppressed* (New York: Seabury Press, 1970).

105. Stanley Aronowitz, "Working Class Displacements and Postmodern Representations," *Postmodern Education: Politics, Culture, and Social Criticism*, Stanley Aronowitz and Henry Giroux (Minneapolis: University of Minnesota Press, 1991) 165.

106. Peter Greenaway, "The Role of Media Studies and Arts Education in Visual and Cultural Literacy," 8 Aug. 2002 <http://www.sirius.com/~medialit.green.htm>.

107. Kathleen Tyner, "Representing Diversity–Media Analysis in Practice," 8 Aug. 2002 <http://www.sirius.com/~medialit.tyner2.htm>.

108. David Buckingham and Julian Sefton-Green, *Cultural Studies Goes to School Reading and Teaching Popular Media* (Bristol: Taylor & Francis, 1994) 59.

109. Renee Hobbs, "The Seven Great Debates in the Media Literacy Movement," 1 Oct. 2002 <http://www.medialit.org/reading_room/article2.html>.

110. Tyner, *Literacy* 4.

111. Patricia Aufderheide, *Media Literacy: A Report of the National Leadership Conference on Media Literacy* (Queenstown: Aspen Institute, 1993) v, emphasis added.

112. Texas Education Agency, "Texas Essential Knowledge and Skills for English, Language Arts, and Reading, Viewing/Representing Strands, Grades 4–12," 8 Aug. 2002 <http://www.tea.state.tx.us/teks>.

113. Other coed community-based youth media education programs include the Center for Young Cinema in Austin, Texas; Children's Media Project in Poughkeepsie, New York; Global Action Project in New York, New York; Just Think in San Francisco, California; the Mirror Project in Somerville, Massachusetts; Reach LA in Los Angeles, California; Teen Producer's Project in San Diego, California; and Youth Radio in Berkeley, California.

114. Brian Goldfarb, *Visual Pedagogy: Media Cultures In and Beyond the Classroom* (Durham: Duke University Press, 2002) 72.

115. Notable exceptions are Kristen Drotner, "Girl Meets Boy: Aesthetic Production, Reception, and Gender Identity," *Cultural Studies* 3.2 (1989) 208–25; and Jenny Grahame, "*Playtime*: Learning about Media Institutions through Practical Work," *Watching Media Learning: Making Sense of Media Education*, David Buckingham, ed. (Bristol: Taylor & Francis, 1990) 101–23. Anne Orwin and Adrianne Carageorge discuss gender in media production training in relation to college-level programs. See "The Education of Women in Film Production," *Journal of Film and Video* 53.1 (Spring 2001) 40–53.

116. Goodman 58.

117. Kathleen Tyner, "The Media Education Elephant," *Proceedings of the 1992 UNESCO Conference on Media Education*, Cary Bazalgette, ed. (London: BFI and CLEMI, 1992), 1 Oct. 2002 <http://www.interact.uoregon.edu/MediaLit/FA/mltyner/elephant.html.

118. Buckingham, *Media Education* 84.

119. Grahame 101.

120. Goodman 53.

121. Doriss quoted in Dean.

122. Barbara Hudson, "Femininity and Adolescence," *Gender and Generation*, Angela McRobbie and Mica Nava, eds. (London: Macmillan, 1984) 31–53.

123. Zander, email, 20 Apr. 2001.

124. Donnelly, email, 2 Feb. 2005.

125. Zander, email, 22 Sept. 2002.

126. Drotner 210.

127. Ross, email, 30 Sept. 2002.

128. Fort quoted in Baker. See also Orwin and Carageorge.

129. Drotner 212.

130. Orwin and Carageorge 49.

131. Zander, email, 22 Sept. 2002.

132. Donnelly, email, 2 Feb. 2005.

133. Marilyn Frye, "Some Reflections on Separatism and Power," *The Politics of Reality: Essays in Feminist Theory* (Trumansburg: Crossing Press, 1983) 107.

134. Orwin and Carageorge 41.

135. Lotz, email, 21 Jun. 2001.

136. "Girls Making Headlines" student survey, 18 June 2001.

137. Lindsay Carver quoted in Heil.

138. Megan Peters quoted in Dean, "Film School."

139. Moore, email, 22 Apr. 2001.

140. Ross, email, 30 Apr. 2001.

141. Jamie Wheeler quoted in Candy Hatcher, "Empowered Young Women Are Passing It On," *Seattle Post-Intelligencer* (4 Feb. 2002), 15 Oct. 2002 <http://www.911media.org/youth/reelgrrls.html>.

142. Fort quoted in "iMovie."

143. Ramirez quoted in Hatcher, "Girls' Film."

144. Liana Gonzales quoted in "Girls Film School," *Pasatiempo* (5 Apr. 2001), 11 Aug. 2002 <http://girlsfilmschool.csf.edu/gfspress/Pasa4-5-01.html>.

145. Jennifer Kwok quoted in Baker.
146. Unidentified Reel Grrls' participants quoted in Hatcher, "Girls' Film."
147. Latinitas, "What People Are Saying."
148. Girls Making Headlines student survey (15 June 2001).
149. Graham quoted in Levin.
150. Wheeler quoted in Hatcher, "Girls' Film."
151. Time Warner, "Time Warner Foundation Awards 21st Century Media and Technology Literacy Grant to Girls Incorporated" (20 Nov. 2003), 15 Jan. 2005. <http://www.timewarner.com/corp/print/0,20858,670124,00.html>. The Foundation determined the focus on high school girls. At this time, Girls Inc. has no plans to expand its Girls Make the Message curriculum to younger girls.
152. Deborah Aubert, telephone interview with the author, 28 Jan. 2005.

CHAPTER 4

1. Virginia Woolf, *A Room of One's Own* (1929; New York: Harcourt Brace Jovanovich, 1981) 52.
2. Darby Romeo, "Ben Is Dead Is Born," *A Girl's Guide to Taking Over the World: Writings from the Girl Zine Revolution*, Karen Green and Tristan Taormino, eds. (New York: St. Martin's Press, 1997) 70.
3. Lyn Mikel Brown, "Telling a Girl's Life: Self-Authorization as a Form of Resistance," *Women, Girls, and Psychotherapy: Reframing Resistance*, Carol Gilligan, Annie G. Rogers, and Deborah L. Tolman, eds. (New York: Harrington Park, 1991) 72.
4. Brown 72.
5. For this study, I examined approximately seventy-five girl zines produced between 1990 and 2003.
6. Kate Peirce, "Socialization of Teenage Girls through Teen-Magazine Fiction: The Making of a New Woman or an Old Lady," *Sex Roles* 29.1/2 (1993) 66–67.
7. As noted in Chapter 2, such connections between Sassy and Riot Grrrl were likely the result of Erin Smith's simultaneous work for the magazine and involvement in the punk feminist community.
8. Angela McRobbie, "More!: New Sexualities in Girls' and Women's Magazines," *Cultural Studies and Communications*, James Curran, David Morley, and Valerie Walkerdine, eds. (London: Arnold, 1996) 186, 183.
9. Janice Winship, "'A Girl Needs to Get Street-Wise': Magazines for the 1980s," *Feminist Review* 21 (1985) 40.
10. Winship 37.
11. Jay Cole quoted in Deidre Carmody, "Petersen Will Restart Sassy with Push for Older Readers," *The New York Times* (8 Dec. 1994) D19.
12. Kim Whiting, publisher's welcome message, *Empowered* (Feb.–Mar. 1997) i.
13. *blue jean magazine* (Jan.–Feb. 1998) i.
14. "About Teen Voices," *Teen Voices* 5.3 (1996) 2.
15. For example, *Teen Voices* 5.2 includes a guide on how to produce zines.
16. *blue jean magazine* was published from 1996 to 1998. Its online version was active from 2001 to 2003.

17. The title *Nolite te Bastardes Carborundorum* comes from Margaret Atwood's novel, *The Handmaid's Tale*, and means, "Don't let the bastards get you down."

18. *Nolite te Bastardes Carborundorum #2*, Nikki Atwell, ed. (Melbourne, AR: self-published, 1997) n.p. Note: Bibliographic information for zines is often incomplete, due to the absence of information about editors, geographical location, and publication date within such documents.

19. "Sassy: Then and Now," *Bitch #1*, Lisa Jervis, ed. (Oakland: self-published, Winter 1996) n.p.

20. *Little Big Sister Zine #2*, Caroline and Libs, eds. (Lindsay: self-published, c. 1993) n.p.

21. *Ben Is Dead #23*, Darby Romeo, ed. (Hollywood: self-published, Spring 1994). For a more detailed analysis of this zine's *Sassy* parody, see Mary Celeste Kearney, "Producing Girls: Rethinking the Study of Female Youth Culture," *Delinquents and Debutantes: Twentieth-Century American Girls' Cultures*, Sherrie A. Inness, ed. (New York: New York University Press, 1998) 285–310.

22. Amanda Burr, "Competition? What Competition?" *Ben Is Dead #23* (Hollywood: self-published, Spring 1994) 41.

23. Darby Romeo, "Zines: Girl Powered!" *Ben Is Dead #23* (Hollywood: self-published, Spring 1994) 43–44

24. Eric Swenson, "DIY Hypermedia Publishing: A Primer," *Ben Is Dead #23* (Hollywood: self-published, Spring 1994) 103–6.

25. For example, in the late 1990s, *Factsheet Five's* online list of girl zines was titled "Riot Grrrlz." See 12 Aug. 1998 <http://www.factsheet5.com>. Mark Fenster relates girl zines to both Riot Grrrl and the homocore movement. See "Queer Punk Fanzines: Identity, Community, and the Articulation of Homosexuality and Hardcore," *Journal of Communication Inquiry* 17.1 (Winter 1993) 73–94.

26. Stephen Duncombe, *Notes from the Underground: Zines and the Politics of Alternative Culture* (New York: Verso, 1997).

27. Pander Zine Distro website, 18 Jan. 2003 <http://www.panderzinedistro.com>, and Grrrl Style! Distro website, 18 Jan. 2003 <http://grrrlstyle.org>.

28. Grrrl Zines a Go-Go website, 1 May 2005 <http://grrrlzines.net/agogo.htm>.

29. As a way of honoring and promoting other young zinesters, Cecilia Moss compiled a list of zinemakers fifteen years old and younger that she published periodically in *Suburbia*.

30. My survey of members of the Pander Zine and Grrrl Style! distros was conducted in February 2003. My survey of distro owners was conducted in May–June 2005. The seventeen survey respondents reported 17.9 years old as the average age of initial zinemaking.

31. Fredric Wertham, *The World of Fanzines: A Special Form of Communication* (Carbondale: Southern Illinois University Press, 1973); Stephen Schwartz, "History of Zines," *Zines!,* Vol. 1, V. Vale, ed. (San Francisco: V/Search, 1996) 155–59.

32. Michel de Certeau, *The Practice of Everyday Life*, Steven Rendall, trans. (Berkeley: University of California Press, 1984) 25–26.

33. Fredric Jameson, "Postmodernism and Consumer Society," *The Anti-Aesthetic: Essays on Postmodern Culture*, Hal Foster, ed. (Port Townsend: Bay Press, 1983) 114.

34. Stanley Aronowitz, *Dead Artists, Live Theories and Other Cultural Problems* (New York: Routledge, 1994) 197–98.

35. Stuart Hall, "Cultural Identity and Cinematic Representation," *Framework* 36 (1989) 68.

36. Hall 68, 70.

37. Stuart Hall, "New Ethnicities," *Stuart Hall: Critical Dialogues in Cultural Studies*, David Morley and Kuan-Hsing Chen, eds. (London: Routledge, 1996) 442.

38. Barbara Crowther, "Writing as Performance: Young Girls' Diaries," *Making Meaning of Narratives in the Narrative Study of Lives*, Ruthellen Josselson and Amia Lieblich, eds. (Thousand Oaks: Sage, 1999) 208.

39. See note 30 above.

40. Romeo, "Ben Is Dead Is Born" 70.

41. Duncombe 37, 43.

42. Duncombe 39.

43. Prior to the proliferation of mass media, W. E. B. DuBois wrote of African American's double-consciousness in *The Souls of Black Folk: Essays And Sketches* (Chicago: A. C. McClurg, 1903).

44. Teresa de Lauretis, *Technologies of Gender: Essays on Theory, Film, and Fiction* (Bloomington: Indiana University Press, 1987) 10.

45. Marion Leonard, "Paper Planes: Travelling the New Grrrl Geographies," *Cool Places: Geographies of Youth Cultures*, Tracey Skelton and Gill Valentine, eds. (New York: Routledge, 1998) 107, 101.

46. Ednie Kaeh Garrison, "U.S. Feminism—Grrrl Style!: Youth (Sub)cultures and the Technologics of the Third Wave," *Feminist Studies* 26.1 (Spring 2000) 141–70. Garrison, like Leonard, includes online forms of communication as part of this process.

47. Michelle Comstock, "Grrrl Zine Networks: Re-Composing Spaces of Authority, Gender, and Culture," *Journal of Advanced Composition* 21.2 (Spring 2001) 386.

48. Comstock 388, 383.

49. Marion Leonard, "'Rebel Girl, You Are the Queen of My World': Feminism, 'Subculture' and Grrrl Power," *Sexing the Groove: Popular Music and Gender*, Sheila Whiteley, ed. (New York: Routledge, 1997) 231.

50. Henry Jenkins, *Textual Poachers: Television Fans and Participatory Culture* (New York: Routledge, 1992) 23.

51. Jenkins 158, 154, 156.

52. Fred Wright, "Identity Consolidation in Zines," *Journal for the Psychoanalysis of Culture and Society* 1.1 (1996) 137.

53. For feminist work in this area, see Janice A. Radway, *Reading the Romance: Women, Patriarchy, and Popular Literature* (Chapel Hill: University of North Carolina Press, 1984); Jackie Stacey, *Star Gazing: Hollywood Cinema and Female Spectatorship* (New York: Routledge, 1994); Ien Ang, "Melodramatic Identifications: Television Fiction and Women's Fantasy," *Feminist Television Criticism: A Reader, Charlotte Brunsdon*, Julie D'Acci, and Lynn Spigel, eds. (Oxford: Oxford University Press, 1997) 155–66.

54. Constance Penley, "Feminism, Psychoanalysis, and the Study of Popular Culture," *Cultural Studies*, Lawrence Grossberg, Cary Nelson, and Paula Treichler, eds. (New York: Routledge, 1992) 480.

55. Penley 493.

56. Jean Laplanche and Jean-Bertrand Pontalis, "Fantasy and the Origins of Sexuality," *International Journal of Psycho-Analysis* 49 (1968) 17.

57. Elizabeth Cowie, "Fantasia," *m/f* 9 (1984) 79.

58. Ien Ang argues that the pleasure gained from consuming fictional fantasies "is not so much a denial of reality as a *playing with it*. A game that enables one to place the limits of the fiction and the real under discussion and make them fluid." See *Watching Dallas: Soap Opera and the Melodramatic Imagination*, Della Couling, trans. (New York: Methuen, 1985) 49, emphasis added.

59. This cultural practice is popularly known as "slash."

60. Penley 488.

61. Richard Dyer, "Believing in Fairies: The Author and the Homosexual," *Inside/Out: Lesbian Theories, Gay Theories*, Diana Fuss, ed. (New York: Routledge, 1991) 186, emphasis added.

62. Dyer 186–87.

63. Dyer 185–86.

64. Dyer 188.

65. Dyer 196.

66. Dyer 187–88.

67. Dyer 188.

68. Wendy Hollway, "Gender Difference and the Production of Subjectivity," *Changing the Subject: Psychology, Social Regulation and Subjectivity*, Julian Henriques, Wendy Hollway, Cathy Urnwin, Couze Venn, and Valerie Walkerdine, eds. (London: Methuen, 1984) 236.

69. Hollway 238.

70. Hollway 239.

71. Pierre Bourdieu, *Distinction: A Social Critique of the Judgment of Taste*, Richard Nice, trans. (Cambridge: Harvard University Press, 1984).

72. Judith Butler, *Gender Trouble: Feminism and the Subversion of Identity* (New York: Routledge, 1990) 145.

73. Stuart Hall, "The Question of Cultural Identity," *Modernity and Its Futures: Understanding Modern Societies*, Stuart Hall, David Held, and Tony McGrew, eds. (London: Polity Press, 1992) 277.

74. Mary Bucholtz, A. C. Laing, and Laurel A. Sutton, eds., *Reinventing Identities: The Gendered Self in Discourse* (New York: Oxford University Press, 1999).

75. Cowie 83.

76. Barbara Hudson, "Femininity and Adolescence," *Gender and Generation*, Angela McRobbie and Mica Nava, eds. (London: Macmillan, 1984) 51.

77. Butler 145–47.

78. This common foregrounding of musical discourse is not surprising given that music served as the most privileged medium in punk scenes during this period.

79. Fenster 74.

80. The first issue of *Action Girl Newsletter* contains reviews of such zines as *GirlFrenzy*, *MadWoman*, and *Riot Grrrl*, as well as resources for female youth, such as Youth Hotline and Planned Parenthood. *Action Girl Newsletter #1*, Sarah Dyer, ed. (Staten Island: self-published, 1992).

81. Dyer quoted in Tristan Taormino, "An Interview with Action Girl's Sarah Dyer," *A Girl's Guide to Taking Over the World: Writings from the Girl Zine Revolution*, Karen Green and Tristan Taormino, eds. (New York: St. Martin's Press, 1997) 168.

82. On the difference between sex and gender display, see Candace West and Don H. Zimmerman, "Doing Gender," *The Social Construction of Gender*, Judith Lorber and Susan A. Farrell, eds. (Newbury Park: Sage, 1991) 13–37.

83. Mukherji quoted in *Evolution of a Race Riot*, Mimi Nguyen, ed. (Berkeley: self-published, 1997) 62.

84. Hanna quoted in *Bikini Kill #2*, Kathleen Hanna, ed. (Washington, D.C.: self-published, 1991) n.p.

85. Gayle Wald, "One of the Boys? Whiteness, Gender, and Popular Music Studies," *Whiteness: A Critical Reader*, Mike Hill, ed. (New York: New York University Press, 1997).

86. *Evolution of a Race Riot; Race Riot #2*, Mimi Nguyen, ed. (Berkeley: self-published, 2002).

87. C/S Distro website, 4 June 2005 <http://www.csdistro.com>; Mamas Unidas Distro website, 17 May 2005 <http://www.geocities.com/mamasunidasdistro/index.html>.

88. Sisi quoted in *Evolution of a Race Riot* 52.

89. Chela Sandoval, "U.S. Third World Feminism: The Theory and Method of Oppositional Consciousness in the Postmodern World," *Genders* 10 (1991) 1–24.

90. Griel Marcus, *Lipstick Traces: A Secret History of the Twentieth Century* (Cambridge: Harvard University Press, 1989). Dick Hebdige made a similar, but less supported, argument in *Subculture: The Meaning of Style* (1979; London: Routledge, 1991).

91. John A. Walker, *Cross-Overs: Art into Pop, Pop into Art* (London: Comedia, 1987) 79.

92. Walter Benjamin, "The Work of Art in the Age of Mechanical Reproduction," 1935, *Illuminations*, Hannah Arendt, trans. and ed. (New York: Harcourt Brace Jovanovich, 1968) 237–38.

93. Guy Debord, "Détournement as Negation and Prelude," *Post-Pop Art*, Paul Taylor, ed. (Cambridge: MIT Press, 1989) 7–9.

94. Such aesthetics are not always successful with all audiences, as many audience members develop a "shock defense" that allows them to absorb the shock into their consciousness, thereby neutralizing its transformative power and making it impossible for any new meanings to be made and heightened awareness to develop. Walter Benjamin, *Charles Baudelaire: A Lyric Poet in the Era of High Capitalism*, Harry Zohn, trans. (London: NLB, 1973) 115–18.

95. For an extended analysis of the Situationists, see Sadie Plant, *The Most Radical Gesture: The Situationist International in a Postmodern Age* (New York: Routledge, 1992).

96. Hebdige 106–12.

97. Hebdige 112.

98. Hebdige 87. See also Dave Laing, *One Chord Wonders: Power and Meaning in Punk Rock* (Milton Keynes: Open University Press, 1985) 29–31.

99. Hebdige 87.

100. Hebdige 111.

101. Punk's historical relation to youth is notable in its etymological development as a term for a young sexual partner of an older gay man, a young male with a low-paying job, and a youthful gangster. See Laing 41–42.

102. Two notable exceptions here are Neil Nehring, *Popular Music, Gender, and Postmodernism: Anger Is an Energy* (Thousand Oaks: Sage, 1997); and Robert D. DeChaine, "Mapping Subversion: Queercore Music's Playful Discourse of Resistance," *Popular Music and Society* 21.4 (Winter 1997) 7–37.

103. For analyses of carnival culture, see Mikhail Bakhtin, *Rabelais and His World*, Helene Iswolsky, trans. (Bloomington: Indiana University Press, 1984); Peter Stallybrass and Allon White, *The Politics and Poetics of Transgression* (London: Methuen, 1986).

104. Mary Russo, "Female Grotesques: Carnival and Theory," *Feminist Studies/Critical Studies*, Teresa de Lauretis, ed. (Bloomington: Indiana University Press, 1986) 218.

105. Russo 215.

106. Stallybrass and White 58.

107. Natalie Zemon Davis, *Society and Culture in Early Modern France* (Stanford: Stanford University Press, 1965) 131.

108. Russo 214, 217.

109. See *Action Girl Newsletter #1*; Romeo, "Zines"; Grrrl Zines Network, 14 Jan. 2003 <http://wwwgrrrlzines.net>. The online version of *Factsheet Five* also contained a "grrrl zine" category in the late 1990s.

110. *Riot Grrrl*, the title of Molly Neuman and Alison Wolfe's second zine, has been used for numerous zines produced by various local Riot Grrrl groups.

111. For a linguistic analysis of the "intentional violations" of writing found in grrrl zines, see Laurel A. Sutton, "All Media Are Created Equal: Do-It-Yourself Identity in Alternative Publishing," *Reinventing Identities: The Gendered Self in Discourse*, Mary Bucholtz, A. C. Liang, and Laurel A. Sutton, eds. (New York: Oxford University Press, 1999) 163–80.

112. *Verboslammed #8*, Rebecca Gilbert, ed. (Portland, OR: self-published, 1996).

113. *Bikini Kill #2*; *Doing Maria #1*, Tricky, ed. (Tennessee: self-published, 2000); *Girl Germs #4*, Molly Neuman and Allison Wolfe, eds. (Olympia: self-published, 1992).

114. For example, see *Bamboo Girl #9*, Sabrina Margarita Sandata, ed. (New York City: self-published, Jan. 2000).

115. *Riot Grrrl NYC #5*, Riot Grrrl NYC, eds. (New York City: self-published, Mar. 1993).

116. *Retail Whore #4*, K. Raz, ed. (Chicago: self-published, 2001) cover.

117. *Korespondances #7.1*, Womyn's Action Coalition, eds. (Memphis: self-published, 1999).

118. *Skunk #4*, Margaret and Steve, eds. (New York: self-published, Fall 1995); *Welcome #8*, Jello and Gloworm, eds. (Ft. Huachuca: self-published, 1996).

119. *Hey There, Barbie Girl #1*, Barbara Kligman, ed. (New York City: self-published, Winter 1994).

120. *Ms. America #2*, Sarah and Jen, eds. (Normal: self-published, c. early 1990s) cover; *Bikini Kill: A Color and Activity Book* (a.k.a. *Bikini Kill #1*), Kathleen Hanna, ed.

(Olympia: self-published, 1991) cover; *Nerd Girl #4*, Marcy, ed. (Seattle: self-published, 1995) cover.

121. bell hooks, *Feminist Theory: From Margin to Center* (Boston: South End Press, 1984) 111.

122. *Aim Your Dick #1*, Mimi and Marike, eds. (Berkeley: self-published, 1993) cover.

123. *Girl Germs #4* cover.

124. *Evolution of a Race Riot* cover.

125. *Slant #5*, Mimi Nguyen, ed. (Berkeley: self-published, 1997) cover.

126. *Housewife Turned Assassin #2*, Dani and Sisi, eds. (North Hollywood: self-published, 1993).

127. *Pixxiebitch #3*, Zoe, ed. (Montrose: self-published, c. mid-1990s).

128. *Twat! #2*, Christine Johnston, ed. (Olympia: self-published, 1996).

129. *Girl Germs #5*, Molly Neuman and Allison Wolfe, eds. (Olympia: self-published, 1993) back cover.

130. For example, see *Gurlz with Gunz #8*, Goofy, Moo, and Bertha, eds. (Havertown: self-published, 1994).

131. Thompson quoted in *Zines!*, Vol. 1, V. Vale, ed. (San Francisco: V/Search, 1996) 168.

132. Marcy quoted in *Nerd Girl #4* n.p.

133. *Bikini Kill #2* n.p.

134. *Girl Infinity #2*, Emelie Feingold-Tarrant, ed. (Venice: self-published, 1996) n.p.

135. Smith quoted in *Girl Germs #3*, Molly Neuman and Allison Wolfe, eds. (Olympia: self-published, 1992) 15.

136. *Housewife Turned Assassin #3*, Dani and Sisi, eds. (North Hollywood: self-published, 1994).

137. *Girl Germs #5* n.p.

138. Tania Modleski, "The Search for Tomorrow in Today's Soap Operas: Notes on a Feminine Narrative Form," *Film Quarterly* 33.1 (Fall 1979) 17.

139. *Survival Guide for Her Repellant #3*, Coni, ed. (Howard Beach, NY: self-published, 1995) back cover.

140. *Nerd Girl #4* n.p.

141. The origins of this list are unclear; however, it has been published several times on the Internet. For example, see "Barbies We Would Like to See," 14 Jan. 2003 <http://monster-island.org/tinashumor/humor/barbie.html>. A slightly different list appears as "Barbies Never Seen," 10 Oct. 2004 <http://www.lotsofjokes.com/cat_242.htm>.

142. *Girl Germs #4* n.p.

143. *Ms. America #2* n.p.

144. *Nolite te Bastardes Carborundorum #2* n.p.

145. Gayle Wald, "Just a Girl?: Rock Music, Feminism, and the Cultural Construction of Female Youth," *Signs: Journal of Women in Culture and Society* 23.3 (Spring 1998) 596–97.

146. *Ms. America #2* n.p.

147. *Marika #2*, Erika Reinstein and May Summer, eds. (Reston: self-published, 1993).

148. *Girlie Jones #2.2*, Aimée Gagnon, Sarah Miller, Collen Sumner, Zoë Miller, eds. (Springfield, ME: self-published, Fall 1996) 5.

149. *Verboslammed #6*, Rebecca Gilbert, ed. (Portland, OR: self-published, 1995).

150. *Girl Germs #2*, Molly Neuman and Allison Wolfe, eds. (Olympia: self-published, 1991) 25.

151. *Fantastic Fanzine #3* 1/2, Erika Reinstein, ed. (Olympia: self-published, 1993) n.p. Trinh T. Minh-ha, *Woman, Native, Other: Writing Postcoloniality and Feminism* (Bloomington: Indiana University Press, 1989); Rita Mae Brown, *Rubyfruit Jungle* (Plainfield: Daughters, 1973); Susan Faludi, *Backlash: The Undeclared War Against American Women* (New York: Crown Publishers, 1991).

152. *Housewife Turned Assassin #3* n.p.

153. Annette Kuhn, *The Power of the Image: Essays on Representation and Sexuality* (London: Routledge & Kegan Paul, 1985); Cherríe Moraga and Gloria Anzaldúa, eds., *This Bridge Called My Back: Writings by Radical Women of Color* (Watertown: Persephone Press, 1981).

154. *Korespondances #6.2*, Womyn's Action Coalition, eds. (Memphis: self-published, 1998).

155. Barbara Findlen, ed., *Listen Up: Voices from the Next Feminist Generation* (Seattle: Seal Press, 1995); Robin Morgan, ed., *Sisterhood Is Powerful: An Anthology of Writings from the Women's Liberation Movement* (New York: Random House, 1970); Raya Dunayevskaya, *Women's Liberation and the Dialectics of Revolution* (Atlantic Highlands: Humanities Press, 1985).

156. Nguyen quoted in *Evolution of a Race Riot 4*.

157. hooks 12.

158. Martin quoted in *Evolution of a Race Riot 16*.

159. "Women in Punk 1975–1980, Part 1," *Interrobang?!* #2, ed. Sharon Cheslow (Washington, D.C.: self-published, 1994); and "Women in Punk 1975–1980, Part 2," *Interrobang?!* #3, ed. Sharon Cheslow (Washington, D.C.: self-published, 1996–1997) 23 Oct. 2004 <http://www.mindspring.com/~acheslow/AuntMary/bang/wip.html>.

160. Vail quoted in *Bikini Kill #1* n.p.

161. Kile quoted in *Girls Can Do Anything #1*, Crystal Kile, ed. (Bowling Green: self-published, Summer 1994) n.p.

162. Jenny quoted in *Not Sorry #1*, Jenny, ed. (Chula Vista: self-published, 2002) n.p.

163. For example, see *Ms. America #2* n.p.

164. *Housewife Turned Assassin #3* n.p.

165. *The Bad Girl Club*, Amy Hixon, ed. (Minneapolis: self-published, c. mid-1990s) n.p.

166. *Bikini Kill #1*, n.p.; *Girl Germs #4*, n.p.; *Nolite te Bastardes Carborundorum #2* n.p.; *Suburbia #6*, Cecilia Moss, ed. (Richmond, CA: self-published, 1996) n.p.

167. *Skunk #4* n.p.; *Suburbia #6* n.p.

168. Kim France, "Rock-Me Feminism," *New York* (3 June 1996) 36–41.

169. Mukherji quoted in *Evolution of a Race Riot 62*.

170. *Bamboo Girl #9* 10–14.

171. Robin quoted in *Korespondances #6.2* n.p.

172. May quoted in *Marika #2* n.p.

173. Erika quoted in *Riot Grrrl #7*, Ed. Erika Reinstein (Washington, D.C.: self-published, 1992) n.p.

174. Anonymous quoted in *Housewife Turned Assassin #3*, Dani and Sisi, eds. (North Hollywood: self-published, 1994) n.p.

175. *Girlie Jones #2.2*, 15.
176. Marcy quoted in *Nerd Girl #4* n.p.
177. *Ms. America #2* n.p.
178. *Meat Hook #4*, Tye, ed. (Los Angeles: self-published, 1993).
179. *Welcome #8* n.p.
180. Gilbert quoted in *Verboslammed #8* n.p.
181. Moon quoted in *Korespondances #7.1*, n.p.
182. *Housewife Turned Assassin #3* n.p.
183. Allison quoted in *Bikini Kill #2* n.p.
184. Jenny quoted in *Not Sorry #1* n.p.
185. Ray quoted in *Evolution of a Race Riot* 8.
186. Melissa quoted in *Evolution of a Race Riot* 15.
187. Bishon quoted in *Evolution of a Race Riot* 30.
188. Whang quoted in *Girl Germs #5* n.p.
189. Sisi quoted in *Housewife Turned Assassin #3* n.p.
190. Mengshin quoted in *Evolution of a Race Riot* 35.
191. *Ms. America #2* n.p.
192. *Bamboo Girl #10*, Sabrina Margarita Sandata, ed. (New York City: self-published, Jan. 2001) 54–61.
193. *Skunk #4* n.p.
194. Romeo, "Zines" 43.

CHAPTER 5

1. Coppola quoted in *Hearts of Darkness: A Filmmaker's Apocalypse*, dirs. Fax Bahr, George Hickenlooper, Eleanor Coppola (Triton Pictures, 1991).
2. *It Wasn't Love*, dir. Sadie Benning (Video Data Bank, 1992).
3. *If Every Girl Had a Diary*, dir. Sadie Benning (Women Make Movies, 1990); *A Place Called Lovely*, dir. Sadie Benning (Women Make Movies, 1991); *Girl Power*, dir. Sadie Benning (Video Data Bank, 1992).
4. Kim Masters, "Auteur of Adolescence: Sadie Benning, Talking to the Camera," *Washington Post* (17 Oct. 1992) D1.
5. *Hazel, the Guinea Pig's Package*, dir. Alyssa Buecker (Milbo Productions and HBO Family, 1996).
6. *Figure It Out, Guinea Pig Style*, dir. Alyssa Buecker (Milbo Productions and HBO Family, 1999).
7. *Benny*, dirs. Ashli and Callie Pfeiffer and Maggie and Sabrina Kelley (YaYa Productions, 1998).
8. *Gimme Cookies*, dirs. Ashli and Callie Pfeiffer and Maggie and Sabrina Kelley (YaYa Productions and HBO Family, 2000).
9. Hagins also wrote and edited the film. See *Pathogen's* website, 12 Dec. 2005 <http://www.cheesynuggets.com>.
10. This campaign is discussed in this book's Introduction.
11. For this project, I analyzed approximately seventy films produced in the mid-1990s to early 2000s by female youth between nine and nineteen years old. I gained access to these films via online distributors, film festivals, girls' media workshops, and HBO Family's *30 x 30: Kid Flicks*.

12. Andrea Richards, email correspondence with the author (23 June 2001). Andrea Richards, *Girl Director: A How to Guide for the First Time Flat Broke Filmmaker (and Videomaker)* (Los Angeles: Girl Press, 2001).

13. Christine Spines, "Behind Bars," *Women in Hollywood* (Jan. 2000) 45.

14. Citron quoted in Alexandra Juhasz, ed., *Women of Vision: Histories in Feminist Film and Video* (Minneapolis: University of Minnesota Press, 2001) 147.

15. Godmilow quoted in Janis Cole and Holly Dale, *Calling the Shots: Profiles of Women Filmmakers* (Kingston: Quarry Press, 1993) 72.

16. Coolidge quoted in Cole and Dale 52.

17. A "grip" is a cinematic stagehand.

18. Ruane quoted in Katie Dean, "Women Behind the Camera: Where?" *Wired News* (17 June 2002), 12 Aug. 2002 <http://www.wired.com/news/print/0,1294,53209,00.html>.

19. Arthur quoted in Cole and Dale 28.

20. Wilson quoted in Cole and Dale 252.

21. Hammer quoted in Juhasz 83.

22. Reichert quoted in Juhasz 132.

23. Haines quoted in Cole and Dale 104.

24. Heckerling quoted in Cole and Dale 116.

25. Seidelman quoted in Cole and Dale 194.

26. Tewkesbury quoted in Cole and Dale 232.

27. Foster quoted in Spines 47.

28. Seidelman quoted in Cole and Dale 194.

29. Bird quoted in Spines 46.

30. Spines 46.

31. Godmilow quoted in Cole and Dale 77.

32. Borden quoted in Cole and Dale 39.

33. Julia Lesage, "Political Aesthetics of the Feminist Documentary Film," *Issues in Feminist Film Criticism*, Patricia Erens, ed. (Bloomington: Indiana University Press, 1990) 222–37; and Annette Kuhn, *Woman's Pictures: Feminism and Cinema* (1982; New York: Verso, 1994).

34. Hammer quoted in Juhasz 83.

35. Michelle Citron, "Women's Film Production: Going Mainstream," *Female Spectators: Looking at Film and Television*, E. Deidre Pribram, ed. (New York: Verso, 1990) 54–55.

36. Caples quoted in Juhasz 115.

37. Patricia R. Zimmerman, *Reel Families: A Social History of Amateur Film* (Bloomington: Indiana University Press, 1995) 43, 61, 66.

38. Zimmerman 123.

39. Zimmerman 112–13.

40. Michelle Citron, *Home Movies and Other Necessary Fictions* (Minneapolis: University of Minnesota Press, 1999) 11.

41. Elaine Tyler May, *Homeward Bound: American Families in the Cold War Era* (New York: Basic Books, 1988).

42. Stereophile Staff, "CEA Study: Shrinking Difference in Technology Use by Men, Women" (26 Nov. 2000) 15 Nov. 2004 <http://stereophile.com/news/10901>.

43. Good Housekeeping, "Women and Consumer Technology: Good Housekeeping Reader Panel Results" (Dec. 2004) 18 Jan. 2005 <http://www.goodhousekeeping-seal.com/hotdata/publishers/hearst5880925/promos/women_consumer_tech.pdf>.

44. Mary Ann Clawson, "Masculinity and Skill Acquisition in the Adolescent Rock Band," *Popular Music* 18.1 (1999) 102.

45. Claire Johnston, "Women's Cinema as Counter-Cinema," 1973, *Feminist Film Theory: A Reader*, Sue Thornham, ed. (New York: New York University Press, 1999) 36–37.

46. Laura Mulvey, "Visual Pleasure and Narrative Cinema," *Screen* 16.3 (Autumn 1975) 6–18.

47. E. Ann Kaplan, *Women and Film: Both Sides of the Camera* (New York: Routledge, 1983) 30.

48. Mulvey 11.

49. John Berger, *Ways of Seeing* (1972; London: BBC and Penguin, 1977) 47.

50. Berger 46–47.

51. Kaplan 31.

52. Susan Bordo, *Unbearable Weight: Feminism, Western Culture, and the Body* (Berkeley: University of California Press, 1993) 12.

53. Mavis Bayton, "Women and the Electric Guitar," *Sexing the Groove: Popular Music and Gender*, Sheila Whiteley, ed. (New York: Routledge, 1997) 43.

54. Steve Waksman, *Instruments of Desire: The Electric Guitar and the Shaping of Musical Experience* (Cambridge: Harvard University Press, 1999) 188, 247.

55. Patricia R. Zimmerman, "Video and the Counterculture," *Global Television*, Cynthia Schneider and Brian Wallis, eds. (New York: Wedge Press, 1988) 219.

56. Bayton, 42.

57. Sara Cohen, "Men Making a Scene: Rock Music and the Production of Gender," *Sexing the Groove: Popular Music and Gender*, Sheila Whiteley, ed. (New York: Routledge, 1997) 22.

58. Clawson 106.

59. Bayton 41.

60. Bayton 41–42.

61. Bayton 38.

62. Cohen 24.

63. For example, see Roger Ebert, Review of *Straight Out of Brooklyn*, Chicago Sun-Times (28 June 1991).

64. Marc Savlov, "Small Wonders: Children's Filmmaking Grows Up," *Austin Chronicle* (12 Nov. 1999) 62; Paul Wisenthal, "Pint-Size Producers Get Focused, Mini-Spielbergs Bloom," *USA Today* (6 June 2000) 1D. Wisenthal repeats his skewed focus on young male filmmakers in "The Rising Career of a Young Director. No, Really Young," *The New York Times* (28 Oct. 2001) 11+.

65. Jack Hitt, "Film at 11 (or 12, or 13)," *The New York Times Magazine* (5 Mar. 2000) 79.

66. Chris Garcia, "Direct from Kids," *Austin American-Statesman* (15 Dec. 2002) K13.

67. For example, see Robin Clark, "Girl Behind the Camera," *Sante Fe New Mexican* (23 June 2000), 11 Aug. 2002 <http://www.girlsfilmschool.csf.edu/gfspress/

SFNewMex-6-23-00.html>; Katie Dean, "Film School for Girls' Eyes Only," *Wired News* (17 June 2002), 12 Aug. 2002 <http://www.wired.com/news/print/0,1294,53171,00.html>; Candy Hatcher, "Girls' Film Shatters Old Images of Women," *Seattle Post-Intelligencer* (20 June 2001), 15 Oct. 2002 <http://seattlepi.nwsource.com/hat.cher/28188_candy20.shtml>.

68. Julie Bourbon, "School Producing Young Filmmakers," *The Washington Post* (11 Apr. 2002) 3+.

69. Coolidge quoted in Richards 76.

70. Spines 45.

71. Anne Orwin and Adrianne Carageorge, "The Education of Women in Film Production," *Journal of Film and Video* 53.1 (Spring 2001) 45.

72. Clawson 106.

73. Dean, "Women Behind the Camera."

74. Anders quoted in Richards 1.

75. See "Evan and Jaron," *YM* (July 2001) 6; "Coolest Boys in America," *YM* (Nov. 2001) 118.

76. "She's Way Sassy!" *Sassy* (Apr. 1996) 24. Big Miss Moviola is discussed in more detail in Chapter 2.

77. See notes 67 and 68.

78. Kaye Black, *Kid Vid: Fun-damentals of Video Instruction* (Tucson: Zephyr Press, 2000).

79. Angela McRobbie, "Shut Up and Dance: Youth Culture and Changing Modes of Femininity," *Cultural Studies* 7.3 (Oct. 1993) 408.

80. Jan Biles, "Makin' Movies," *Examiner.net* (13 Feb. 1999), 30 Aug. 2002 <http://www.examiner.net.stories/021399/lif_movies.html>.

81. Welbon quoted in Juhasz 273.

82. Richards, email.

83. Richards, *Girl Director* 3.

84. Katie Hutchinson and Kellen Sheedy, "Dash of Cinema," *New Moon* (May–June 1999) 28–29.

85. Ruth Young, "Hollywood Behind the Scenes," *New Moon* (Nov.–Dec. 2002) 11.

86. San Diego Women Film Foundation website, "San Diego Girl Film Festival," 15 Oct. 2004 <http://sdgff.org/sdgff.htm>.

87. Listen Up!, a youth media network, organized a film program curated by nine girl filmmakers for the 2000 DocSide Short Film Festival. See the Listen Up! website, 23 Jan. 2003 <http://www.listenup.org/grrrl>.

88. *Smashing the Myth (or Not Just White, Rich, and Dangerously Thin)* (Listen Up!, 2001).

89. "Teen Girls Get Their Version of Sundance," *Girl Zone* (26 Feb. 2001) 23 Jan. 2003 <http:www.girlzone.com/html/flix.html>.

90. Joanie 4 Jackie website, 25 Jan. 2003 <http://www.joanie4jackie.com>.

91. Peter Humm, "Real TV: Camcorders, Access, and Authenticity," *The Television Studies Book*, Christine Geraghty and David Lusted, eds. (New York: St. Martin's, 1998) 228–49.

92. Richard Dyer, "Believing in Fairies: The Author and the Homosexual," *Inside/Out: Lesbian Theories, Gay Theories*, Diana Fuss, ed. (New York: Routledge, 1991) 185–201.

93. Wendy Hollway, "Gender Difference and the Production of Subjectivity," *Changing the Subject: Psychology, Social Regulation and Subjectivity*, Julian Henriques, Wendy Hollway, Cathy Urnwin, Couze Venn, and Valerie Walkerdine, eds. (London: Methuen, 1984) 226–63.

94. Dyer 188.

95. Georganne Scheiner, *Signifying Female Adolescence: Film Representations and Fans, 1920–1950* (Westport: Praeger, 2000) 90–115.

96. Mary Celeste Kearney, "Girlfriends and Girl Power: Female Adolescence in Contemporary U.S. Cinema," *Sugar, Spice, and Everything Nice: Cinemas of Girlhood*, Frances Gateward and Murray Pomerance, eds. (Detroit: Wayne State University Press, 2002) 125–42.

97. *What if Barbie Had a Voice?*, dir. Lillian Ripley (Reel Grrls, 2004).

98. *Barbie*, dirs. Anna Bulley and Katie McCord (Reel Grrls, 2003).

99. The film seems to be a visual reconstruction of the "Barbies We Would Like to See" list that has appeared in several grrrl zines and on the Web. See "Barbies We Would Like to See," 14 Nov. 2004 <http://monster-island.org/tinashumor/humor/barbie.html>.

100. *Barbie Resized*, dir. Kat Bauman (Reel Grrls, 2001).

101. *Fight Girl Poisoning* (Project Chrysalis and Listen Up!, 1996). The girls who participated in making this film were adjudicated. Therefore, their identities are protected.

102. *Girls Making Headlines*, dirs. Beth Cortez-Neavel, Elena Cortez-Neavel, Jessica Garcia, Meredith Gibson, Rachel Greenberg, Annie Hicks, Adianez Martinez, Elizabeth McGinnis, Wynden Rogers, and Caitlin Sherrill (RTF/AFF Summer Camp, 2000).

103. *Silicone Bone*, Heather Altherr, Rachel Detrinis, Samantha Goble, Thea Heilbron, Aja Longi, Aileen Mell, and Sawyer Perry (Girls Film School, 2004).

104. *Baywatch Babes … or Not*, dir. Emily Vissette (Reel Grrls, 2001).

105. *Listen to Your Angel*, dirs. Leah Ruthrauff and Miquela Suazo (Reel Grrls, 2001).

106. *Body Rhapsody*, dirs. Sina Gedlu, Louisa Jackson, Marianne Maksirisombat, and Emily Zisette (Reel Grrls, 2001).

107. *I Am Beautiful*, dir. Jennifer Sugg (Girls Film School, 2002).

108. Marilyn Manson, "Beautiful People," *Antichrist Superstar* (Interscope Records, 1996).

109. *Mirror*, dir. Alix Brown (Reel Grrls, 2001).

110. *Beauty Marks*, dir. Tess Jubran (Reel Grrls, 2003).

111. *Girl Power* (Project Chrysalis and Listen Up!, 1996). The girls who participated in making this film were adjudicated. Therefore, their identities are protected.

112. *Prufrock and Me*, dir. Ilana Urbach (California State Summer School for the Arts, 1997).

113. *Body Image*, dir. Mieko Krell (911 Media Arts Center and Listen Up!, 2000).

114. Reel Grrls website, 22 Feb. 2005 <http://reelgrrls.org/>.

115. Diane Zander, email response to author's questionnaire (20 Apr. 2001).

116. Reel Grrls website.

117. Zander.

118. *Video Icons* was collectively produced by Coco Massengale, Tenzin Tingkhye, Leela Townsley, Zoe Euster, Bana Abera, Victoria Wilson, Emilie Collier, and Kendra Terry (Reel Grrls, 2003).

119. *What if Men Menstruated?*, dirs. Theresa Benkman and Leela Townsley (Reel Grrls, 2003).

120. *Girls*, dir. Ryan Davis (John Jay High School and Listen Up!, 2000).

121. Beastie Boys, "Girls," *Licensed to Ill* (Def Jam Records, 1986).

122. *The Ultimate Guide to Flirting*, dir. Tricia Grashaw (California State Summer School for the Arts, 1996).

123. *Tomboygirl*, dir. Candice Yoo (Reach LA, 2002).

124. *Love Shouldn't Hurt*, dir. Tamara Garcia (5 Points Media Center and Listen Up!, 2000); *It's Never OK*, dir. Arielle Davis (Reel Grrls, 2003); *No More Silence*, dirs. Cassie Reeder, Kim Phillips, Natalie Camavati, and Kelly Rolfes (Communications Arts High School and Listen Up!, 2000).

125. *Now You Know How We Feel*, dir. Natasha Norton (Reel Grrls, 2003).

125. *What Would Your Family Do?*, dir. Tenzin Tingkhye (Reel Grrls, 2003).

127. *Pushing Back the Limits*, dirs. Ashli and Callie Pfeiffer and Maggie and Sabrina Kelley (YaYa Productions, 1999).

128. *Femininity*, dir. Lauren Dowdall (St. Charles High School and Listen Up!, 2000).

129. Bruno Bettelheim, "The Problem of Generations," *The Challenge of Youth*, Erik H. Erikson, ed. (Garden City: Anchor Books, 1965) 76–109.

130. *Pick Me*, dir. Stephanie Dunn (Animation Stewdio, 2003).

131. *Are You a Boy or a Girl?* dir. Taizet Hernandez (Reach LA, 2002).

132. *Looks Like a Girl*, dir. Ana Lopez (Reach LA, 2004).

133. *Scary Movie Spot*, dir. Emily Vissette (Reel Grrls, 2001).

134. *I Popped His Cherry*, dir. Cesy Urbina (California State Summer School for the Arts, 1997).

135. *Paybax*, dir. Ginny Habereder (California State Summer School for the Arts, 1997).

136. *The Sensible Girl*, dir. Elizabeth Mims (independently produced in Austin, 2002).

137. *A Story of Hope*, dirs. Meghan Baker, Adriana Medine, Kimani Nagurski, and Julia Wells (Girls Film School, 2002).

138. *A Party*, dir. Kimberly Po (California State Summer School for the Arts, 1998).

139. *The Nightcrawlers*, dir. Carley Steiner (HBO Family, 1998).

140. *The Commitments*, dir. Alan Parker (United Artists, 1991).

141. For analyses of Benning's videos, see Mia Carter, "The Politics of Pleasure: Cross-Cultural Autobiographic Performance in the Video Works of Sadie Benning," *Signs: Journal of Women in Culture and Society* 23.3 (Spring 1998) 745–69; Christie Milliken, "The Pixel Visions of Sadie Benning," *Sugar, Spice, and Everything Nice: Cinemas of Girlhood*, Frances Gateward and Murray Pomerance, eds. (Detroit: Wayne State University Press, 2002) 285–302.

142. *Gay Girls on the PL*, dir. Ana Lopez (Reach LA, 2002); *Looks Like a Girl*, dir. Ana Lopez (Reach LA: 2004).

143. *Double Consciousness*, dir. Amber Friedlander (Nathan Hale High School, 2000).

144. *We Love Our Lesbian Daughters*, dir. Taizet Hernandez (Reach LA, 2004).

145. *Love Knows No Gender*, dir. Zoe Euster (Reel Grrls, 2003).
146. *Coming Out*, dirs. Kali Snowden, Tina Huang, and Dharma Sa (Reel Grrls, 2004).
147. *3 Bitches*, dir. Gina Podesta (California State Summer School for the Arts, 1997).
148. *First Impressions from Seven Friends*, dirs. Tomekeh Porter (Watkins), Tiffany Spence, Tiffany Webb, and Shara Williams (Reagan High School, 2003).
149. *Skipping Rope*, dir. Katie Long (Kealing High School, 2003).
150. *Sisters*, dir. Linzi Silverman (Clarkstown High School North, 2003).
151. *La Gazelle: The Wilma Rudolph Story*, dir. Amina Jones (HBO Family, 1998).
152. *Baking Bread at Santa Clara Pueblo*, dir. Hollie Jenkins (Española Valley High School, 2002).
153. *Mi Nombre*, dir. Astrid Maldonado (Video Machete, 2002). Sandra Cisneros, *The House on Mango Street* (Houston: Arte Publico Press, 1983).
154. *Share Our World*, dir. Ramalah Yusufzai (Downtown Community Television Center, 2004).
155. *B.A.M. (Black As Me)*, dirs. Triniti Eberhardt-Corbin, Rachel Johnson, and Jomiah Price-Simpson (Reel Grrls, 2004).
156. *Name*, dir. Miyo Ann Tubridy (911 Media Arts Center and Listen Up!, 2000).
157. *Seventeen*, dir. Komal Herkishnami (Reel Grrls, 2004).
158. *Latinas Proving Themselves*, dirs. Ilianna Avila, Indhira Ben, Annette Gutierrez, Sandra Guzman, Melissa Menendez, Yaltiza Miranda, Juanita Molina, and Francis Solis (Skyline Youth Producers, 1999).
159. Unidentified creator of *Life through Shakira's Eyes* quoted on HBO Family's *30 x 30 Kid Flicks* (Feb. 2000).
160. Palcy quoted in Cole and Dale 158.
161. *My Name Is Ruth*, dir. Ruth Smith (HBO Family, 2000).
162. Barbara Hudson, "Femininity and Adolescence," *Gender and Generation*, Angela McRobbie and Mica Nava, eds. (London: Macmillan, 1984) 51.
163. See note 8.
164. *Twin Tales*, dir. Erica Shapiro (Tisch School of the Arts Summer Filmmakers' Workshop, 1999).
165. *Zerzura*, dir. Natalie Neptune (Downtown Community Television Center and Listen Up!, 2000).

CHAPTER 6

1. Karen Coyle, "How Hard Can It Be?" *Wired Women: Gender and New Realities in Cyberspace*, Lynn Cherny and Elizabeth Reba Weise, eds. (Seattle: Seal Press, 1996) 54.
2. Reddy quoted in Laurel Gilbert and Crystal Kile, *Surfergrrrls: Look Ethel! An Internet Guide for Us!* (Seattle: Seal Press, 1995) 205.
3. Online Computer Library Center, 10 May 2005 <http://www.oclc.org/research/projects/archive/wcp/stats/size.htm>.
4. Julian Sefton-Green and Vivienne Reiss, "Multimedia Literacies: Developing the Creative Uses of New Technology with Young People," *Young People, Creativity and New Technologies: The Challenge of Digital Arts*, Julian Sefton-Green, ed. (New York: Routledge, 1999) 2.

5. U.S. Department of Education, National Center for Education Statistics, *The Condition of Education 1999* (June 1999), 12 May 2005 <http://nces.ed.gov/pubs99/condition99/pdf/1999022.pdf>.

6. U.S. Department of Education, National Center for Education Statistics, *Internet Access in Public Schools and Classrooms, 1994–2003* (Feb. 2005), 4 May 2005 <http://www.nces.ed.gov/pubs2005/2005015.pdf>.

7. U.S. Department of Commerce, National Telecommunications and Information Administration, *Falling through the Net* (July 1995), 7 May 2005 <http://www.ntia.doc.gov/ntiahome/fallingthru.html>.

8. U.S. Department of Commerce, National Telecommunications and Information Administration, *A Nation Online* (Feb. 2002), 7 May 2005 <http://www.ntia.doc.gov/ntiahome/dn/>.

9. Digital Future Project, "Year Four: Surveying the Digital Future" (Sept. 2004), 7 May 2005 <http://www.digitalcenter.org/downloads/DigitalFutureReport-Year4-2004.pdf>.

10. U.S. Department of Commerce, Economics and Statistics Administration, *Home Computers and Internet Use in the United States: August 2000, Special Studies* (Sept. 2001), 7 May 2005 <http://www.census.gov/prod/2001pubs/p23-207.pdf>.

11. U.S. Department of Commerce, *Home Computers*.

12. Digital Future Project.

13. Pew Internet and American Life Project, *Internet: The Mainstreaming of Online Life* (2005), 7 May 2005 <http://www.pewinternet.org/pdfs/Internet_Status_2005.pdf>. For information on the Media Metrix report, see Lori Enos, "One Year Ago: Report: Kids Surf Online, Spend Offline," Ecommerce Times (13 Sept. 2001), 17 Dec. 2005 <http://www.ecommercetimes.com/story/13495.html>.

14. Virginia J. Rideout, Donald F. Roberts, and Ulla G. Foehr, "Generation M: Media in the Lives of 8-18 Year Olds" (Kaiser Family Foundation, Mar. 2005), 38, 10 May 2005 <http://www.kff.org/entmedia/loader.cfm?url=/commonspot/security/getfile.cfm&PageID=51805>.

15. Rideout et al. 16.

16. Rideout et al. 13.

17. Anne Rickert and Anya Sacharow, "It's a Woman's World Wide Web" (Media Metrix and Jupiter Communications, Aug. 2000), 4 May 2005 <http://www.rcss.ed.ac.uk/sigis/public/backgrounddocs/womenontheweb2000.pdf>.

18. U.S. Department of Commerce, *Home Computers*.

19. National School Boards Foundation, "Safe and Smart: Research and Guidelines for Children's Use of the Internet" (2003), 4 May 2005 <http://www.nsbf.org/safe-smart/equally.htm>.

20. Rideout et al. 38.

21. Rideout et al. 31.

22. National School Boards Foundation.

23. Victoria J. Rideout, Ulla G. Foehr, Donald F. Roberts, and Mollyann Brodie, "Kids and Media @ the New Millennium" (Kaiser Family Foundation, Nov. 1999) 51, 9 May 2005 <http://www.kff.org/entmedia/upload/13265_1.pdf>.

24. Andrea M. Matwyshyn, "Silicon Ceilings: Information Technology Equity, the Digital Divide and the Gender Gap among Information Technology Professionals,"

Northwestern Journal of Technology and Intellectual Property 2.1 (Fall 2003), 15 May 2005 <http://www.law.northwestern.edu/journals/njtip/v2/n1/2/#note4>.

25. Tracy Camp, "The Incredible Shrinking Pipeline," *Communications of the ACM* 40.10 (Oct. 1997) 103–10.

26. American Association of University Women, *Tech-Savvy: Educating Girls in the New Computer Age* (2000) 42, 12 Apr. 2005 <http://www.aauw.org/research/girls_education/techsavvy.cfm>.

27. Tracy Camp, Keith Miller, and Vanessa Davies, "The Incredible Shrinking Pipeline Unlikely to Reverse" (1999), 6 Mar. 2005 <http://www.mines.edu/fs_home/tcamp/new-study/new-study.html>.

28. Valerie Clarke, "Strategies for Involving Girls in Computer Science," *In Search of Gender Free Paradigms for Computer Science Education*, C. Dianne Martin and Eric Murchie-Beyma, eds. (Eugene: International Society for Technology in Education, 1992) 72.

29. Sherry Turkle, *The Second Self: Computers and the Human Spirit* (New York: Simon and Schuster, 1984) 210.

30. Sara Kiesler, Lee Sproull, and Jacquelynne Eccles, "Poolhalls, Chips, and Wargames: Women in the Culture of Computing," *Psychology of Women Quarterly* 9 (1985) 451–62; Eileen Green, Jenny Owen, and Den Pain, eds., *Gendered by Design? Information Technology and Office Systems* (London: Taylor and Francis, 1993).

31. Liesbet Van Zoonen, "Gendering the Internet: Claims, Controversies, and Cultures," *European Journal of Communication* 17.1 (2002) 11.

32. Sheila E. Widnall, "Voices from the Pipeline," *Science* 214 (1988) 1740–45.

33. Stephen Zweben and William Aspray, "2002–03 Taulbee Survey," *Computing Research News* (May 2004), 6 Mar. 2005 <http://www.cra.org/statistics/survey/03/03.pdf>.

34. Gail Crombie and Patrick Ian Armstrong, "Effects of Classroom Gender Composition on Adolescents' Computer-Related Attitudes and Future Intentions," *Journal of Educational Computing Research* 20.4 (1999) 321.

35. American Association of University Women 7.

36. Camic quoted in American Association of University Women 54.

37. Valerie Clarke, "Sex Differences in Computing Participation: Concerns, Extent, Reasons, and Strategies," *Australian Journal of Education* 34.1 (1990) 52–66.

38. Melanie Stewart Millar, *Cracking the Gender Code: Whole Rules the Wired World?* (Toronto: Second Story Press, 1998) 77.

39. Matthew Weinstein, "Computer Advertising and the Construction of Gender," *Education/Technology/Power: Educational Computing as a Social Practice*, Hank Bromley and Michael Apple, eds. (New York: State University of New York Press, 1998) 85–100.

40. Judy Wajcman, *Feminism Confronts Technology* (University Park: University of Pennsylvania Press, 1991) 158.

41. Jo Sanders, "Girls and Technology: Villain Wanted," *Teaching the Majority: Breaking the Gender Barrier in Science, Mathematics, and Engineering*, Sue V. Rosser, ed. (New York: Teacher College, Columbia University, 1995) 151.

42. Lilith Computer Group website, 2 Mar. 2005 <http://www.madison.k12.wi.us/lilithclub/mission.htm>.

43. Camic quoted in Dave Becker, "Lilith Computer Club? It's a Girl Thing," *Wisconsin State Journal* (4 Oct. 1997), 3 Mar. 2005 <http://axle.doit.wisc.edu/%7Esss/affiliations/lilith/lilith1.htm>.

44. American Association of University Women 10.

45. Camic quoted in American Association of University Women 54.

46. McClain quoted in Kathy Foster, "Club Gets Girls to Delve into Computers," *Capital Times* (6 Jan. 2000), 3 Mar. 2005 <http://axle.doit.wisc.edu/%7Esss/affiliations/lilith/lilith5.htm>.

47. Papers from this workshop are included in C. Dianne Martin and Eric Murchie-Beyma, eds., *In Search of Gender Free Paradigms for Computer Science Education* (Eugene: International Society for Technology in Education, 1992).

48. Clarke, "Strategies" 72–82.

49. C. Dianne Martin, "Report on the Workshop," *In Search of Gender Free Paradigms* 6–7.

50. In addition to Sanders, and Crombie and Armstrong, see: Denise E. Agosto, "Connecting Girls to the World Wide Web: An Investigation of Girls' Website Design Preferences," *SCAN: The Journal of the New South Wales Department of Education and Training* 22.1 (2003) 27–33; John Beynon, "Computer Dominant Boys and Invisible Girls: or 'Hannah, It's Not a Toaster, It's a Computer,'" *Computers into Classrooms: More Questions than Answers*, John Beynon and Hughie Mackay, eds. (Washington, D.C.: Falmer Press, 1993) 160–89; Justine Cassell and Henry Jenkins, eds., *From Barbie to Mortal Kombat: Gender and Computer Games* (Cambridge: MIT Press, 1998); Ann L. Davidson and Janet Schofield, "Female Voices in Virtual Reality: Drawing Young Girls into an Online World," *Building Virtual Communities: Learning and Change in Cyberspace*, K. Ann Renninger and Wesley Shumar, eds. (New York: Cambridge University Press, 2002) 34–59; Brad R. Huber and Janet Schofield, "I Like Computers, But Many Girls Don't: Gender and Sociocultural Contexts in Computing," *Education/Technology/Power: Educational Computing as a Social Practice*, Hank Bromley and Michael Apple, eds. (New York: State University of New York Press, 1998) 103–32; Kathleen Lynn, Chad Raphael, Karin Olefsky, and Christine Bachen, "Bridging the Gender Gap in Computing: An Integrative Approach to Content Design for Girls," *Journal of Educational Computing Research* 28.2 (2003) 143–62; Sharon R. Mazzarella, ed., *Girl Wide Web: Girls, the Internet, and the Negotiation of Identity* (New York: Peter Lang, 2005); Leslie Miller, Melissa Chaika, and Laura Groppe, "Girls' Preferences in Software Design: Insights from a Focus Group," *Interpersonal Computing and Technology* 4.2 (Apr. 1996) 27–36; Krista Scott, "'Girls Need Modems!': Cyberculture and Women's Ezines," *Master's* report (York University, Jan. 1998), 17 Feb. 2002 <http://www.stumptuous.com/mrp.html>; Ellen Tarlin, "Computers in the Classrooms: Where are All the Girls?" *Harvard Educational Review, Focus Series* 3 (1997) 20–21.

51. Sherry Turkle, "Computational Reticence: Why Women Fear the Intimate Machine," *Technology and Women's Voices: Keeping in Touch*, Cheris Kramarae, ed. (New York: Routledge, 1988) 41–61.

52. See note 26. Another nonprofit report on girls' computing is *The Net Effect: Girls and New Media*, published by the Girl Scout Research Institute in 2002.

Conducted by Whitney Roban in conjunction with staff at Girl Games, this study examined the effects of online culture on girls' social and emotional lives.

53. American Association of University Women, *Gender Gaps: Where Schools Still Fail Our Children* (1998), 19 Oct. 2003 <http://www.aauw.org/research/GGES.pdf>.

54. American Association of University Women, *Tech-Savvy* 71.

55. American Association of University Women, *Tech-Savvy* ix–x.

56. American Association of University Women, *Tech-Savvy* xii–xiii.

57. American Association of University Women, *Tech-Savvy* 7–8.

58. American Association of University Women, *Tech-Savvy* xii.

59. American Association of University Women, *Tech-Savvy* 4 and 41.

60. *Tech-Savvy* has recommendations for improving home computing so as to facilitate girls' engagements with digital technologies; however, the scope and depth of these recommendations (two pages) pale in comparison to those related to schools (two chapters).

61. Nancy Kaplan and Eva Farrell, "Weavers of Webs: A Portrait of Young Women on the Net," *Arachnet Electronic Journal in Virtual Culture* 2.3 (26 July 1994), 6 May 2005 <http://www.kovacs.com/EJVC/kaplan.htm>.

62. These are the "dual visions" of AAUW's commission. See American Association of University Women, *Tech-Savvy* 3.

63. Turkle 57–58.

64. Paul Willis, *Common Culture: Symbolic Work at Play in the Everyday Cultures of the Young* (Buckingham: Open University Press, 1990) 15.

65. Kimberley S. Gregson, "What If the Lead Character Looks Like Me?: Girl Fans of Shoujou Anime and Their Websites," *Girl Wide Web: Girls, the Internet, and the Negotiation of Identity*, Sharon R. Mazzarella, ed. (New York: Peter Lang, 2005) 121–40; Sharon R. Mazzarella, "Claiming a Space: The Cultural Economy of Teen Girl Fandom on the Web," *Girl Wide Web: Girls, the Internet, and the Negotiation of Identity*, Sharon R. Mazzarella, ed. (New York: Peter Lang, 2005) 141–60; Jacqueline Reid-Walsh and Claudia Mitchell, "Girls' Websites: A Virtual 'Room of One's Own'," *All About the Girl: Power, Culture, and Identity*, Anita Harris, ed. (New York: Routledge, 2004) 173–82; Susannah Stern, "Adolescent Girls' Expression on Web Home Pages: Spirited, Sombre and Self-Conscious Sites," *Convergence* 5.4 (Winter 1999) 22–41; Susannah Stern, "Adolescent Girls' Home Pages as Sites for Sexual Self-Expression," *SIECUS Report* 28.5 (June–July 2000) 6–15; Susannah Stern, "Sexual Selves on the World Wide Web: Adolescent Girls' Home Pages as Sites for Sexual Self-Expression," *Sexual Teens, Sexual Media: Investigating Media's Influence on Adolescent Sexuality*, Jane D. Brown, Jeanne R. Steele, and Kim Walsh-Childers, eds. (Mahwah: Lawrence Erlbaum Associates, 2002) 265–85; Susannah Stern, "Virtually Speaking: Girls' Self-Disclosure on the WWW," *Women's Studies in Communication* 25.2 (Fall 2002) 223–53.

66. Pamela Takayoshi, Emily Huot, and Meghan Huot, "No Boys Allowed: The World Wide Web as a Clubhouse for Girls," *Computers and Composition* 16.1 (1999) 89–106.

67. Michelle Comstock, "Grrrl Zine Networks: Re-Composing Spaces of Authority, Gender, and Culture," *Journal of Advanced Composition* 21.2 (Spring 2001) 383–409; Marion Leonard, "Paper Planes: Travelling the New Grrrl Geographies,"

Cool Places: Geographies of Youth Cultures, Tracey Skelton and Gill Valentine, eds. (New York: Routledge, 1998) 101–18; Elke Zobl, "Persephone is Pissed! Grrrl Zine Reading, Making, and Distributing across the Globe," *Hecate* 30.2 (Oct. 2004) 156–75; Doreen Piano, "Congregating Women: Reading 3rd Wave Feminist Practices in Subcultural Production," *Rhizomes* 4 (Spring 2002), 15 July 2002 <http://www.rhizomes.net/issue4/piano.html>.

68. Reid-Walsh and Mitchell briefly discuss younger girls' reliance on free authoring software, and analyze one girl's website. Stern's essay, "Adolescent Girls' Expression," looks specifically at three types of "tone" girls construct in their websites through language, color, and imagery.

69. Mazzarella, as well as Reid-Walsh and Mitchell, briefly discuss the different levels of skill suggested by girls' websites.

70. Kaplan and Farrell.

71. As explained in more depth in Chapter 2, I use "micro" rather than "alternative" to describe media texts, producers, and infrastructures independent of corporate culture.

72. This study was conducted May–June 2005 via email questionnaires and correspondence. The subjects are young females who were twenty-one or younger when they first went online, and whose distros are linked to Distrokids (http://www.violeteyes.net/distrokids/), or the Grrrl Zine Network (http://grrrlzines.net/zines/distros.htm?source=zinebook#us).

73. C/S Distro <http://www.csdistro.com/>; Dreamer's Distro <http://www.dreamersdistro.com/>; Fork 'n Spoon Mail Order <http://www.retrobugs.com/forknspoon/>; HousewifeXcore Distro <http://www.freewebs.com/housewifexcore>/; Ladymen Distro <http://www.ladymen.8m.com/>; Mad People Distro <http://www.madpeople.net/>; MY MY Distro <http://mymy.girlswirl.net/>; Neon Pavement Distro <http://www.freewebs.com/neonpavementdistro/>; Spy Kids Distro <http://www.skdistro.cjb.net/>; Supernova Distro <http:// violeteyes.net/supernova/>; Wingless Zine Distro <http://wingless.xexix.net/>; and Wrong Number Distro <http://wrong-number.net/>.

74. The Internet Archive: WayBack Machine website <http://www.archive.org/web/web.php> contains some of the older iterations of the distros studied here.

75. Taryn Hipp, email response to author's questionnaire, 23 May 2005.

76. Arianna Perezdiez, email response to author's questionnaire, 11 May 2005.

77. Sarah Ketcham, email response to author's questionnaire, 14 May 2005.

78. Meredith Wallace, email response to author's questionnaire, 12 May 2005.

79. Taryn Hipp, email response to author's questionnaire, 10 May 2005.

80. Ketcham.

81. For example, see National School Boards Foundation.

82. Davidson and Schofield 52.

83. Davidson and Schofield 55.

84. "Tabling" is the practice of displaying products on tables at cultural events, such as musical shows and zine conventions, for promotion and distribution purposes.

85. Perezdiez.

86. Jen Venegas, email response to author's questionnaire, 12 May 2005.

87. Noemi Martinez, email response to author questionnaire, 3 June 2005.

88. Martinez.
89. Hypertext codes can be viewed in web browsers by clicking on the View menu and selecting Source or Page Source.
90. Chris Abbott, "Web Publishing by Young People," *Young People, Creativity, and New Technologies: The Challenge of Digital Arts*, Julian Sefton-Green, ed. (New York: Routledge, 1999) 112.
91. Several respondents identified the Pander Forums, on the Pander Zine Distro <http://panderzinedistro.com>, as a message board in which they participated frequently as teenagers.
92. For example, see Clarke, "Strategies"; and American Association of University Women, *Tech-Savvy*.
93. Ketcham.
94. Martinez.
95. American Association of University Women, *Tech-Savvy* 10.
96. Live Journal <http://www.livejournal.com>; Laundromatic <http://www.laundromatic.net>; The Switchboards <http://www.theswitchboards.com>.
97. Wallace.
98. Wallace.
99. Ketcham.
100. Wallace.
101. Maria Struk, email response to author's questionnaire, 12 May 2005.
102. Ashley (Pixie) Chapman, email response to author questionnaire, 6 June 2005.
103. Stephanie Basile, email response to author's questionnaire, 22 May 2005.
104. Sarah Lynne Wells, email response to author's questionnaire, 14 May 2005.
105. Perezdiez. Dreamweaver is an authoring tool developed by Macromedia.
106. Venegas.
107. Lisa, email response to author's questionnaire, 12 May 2005. For reasons of privacy, this research subject chose not to report her full name.
108. Arianna Perezdiez, email correspondence with author, 11 May 2005.
109. Hipp, 10 May 2005.
110. Taryn Hipp, email correspondence with author, 12 May 2005.
111. Meredith Wallace, email response to author's questionnaire, 22 May 2005.
112. Maria Struk, email response to author's questionnaire, 24 May 2005.
113. Sarah Ketcham, email response to author's questionnaire, 22 May 2005.
114. Basile.
115. Lisa, email response to author's questionnaire, 24 May 2005.
116. Wells, email response to author's questionnaire, 22 May 2005.
117. Chapman.
118. Martinez.
119. Wallace, 22 May 2005.
120. Stephanie Scarborough, email response to author's questionnaire, 22 May 2005.
121. Ketcham, 22 May 2005.
122. Lisa, 12 May 2005.
123. Martinez.
124. Perezdiez, email response. PayPal <http://www.paypal.com> is an online service that transfers payment for goods and services via credit cards and bank accounts.

125. Venegas.

126. Ketcham, 14 May 2005.

127. Stern, "Adolescent Girls' Expression" 23–24. Today, "home page" typically refers to the first page that loads when a website is accessed; in the late 1990s, this term was used more generally to describe personal websites.

128. Stern, "Adolescent Girls' Expression" 25.

129. Web authoring programs are also available commercially.

130. Ketcham, 14 May 2005.

131. Stephanie Scarborough, email response to author's questionnaire, 10 May 2005.

132. Spy Kids Distro website, 2 June 2005 <http://www.skdistro.cjb.net/>.

133. As discussed below, websites are often divided into separate sections, referred to as "pages."

134. Neon Pavement Distro website, 7 May 2005 <http://www.freewebs.com/neonpavementdistro/>.

135. Fork 'n Spoon Mail Order website, 8 May 2005 <http://www.retrobugs.com/forknspoon/>.

136. Margaret Batschelet, *Web Writing, Web Designing* (Boston: Allyn and Bacon, 2001) 63.

137. Such components are available through PayPal. See note 124.

138. Batschelet 73.

139. Batschelet 118.

140. For these two iterations of Supernova Distro's website, see <http://web.archive.org/web/20020317223533/violeteyes.net/supernova>; <http://web.archive.org/web/20030805003406/violeteyes.net/supernova>.

141. Batschelet 171.

142. Hipp, 10 May 2005.

143. Lisa, 12 May 2005.

144. Ketcham, 14 May 2005.

145. Wells, 14 May 2005.

146. Scarborough, 10 May 2005.

147. Venegas.

148. A URL (Uniform Resource Locator) is the location or "address" of a file on the Internet.

149. Martinez.

150. Batschelet 103.

151. Hipp, 10 May 2005.

152. Struk, 12 May 2005.

153. Venegas.

154. Wells, 14 May 2005.

155. Abbott 116.

156. Basile.

157. Scarborough, 10 May 2005.

158. Basile.

159. Straight edge is a punk sub-community whose members typically are vegetarians, do not consume drugs or alcohol, and do not engage in promiscuous sexual behavior.

160. Perezdiez, email response.

161. Wallace, 12 May 2005.
162. Meredith Wallace, email correspondence with author, 6 June 2005.
163. Meredith Wallace, email correspondence with author, 7 June 2005.
164. Struk, 12 May 2005.
165. A "splash page" appears before a home page and is utilized primarily to attract user attention.
166. Perezdiez, email response.
167. Hipp, 10 May 2005.
168. Lisa, 12 May 2005.
169. Scarborough, 10 May 2005.
170. Perezdiez, email response.
171. MY MY Distro website, Home page, 1 June 2005 <http://mymy.girlswirl.net/>.
172. Piano ¶3.
173. Record stores have served a similar community function for members of youth countercultures, such as punk and hip-hop.
174. Linda Steiner, "The History and Structure of Women's Alternative Media," *Women Making Meaning: New Feminist Directions in Communication*, Lana F. Rakow, ed. (New York: Routledge, 1992) 135.
175. Piano ¶18.
176. Dreamer's Distro website, Home page, 9 May 2005 <http://www.dreamersdistro.com/>.
177. Stern, "Adolescent Girls' Expression" 28.
178. MY MY Distro website, Home page, 1 June 2005 <http://mymy.girlswirl.net/>.
179. An "about page" typically identifies the website owner, the history of the site, and/or its purpose.
180. Neon Pavement Distro website, About page, 7 May 2005 <http://www.freewebs.com/neonpavementdistro/aboutcontact.htm>.
181. Wrong Number Distro website, About page, 14 May 2005 <http://wrong-number.net/>.
182. Mad People Distro website, Information page, 10 May 2005 <http://web.archive.org/web/20040528220645/madpeople.net/distro/index>.
183. HousewifeXcore Distro website, Home page, 13 May 2005 <http://www.freewebs.com/housewifexcore/>.
184. Dreamer's Distro website, Get Distroed page, 9 May 2005 <http://www.dreamersdistro.com/>.
185. Ladymen Distro website, Home page, 12 May 2005 <http://www.ladymen.8m.com/>.
186. C/S Distro website, Why page, 4 June 2005 <http://www.csdistro.com/why.shtml>.
187. C/S Distro website, About page, 4 June 2005 http://www.csdistro.com/aboutus.shtml.
188. Piano ¶18.
189. Though zinesters are the primary individuals externally linked to the distros in this study, several distros reveal their owners' commitment to other producers of handcrafted goods. For example, the vast majority of connections on MY MY distro's links page are categorized under "shopping" <http://mymy.girlswirl.net>.

The links page for Fork 'n Spoon is fairly evenly split between zine distros and "crafty places" <http://www.retrobugs.com/forknspoon/2005/03/links.html>.

190. HousewifeXcore Distro website, Links page, 27 May 2005 <http://www.freewebs.com/housewifexcore/links.htm>.

191. Pander Zine Distro website, 8 May 2005 <http://panderzinedistro.com>.

192. Pander Zine Distro website, Pander Forums, 15 May 2005 <http://messageboard.panderzinedistro.com/cgi/ikonboard.cgi>. Several distros in this study have guestbooks or customer feedback pages; however, none of these pages is as active as Pander Forums.

193. See note 72. Elke Zobl, a zinester and feminist media scholar, runs this site.

194. Distrokids.

195. Piano ¶25.

196. American Association of University Women, *Tech-Savvy* xii.

197. Sefton-Green and Reiss 3.

CONCLUSION

1. Bratmobile, "Girls Get Busy," *Girls Get Busy* (Lookout Records, 2002).

2. This figure is approximate and is based on my six years as director of Cinemakids, a special program for youth-made films that is part of the larger Cinematexas International Short Film Festival.

3. DiFranco quoted in *The Righteous Babes*, dir. Pratibha Parmar (Women Make Movies, 1998).

4. Sara Cohen, "Men Making a Scene: Rock Music and the Production of Gender," *Sexing the Groove: Popular Music and Gender*, Sheila Whiteley, ed. (New York: Routledge, 1997) 17.

5. Cohen 17.

6. Lucy Green, "Affirming Femininity: Women Singing, Women Enabling," *Music, Gender, Education* (Cambridge: Cambridge University Press, 1997) 28–29.

7. Mavis Bayton, "Women and the Electric Guitar," *Sexing the Groove: Popular Music and Gender*, Sheila Whiteley, ed. (New York: Routledge, 1997) 47.

8. Green 28.

9. Bayton 39.

10. Bayton 41.

11. Carol Jennings, "Girls Make Music: Polyphony and Identity in Teenage Rock Bands," *Growing Up Girls: Popular Culture and the Construction of Identity*, Sharon R. Mazzarella and Norma Odom Pecora, eds. (New York: Peter Lang, 2001) 187.

12. Bayton 38.

13. David Uskovich, "Gear for Grrrls," Unpublished paper, University of Texas at Austin, 2000.

14. Bayton 42–43.

15. Robin D. G. Kelley, *Yo' Mama's Disfunktional!: Fighting the Culture Wars in Urban America* (Boston: Beacon, 1997) 69–70.

16. Bayton 39.

17. Mary Ann Clawson, "Masculinity and Skill Acquisition in the Adolescent Rock Band," *Popular Music* 18.1 (1999) 105.

18. Clawson 106.
19. Cohen 20.
20. Clawson 108.
21. Bayton 40.
22. Will Straw, "Sizing Up Record Collections: Gender and Connoisseurship in Rock Music Culture," *Sexing the Groove: Popular Music and Gender*, Sheila Whiteley, ed. (New York: Routledge, 1997) 9.
23. Tina quoted in Clawson 178.
24. Bayton 40.
25. Clawson 111.
26. Clawson 103.
27. Carly quoted in Jennings 182.
28. Carly quoted in Jennings 184.
29. Clawson 102.
30. Mavis Bayton, *Frock Rock: Women Performing Popular Music* (New York: Oxford University Press, 1998).
31. See Cynthia Lont, "Redwood Records: Principles and Profit in Women's Music," *Women Communicating: Studies of Women's Talk*, Barbara Bate and Anita Taylor, eds. (Norwood: Ablex Publishing, 1988) 233–50; Cynthia Lont, "Women's Music: No Longer a Small Private Party," *Rockin' the Boat: Mass Music and Mass Movements*, Reebee Garofalo, ed. (Boston: South End Press, 1992) 241–53; Boden Sandstrom, "Women Mix Engineers and the Power of Sound," *Music and Gender*, Pirkko Moisala and Beverley Diamond, eds. (Chicago: University of Illinois Press, 2000) 289–305.
32. Information about McElroy and the Rock'n'Roll Camp for Girls was obtained through a telephone interview on 6 Sept. 2002 and email correspondence on 30 Sept. 2002 with the author, as well as the Rock'n'Roll Camp for Girls website, 28 Aug. 2002 <http:// www.girlsrockcamp.org>.
33. McElroy, telephone conversation.
34. Rock'n'Roll Camp for Girls promotional flyer (Portland: self-published, 2002).
35. McElroy, email correspondence.
36. McElroy, email correspondence.
37. McElroy, telephone interview.
38. Southern Girls Rock'n'Roll Camp website, 10 Nov. 2004 <http://www.mtsu.edu/~w4w>.
39. Institute for Musical Arts' Rock & Roll Girls Camp website, 1 June 2005 <http:// www.ima.org/rockcamp/aboutus.htm>.
40. Willie Mae Rock'n'Roll Camp for Girls website, 1 June 2005 <http://www.wil-liemaerockcamp.org/>.
41. Daisy Rock website, 1 June 2005 <http://www.daisyrock.com/news/tish2.htm>.
42. For example, Trish Ciravolo, *Girl's Guitar Method* 1 (Van Nuys: Alfred Publishing, 2002).
43. *Guitar for Girls: Start Playing with Alex Bach* (Rock House and Amsco Publishing, 2005).
44. Walter Benjamin, "The Author as Producer," 1934, *Walter Benjamin: Selected Writings, Volume 2, 1927–1934*, Rodney Livingstone, trans., Michael W. Jennings,

Howard Eiland, and Gary Smith, eds. (Cambridge: Harvard University Press, 1999) 768–82.

45. Erika Falk and Erin Grizard, "The Glass Ceiling Persists: The 3rd Annual APPC Report on Women Leaders in Communication Companies," *Annenberg Public Policy Center* (Dec. 2003), 2 June 2005 <http://www.annenbergpublicpolicycenter.org/04_info_society/women_leadership/2003_04_the-glass-ceiling-persists-corrected_pr.pdf>.

46. Rachel Abromowitz, "A Hollywood League of Their Own," Los Angeles Times (30 Apr. 2002), 11 Aug. 2003 <http://www.latimes.com/news/local/la-000030626apr30story?coll-la-hedlines-california>.

47. Martha M. Lauzen and David M. Dozier, "Equal Time in Prime Time?: Scheduling Favoritism and Gender on the Broadcast Networks," *Journal of Broadcasting and Electronic Media* 46.1 (Mar. 2002) 145. This study shows that primetime shows on the newer networks, UPN and the WB, had considerably more women in these positions (25%) than FOX (15.2%) or the three traditional networks, ABC, CBS, and NBC (14%).

48. Radio-Television News Directors Association 2001 study and American Society of Newspaper Editors 2002 study quoted in *Media Report to Women*, "Industry Statistics," 11 Nov. 2004 <http://www.mediareporttowomen.com/statistics.htm>.

49. Joe Strupp, "A Feminine Touch," *Editor and Publisher* (16 Sept. 2002) 10.

50. Terry Barnes, "Despite the Restrictions of Glass Ceilings and Mommy Tracks, Women Executives are Making Music Their Business," *Billboard* 105.17 (24 Apr. 1993) W3+. Unfortunately, this is the most recent data I could find on women leaders in the recording industry.

51. Kathleen Hall Jamieson, Lorie Slass, and Nicole Porter, "Progress or No Room at the Top?: The Role of Women in Telecommunications, Broadcast, Cable, and E-Companies," *Annenberg Public Policy Center* (Mar. 2001) 8 Aug. 2003 <http://www.annenbergpublicpolicycenter.org/04_info_society/women_leadership/telecom/2001_progress-report.pdf>.

52. Men have historically dominated as the publishers of such texts, however.

Index